THE

SERPENT

AND THE

SACRED

FIRE

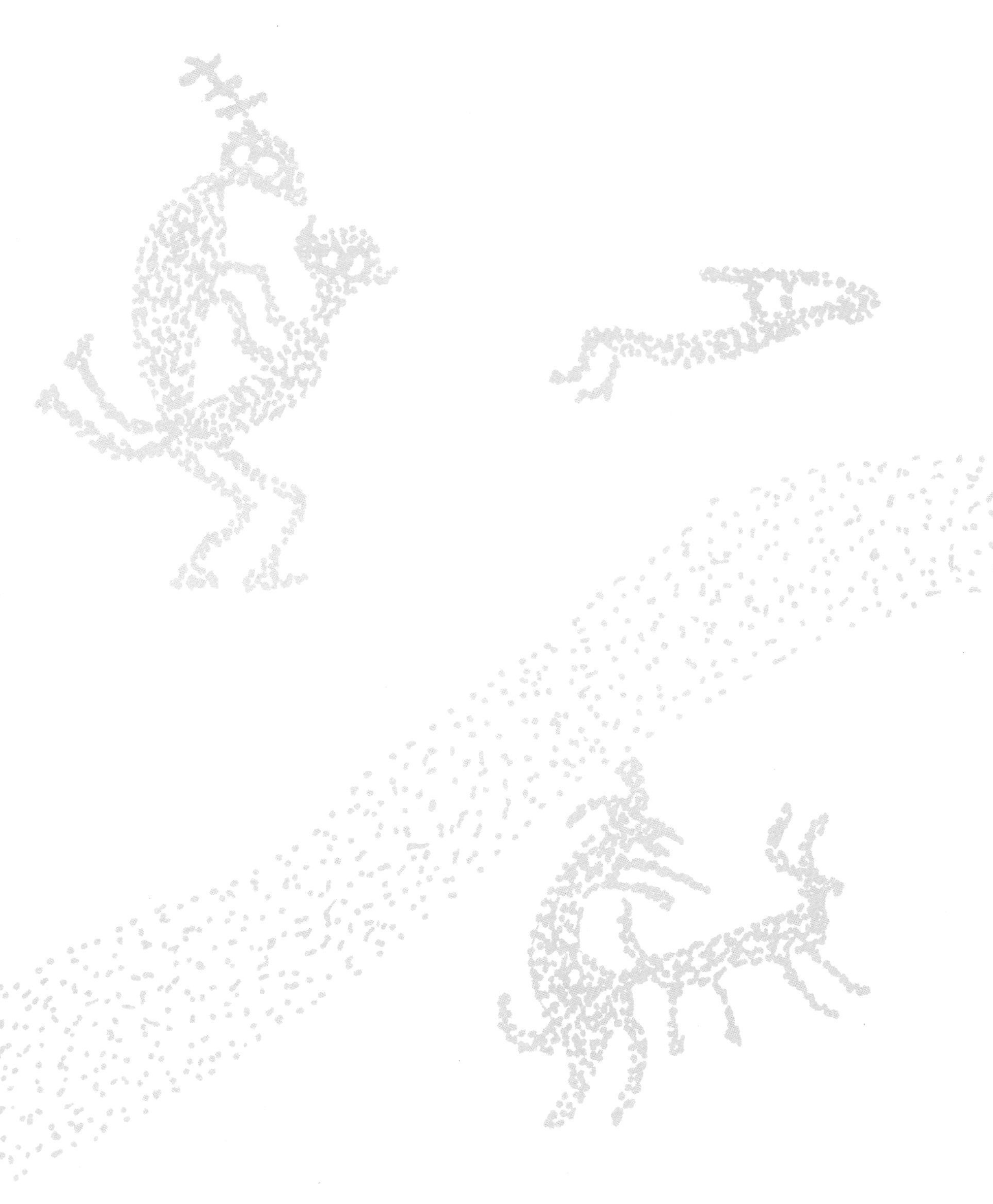

MUSEUM OF NEW MEXICO PRESS
SANTA FE

THE SERPENT AND THE SACRED FIRE

FERTILITY IMAGES IN SOUTHWEST ROCK ART

DENNIS SLIFER
with photographs
and drawings by the author

Project editor: Mary Wachs
Manuscript editor: Ann Mason
Design and production: David Skolkin
Layout: Bruce Taylor Hamilton
Map: Deborah Reade

Manufactured in Korea
10 9 8 7 6 5 4 3 2 1

Library of Congress Control Number:
00–133693

Museum of New Mexico Press
Post Office Box 2087
Santa Fe, New Mexico 87504

CONTENTS

ACKNOWLEDGMENTS

I am grateful to everyone who aided my research and writing of this book. There were many of you, and if I omit any names here please forgive the mistake. Jim Duffield and Chris Larsen accompanied me on many field trips and shared photographs and site information. So did Larry Larason, Ron Lee, Paul Williams, Alain Briot, and Sheila Brewer. Ekkehart Malotki provided a photograph of the Cave of Life. Bart Durham shared site information and photographs and guided me to a cave with vulva symbols in it. Brad Draper, Clay Martin, Burt Alpert, and Ruth Burton also provided photographs to me. I am grateful to Manfred Knaak for helping me with site information in Anza-Borrego Desert, and to Louise Ross and Carol Milligan for sharing information about birthing scenes. Barbara Alpert and Orit Tamir shared information about foreign sites. Veronika Holzer provided a photograph of the Venus of Willendorf. I appreciate advice given by Jerry Brody about Mimbres designs and am grateful to Eric Blinman, Curt Schaafsma, Orit Tamir, and Barbara Alpert for reviewing the manuscript. Rev. Galal Gough provided copies of his papers on fertility symbols. Mary and Alan Wreyford permitted me to photograph Huichol yarn paintings in their Santa Fe art gallery. Katherine Wells was always gracious in granting me access to the sites on her property. The manuscript was improved by the expert editing of Ann Mason, who is a joy to work with, and the project would not have happened at all without the support and professionalism of Mary Wachs at the Museum of New Mexico Press. And of course my last words of gratitude are reserved for my wife, Dena, for pleasantly carrying more than her share of the chores at home while I was in the field or sequestered in my study.

In prehistoric art, pregnant women . . . and excited men are not sex symbols in the twentieth century sense. Our forebears were more philosophical; there was no element of obscenity in their art. Prehistoric fertility symbols are symbols of potency, abundance, and multiplication, concerned with the perpetuation of life and the preservation of life forces constantly threatened by death. . . . Fertility symbols are seasonal, representing dying and awakening nature.[1]

—Marija Gimbutas
The Language of the Goddess

The beginning of art, like that of religion, arose from a profound but bewildered concern for life and death, and the unknown processes that controlled them. Origins, continuity, fertility, security, and assurance of survival are universal themes.[2]

—Jay von Werlhof
Spirits of the Earth

No idle fancy is the concept of Earth Mother. Wide as the world is the idea that all living things, including man, issued from Mother Earth. . . . Life is seen germinating in the earth, emerging from the earth, dependent upon the earth for maintenance. Earth is seen quickening life, nourishing life, preserving life. . . .[3]

—Edgar L. Hewett
Pajarito Plateau and Its Ancient People

The Earth is like the breasts of a woman, useful as well as pleasing.[4]

—Sotho proverb

INTRODUCTION

THE RENEWING AND SUSTAINING EARTH

The American Southwest abounds in prehistoric rock art. The fascinating images of petroglyphs and pictographs span thousands of years of American Indian culture. Although the meaning of many of the symbols eludes us, fertility has been identified as one of the most obvious and persistent themes in rock art of prehistoric cultures in the Southwest and around the world. In the broadest sense, these images suggest that their ancient creators were concerned with appeasement of the supernatural to ensure that procreant forces continued to sustain the sacred fire that animates all life. In addition to the obvious desire for successful human reproduction, their concerns extended to the fertility of earth itself and the fecundity of plants and animals—the community of life upon which physical and spiritual well-being depended.

Because much rock art is thought to be sacred and connected to religious beliefs of the cultures that made it, notions such as fertility, abundance, and creation are imbued with spiritual potency and universal significance. Thus in the rock art record are found not only images of human sexuality and reproduction but also portrayals of pregnant game animals and successful hunts, seeds and edible plants both wild and cultivated, symbols of rain and moisture upon which all life depends, of sexual rituals intended to ensure a fruitful earth, and of supernatural beings who empower and control lifeforms. Even portrayals of origin myths can be seen as related to fertility since the Earth Mother was fertilized by the sun or Father Sky and gave birth to all creatures in the world.

People of all cultures, from nomadic hunter-gatherers to settled agriculturalists, have expressed awe for the creative principle in their art. Man's efforts to understand the great mysteries of birth, death, and sexuality have inspired graphic images and vivid mythologies. Modern people, having lost intimacy with the earth and her life-giving magic, would do well to study these messages in the ancient rock art. The ancestors of us all at one time participated in rituals that venerated fertility. When the oldest rock art in the Southwest was being created, people in what is now Europe and the British Isles were also being led by their shamans in rites celebrating regeneration, death and rebirth, healing, seasonal changes, the powers of vegetation, human mating, and the fertilizing of animals and the soil. In old Germanic languages, the word *Lust* meant "religious joy." The recurrent themes of sexuality, death, and regeneration are, in fact, archetypal, occurring in

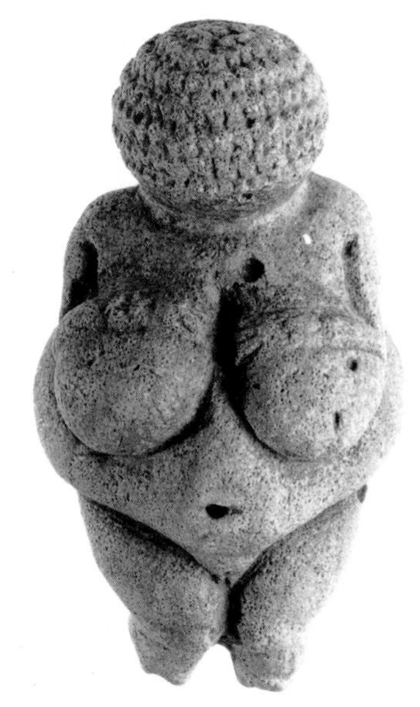

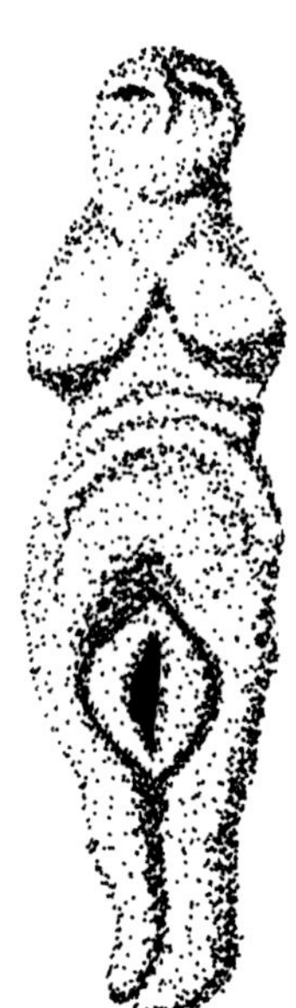

Fig. 1. (left) The Venus of Willendorf, a Paleolithic figurine carved in limestone dating to approximately 24,000 B.C., is one of the earliest known representations of the mystery of female fertility. With permission Naturhistorisches Museum Wien; photo: Alice Schumacher.

Fig. 2. (right) A Paleolithic figurine with a greatly emphasized vulva, Monpazier, Dordogne, France (after Gimbutas 1989, 103).

Fig. 3.(opposite page) Basketmaker III female figurines of unfired clay from various sites in northeastern Arizona (after Morss 1954:fig.19; adapted from Morris 1927 and 1951, Renaud 1929, and Parsons 1919). Reprinted courtesy of the Peabody Museum of Archaeology and Ethnology, Harvard University.

myths and prehistoric images from cultures around the planet. The Southwest is an excellent region to study examples of these themes because of the abundance of rock art and of ethnographic accounts from the descendants of some ancient cultures; and comparison of motifs in rock art of other parts of the world provides additional context.

To primitive man the earth was everything, the source of all sustenance. She was the mother of generations, and in her womb dwelt ancestral spirits. Mother Earth was the origin of religious beliefs, for all things were animated and had a spiritual force. It is not surprising that early humans perceived the earth as female, seeing caves or fissures as both womb and tomb—places to access supernatural forces for the perpetuation and renewal of life.

Since prehistoric times mankind has been preoccupied with the mysteries of birth, sex, fertility, and death. In response to these mysteries our ancestors developed a dynamic relationship with the earth as a sacred source of sustenance. These themes have greatly influenced our physical and cultural evolution and are manifest in the art and religion of every culture. All religions have developed around and acknowledged the power of sex—by either restraining it through chastity and monasticism or by licensing it through rituals. Thus it is not surprising that traces of archaic fertility rituals are found, however attenuated, in nearly every surviving religion. It has been suggested that all major manifestations of the human spirit, including religion, art, and culture, are probably sublimations of the sex drive (Bishop 1996, 7).

There is evidence in ancient artifacts and cave art that fertility was among humanity's first great psychological and spiritual concerns. This evidence suggests a profound and widespread association for ancient people between human sexuality and the abundance of animals and plants upon which their lives depended.

Some of the earliest human artistic expression involves procreation, as seen in phallic symbols carved in antler and wood and especially by the Great Mother or Great Goddess carvings (the so-called Venus figurines). More than two hundred of these female statuettes in stone, bone, clay, and ivory have been unearthed throughout the European continent from sites dating between 35,000 and 10,000 B.C. Their female sexual characteristics (breasts, buttocks, bellies, and vulvas) are exaggerated, suggesting enhanced fertility (figs. 1 and 2). Even in the dawn of human development, the female was perceived as the primary source of procreative power. As symbols, these figurines and other painted or carved images of females (Plate 1) were potent magic representing renewal of all life. That these images were sometimes buried with the dead implies that concepts of an afterlife and rebirth were present in the early Stone Age. An awareness of the periodicity of nature, the cycles of the moon and the female body, probably led to beliefs in regeneration of life after death, a theme reflected in mankind's first art. Along with the female figures, the images of vulvas and phalli in prehistoric cave sanctuaries represent our ancestors' concern with birth—or, more accurately, with rebirth.

As potent, magic symbols, such female images are not unique to Europe but occur in analogous forms around the world, including North and South America. In the American Southwest, clay figurines depicting females, with breasts and vulvas, have been found in Basketmaker caves and at burial sites in northeastern Arizona and southern Utah (fig. 3) (Morss 1954). Similar clay figurines depicting pregnant females have been discovered in the ruins of Pecos Pueblo in New Mexico and at Snaketown, Arizona. In southern California bulbous clay figurines molded over acorn kernels may have been used in a fertility ritual (True, Meighan, and Crew 1974, 66–67). Some of the clay Venus figurines may also contain a seed—ritually sown in the earth—material that was molded into these images of fertility with the notion that the earth brings forth crops as the woman brings forth children.

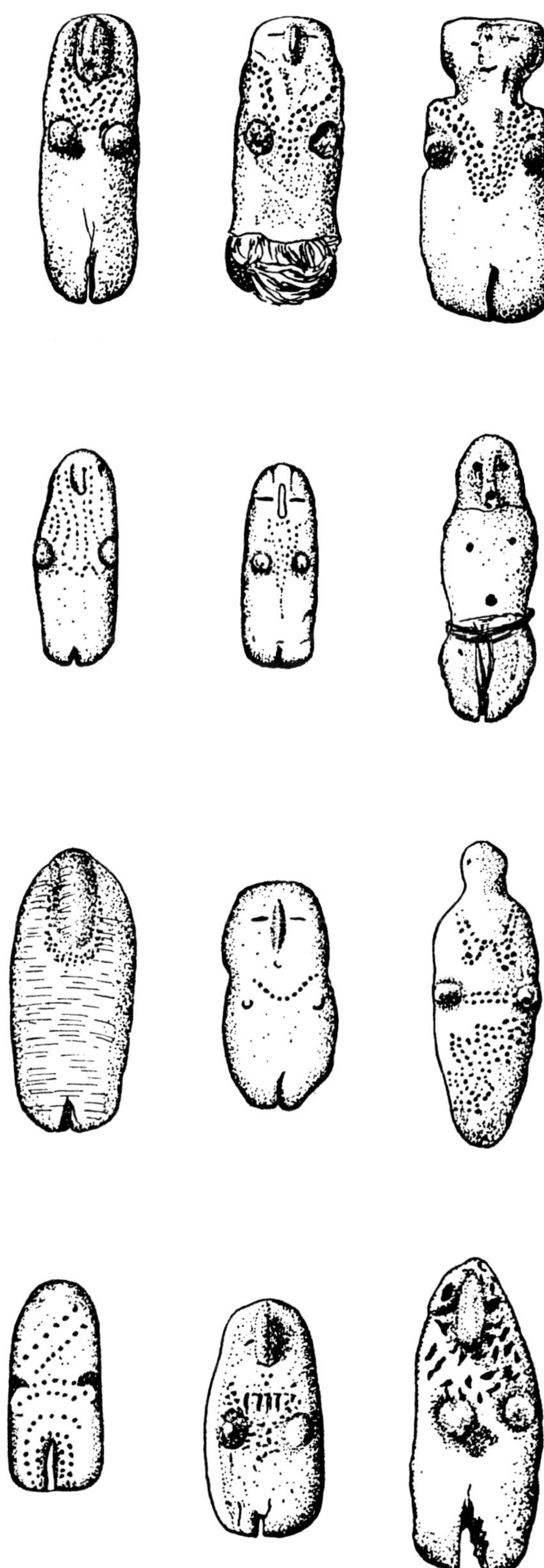

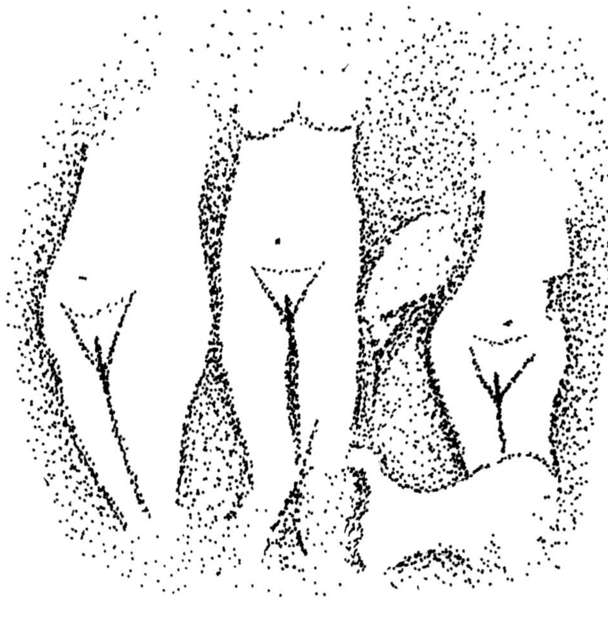

The famous Paleolithic cave paintings of Europe, some 30,000 years old, were created by the same cultures that carved the female figurines, and they express similar concerns about fertility. The murals are exquisite renderings of animals and suggest an intimate relationship with the animal world and its spirits. The dark, womblike caves provided a location for magic to support the regeneration of life—a place to spiritually incubate the great herds of animals upon which these Ice Age hunters depended. These symbolic landscapes of imagery conveyed fundamental ideas about nature. The sacredness of caves as wombs of the earth was perhaps suggested by observing animals such as bears that hibernate in winter and then emerge with their newborn in spring—a time when the earth itself reawakens.

In addition to images of animals, the painted caves of Ice Age Europe contain carvings and scratched designs representing the female form (figs. 4 and 5). Some of these markings may have been records of menstruation, and one such carving may depict a birth scene. Other rock art of similar antiquity from Africa and Australia also expresses analogous concepts about fertility, sex, and supernatural power associated with procreative forces and is discussed further in Chapter 5.

Fertility images can take many forms. In addition to images of women, vulva symbols came to represent the female and

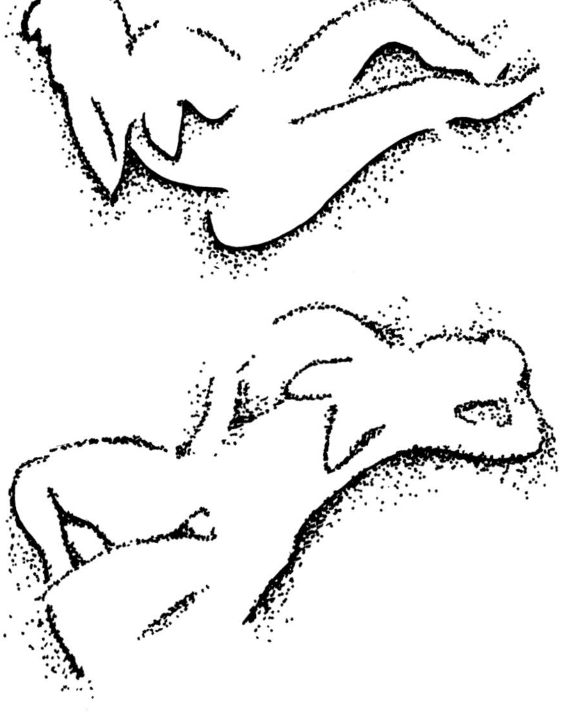

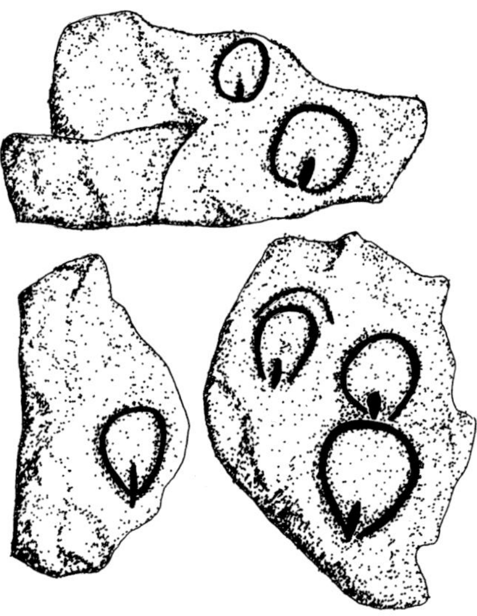

fertility generally in the art of many cultures around the world (fig.s 6 and 7). Anthropologist Alexander Marshack, in one of the first scholarly studies of this symbol, wrote that the vulva became

> isolated, abstracted, and symbolic to the point where it could be recognized in a simple circle with a single mark. One assumes, then, that the image and story were so well known they were "understood" by every adult in the culture, that it was a traditional image with a traditional story. This argues for use of this symbol over many generations, a use so ancient it could be decorated or embellished without loss of recognition or meaning (Marshack 1972, 297).

This concept is beautifully illustrated by a story from South Africa, where Adrian Boshier was exploring the symbolic content of rock paintings. He took Credo Mutwa, a Zulu *sangoma* (spirit-diviner), to see a site he had discovered in the bush:

> "Look there," said Mutwa, pointing to a sign painted on the village wall, an oval design surrounding a very stylized face. "That is the symbol of birth. No one but a midwife would paint such a thing on her wall." And, indeed, the village was occupied by two ancient *babelegisi* or midwives. A short while later Adrian Boshier led Credo Mutwa into a cave containing a similar design in red ochre—a sixteen-inch high, somewhat vulvar oval, this time without a face, but surrounded by a pattern of red thumbprints. Ecstatic, Mutwa fell on his knees in front of the crude painting. "How wonderful! This place is very special. The symbol is that of the goddess, the great mother, the sign of birth and life. It shows the female part," he added, rather unnecessarily. "What about the thumbprints?" asked Boshier. "They are the number of births. They tell how many babies were born here." He counted 92 dots and announced that the cave was certainly a popular maternity ward. "Serapa bana, a garden of babies" (Watson 1982, 104–5).

For many years there was a common misconception that North America's rock art was relatively lacking in sexual symbolism compared to that of Europe, Africa, and elsewhere. However, we now know that the symbolic content of prehistoric images, especially in the American Southwest, is rich with fertility themes, not surprising since it has been well established that these themes are universal and archetypal. Early misconceptions owed partly to a limited awareness of the true range of rock art imagery, but were also the result of religious zealotry and sexual prudery that characterized the first centuries of exploration on our continent, especially in the Spanish Catholic Southwest. While explicit erotic scenes are not abundant among the thousands of rock art sites in North America, they can be found in many rock art regions of the continent, including the Southwest.

Early observers chose to overlook, misinterpret, or destroy scenes they found offensive or threatening to their worldview. An example, an 1821 Spanish expedition in southern California that encountered pictographs "of a venal nature" in a

fig. 4.(opposite page, top left) Paleolithic rock carvings of female torsos in the wall of a rock shelter, Le Roc-aux-Sorciers, Vienne, France (after Anati 1994, 79).

fig. 5. (opposite page, bottom left) Fifteen thousand-year-old rock carvings in La Magdeleine Cave, Aveyron Valley, France (after Campbell 1988, I(1):69).

fig. 6. (opposite page, bottom right) Rock carvings of vulvas from the Aurignacian period (30,000 B.C.), Abri Blanchard, Castelmerle, Dordogne, France (after Gimbutas 1989, 99).

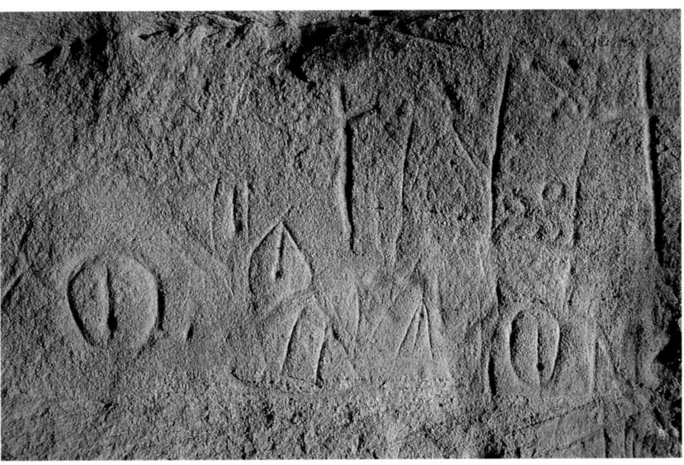

fig. 7. (below) Petroglyphs of vulva symbols inside a small cave, Galisteo Creek, New Mexico.

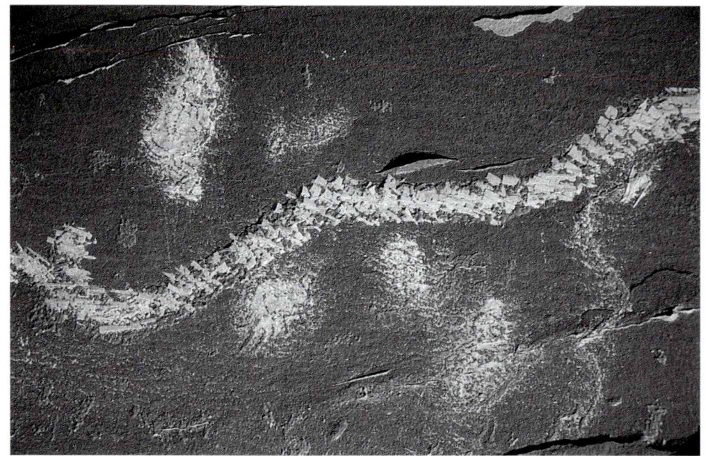

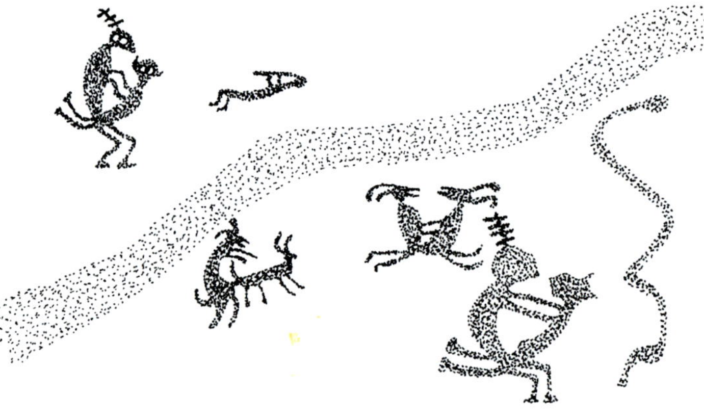

fig. 8. (top) Destruction of Anasazi petroglyphs depicting sexual activity at Inscription Point, Arizona.

fig. 9. (bottom) Drawing of the petroglyphs at Inscription Point, Arizona, before they were vandalized (after Hunger 1983, 116).

canyon near San Antonio de Pala relates how: "[the men] discovered a stone which without doubt had served and still serves these unhappy Indians as an occasion of sin. One look sufficed, owing to its many huge figures and the adjoining thicket, to make it clear what it might signify. The Reverend Friar Prefecto commanded Friar Peyri to have it destroyed" (Englehardt 1921, 44). Other historical records also document similar efforts by early Spanish priests in New Mexico to destroy rock art in order to exorcize evil spirits from the pagan images.

Even the early anthropologists, archaeologists, and ethnographers, with a few notable exceptions, may have declined to report some of the more prurient (to their Victorian sensibilities) images. Consequently, discussions of sexual intercourse are rare in most of the ethnographic and historic literature, much of which was produced during this period. The few that occur are downplayed, and some were even published in Greek, Latin, and German—ostensibly to lend them a veneer of intellectual objectivity. Nonetheless, they strongly suggest the significance of sexual symbolism in the greater Southwest (Whitley 1994, 21). Even in the 1970s, editors of journals dealing with the science of man have been loath to publish any such "dirty pictures," for fear of offending their readers. An author of rejected material wrote:

> While such sentiments accurately reflect the prejudicial notions of propriety valid in our own culture, they should, nevertheless, have no place in the dispassionate examination of the cultural manifestations of other peoples who follow their own rules of etiquette and have fared well in doing so (Wellman 1974a, 2).

Some anthropologists have claimed as recently as 1975 that avoidance of sexual material is endemic in their profession, and that even when sexuality has been explored, "description has tended to be brief and perfunctory, analysis wary" (Duberman 1979, 130).

Such attitudes are symptomatic of Western morality, the keynote of which has been inhibition of sexual impulses. Christianity made all Europe and the Americas a vast experiment in sexual inhibition and suppression with its doctrine of original sin and its anti-pleasure philosophy:

> Even today it is hardly possible for anyone brought up in one of the western nations to comprehend the ancient world's opinion of sex as an experience of divine pleasure or a preview of heaven, without deliberate, laborious intellectual progress toward such an opinion (Walker 1983, 912).

Although we like to think we live in a more enlightened and tolerant time, as recently as the 1980s in Arizona petro-

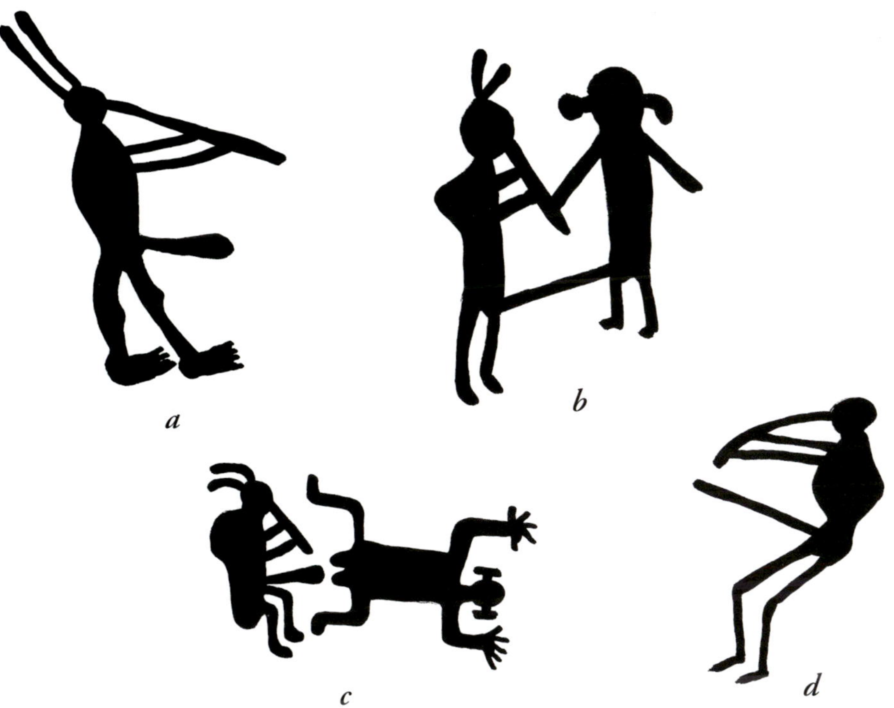

fig. 10. Petroglyphs of humpbacked, phallic flute players emphasizing the sexual nature of this important fertility symbol in southwestern rock art: a. San Juan River, Utah; b. and c. Santa Fe River, New Mexico; d. Galisteo Basin, New Mexico.

glyphs of a sexual nature were still being destroyed by religious zealots (figs. 8 and 9).[5] In another account from Michigan's Fayette Peninsula, pictographs of exaggeratedly phallic figures "Had been so blatantly male that the management of a girl's camp nearby had them defaced" (Dewdney, quoted in Vastokas 1973, 86). Even as recently as 1999 an outstanding petroglyph site in Largo Canyon, New Mexico, was vandalized when someone obliterated the phallic nature of a prominent antrhopomorphic figure. Despite our society's obsession with sexual topics, we still lack understanding of the true, spiritual nature of prehistoric sexual images. Even the wildly popular rock art figure Kokopelli—the humpbacked flute player and ultimate southwestern fertility icon—is usually sanitized and censored (as if it was petro-porn) for the ubiquitous commercial displays; in rock art depictions he is commonly shown with exaggerated phallic attributes and in various fertility contexts (fig. 10).

Regardless of its content, the subject of southwestern rock art did not receive much serious attention by scholars until a few decades ago. Because much of the iconography was considered inscrutable and accurate dating was problematic, most archaeologists overlooked rock art in their professional activities. Today, all that has changed, and a great deal of serious study has vastly improved our understanding of rock art and its value as a cultural artifact of prehistoric people—it affords us our only view of early ceremonial life and other activities as seen through the eyes of these ancient artists.

The American desert was discovered by an unknown people. They tried its deepest secrets. Now they have vanished, extinct as the tapir and coryphodon. But the undeciphered message that they left us remains, written on the walls. A message preserved not in mere words and numbers, but in the durable images of line on stone. We were here.[6]

—Edward Abbey
The Serpents of Paradise

Art outlives governments, creeds, societies, even civilizations. Art is what we find again when the ruins are cleared away. [7]

—Katherine Anne Porter

Symbols stand for or suggest something by reason of relationship, convention, or accident, including something invisible or intangible such as concepts of death and fertility.

—*Webster's Third New International Dictionary*

CHAPTER 1

SOUTHWESTERN ROCK ART AND CULTURAL TRADITIONS

THE MEANING AND FUNCTION OF ROCK ART

There are basically two kinds of rock art—petroglyphs and pictographs. Petroglyphs are pecked, carved, or abraded images whereas pictographs are painted onto rock surfaces with natural pigments, usually under protective ledges or in caves, locations that have helped them survive through the ages. Petroglyphs usually occur on rocks such as sandstone or basalt that have a dark surface or patina, known as desert varnish, which forms slowly as a result of weathering and microbial/chemical alterations. When the desert varnish is removed by pecking or carving with another stone, the lighter-colored unweathered rock is exposed, producing a visual contrast. Sometimes smoke-blackened walls of caves or ceremonial chambers provided the same effect for producing petroglyphs. Petroglyphs will eventually darken, or repatinate, as the weathering process continues on the rock surface, although it can take hundreds to thousands of years for the process to completely repatinate petroglyphs, depending on microclimatic factors at specific sites. The degree of patination between different petroglyphs on the same rock provides a relative means of dating, with the fresher-looking ones younger than the darker ones.

Pictographs, or rock paintings, are obviously more vulnerable than petroglyphs, and, unless protected from the weather, will not usually last as long.[8] Natural pigments such as iron oxides (hematite or limonite), white or yellow clays and soft rock, charcoal, and copper minerals were used to produce a palette of red, yellow, white, black, blue, and green. Organic binders were used to mix the powdered mineral pigments into a paint. Binders could be some combination of fluids such as plant juices, egg, animal fat, saliva, blood, urine, and water. Most pictographs are relatively small, although there are some life-size exceptions.

One of the most frequently asked questions about rock art is what it means. Accurate interpretation is difficult, however, because exact meaning cannot be proven, only assumed or extrapolated from ethnographic sources, such as existing Pueblo tribes. Because rock art now exists out of its cultural context, attempting to explain how it functioned and what it meant to past societies is tentative at best. This uncertainty is further complicated by the fact that archaeological records are incomplete, especially regarding the earliest societies. Only in the case of historic Indian rock art is it possible to make relatively certain interpretations based on historic records and ethnographic informants. As symbols, rock art images must be examined in the contexts of time, place, and culture. On a broad scale we know that these symbols functioned in information exchange and as a means of expressing group identities, but few studies have demonstrated more precise meaning of prehistoric rock art.

Reasons for making rock art could include marking territory and features such as trails, springs, and shrines; recording special events, rituals, successful hunts, and battles; ensuring rain, bountiful harvests and fertility; creating something of beauty; or simply saying "I was here." No matter what the motivation, rock art is generally aesthetically pleasing and seems to have been creatively inspired, even if that was not always the primary intention. Moreover, it is nearly always located in special places of grandeur or power, something undoubtedly not coincidental. Whatever its function, it seems clear that the elements of rock art are complex and powerful symbols rather than being merely decorative. The making of rock art was primarily related to concerns about the supernatural and spiritual, with sites selected because they were considered numinous—inhabited by spirits.

Perhaps rock art is best defined as an artifact of ideas. As ancient records of sacred concepts and former worldviews, rock art images are tangible manifestations of beliefs and visions. These symbols provided communication and a record for future generations about cultural values and ideas. Thus rock art reflects the minds and souls of ancient, vanished people and allows us to examine aspects of the most basic mode of early human existence—that of the hunter-gatherer. We are all descended from ancestors with similar cultural practices, and themes in rock art of all continents reflect this universal connection.

There is consensus among scholars that rock art is not "writing" and cannot be "read" as such. It is a language only in the sense that symbols are used to represent things in a nonliteral, symbolic manner. There is no doubt that rock art contains messages of many kinds, including ownership, warnings, signatures, demarcations, exhortations, and commemorations, as well as stories and myths. But we cannot read them, and without the ancient artists to inform us, how would we know if we were right or wrong? Today, we can understand certain rock art styles to varying degrees. For example, the more recent Pueblo rock art is more readily interpreted through ethnographic accounts, because the beliefs of the artists who created it have been preserved by their recent descendants. By contrast, millennia-old rock art of Archaic peoples is relatively inscrutable, because there is no other record of their beliefs passed down to descendants. However, despite some intriguing suppositions about its meaning, any interpretation of rock art remains conjecture. Yet although rock art elements may remain ambiguous, they will always engage us because they represent mysterious, intangible realms and because they challenge us to integrate our own physical and spiritual worlds.

One of the more intriguing explanations for some types of nonrepresentational abstract or geometric rock art is the neuropsychological model that suggests it mirrors entoptic (within the eye) phenomena. This concept holds that certain geometric visual imagery is projected by the optic nervous system and is caused by an altered state of consciousness. Altered states of consciousness can be induced by psychoactive drugs such as peyote, datura, and mescal; drumming; chanting; dance; sensory deprivation, as in the vision quest; hyperventilation; or meditation. Through such activities, many of which are employed in shamanic practice, people tend to perceive relatively common, fundamental forms such as grids, dots, parallel and zigzag lines, nested curves, concentric circles, and thin meandering lines. According to the neurological model, some rock art motifs that exhibit these forms may be products of shamanic or trancing traditions or other altered states of consciousness. They may be the record of someone's vision or mental imagery. The model cannot, however, accurately ascribe the role that different cultural meanings would affix to such perceptual phenomena. For instance, it cannot indicate whether some rock art was made by an experienced shaman, by a shaman's apprentice, or by a shaman's patient as part of a curing ceremony; what rock art was produced by a group of artists and what was produced by a lone individual; how much acceptability there was for individual, idiosyncratic expression within culturally defined norms of expression; or how much of a particular style was instinctual and how much was consciously produced.

In addition to the questions raised by shamanic rock art that is abstract or entoptic, there are also significant numbers of shaman-influenced styles that are representational rock art images in the Southwest, and that contain some of the most intriguing and enigmatic depictions of fertility themes.

The locations of some rock art sites provide clues as to its possible meaning. We know that Pueblo/Anasazi rock art, and probably most other, was often made near places in the landscape imbued with mythic significance, or at shrines where ritual took place. Many are near villages, but some are quite remote and hidden. Prominent high points and tributary confluences of streams or canyons are other favored places. Caves and rock shelters were thought to be entrances to the underworld and so often contain rock art. Yet in addition to being situated at places of ritual significance, rock art occurs in many other places as different as the landscape itself.

Despite the varied locations of rock art, it seems clear that many rock art sites are in places considered sacred or that have power of some kind. Some sites seem to be around prominent cracks or openings in the rock. Some of these may be rocks that have been struck by lightning, an obvious source of power. Further, openings in the rock have been described as locales where supernaturals or shamans' spirits enter the underworld or emerge into this one (fig. 11). Moreover, in many indigenous cultures, the surface of rock is seen as a veil separating this world and the supernatural realm, which lies behind. The placement of images near rock features is thus significant, as are prevalent symbols such as lizards and snakes, which may represent spirit messengers that can enter the supernatural realm via cracks and holes in rock.

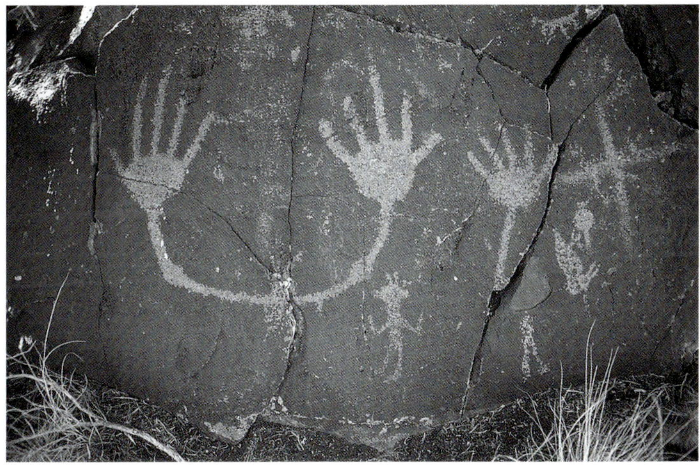

fig. 11. Pueblo petroglyphs of hands and arms emerging from rock cracks to suggest connection with the supernatural realms of the underworld inside the rock, Velarde, New Mexico.

Further, hunting magic or ritual is suggested by the placement of some rock art near prominent game trails at narrow passes, canyons, or at jump sites where animals could be driven over cliffs. Scenes with game animals pierced by arrows or spears have traditionally been interpreted in this way.

Another intriguing possibility is that rock art focused on prominent rock features could thus reflect aspects of Native American cosmology in a graphic way similar to the image of the *axis mundi*. In ancient cosmology, the *axis mundi* (axle of the world) pictured the world spinning on a shaft that penetrated the earth at its center/navel. Each nation placed this hub at the center of its own territory; each pueblo regards its ceremonial plaza as the focal point of activities. It is conceivable that some rock art which is focused on prominent vertical cracks (or other special features of the landscape) reflects aspects of Native American cosmology. Native concepts of a vertically layered cosmos, of which the earth is but one layer in a series between the sky and underworld, tend to support such interpretation.

In addition to significant locations, some rock art sites seem to have special acoustical properties. Rock overhangs, alcoves, caves, and canyon walls can have dramatic resonance and echo-producing qualities, which would accentuate the effects of drums, chants, flutes, or other

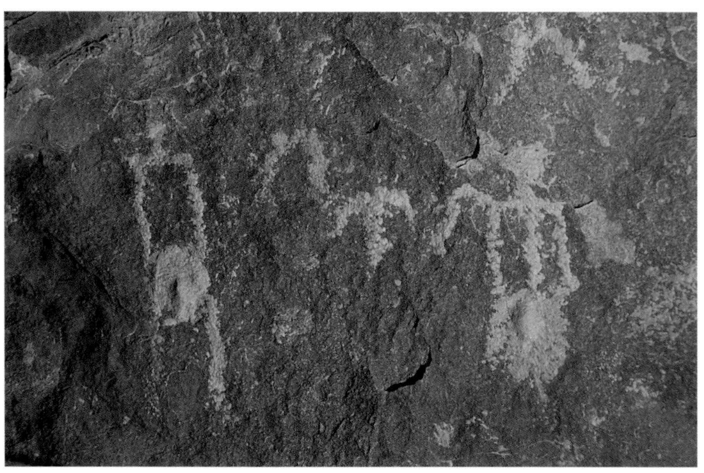

fig. 12. Petroglyphs of anthropomorphs with deeply pecked genital area, suggesting ritual activity related to fertility. Rasmussen Cave, Nine Mile Canyon, Utah.

ritual sounds. Further, some large rock slabs seem to have special acoustical properties that make them ring like a bell or gong when struck with another rock. Moreover, rocks with deeply worn grooves or pits (cupules) were probably ritual sites where contact with supernatural forces was facilitated by the act of rubbing or striking the rock. For example, images related to fertility sometimes have deep pits in the genital areas (fig. 12), and depictions related to hunting may have evidence of ritual repecking on certain animals. Thus certain petroglyphs may have been created at specific sites, or used repeatedly, as a way of addressing the earth or contacting earth spirits.

Still another function of rock art may have been astronomical observations. In recent years substantial research in the field of archaeoastronomy has been focused on rock art sites that may have been created to function as solar observatories or calendrical markers. For horticultural people concerned with planting and harvesting times in a land of quirky growing seasons, accurate knowledge of solstices and equinoxes would have been invaluable. One of the first examples of such a site was the discovery of the "sun dagger" petroglyphs that seemed to mark the solstices and equinoxes at Fajada Butte in Chaco Canyon, New Mexico.

Despite the difficulties of interpreting most rock art, in recent decades our understanding of the iconography of some older rock art has significantly increased —rock art depicting shamanistic themes related to hunter-gatherer and early agricultural societies. Shamanism is an ancient, worldwide religious system practiced by most hunter-gatherer and some agricultural societies. The shaman is the tribal specialist in sacred matters, healing, fertility, death, and balancing universal forces. As scholars examine rock art images in this context, it is becoming more apparent that rock art was used by many past cultures to record shamanistic experiences and related spiritual events throughout the world, including the Southwest.

In contrast to the interpretation of representational styles of rock art, such as those where shamanistic elements are apparent, the relatively inscrutable imagery of abstract rock art styles is problematic. Without an understanding of the cultural processes that produced conventionalized symbols, we can only guess at their intended meaning. Even within a given society that created abstract rock art, perhaps only the specialists or initiates could understand the symbols. Studies of abstract rock art and symbology only conclude that the images symbolize certain aspects of the natural and supernatural realms or served as mnemonic devices to trigger memory and narrative accounts. The exception to this inability to grasp the meaning of abstract rock art is the relatively recent theory about entoptic phenomena related to visions experienced in trance and altered states of consciousness.

Despite possible interpretations, the meaning of rock art remains elusive. However, whatever its function, its aesthetic quality is apparent. In *The Serpents of Paradise*, Edward Abbey expressed a central issue about controversy surrounding the meaning of rock art:

> Perhaps meaning is not of primary importance here. What is important is the recognition of art, wherever we may discover it, in whatever form. These canyon paintings and canyon inscriptions are valuable for their own sake, as work of elegance, freshness, originality (in the original sense of the word),

economy of line, precision of point, integrity of materials. They are beautiful. And all of them are hundreds of years old—some may be much, much older.

The artist Paul Klee, whose surreal work resembles some of this desert rock art, wrote in his *Diaries 1898–1918:* "There are two mountains on which the weather is bright and clear, the mountain of the animals and the mountain of the gods. But between lies the shadowy valley of men." How's that for meaning (Abbey 1995, 309)?

CULTURAL TRADITIONS OF SOUTHWESTERN ROCK ART

The American Southwest has a special allure—its beautiful, mysterious landscape is imbued with magical charm and a tangible presence of ancient peoples. Sculpted by eons of erosion, the incredible desert vistas, broken by canyons, mesas, and majestic mountain ranges overwhelm the senses. A land of stunning topographic contrasts and environmental and cultural diversity, it is a region where many prehistoric cultures have thrived for millennia. The prehistory of the Southwest falls into three broad categories—the Paleo-Indian, the Archaic, and the later periods consisting of at least five major cultural traditions: the Anasazi, Fremont, Hohokam, Mogollon, and Patayan. In the following sections, the principal cultural traditions are discussed, including brief descriptions of the rock art styles attributable to these cultures as well as protohistoric cultures present at European contact (see map, fig. 13).

Rock art was created over a long span of time. It was continually produced in constantly evolving styles from the period of early hunter-gatherers to that of later, more complex agricultural societies. To understand its origin, age, and possible meaning, rock art has been classified by styles. Further, rock art styles can be divided into two basic categories, representational and abstract. Representational rock art depicts life-forms (humans, animals, plants, supernatural beings) but is more often highly stylized than naturalistic. Abstract elements, whether geometric or free-form shapes, are not recognizably related to the real world. Generally speaking, abstract rock art is older and was created by hunter-gatherers, whereas most representational rock art is more recent and was produced by primarily agricultural societies, although in some areas abstract rock art was made continuously up to the time of European contact. Much rock art of the Archaic period and some that is transitional between the Archaic and agricultural periods, such as early Basketmaker Anasazi, has shamanistic elements.

The basis for organizing rock art into stylistic categories involves patterns observed in systematic investigations of human cultures. The art of any culture group is bound by the confines of a style. In regard to rock art, the main components of style are element inventory and figure types. General aesthetics and technical production are also part of what constitutes a style. Once these are determined, the distribution in space and time of a rock art style can be used within cultural and archaeological contexts to infer limited meaning to the rock art and its development. Rock art styles usually span broad periods measured in centuries. In areas where a number of styles share similar traits over time, the concept of style tradition is employed. For example, in eastern Utah there is a tradition of shamanic anthropomorphic figures in the rock art of a number of different styles—collectively known as the Utah Anthropomorphic Tradition. In areas of great physical and cultural diversity, all rock art does not fit neatly into existing style categories. Nevertheless, rock art styles provide a general conceptual framework useful for comparison and observation of contextual changes. Currently accepted ideas about rock art styles are broadly correlated to the various cultures known to have inhabited the region.

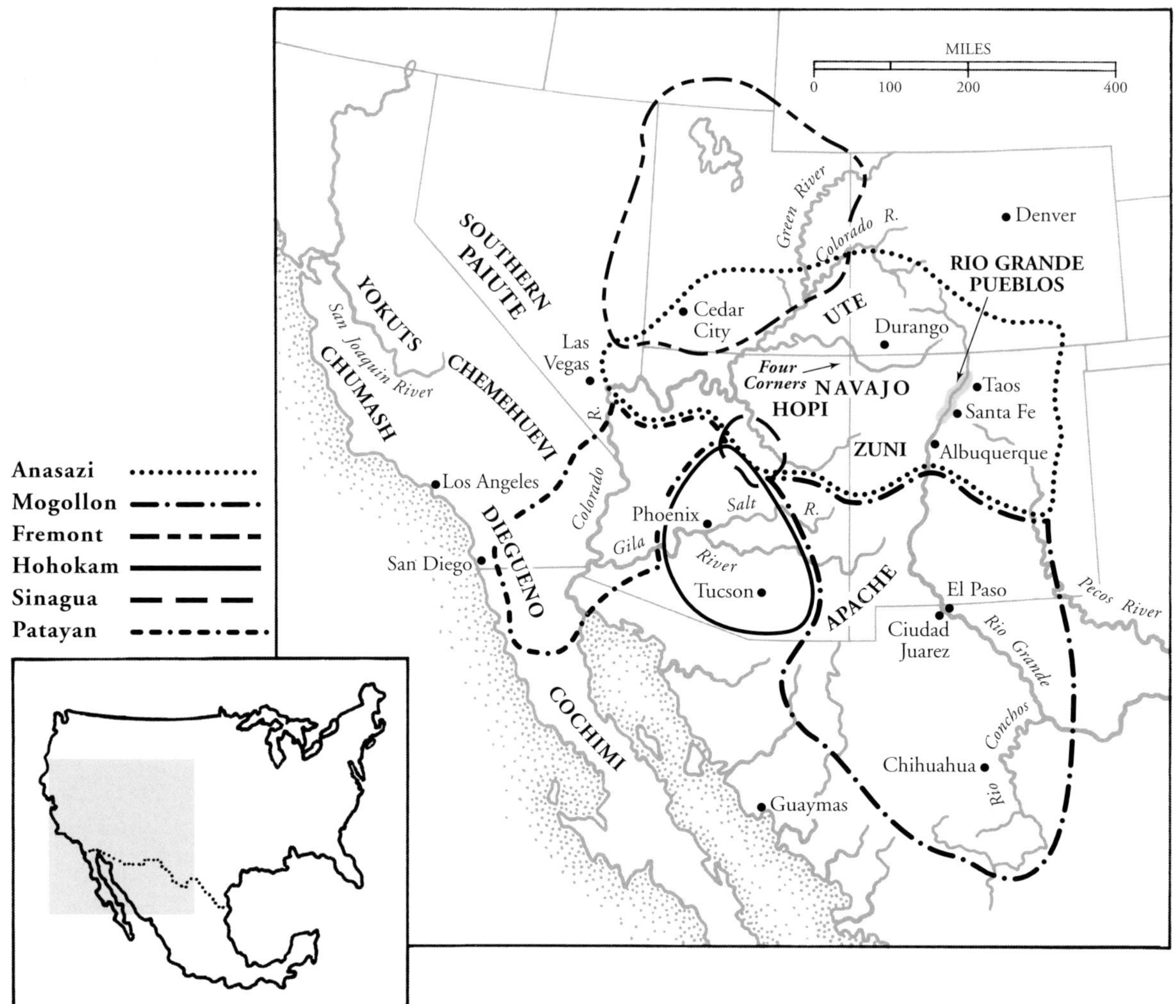

fig. 13. Map of the greater Southwest showing regions and culture areas discussed in this book (adapted from Cordell 1984, 15).

To most people today, the term Southwest probably conjures up visions of the Four Corners states of New Mexico, Arizona, Utah, and Colorado. That area constitutes the core of the Southwest, but because state lines are recent, artificial concepts, the Southwest is more broadly defined here on a cultural and geographic basis in order to include the rock art of adjacent and overlapping provinces. This book looks at sites from Texas to California, and from northern Mexico to the Rocky Mountains and Great Basin. This large area of the greater Southwest contains thousands of rock art sites, representing dozens of distinct styles that were produced by many different cultures.

A land of extreme physical contrasts, the Southwest necessarily forged enduring and adaptable societies. Before contact with Europeans, unbroken land, despite its harshness, sustained humans and animals in the sacred web of life. The land was marked with hallowed places and signs in many languages, and the spirit world was integrated with the physical. The map in fig. 13 shows the region's principal features and the primary cultural provinces that produced the rock art later discussed in connection with its fertility themes.

The Paleo-Indians

People have been in the Southwest for at least 12,000 years. According to the archaeological community, the first Native Americans are thought to have crossed a land bridge between Asia and Alaska that was exposed intermittently during the Pleistocene Ice Ages between 8,000 and 23,000 years ago. By contrast, many Indians believe their people have always been here in sacred places or that their ancestors came here from the underground or spirit world. The land bridge theory says that successive waves of immigration eventually peopled all of North and South America. In the Southwest, these first Paleo-Indians are known from their distinctive fluted stone lance heads (Clovis and Folsom points) that have been found with the remains of the big game animals they stalked. As long as 12,000 years ago they hunted mammoth, giant bison, camels, sloth, antelope, and tapirs. Nearly all of these Ice Age megafauna were extinct by about 8500 B.C., perhaps due in part to successful hunting strategies by the Paleo-Indians. No rock art is known in the Southwest from Paleo-Indians; the earliest is from the Archaic people who followed.

The Archaic Period Peoples

The Archaic Period (typically known as the Western Archaic or Desert Archaic in the Southwest) began with the final drying cycle of the cool, wet glacial climate that had preceded and with the commencement of desert and semiarid climates that prevail today. As the climate became more arid, people of necessity became more dependent on the fewer existing perennially flowing streams and springs, and habitation as well as rock art distribution may reflect this.

The Archaic Period spans from about 5500 B.C. to A.D. 100. Evidence of the Archaic way of life has been documented from most parts of the Southwest, where slight regional variations have been described. During this time, people in the Southwest were hunter-gatherers and typically were nomadic, at least seasonally, as a function of food supply. There was more emphasis on gathering wild plants and killing small animals such as rabbits, in contrast to the large game hunting of the Paleo-Indians. Populations remained small and unconcentrated. From their artifacts found in dry caves in the Southwest, we know they were skilled in basketry, textiles, and woodworking. Housing was impermanent, and natural shelters such as caves and rock overhangs were often used. Many impressive rock paintings and engravings of this era are found in caves and on cliffs. The earliest known rock art in the region is attributed to this culture, as are some of the most interesting fertility-related images.

The earliest Western Archaic rock art was abstract, followed later by the addition of zoomorphic and anthropomorphic

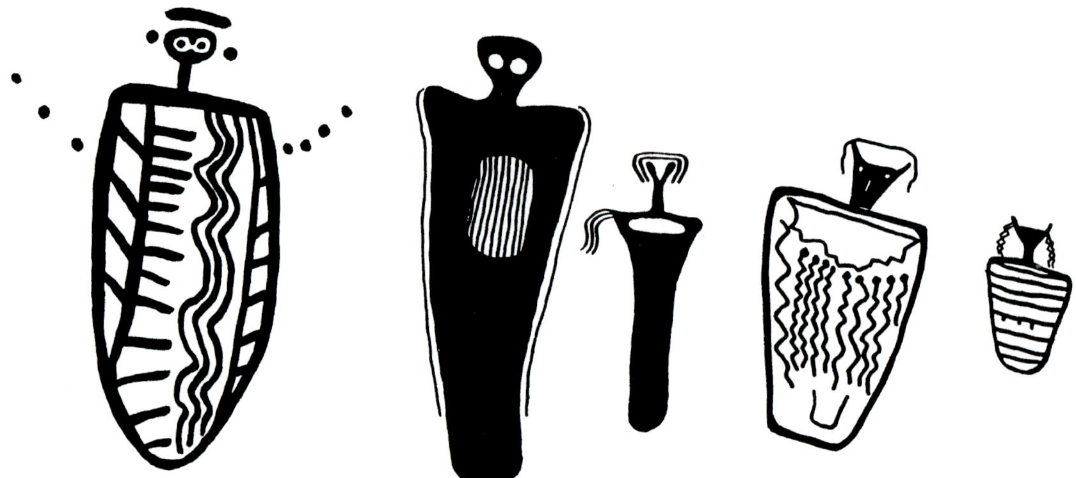

fig. 14. Composite of various Barrier Canyon Style anthropomorphic images that represent shamans or supernatural figures, from southeastern Utah.

elements in both petroglyphs and pictographs. The ideography of their rock art was heavily influenced by shamanism. The shaman was a priest-healer who was believed to possess supernatural or psychic powers received through trances and dreams, frequently achieved by the use of hallucinogens. He was responsible for healing the sick, revealing the arcane, and using his power to control events that affected the fertility of crops, game animals, and the tribe itself. Bird symbolism was important in shamanism, hence the concept of magical "soul-flight." Snakes were also commonly depicted in shamanistic imagery; it was believed that as spirit helpers snakes could access the underworld by entering cracks in the rocks, and their ability to shed their skins represented powerful regenerative magic. Shamans used masks to give tangible form to the power of their relationship to spirit helpers (in contexts of magical "soul-flight," hunting magic, healing, and so forth) and evidently represented themselves in rock art to fix their power in concrete expression. Horns on human figures may indicate their shamanic powers.

In the Southwest, numerous rock art styles are ascribed to the Archaic Period, including Desert (Great Basin) Abstract Style, Great Basin Representational Style, Chihuahuan Polychrome Style, Glen Canyon Linear Style, Diablo Dam Petroglyph Style, Barrier Canyon Style, Pecos River Style, and Red Linear Style. Rock art of the Desert Abstract Style is found throughout much of the Southwest, but its boundaries are not currently known. This style consists of zigzags, circles, triangles, wavy lines, sun disks, rakes, and snakelike designs. As petroglyphs, they typically occur on boulders or outcroppings, usually filling most of the rock faces on which they are placed. Pictographs of the Chihuahuan Polychrome Style are similar and may be analogous to the Desert Abstract Style petroglyphs. The function of these Archaic rock art sites is not well understood. Some petroglyph sites occur near springs and may thus be related to concerns with moisture. In the Great Basin of Nevada and western Utah, rock art of this style is linked to hunting magic (Heizer and Baumhoff 1962). It seems apparent that creating petroglyphs was an important part of the rituals performed at these Archaic sites, and they could have incorporated ideas about territorial rights or water, or pertained to appeasement of the supernatural.

Other major Archaic rock art styles are representational and typically express strong shamanic contexts—featuring large anthropomorphic figures that represent shamans or supernaturals, along with their spirit helpers. The Barrier Canyon Style of southeastern Utah exemplifies this genre with prominent, elaborately decorated anthropomorphs (fig. 14). These figures are commonly described as ghostly, spectral, otherworldly, powerful, and mysterious. Edward Abbey, who explored and wrote passionately about many of the canyons where these figures are painted, described them as follows:

> These are sinister and supernatural figures, gods from the underworld perhaps, who hover in space, or dance. . . . Most are faceless but some stare back at you with large, hollow, disquieting eyes. Demonic shapes, they might have meant protection to their creators and a threat to strangers: Beware, traveler. You are approaching the land of the horned gods (Abbey 1990, 101).

Demonic or beneficent, there is no doubt these images represented special beings to the Archaic people who created them. The usual iconography of this style involves tall, normally armless, broad-shouldered anthropomorphs, often occurring in rows or groups. Facial features are commonly missing; however, prominent, bulging eyes are occasionally depicted. Anthropomorphic figures are frequently associated with snakes, birds, rabbits, and bighorn sheep, as well as with other types of abstract anthropomorphs. These images are distributed over a large area, from the Grand Canyon north to the White River drainage in northwest Colorado. The Barrier Canyon Style is dated approximately 5000 to 500 B.C. but there are reasons to suspect an even older origin (Schaafsma 1994, 45). Early dates are supported by archaeological materials and radiocarbon dates from sites in eastern Utah. Clay figurines that resemble the Barrier Canyon Style anthropomorphs have been excavated from caves and dated between 6000 and 4000 B.C. (Cole 1990, 70; Schaafsma 1971, xii). At another site, midden materials that may have been related to a Barrier Canyon pictograph have been dated approximately 1400 B.C. It is likely that Barrier Canyon Style sites served as religious shrines or ceremonial places, due to the remote and special locations selected and the depictions of large, striking shamanistic figures that convey a sense of spiritual power. The ghostly aspect of many of these figures may indicate the metaphorical death which the shaman experiences in trance and in his initiatory journey to the underworld; in some shamanic cultures skeletal imagery is used for this purpose. At some sites the rock paintings appear to be the work of one person or a limited number of people, suggesting that they were probably made by a select few artists or shamans. This style predates Anasazi and Fremont rock art, but it influenced both of them, as well as other styles on the Colorado Plateau that are part of a 2,000-year-old rock art tradition that emphasizes large, powerful anthropomorphic forms.

The pictographs of the Pecos River Style in Texas are remarkably similar in iconographic content to Utah Barrier Canyon Style rock paintings, and the two styles are roughly contemporaneous. Present at some Pecos River Style sites are other, peculiar images of the Red Linear Style—also ascribed to the Archaic Period (Turpin 1990, 104). Some of these pictographs seem to be especially concerned with fertility themes or rituals. Also in west Texas along the Rio Grande, the Diablo Dam Petroglyph Style consists of petroglyphs depicting primarily shamans and hunters with an emphasis on large spear points, perhaps indicating a concern with hunting and animal fertility.

The Glen Canyon Linear Style is another archaic, representational petroglyph style that was identified from type sites on the Colorado River in Utah and Arizona. Beginning dates are still uncertain but could have originated as early as 4000 B.C., based on similarities of animal figures portrayed in this style and split-twig animal figurines that have been found in the Grand Canyon and Utah that date between 1,500 and 4,000 years old (Turner 1971, 469–71). This style is widely distributed across the Colorado Plateau, with most sites occurring in canyons along major river corridors. This rock art is also part of the Utah Anthropomorphic Tradition referred to above, and as such has similarities with other styles of rock art in the region. In addition to pecked shamanistic figures having a ceremonial or supernatural appearance, it includes a variety of animals and occasional abstract elements.

The Great Basin Representational Style seems to have originated from Archaic groups in the Great Basin, where it is found along the Colorado River in southern California and Nevada. Examples of this style are present, however, in eastern Utah, where it either replaced the old Great Basin Abstract Style or was added to the Archaic repertoire sometime after A.D. 1 (Schaafsma 1980, 55). It is believed to have been transmitted to this region by tribal commerce or by the migration of Great Basin peoples, probably by movement along the Colorado River corridor. Typical elements consist of skillfully drawn bighorn sheep and other quadrupeds, anthropomorphs, and hands and feet. Both petroglyphs and pictographs occur, and this style frequently occurs with the Great Basin Abstract Style.

The development of representational styles of rock art in the late Archaic Period suggests the emergence of ideological changes. In representational elements we are able to discern the development of stylistic diversity or similarities—for example, there are resemblances between the art of the Glen Canyon Linear and the Great Basin Representational styles, and the influence of the Barrier Canyon Style can be seen in the Anasazi and Fremont rock art that followed. It is with these Archaic representational styles that the depiction of anthropomorphs with supernatural or shamanistic features originated on the Colorado Plateau and influenced the subsequent rock art of the Anasazi and Fremont cultures (Cole 1990, 59).

By 1000 B.C. the life-style of southwestern hunter-gatherers began to change as they learned to cultivate corn (maize), beans, and squash, which were introduced to the area by trading contacts with the ancient societies in Mexico. Gradually becoming more sedentary with dependence on crops and irrigation, the next distinctive regional cultures of the region were taking shape by 300 B.C. with the advent of village living and the use of pottery. At first, small communities were scattered across huge territories; then after A.D. 750 small villages began to grow into towns and even cities (pueblos) with distinctive stone or adobe architecture. In the core area of the Southwest, several approximately contemporaneous cultures evolved, including the Mogollon in southern New Mexico, the Anasazi in the Colorado Plateau and upper Rio Grande, the Sinagua and Hohokam in central and southern Arizona, and the Fremont in Utah—all of which produced rock art that depicts fertility themes.

The Mogollon People

The Mogollon culture region covers approximately the southern half of New Mexico as far east as the Pecos River, northern parts of Chihuahua and Sonora, Mexico, and extends into southeastern Arizona as far north as the Little Colorado River. This mountain and desert culture involved a complex series of developments and a period of major changes with far-reaching consequences for the history of the Southwest. Horticultural activities began very early in the Mogollon region, but village living did not commence until around 300 B.C. These villages consisted of relatively small group of pit houses until about A.D. 1000, after which above-ground, pueblo-type structures became prevalent.

Mesoamerican civilization strongly influenced the Mogollon culture development, including the symbols in its rock art. In turn, some of the ideologies of Mogollon rock art were apparently adopted by the Anasazi peoples to the north—in particular the masks associated with the kachina cult. The Western, or Mountain, Mogollon territory encompassed the rugged, wooded highlands of southwestern New Mexico and southeastern Arizona. The Eastern, or Desert, Mogollon territory extended east to the arid basin and range country of the Chihuahuan Desert. The Desert Mogollon are further divided into the Mimbres and Jornada regions.

The rock art of the Jornada and Mimbres regions, collectively known as the Jornada Style, was influential in the development of Pueblo rock art to the north, as well as modern ceremonial art throughout much of the Southwest (Schaafsma 1980, 186–87). The Jornada Style, datable from its appearance on decorated Mimbres ceramics, reflects a significant cultural shift in the region due to contacts with the high cultures of Mesoamerica. This Style is known for its rich inventory of visually stunning figures, including masks and faces, mythical beings, animals, blanket designs, horned serpents, fish, insects, and cloud terraces.

The Jornada Style persisted in southern New Mexico until approximately A.D. 1400 (Schaafsma 1980, 72). The function of Jornada Style sites is undoubtedly complex, but the near universal appearance of moisture-associated elements such as Tlaloc (a Mesoamerican rain deity), crested serpents, and cloud imagery suggests that the rock art was placed, in part, to ensure adequate rain and good harvests in this harsh desert land. Other water-loving figures found in Jornada Style sites are fish, tadpoles, turtles, and dragonflies. Many rock art enthusiasts consider the Jornada Style depictions of animals and humans to be the most imaginative, stylized, and creative of all southwestern rock art.

The Anasazi/Pueblo Peoples

The people we call Anasazi (a Navajo word meaning "Ancient Ones" or "Ancient Enemies") originated on the Colorado Plateau from Desert Archaic people about 2,000 years ago. They became the largest and best known of all prehistoric southwestern cultures and were primarily a horticultural society, growing corn, beans, and squash for food staples. Spectacular cliff dwellings and multistoried masonry pueblos with underground ceremonial chambers known as kivas are the architectural tradition of the classic Anasazi era. The Anasazi tradition spans a period from at least as early as 200 B.C. to approximately A.D. 1540, when the Spanish entered the Southwest. Modern Pueblo peoples living along the Rio Grande, and at Hopi, Zuni, and Acoma, are descendants of the Anasazi. Some Pueblo peoples today prefer the name Hisatsinom instead of Anasazi to refer to their ancestors.

Unlike many of their neighbors who shared common Desert Archaic origin and lifeways, the Anasazi culture exhibited a tendency for radical change throughout its history. It became more complex with time, perhaps due in part to the well-documented contacts with the cultures of Mexico across the desert to the south. Many developments from Mexico, and elsewhere, shaped Anasazi life: pottery, irrigation techniques, the bow and arrow, cotton and loom weaving, as well as esoteric knowledge and religious ideas.[9]

Stages of cultural development for the Anasazi and their descendants, the Pueblo peoples, are described by the Pecos Classification system based on archaeological remains. These cultural stages, with generalized dates, are as follows (Cole 1990, 13):

Basketmaker I: This was a postulated preagricultural stage, but this category is no longer used, and these traits are now attributed to the late Archaic stage (pre-A.D. 100).

Basketmaker II: Evidence of agriculture, use of atlatl, no pottery, no cranial deformation, pre-A.D. 1–A.D. 500 to 700.

Basketmaker III: Pit or slab houses, undecorated pottery cooking ware, no cranial deformation, A.D. 450–A.D. 750 to 800.

Pueblo I: Aboveground masonry villages, neck-banded cooking ware, cranial deformation, A.D. 750–A.D. 900 to 1000.

Pueblo II: Widely distributed small villages, corrugated cooking ware, A.D. 850–A.D. 1100 to 1150.

Pueblo III: Large communities, artistic elaboration and specialization, A.D. 1100–A.D. 1300.

Pueblo IV: Decline in artistic elaboration, plain wares instead of corrugated cooking wares; after A.D. 1300 the Colorado Plateau area was abandoned.

Pueblo V: Historic period from European contact in A.D. 1540 to the present, primarily in the Rio Grande drainage.

There was significant regional variation within Anasazi culture, and this is reflected in their distinctive cultural remains, including pottery, architecture, and rock art. The Anasazi rock art tradition of the Colorado Plateau endured for about 1,300 years. Although it evolved through a continuum of stylistic developments, there are great differences between the art of the early Basketmakers and that of the later periods that followed. From its origins in the San Juan Basin, Anasazi rock art eventually extended from Nevada to the Rio Grande in New Mexico.

Rock art of the Anasazi spans from the Basketmaker II and III periods through Pueblo I, II, and III. After Pueblo III times (A.D. 1300), major changes in the Anasazi world produced a new rock art tradition known as the Rio Grande Style, which dominates the rock art of the upper Rio Grande but which is lacking in the ancestral Anasazi territories of the Colorado Plateau. This style is quite different from early Anasazi rock art that preceded it. Kachina-like masks are common, anthropomorphs are large and often stylized, shield bearers and humpbacked flute players are prevalent and highly varied. Many types of animals are represented, with birds and snakes being more common. Cloud terraces, crosses, stars, corn plants, and handprints are also found. The elements of Rio Grande Style rock art are still maintained in ceremonial art by modern Pueblos.

Most Basketmaker II rock art occurs on the Colorado Plateau. Along the San Juan River in the southeastern part of Utah are a number of outstanding San Juan Anthropomorphic Style sites. This style is characterized by large, broad-shouldered anthropomorphs in frontal attitudes, usually wearing elaborate ceremonial regalia and replete with symbolism of shamans. Anasazi rock art of later periods (Basketmaker III through Pueblo III) is similar across a much larger area from Nevada to the Rio Grande Basin of New Mexico. There are petroglyphs and pictographs of animals, stick figures, lizards, flute players, tracks, birds, and textile and pottery motifs, which are thought to date between A.D. 1000 and 1300 (Schaafsma 1980, 160).

The role of rock art in the Pueblo world is probably comparable to that of other cultures in the Southwest, but due to the traditional continuity of the modern Pueblos it is possible to infer more meaning from many of the elements at Rio Grande Style sites. The religious context of most of the rock art expresses the Pueblo worldview and rituals. Some of it is associated with shrines, clan use areas, war, protective power, and hunting. One of the few symbolic carryovers from earlier Anasazi rock art to the Rio Grande Style is the continued presence of the flute player as a fertility symbol.

The Sinagua People

Most rock art sites in the area centered around the Verde River and Flagstaff, Arizona, are part of the Sinagua tradition, a culture on the fringes of the Western Anasazi, with Mogollon and Hohokam relationships. The Sinagua people appeared in this region in the seventh century A.D. and maintained their complex tradition until the fourteenth century, when their culture began to merge into that of the Hopi, now considered descendants of the Sinagua people. Their rock art iconography was influenced by the Anasazi to the northeast, as well as the Hohokam, from whom the Sinagua apparently adapted the beautifully executed and elaborate textile and formal abstract designs seen on petroglyph panels in the area.

The Hohokam People

The Hohokam area occurs in south-central Arizona, centered around the lower Gila and Salt rivers and their tributaries (fig. 13). It is believed that the Hohokam people had Mesoamerican origins, arriving in the area from the south around 300 B.C. At the time of their migration to this region, they already lived in villages and had developed pottery making and an extensive irrigation system to support their horticulture. The Hohokam people evidently imported the use of ball courts and temple mounds from the south. Their villages consisted of small groups of houses until the Classic Period (A.D. 1100–1450) at which time sizable adobe complexes and large houses began to predominate. The Papago and Tohono O'odham Indians (formerly Pima) are probably descendants of the Hohokam people.

In the rock art of the Hohokam area, petroglyphs are more common than pictographs; the petroglyph complex in this region has been described by Schaafsma as the Gila Petroglyph Style (Schaafsma 1980, 83). Both abstract and representational designs are present. Humans, game animals, and quadrupeds that may represent dogs are all found in Hohokam rock art. These are sometimes depicted with swollen abdomens suggesting pregnancy. The spiral is nearly ubiquitous in Hohokam rock art—probably occurring more frequently than in any other area of the Southwest.

The Fremont

The Fremont culture area includes that part of Utah northwest of the Colorado River and overlaps the Anasazi area in some locations; the approximate Fremont date range is A.D. 400–1300. Related to other Southwest cultures, the Fremont, although practicing horticulture, relied more on wild food gathering than did the neighboring Anasazi. Fremont settlements were quite small and did not have kivas. The Fremont area is divided into five major cultural regions: Sevier, Parowan, Southern San Rafael, Northern San Rafael, and Uintah. Each region is characterized by its own variations in rock art iconography and style.

Most Fremont rock art is in the eastern third of Utah. This rock art style was strongly influenced by Anasazi motifs from the south, such as realistic human figures and frequent depiction of shields, and is illustrated by some of the most spectacular and superbly executed panels in the Southwest. Fremont rock art styles fall within the Utah Anthropomorphic Tradition discussed earlier. Style overlaps between Fremont rock art and that of the Barrier Canyon, San Juan Anthropo–morphic, and later Anasazi styles is apparent, especially with regard to the portrayals of anthropomorphic figures (although Fremont rock art has certain geometric and angular qualities that distinguish it from the other styles). These and other similarities indicate there was cultural interaction between the Fremont and the Anasazi peoples.

Fremont rock art includes well-crafted petroglyphs, pictographs, and sometimes a combination of both. Heroic, supernatural-appearing anthropomorphs are a hallmark, and they often feature details in their clothing, body decorations and jewelry, facial features, and distinctive headdresses. They are typically broad-shouldered with tapering torsos, although some have other body shapes, and they frequently occur in rows similar to many Archaic and Anasazi styles. Fremont figures often are shown holding objects such as staffs, shields, weapons, bags, and even heads and scalps (Cole 1990, 191).[10] Many examples of Fremont rock art are located very high on cliff walls in nearly inaccessible locations. The artists took considerable risks to place the rock art in these locales, and the settings and care taken to make these images seem to attest to the ceremonial importance of some Fremont rock art sites. Fremont rock art appears to contain themes of shamanism, fertility, warfare, hunting, and mythology. In many panels the subject matter seems to be organized, and some even appears to be narrative.

The Apaches and Navajos

Between A.D. 1000 and 1500. people speaking Athabaskan languages migrated south on the Great Plains from Canada and soon moved westward into the Pueblo area of central New Mexico. These Plains-oriented buffalo hunters were ancestral to the Apaches and Navajos. By 1540 they had established extensive trading contacts with the Pueblos. Originally referred to as Apaches or Querechos by Spanish chroniclers, by 1626 the Navajos were apparently seen as a separate Athabaskan group living and farming on the upper Chama River (Schaafsma 1980, 302). The Athabaskans borrowed ideology and art from the Pueblos (who in turn had borrowed from the Mogollons) and forged their own unique expression. The lifeway of the Athabaskans changed dramatically with their acquisition of the horse from Spanish stock in the early 1600s. This development allowed revolutionary mobility for hunting and raiding their neighbors. Depictions of horses in their rock art is thus relatively datable. Today, the Navajos are the largest Indian tribe in the United States and occupy a huge area in the old Anasazi territory of the Colorado Plateau. Their homeland, before their current reservation, was known as the Dinetah, a vast and beautiful system of canyons draining through Gobernador and Largo canyons into the San Juan River in northwest New Mexico.

Navajo rock art is a result of acculturation and intermarriage between Athabaskan peoples and a number of Pueblo groups (Jemez, Cochiti, Tewa) who fled the Rio Grande area after the Pueblo Revolt of 1680 to escape Spanish reprisal and to join the Navajos in the Dinetah area of northwestern New Mexico. The Navajos apparently adopted aspects of Pueblo religion and ritual during what is known as the Gobernador Phase (approximately 1696 to 1775), and it is from this time that the first Navajo rock art is known (Schaafsma 1980, 305).

The Gobernador Representational Style occurs in the upper San Juan and the Gobernador and Largo Canyon drainages of northwestern New Mexico. It has similarities to Pueblo art of the time, as would be expected. Depictions of ceremonial figures and Navajo deities (*Ye'is*), shield bearers, cloud terraces, birds, and corn plants are found in seventeenth-century Navajo rock art. Both petroglyphs and pictographs occur in this style and are often beautifully executed. Canyon junctions were favored locations; much Navajo rock art probably functioned as shrines. The sand paintings for which the Navajos are well known evolved from earlier rock art ceremonial motifs of the Gobernador Phase.

By contrast, Apache rock art is less well known than that of the Navajos. Rock art believed to be attributable to Apaches is not concentrated in a particular region such as the Dinetah, but instead is found at relatively few sites scattered over a large area, primarily from southern Arizona through southern New Mexico and in west Texas and northern Chihuahua. Through a combination of raiding and trading with their Pueblo neighbors, the Apaches acquired some of the Pueblos' ideas about religion and its expression in ceremonial art. Polly Schaafsma states " . . . the work at these sites represents a rather miscellaneous collection of rock paintings and petroglyphs obviously relatively recent in origin, but often so limited or undiagnostic in context and style that . . . one cannot always be certain who made them" (Schaafsma 1980, 335). The horse and rider are common elements, as are bison, shields, snakes, lizards, masks, small animals, and abstract designs. There are probable shamanistic contexts to the anthropomorphic figures depicted with sunburst head motifs, horned headdresses, and carrying staffs.

The Utes

The Numic-speaking Ute Indians were apparently also recent newcomers to the Southwest region, although their ancestors were probably Desert Archaic residents of the Great Basin and the northern periphery of the Southwest for thousands of years. Their primary territory was the western slope of Colorado and eastern Utah. After acquiring the horse in the 1800s, they began raiding their Pueblo neighbors and eventually joined with their Comanche cousins to raid Spanish settlements, too. Anglo settlement of Colorado and the gold rushes of the nineteenth century spelled doom for the raiding and roaming Utes.

Ute rock art has been studied mainly in western Colorado and eastern Utah—the area that was their principal territory at the time of historic contact. In terms of general archaeological knowledge, there seem to be more questions than answers about the Utes. Their mobile life-style may partly explain this paucity in the archaeological record. At the time of historic contact, Utes were making rock art of a distinctive style, as well as imitating some earlier rock art. Often they imitated the older figures "just for fun" (Heizer and Baumhoff 1962, 222). They may have incorporated symbolism and styles of various cultures as a result of their mobility. Ute rock art can sometimes be identified by the historic context of elements such as horses, tipis, trains, and guns. Petroglyphs and pictographs are both present, and sites occur in diverse settings. The alpine cave sites are particularly interesting as only Ute rock art is found at these higher elevations (Cole 1990, 224). Their art typically is superimposed on other styles.

The subject matter of early historic Ute rock art includes anthropomorphs (both on foot and mounted), shield figures, horses, bears and bear shamans, female fertility symbols (fig. 15), birds, weapons, and abstract linear designs. Themes of this style include battles and raids, individual power, and hunting. Biographical or narrative content is implied in some panels. Late historic Ute rock art exhibits some continuity with the earlier, but with more detail, realism, and naturalism in life-forms. Although subject matter is similar to the earlier, there is less abstraction. In some regards it is similar to contemporaneous Plains Indian rock art: panels tend to be crowded, and themes include aggression, male prestige, horses, and ceremonies.

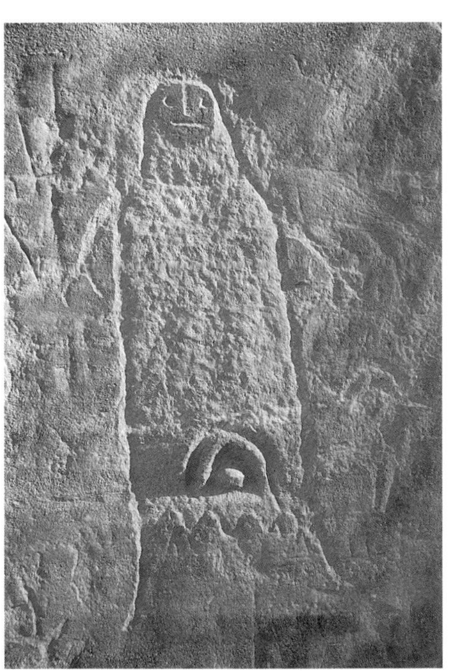

fig. 15. Ute rock art often contains elements of female fertility such as this petroglyph with a prominent vulva, Cottonwood Canyon, Bluff, Utah.

The Paiutes and Shoshones

The Numic-speaking Paiutes and Shoshones inhabited the Great Basin, including the areas covering much of Nevada and the Mojave Desert, Death Valley, and Owens Valley of southeastern California. Among the Southern Paiutes are the Chemehuevis, whose rock art and lore contain notable fertility-related themes. The Great Basin is a very arid, harsh environment that did not support agriculture or large prehistoric populations. These people were hunter-gatherers with seasonal, migratory lifestyles who were heavily dependent on piñon nuts, wild seeds, rodents, and rabbits. Their rock art consists of petroglyphs and pictographs, and much of it contains shamanistic elements, along with an emphasis on rainmaking.

The Patayans

The Patayan cultural province includes western Arizona and the valley of the lower Colorado River. The term Yuman has also been applied to these people, because of the Yuman-speaking inhabitants of the area who lived there at the time of European contact. Although the prehistory of this area is relatively poorly understood, it is thought that the Patayan or Yuman represents a basic culture of status similar to Anasazi or Hohokam. These people, unlike other far western groups, were agriculturalists who farmed, at least part time, the rich floodplains to raise corn, beans, and squash. Their settlements were spread widely over the area, and relatively few material remains have been found by archaeologists. Their rock art

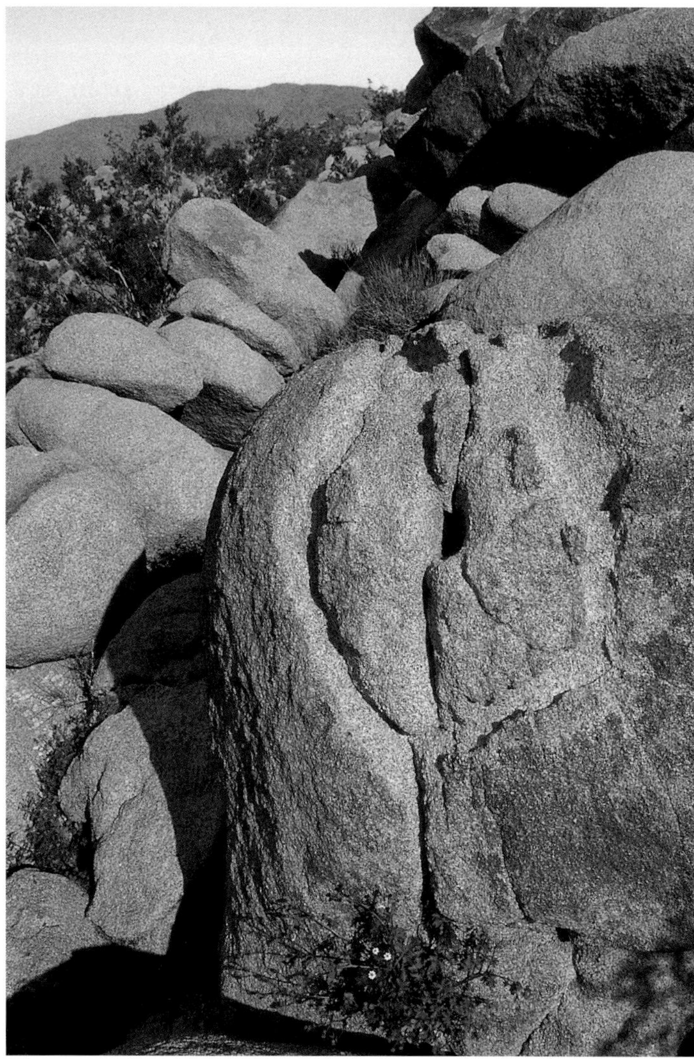

fig. 16. In the desert of southern California, giant vulva formations, known locally as yoni rocks, may have been connected with Native American puberty initiation rites, Anza-Borrego State Park, California.

consists primarily of rather crude petroglyphs, some of which depict shamanistic visions and supernatural power and also seem to portray aspects of the mythic world (Whitley 1996, 17).

The South-Central California Peoples

The Sierra Nevada of California separates the San Joaquin Valley and the Great Basin and also divides rock art types in a broad sense. Petroglyphs are dominant east of the Sierra in the Great Basin, while pictographs are primarily found west of the mountains. Similarly, it seems that the northern half of the state contains mostly pecked or incised rock art, whereas in the southern half (south of the San Joaquin Valley) the rock art is mainly painted (Grant 1967, 114).[11]

The cultural province of the southern Sierra Nevada, San Joaquin Valley, and Santa Barbara coastal area, because of the extraordinarily rich natural resources there, contained what may have been the densest hunter-gatherer population ever to occur anywhere. Permanent villages as large as 1,000 people occurred in some of the more productive areas. The Chumash Indians created what many consider to be the finest rock paintings in North America. They occupied the area of present-day Santa Barbara, Ventura, and San Luis Obispo counties, centered around the Santa Barbara Channel and extending inland to include the coastal ranges. The Chumash's neighbors to the northeast were the Yokuts, whose territory included the San Joaquin Valley and Southern Sierra and who also made many polychrome pictographs. The Yokuts were the largest ethnic group in California before being decimated by European settlement. Since the Yokuts and Chumash had a similar lifestyle and traded extensively, it is not surprising that their rock paintings share much similarity.

The rock art of the Chumash was largely a product of their shamans and is thought to be influenced heavily by their use of the hallucinogenic drug toloache, or jimsonweed, in ceremonies, especially puberty and initiation rites (Grant 1967, 34). The beautiful polychrome pictographs of the Chumash are typically located in remote, mountainous terrain away from villages—places selected for their power and ritual significance. Elaborate abstract designs painted in as many as six colors are common and probably represent dreamlike visions or entoptic effects of the shaman. Bizarre anthropomorphic and zoomorphic beings are also depicted in a great variety of shapes.

The Southwestern California Peoples

South of the Chumash territory were people who spoke the Takic and Yuman languages and who lived in the cultural province that ranged from the Los

Angeles Basin and San Gabriel Mountains southward into the Baja Peninsula. Some of these groups included the Gabrielino, Luiseno, Cahuilla, and Kumeyaay Indians, whose rock art and ethnography are later discussed for their fertility themes. With no large permanent villages in this province, subsistence life-styles varied widely with the diverse natural settings of the area and ranged from marine-based economies to those based on the gathering of acorns, piñon, mesquite pods, and cactus. Pictographs are more common than petroglyphs in the rock art of this area, and some have been related to puberty initiation rites. The narcotic plant jimsonweed was also used in ceremonials in this province, and its hallucinogenic effects may be expressed in some of the rock art. In some areas puberty and fertility rituals were also apparently associated with boulders containing large vulva-like clefts (yonis) that were sometimes enhanced to resemble symbolic earth-wombs (fig. 16 and Plate 13).

I am glad I have seen your nakedness;
it is beautiful;
it will rain from now on.[12]
—Talashimtiwa
Hopi Indian from Oraibi, 1920

Eroticism, one may say, is consenting to live.[13]
—Jean-Luc Godard

The omnipresent process of sex, as it is woven into the whole texture of our man's or woman's body, is the pattern of all the process of our life.[14]
—Havelock Ellis
The New Spirit

CHAPTER 2

SEXUALITY AND THE SACRED

In cultures worldwide, male and female have commonly been perceived as two complementary principles, and all phenomena can be attributed to one or another of them. For instance, the sun and sky are typically seen as male, while the moon and earth are female. Sex, then, is portrayed as a kind of magnetic force that unites opposites and achieves balance or completeness. Among different peoples, rituals of sex have been used to unite human spirits with one another, as well as with spiritual forces that course through animals, the earth, or the gods themselves. It is probable that our ancestors celebrated the cyclical return of life each year with religious rites that sanctified the sexual union of male and female.

Before focusing on the topic of sex in the prehistoric Southwest, it is instructive to view the subject in a larger world context. In many societies, sexuality was commonly equated with fertility, regeneration, and the holy.[15] Various scholars have explored this aspect of human nature in which biology and culture are intertwined.[16] In surveying the practices and prejudices of the last five thousand years, it is necessary to consider how societies have been structured in relation to sex, reproduction, gender, and power. It is important to realize that our modern thoughts on sex are no more objective than any other way of thinking about it, and that there is no single, compelling definition of what constitutes sexual behavior in humans; rather it is a function of behaviors and attitudes that are inherited and learned.

Most ancient societies perceived a link between human sexuality and plant and animal fertility and, by sympathetic magic, developed forms of ritualized sex to guarantee the continuation and the fruitfulness of the earth. According to archaeological evidence, in prehistory human sexuality was at least as diverse as it is today. It is possible to document great variations in human sexuality in Eurasia approximately five thousand years ago, including "bestiality, homosexuality, prostitution, transvestism, transexuality, hormone treatments, sadomasochism, a vigorous interest in contraception, ideas about racially pure breeding, sex as an acrobatic and competitive pastime, and sex as a transcendental spiritual discipline" (Taylor 1996, 17). According to one source, "This variation went underground when Christian values were publicly adopted, whereupon the chivalric ideal of romantic, preferably un-consummated love gave rise to a view of physical sex as essentially sinful and forbidden, the legacy of which lingers on" (Taylor 1996, 18).[17] The view that sex has a spiritual dimension is thus rooted in ancient traditions and has been vividly expressed in prehistoric art—which most early scholars found too embarrassing to recognize.

Prior to the repressive influence of European Christian colonization around the world, many other cultures openly celebrated their sexuality, including various American Indian groups. The prudish attitude of missionaries and celibate priests toward sex was puzzling to Indians, who from childhood took sexual expression of all kinds for granted. There is no concept of obscenity among them, and there are no "dirty words" in their languages. For example, names for warriors of the Plains such as Penis or Testicles were considered as honorable as any others. These people were probably no more promiscuous than most Europeans, just less inhibited and more honest about sexual matters.

Thus in most native cultures, there was no conflict between matters of the spirit and the flesh. Sex was regarded as a natural function and as a positive activity that assured the continuance of society and the cosmos. Although each society had standards for acceptable sexual behavior, ranging from strict to unrepressed, in general there was little shame and remorse associated with sex. However, the relationship between sexuality and the sacred in the Indian world was troubling to some of the first European observers, especially the celibate Franciscan priests.

For most American Indian groups, sexuality represented cosmic balance, the union of masculine elements associated with the sky and female forces connected with earth. The Cheyennes, for example, linked women with the Deep Earth—the source of all life. Earth had to be fertilized by the life-giving rain from the High Sky in order to bring forth life (Collier 1988, 132). Rain fertilized seeds just as men fertilized women. This symbolic association is expressed in many ways, not the least of which is language. The Hopi word *poshumi* means both seed corn and young female (because a baby girl is "seed" for future clan posterity).[18] There is much innate sexual symbolism expressed in ritual and art about the father (sky) fertilizing the mother (earth) with rain in order for seeds to germinate and plants to grow. Corn is often perceived as the children and nurtured accordingly. Rituals symbolizing these beliefs are performed at some pueblos to celebrate the sex of babies; for example, a seed-filled gourd is placed over a baby girl's vulva with prayers that she become fruitful, while the boy's penis is sprinkled with water (Parsons 1919, 86).

The function of male and female sexuality is illustrated in a Hopi tale of creation. In the beginning, the male god Sho'tokunungwa ("the heart of the above") created a beautiful virgin who all the supernaturals then coveted for a wife. They feuded over her for a long time until Sho'tokunungwa transformed her into the world: "Her hair became the vegetation; her eyes, the springs; her teeth, gems (white shell beads); her bones, the rocks; her breath, the wind; her secretions, salt" (Stephen 1939, in Tyler 1964, 99). A Hopi informant said that Sho'tokunungwa married the earth, and when they have intercourse, rain is produced, for that is the fertilizing fluid. All the vegetation is the offspring of this union; for example, Sho'tokunungwa puts grass seeds inside hailstones, and when they melt, the seeds go into the earth and soon spring up with the heat of the sun (Tyler 1964, 100).

Many ceremonials were essentially prayers for abundance, but without the sexual functions of nature there can be no abundance. An example of a western Pueblo ritual that celebrated sexuality and its role in fertility is the *Marau* women's ceremony. During the ceremonial days prior to the public dances, both men and women made sexual fetishes—the men carved female genitals out of pumpkin or watermelon rinds, while the women made phallic images of clay or other material. These objects were then presented to members of the opposite sex, constituting an invitation for sexual relations. During the dances, the women wore short tunics that exposed their vulvas when stooping or sitting. Men came from all the villages to see the women bending over while dancing and would point and say, "Iss, iss"—I wish, I wish (Duberman 1979, 109, 111–12).

To maintain the desired cosmic balance between male and female principles, men believed they needed to periodically renew their energy by segregating themselves from women, and by conducting rituals for successful hunts, war, curing, and rainmaking. Because it was thought that feminine power rendered male magic impotent, men avoided sex with women at times before or after rituals (Talayesva 1942).[19] Often masculine energy was perceived as a fragile force that could be overwhelmed by feminine potency, and therefore frequent rituals were necessary to ensure its conservation and renewal: "Just as the spirits provided rain that enabled the Deep Earth to bring forth life, so men provided the semen that enabled women to do so. And just as the rain provided by the spirits sank into the Deep Earth never to reappear, so semen disappeared forever in women" (Collier 1988, 132).

By practicing continence, ceremonial leaders intended to bring rain during and after certain ceremonies. Ideas about sexual abstinence and impotence are thus symbolized in ritual. In one ceremony, the penis was tied down with a cotton string to indicate the participant's impotence at the time. At another, clowns engaged in a phallic game that draws humor from a suggestion of impotence. Women attempted to pile up four cones in competition for prizes, while the clowns cry out, "Don't fall! Don't fall!" After this, the clowns lay down as if dead while a priest sprinkled ashes on their penes—the symbolism of ashes (the fire is out) precludes intercourse (Tyler 1964, 201).

Although associated with spiritual power, sex was also often a subject for humor at public dances and ceremonies, as the following episode recounts:

> Once on a dance day a fun-making Katcina ran into the plaza stark-naked. A Clown caught him and asked him what he was doing. He replied, "I am chasing my penis and can't overtake it; it is always a little ahead of me. I think a person would die if he overtook it." The people laughed. The clowns frequently captured women and imitated the sexual act in the open plaza to entertain the people. On some occasions they fastened long gourd necks in front of them and pursued the women. Aunts would also chase their nephews and jokingly pretend to have intercourse with them (Talayesva 1942, 76).

The uncontrolled sexuality of clowns and tricksters is thus like the fecundity of the natural world and the aimless scattering of millions of seeds. This aspect is depicted literally in some clowns; for example, the Koyemshi clowns at Zuni have bumps on their heads which contain all kinds of seeds, and they paint their bodies with mud from the slime of springs (Tyler 1964, 198).

Further, in most Native American societies sexuality was not viewed as solely for reproduction and was not necessarily restricted by marriage. It was thought to be a gift from the spirit world, and as such was to be enjoyed. Thus these societies were apparently untroubled by sexual variance and polygamy. Relatively casual attitudes about sexuality, although often a subject of humor, prevailed in most native cultures. Their songs and myths celebrated "creeping lovers" and "night prowlers" who seduced women. Personal freedom was too highly regarded for sexual stigma or condemnation to become repressive (Williams 1992, 88–89). This openness was practiced by all, especially children, who from an early age were free to observe and experiment as they pleased, as described in the following:

> We small boys paid close attention to these matters. We also watched the animals about the village. . . . We called to each other to watch dogs, cats, goats, and burros when they mated. We also discovered that it was fun to play housekeeping with the girls and to make believe that we were their husbands, sometimes handling them (Talayesva 1942, 78).

Along with the openness associated with children's sex education, there was storytelling of a sexual nature. These tales seem to have been partly serious and partly humorous but always supported freedom of individual sexual identity. A common sexual story among various Native American groups was about the seduction of a young man by an attractive young woman who was actually a spirit with teeth in her vagina; the plot unfolds in various ways as the young man figures out a way to have intercourse with her without losing his penis.

These Native American views contrast sharply with the Christian morality of early missionaries and settlers. In his autobiography, the Hopi Don Talayesva makes it clear that there was a vast difference between his Hopi mores and the Christian ascetic morality that missionaries tried to impose:

> As a child he was led to believe that sex was the most important function of his body. The katcina clowns he loved were given to joking that, next to eating, love-making was the greatest joy of life. And as an older man, such pleasures even included extramarital "private wives." None of these were ideas to be tolerated in the Christian code. (Talayesva 1942, x).

From such relatively recent historic accounts, it is not difficult to picture the even wider gulf in mores and understanding that must have existed around the time of first European contact with the indigenous populations of the Southwest. Thus early descriptions written by friars were biased by their anxieties over "nefarious sins against nature" and "pagan promiscuities" (Gutierrez 1991, 72–73). Even the positions used in sexual intercourse were criticized. The celibate priests presumptuously tried to enforce the "missionary position" (man on top) because in their opinion "this manner [was] more appropriate for the effusion of the male seed, for its reception into the female vessel" (Sanchez, quoted in Flandrin 1975, 38).

The following examples from ethnographic literature further illustrate the sexual diversity existent in many Native American cultures.

In numerous cultures, although participants may have abstained from sexual relations during ceremonial preparations and enactments, these social events often provided opportunities for both premarital and extramarital activity for nonparticipants.[20] Ethnographic documents collected by the Smithsonian Institution contain ample evidence of "endemic promiscuity" focused around certain Pueblo dances in Arizona and New Mexico. Dances that celebrated or enacted sexual activity were apparently not uncommon, as documented in the following records:

> One of the clowns had protruding from his trousers an artificial penis, perhaps carved out of wood, but with hair, perhaps horse hair, hanging down therefrom; and as he danced he sang a song . . . turning from side to side so as to face in all directions, holding the wooden penis in his hand and pointing it in all directions . . . singing about the penis being the thing that made the women happy (Duberman 1979, 124).

A petroglyph from the Rio Grande in New Mexico depicts a possible example of a ritual participant wearing such an artificial penis—in this case two small flute players seem to assist in the celebration of sexuality (fig. 17).

Among the Chiricahua Apaches, the normal restraints on sexual behavior were lifted during certain ritual activities such as victory dances. Likewise, among the Hurons of the Northeast and the Chumash of California, there were occasionally days of sexual license when adults had sex with as many partners as they wished, often quite publicly. During the Papago Drinking Feast and Maiden's Dance, the usual proprieties were dispensed with and a general sexual orgy ensued. At these "official nights of saturnalia, homosexual tendencies were openly acknowledged and sanctioned" (Williams 1992, 107).

For some Native American cultures, sexual intercourse was a way of transferring power. Among the Mandans, for example, a man desiring power might sleep with the wife of a warrior who had a superior rank. Alternatively, he could achieve increased status by offering his wife to a man of a higher rank—the higher ranking man would pass on some of his power to the woman, who then transferred it to her husband sexually (Bishop 1996, 37).

Some agricultural and hunting societies have incorporated into rituals concepts involving semen as a symbolic natural fertilizer. In some groups, berdaches were taken on a "spring riding" ritual, where they would be masturbated to ensure the fecundity of flora and fauna of a sacred mesa (Taylor 1996, 183).[21] The term berdache is generally used for androgynous males who dress as females and assume nonmasculine roles among the Indian tribes of North America. They may be involved in long-lasting relationships with partners who are considered no different from other married men. It is reported that among some Plains Indians, berdaches may have been created by making young boys ride bareback until their testicles were destroyed, causing feminizing changes in their development (Taylor 1996, 212). Male berdaches have been recorded in more than one hundred North American Indian cultures, and female berdaches in at least thirty. As a sacred joining of male and female attributes, the berdache was a living symbol of cosmic balance. Because the power of menstruating women could affect male ritual, they were excluded from some ceremonies. Instead, during ceremonies berdaches sometimes acted as female impersonators, to the point of smearing their legs with rabbit blood to resemble menstrual flow (Hay 1963, 18). In more purely functional terms, berdaches helped facilitate peace by providing a sanctioned erotic outlet for bachelors as well as married men.

Among the more interesting rites of passage related to fertility is the marking of a man's transition to fatherhood, known as the couvade, during which the man is secluded and acts out labor pains. For example, the Huichol Indians of Mexico believe a man should share in his wife's pain of giving birth. According to Huichol tradition, when a woman has her first child, the husband squats in the rafters of the house or branches of a tree above her with cords tied to his testicles; the woman's contractions and labor pains then cause her to tug on the cords so that the man shares in the painful experience. This sympathetic ritual associated with the birth process is illustrated in a Huichol yarn painting in fig. 18. The sharing of labor pains was apparently not uncommon among native peoples. In certain tribes of southern California, during puberty rituals girls were confined for days in "roasting pits" with hot rocks placed on their abdomens and between their legs to prepare them for the trials of childbirth.

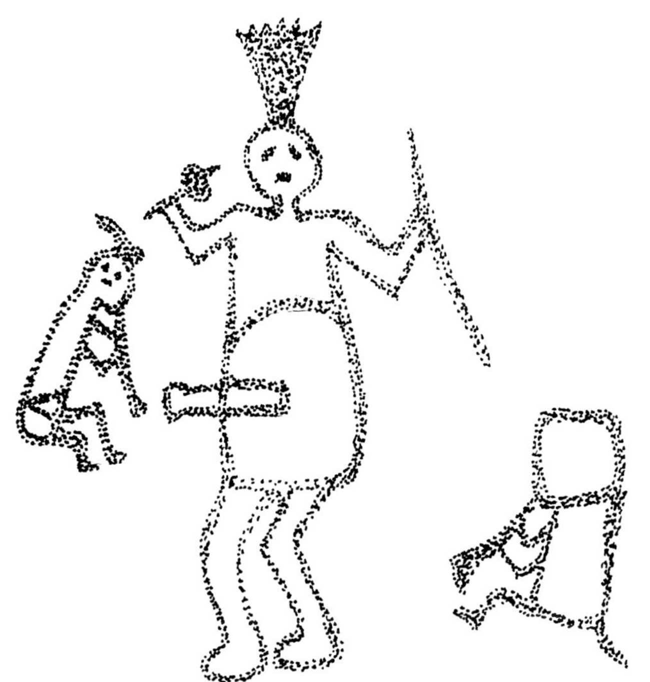

fig. 17. Pueblo petroglyphs perhaps portraying a ritual participant wearing an artificial penis in some aspect of celebrating fertility, West Mesa, Albuquerque, New Mexico.

Native American dances were sometimes erotic because it was recognized that humanity was dependent on sexuality for its survival. Some dances ended in actual or feigned intercourse, as described in the following:

> Two masked Katcinas (Mastops) appeared from the Kwan kiva with their bodies painted black and covered with white hand prints. . . . From their belts dangled bunches of cow hoofs, which rattled when they

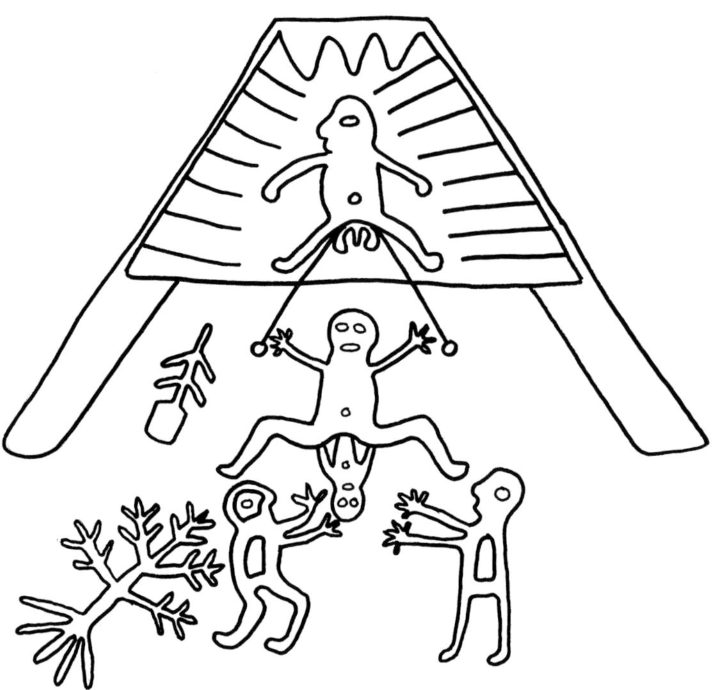

fig. 18. Design from a Huichol Indian yarn painting that illustrates the tradition of couvade, where a man ritually shares in his wife's pains in giving birth, Mexico (after Getty 1990:68).

> ran among the spectators, seizing women from behind and going through vigorous motions of copulation. After each conquest a Katcina would run to the kiva, jabber in a disguised voice, and set out to catch another woman (Talayesva 1942, 172).

Similarly, another source reports that:

> Two Kachinas would appear in the plaza signifying in pantomime that they were being consumed with sexual desire. They would then rush toward a cluster of women spectators and by placing their hands on the shoulders of each of the women pretend to have intercourse with them by jumping up and down in front of them. Then the kachinas rushed over to another cluster of women and continued their pantomime until they had had intercourse with practically every female in the audience. Even women who were normally very shy submitted readily to these public embraces (Niethammer 1977, 212).

Thus, activities perhaps considered offensive at other times were regarded differently during such ceremonies, which may have provided a healthy release of tensions through vicarious or sanctioned participation, such as the following:

> Then the women would form in a row and a clown would drag some young man 18 or 20 years old, out to where the women were standing, and the young man apparently somewhat embarrassed would put his hand under each woman's dress in front. . . . Then some of the women would grab a young man out of the crowd of spectators, put her arms around him and go through the motions of sexual intercourse standing up (Duberman 1979, 107).

Moreover, in the Mandan tribe's autumn buffalo-calling rites, actual sexual intercourse was an important element. During this four-day event, husbands offered their wives to the old men who impersonated the bison. By symbolically having intercourse with the buffalo, the herds were placated and would come near the villages (Niethammer 1977, 212–13).

Such veneration of sexuality was also extended to the natural world. Many landscape features had sexually descriptive names like Clitoris Spring, Girls Breast Point, Buttocks-Vagina, and Shove Penis (Hay 1963, 20). This recognition was reflected in the pantheon of deities, many of whom were bisexual, combining male and female attributes. Bisexual humans were accordingly revered among these cultures.

Further examples of sexuality among Native Americans abound in ribald myths, tales, and legends recorded not only in the Southwest but all over North America. Although all rituals, including those concerning love, had serious intent, many also had a comic component expressed by sacred clowns. Between solemn intervals, the clowns provided comic relief and made lewd jokes (occasionally at the expense of missionaries or tourists). However, despite their sometimes gross antics, the clowns expressed profound sacred ideas.

This is illustrated in the tale "Teaching the Mudheads How to Copulate" (the Mudheads, or Koyemshi, are sacred clowns at Zuni Pueblo). Since the Mudheads are not very bright or knowledgeable, an instructor tries to teach them how to do simple things such as sit in a chair and climb a ladder—actions which they bumble through. Then the instructor decides to show them how to copulate:

> There was a fat old woman who hadn't had a man in her for a long time. "They can all practice on me," she said, "I don't mind." So she lifted up her manta and bent over, and the instructor copulated with her in the simplest way—from the back as dogs do. The Mudheads watched closely, and then they all wanted to try. But none of them could find the right opening. One did it in the anus, another in the knee bend, another in the arm bend, another in the arm pit, another in the navel, another in the ear. They tried and tried. They really wanted to do it right, but they couldn't. "I give up on you," said the instructor. The fat old woman just laughed (Erdoes and Ortiz 1984, 279-80).

Many sexually oriented tales involve mythic tricksters such as Coyote—a buffoon with a gross sexual appetite. One of the more amusing of these stories is about Old Man Coyote deceiving attractive girls picking wild strawberries. He hides in some bushes, leaving only the tip of his penis sticking out:

> Soon the girls came to those bushes. "There's a big berry here," said one girl, "different from the others." She tried to pluck it, but it wouldn't come loose. "This berry has deep roots," she said. All the other girls came and tried to pick the strawberry. Some pulled at it, some nibbled at it. "Oh, my," said one, "this berry weeps." "No," said another girl, "it has milk in it." A third said: "Since we can't pick it, let's look for a sharp piece of flint and cut it off." The girls searched and found a flint, but when they came back to the berry patch, the strange strawberry had disappeared. "It must have been some trick by that nasty Old Man Coyote," the girls said to each other. Deciding to get even, the girls later feign their bloody death with some raw meat and lie in a trail, where Coyote finds them. Fearing that their killers are lurking nearby, he smells their bodies to determine how long they have been dead. Each time he comes near the girls' backsides, they fart in his face. Concluding he must be safe from any enemies because the girls smell so bad, they jump up laughing as this time the joke is on him (Erdoes and Ortiz 1984, 314).

Further examples of sexuality reflected in stories and myths of the Southwest are related in subsequent sections.

Sex . . . pervades art and it produces its spells and magic. It dominates in fact almost every aspect of culture. [22]

—Bronislaw Malinowski

The Sexual Life of Savages in North-Western Melanesia

Symbols were mankind's most effective weapons of survival when confronted by an inimical environment. In no other field was prehistoric man's imagination so abundant as in the invention of symbolic forms. . . . For the overwhelming majority, meaning revolves around an ardent desire for fertility and procreation.[23]

—Siegfried Giedion

Eternal Present: The Beginnings of Art

CHAPTER 3

IMAGES AND RITES OF FERTILITY AND SEXUALITY

In Native American societies, nearly everything was related to concepts of fertility—from sex and reproduction to concerns about rainmaking, hunting, foraging, and horticulture. Even subjects seemingly at odds with the affirmation of life, such as warfare, could have a connection with fertility; to wit, enemy scalps were often used as rain fetishes. Consequently, when discussing the subject of fertility it is important to keep in mind that it encompasses essentially all of the natural and supernatural realms.

Since many topics related to fertility are interconnected in complex ways, the following material has been organized into categories that make them comprehensible without imposing undue artifice on these beautiful portrayals of the life force.

DEPICTIONS OF GENDER

Ancient artists depicted the two sexes in an amazing variety of ways, ranging from simple stick figures to realistic and highly stylized portrayals. Sometimes human attributes are combined with those of animals or supernatural beings. Depictions of humans in rock art are referred to as anthropomorphic figures, and it is not unusual to find ambiguous or androgynous images which cannot be identified as either sex. In rock art of most areas, males and females are not equally represented; images of males (as phallic anthropomorphs) are much more abundant than images of females.

It is usually assumed that most rock art was produced by men due to the themes of male activities that prevail, such as hunting, war, and rituals. Scenes depicting typically female activities, such as carrying water, gathering food plants, or making baskets and pottery, occur less frequently (fig. 19). Where females can be identified, it is often in a context related to sex or fertility, such as intercourse, pregnancy, and birth. Women are seldom portrayed in mundane activities, whereas men are. Emphasis on elaborate depictions of the genitals suggests many female images are intended as symbols of fertility and pro-

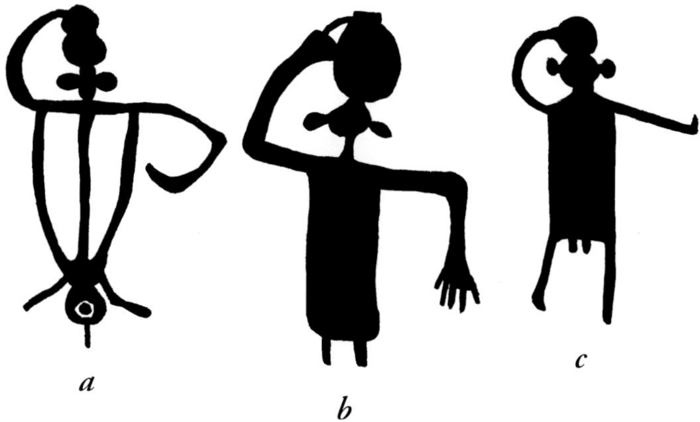

fig. 19. Petroglyphs of females carrying water jugs on their heads: a. North Wash, Utah; b. Galisteo Basin, New Mexico; c. White Rock Canyon, New Mexico.

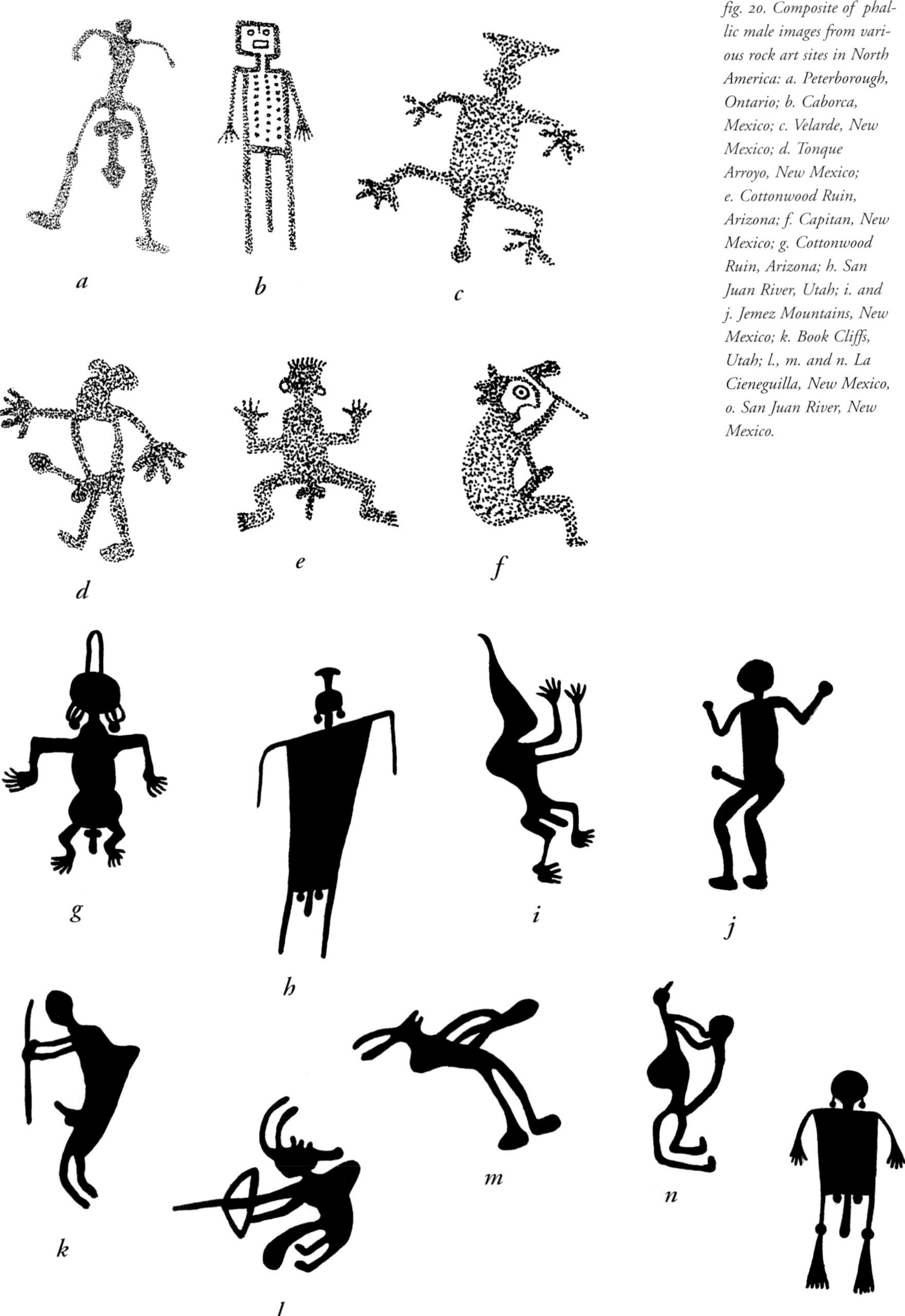

fig. 20. Composite of phallic male images from various rock art sites in North America: a. Peterborough, Ontario; b. Caborca, Mexico; c. Velarde, New Mexico; d. Tonque Arroyo, New Mexico; e. Cottonwood Ruin, Arizona; f. Capitan, New Mexico; g. Cottonwood Ruin, Arizona; h. San Juan River, Utah; i. and j. Jemez Mountains, New Mexico; k. Book Cliffs, Utah; l., m. and n. La Cieneguilla, New Mexico, o. San Juan River, New Mexico.

creation—supporting the notion that most rock art was created by men, who pictured females in terms of life-generating power.

Examples of the range of male images are shown in fig. 20, and of females in fig. 21. Although maleness should be easy to recognize based on anatomy, in some rock art areas this distinction can be confused by the presence of the "lizard-man" figure. Primarily in Pueblo Anasazi rock art of the Four Corners region, but also in Hohokam rock art in southern Arizona, these figures of lizard-like beings with tails tend to merge with other very phallic anthropomorphs (sometimes jokingly called three-legged men). In rock art of the Zuni area, these lizard-man figures may represent ancestral "moss people," who had tails and webbed hands and feet before they emerged from the underworld (Young 1988, 122). However, in most areas, male images are unambiguous and more obvious than those of females. Because female images are less abundant, less obvious, and more typically related to fertility concepts, they merit further discussion.

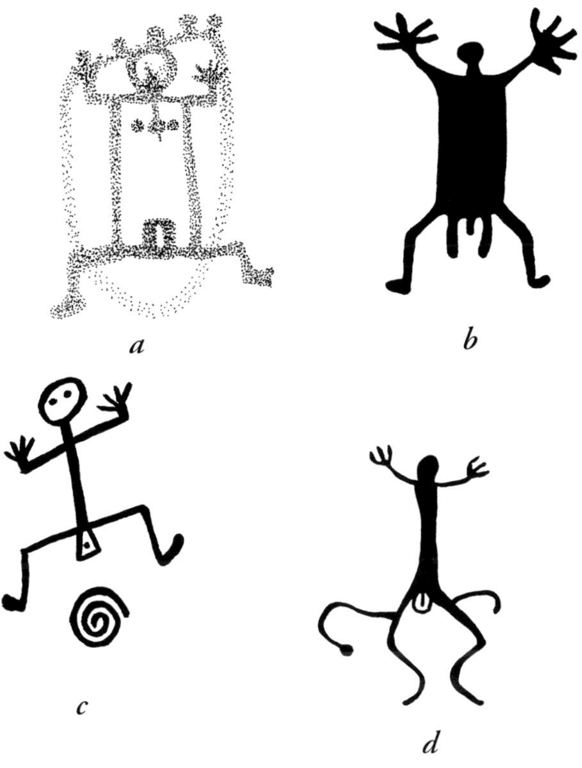

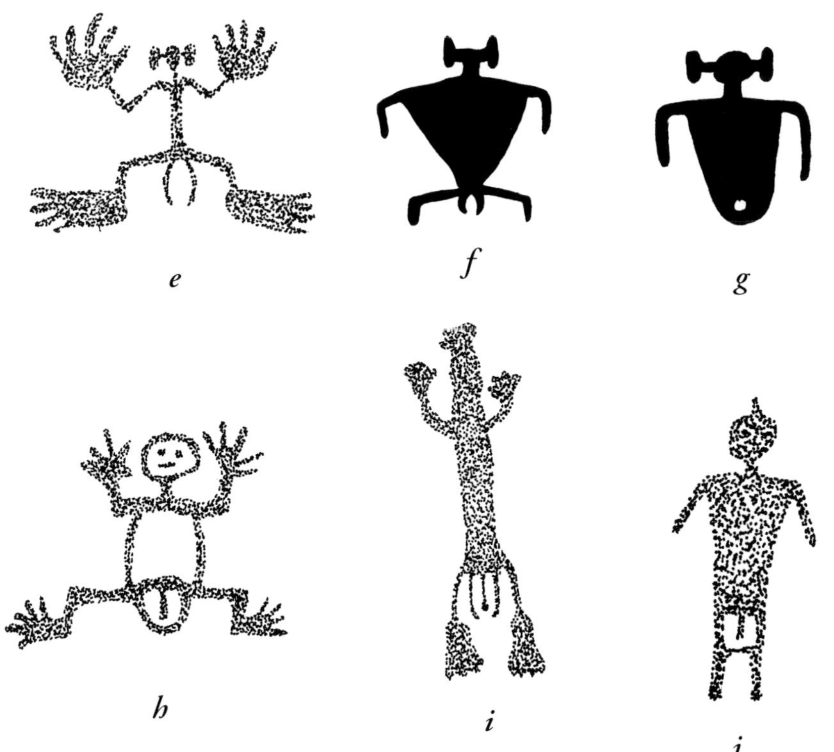

fig. 21. Composite of rock art images of females from various southwestern sites: a. and b. Velarde, New Mexico; c. Cerro Pomo, New Mexico; d. Book Cliffs, Utah; e., f., and g. Canyon de Chelly, Arizona; h. and i. Petrified Forest National Park, Arizona; j. San Juan River, Utah.

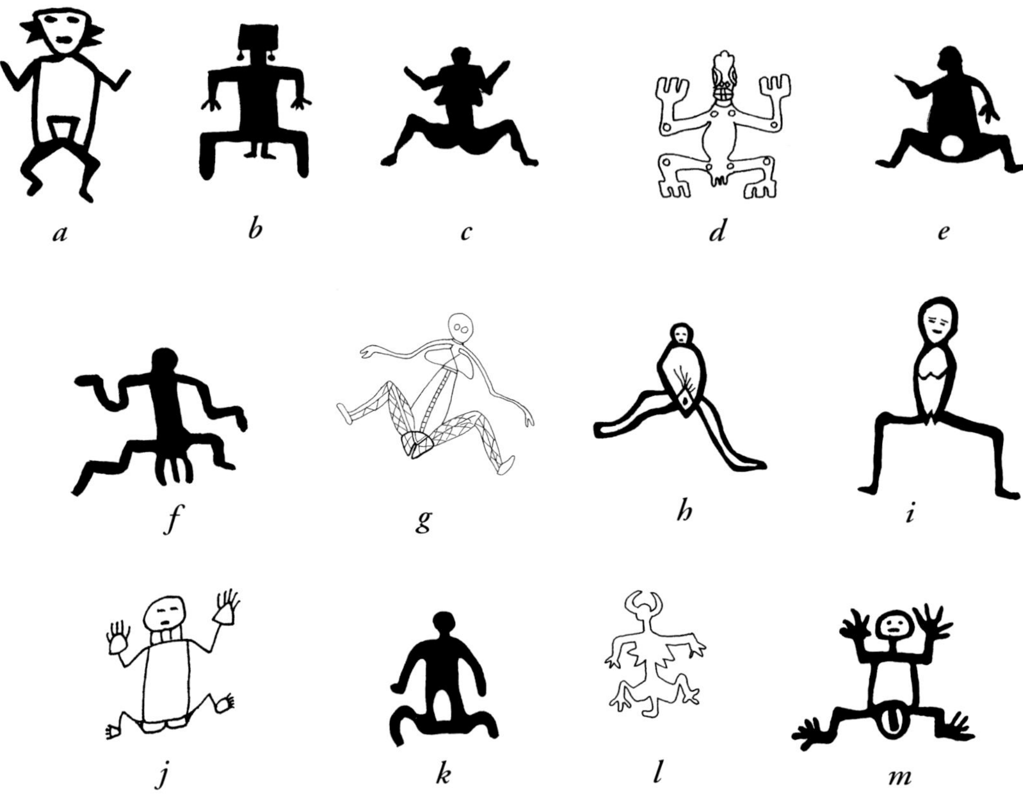

fig. 22. (above) Composite of rock art images of squatting females (hockers), a body posture associated with giving birth or being sexually receptive, from various sites around the world: a. West Mesa, New Mexico; b. Glen Canyon, Utah; c. Syda, Siberia (after Martynov 1991, 272); d. Majaro Island, Brazil (after Campbell 1989 I(1):194); e. Rochester Creek, Utah; f. Kane County, Utah; g. Kunwinjke Bim, Australia (after Getty 1990, 69); h. Anubis Cave, Oklahoma; i. Clenagh Castle, Ireland; j. El Morro, New Mexico; k. Peterborough, Ontario; l. Loy Canyon, Arizona; m. Petrified Forest national Park, Arizona.

Female images can sometimes be identified by genitals and more rarely by the presence of breasts. Further, in the rock art of some cultures, clothing or hairstyles may indicate female gender, as with the "squash blossom" style of hair whorls worn on the side of the head by Hopi maidens and their Anasazi ancestors (fig. 21 e, f, g), or the skirt-like clothing of some Fremont-style females and the supposed menstrual aprons depicted on some Anasazi Basketmaker females (see the section "Menstrual Blood" and figs. 61 to 65).

However, a more universal means of depicting females is through certain body positions; a squatting pose with legs spread is widely used to represent a receptive or birthing female (fig. 22). Such depictions of females have been termed "hockers" (German, "squatters") to indicate that they are sitting on their hocks. A similar-appearing, and possibly related, form of the squatting female figure is also known as the gorgon in ancient European stonework. In the British Isles, they are known as *Sheela-na-Gig* and are carved ornamentally on stonework of ancient churches (fig. 23). These are rare examples

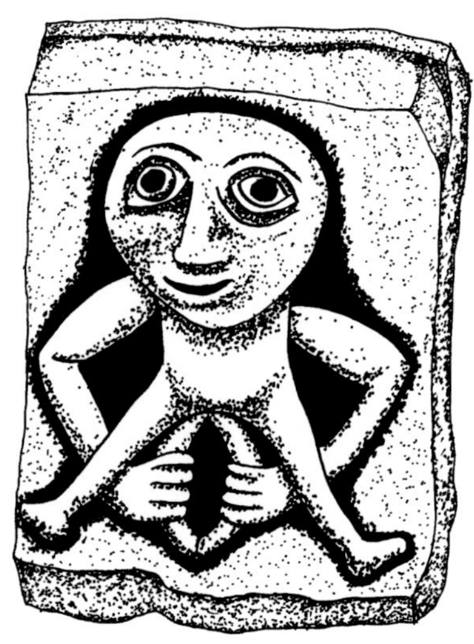

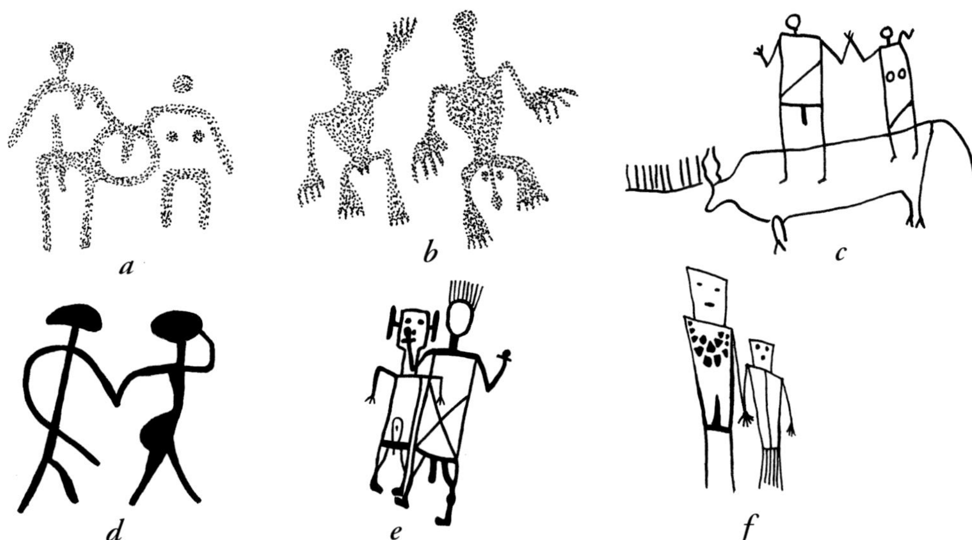

of the ancient Earth Goddess surviving from Celtic culture—figures possibly linked to the goddess Brigit, who presided over spring fertility festivals. Their purpose is uncertain and could be related to ancient goddesses of creation and destruction or to castigating the sins of the flesh and reminding worshipers of the evil that existed before Christianity. Part of the sexual and religious significance of rock art images of squatting females may be concerned with symbolic death and rebirth, since they are sometimes associated with ceremonies of initiation or transition (Vastokas 1973, 90–91).

Another way of distinguishing between males and females in some rock art is color symbolism. The importance of color symbolism for the sexes, in not only pictographs but also body painting and adornment, is known from some cultures and is reflected in myths. Color distinguishes gender in male and female anthropomorphs painted with red and black pigments in the Comondu Great Mural region of central Baja California (Smith 1986a). Moreover, in southern and south-central California, girls' rock art made as part of girls' puberty rites was almost always red. This symbolism relates to menstrual bleeding and to the color of the female direction—west (the color of the sunset). Black was associated with males and their direction—east (the color of night). These colors were also used by shamans in this area, who ritually painted themselves bilaterally black and red to join the principles and power of both sexes (Whitley 1996, 26).

Gender is also expressed in rock art through images of male and female figures shown together as couples, some of which may reflect the concept of marriage (fig. 24). Images of couples with children seem to place value on the nuclear family (fig. 25). Marriage, in its myriad forms, is seen by most cultures as the basis for society, and efforts are made to distinguish it from

fig. 23. (opposite page, bottom) Type of squatting female known as Sheela-na-Gig, carved in stonework decorating a medieval church in Celtic Britain, Church of Saint Mary and Saint David, Kilpeck, Herefordshire, United Kingdom (after Getty 1990, 67).

fig. 24. (top) Rock art depictions of pairs of men and women from various southwestern sites: a. Black Point, Utah; b. Petrified Forest National Park, Arizona; c. southeastern Colorado; d. Canyon del Muerto, Arizona; e. Galisteo Basin, New Mexico; f. Dinosaur National Monument, Utah.

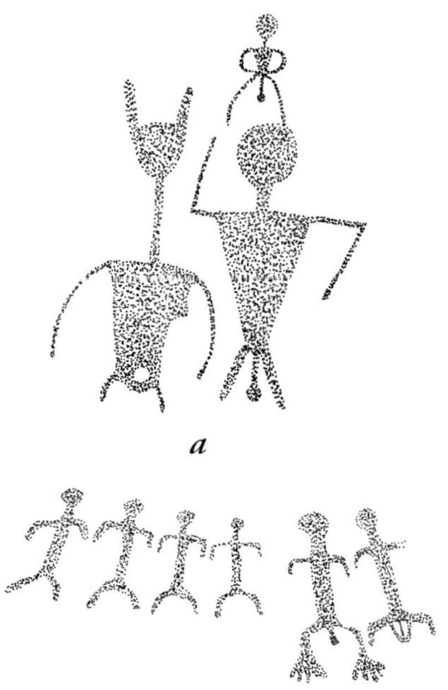

fig. 25. (left) Depictions of couples with children in southwestern rock art sites: a. San Juan Reservoir, New Mexico (after Schaasma 1963, 13); b. Petrified Forest National Park, Arizona (after photo by James Duffield).

fig. 26. (right) Petroglyph panel in the Cave of Life, Petrified Forest National Park, Arizona (after McCreery and Malotki 1994, 110).

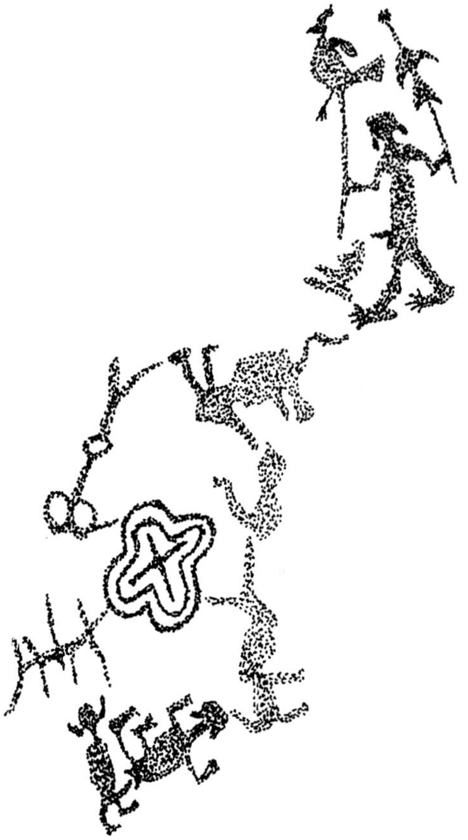

the potentially destabilizing influence of love and passion. Thus cultures throughout the world have devised incentives or punishment to ensure that cultural roles regarding marriage are followed. It is, therefore, reasonable to assume that certain rock art images may promote this concept. It is also possible that some images of couples depict fertility rituals such as the Sacred Marriage, where male and female participants act the parts of god and goddess in a mystical union to sustain life (fig. 26). This religious sacred sexual intercourse is a sacrament that symbolically expresses the creation of the world and stimulates by imitative magic the reproduction of all living things (Frazer 1993, 139–46; Hunger 1982). Further examples of Sacred Marriage and sexual intercourse as illustrated in rock art are discussed in subsequent sections.

Other characteristics that help identify female figures in rock art include widened hips, facial markings, head shape (for instance, in Navajo art, males have round heads and females square), diminutive size or hand-holding with males (fig. 24), and the incorporation of natural holes in rocks as vulvas (fig. 27).

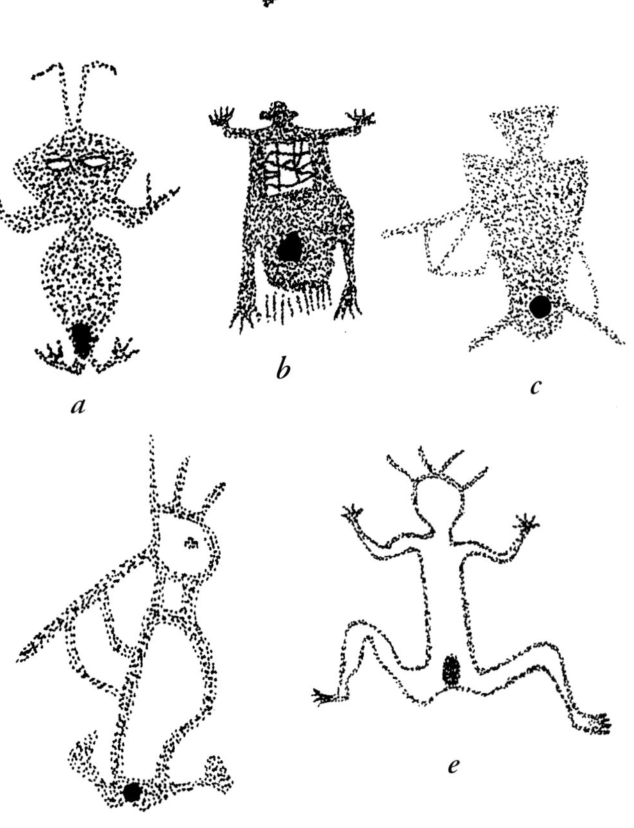

fig. 27. (bottom) Petroglyphs incorporating natural holes in the rock for vulvas; a. Tapia Canyon, New Mexico; b. Coso Range, California; c. Clear Creek Canyon, Utah; d. Cerro Indio, New Mexico; e. Rock Point, Arizona.

Vulva Symbols

The widespread use of the universal vulva symbol to represent females is very important. The concept of female is illustrated in great variety by use of the vulva symbol (fig. 28), and similarly the concept of male is depicted by isolated phallic elements. However, the vulva symbol is much more common than the detached phallic symbol, and in some rock art styles the U- or V-shaped elements are ubiquitous.

The universality of the vulva as symbolic of fertility in rock art of the American Southwest, as well as worldwide, cannot be overstated. In ancient traditions that go back to the dawn of human development, the vulva was revered as the magical portal of life, having the power of physical regeneration and spiritual transformation; it came to represent the sacred manifestation of cre-

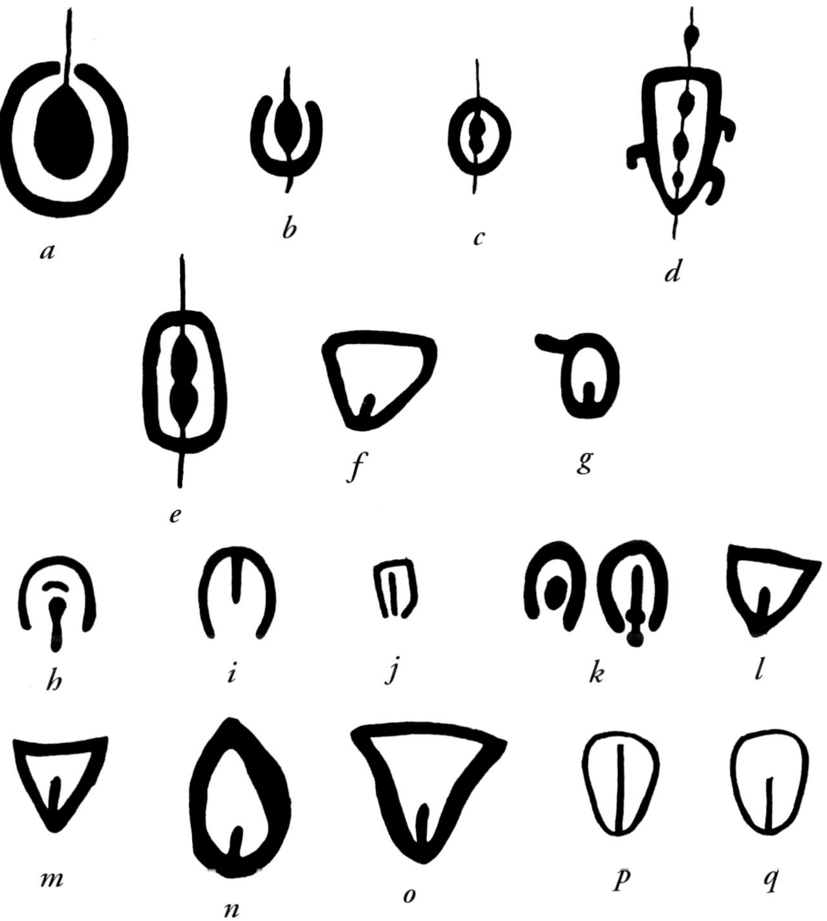

fig. 28. Vulva symbols depicted in rock art from various sites around the world (after Vastokas 1973). a.–g. Peterborough, Ontario; h. British Columbia; i. Washington; j. California; k. Missouri; l.–m. Mexico; n.–o. Siberia; p. Norway; q. France.

ative sexual power. Long before the advent of agriculture, people everywhere used this symbol in their art. The oldest known examples are from the Aurignacian Period of Stone Age Europe, approximately 30,000 B.C. (fig. 6; Gimbutas 1989, 99). An analogous form found throughout much of the world is the cowrie shell as symbolic vulva used in body adornment and ritual paraphernalia. Vulva images were not usually simple expressions of physiology but instead symbolized principles about the creation and regeneration of life: "It is not the anatomic sexual organ that is being symbolized, but the stories, characters, and processes with which the symbol had become associated" (Marshack 1972, 296).

Despite the universality of this symbol, rock art vulvas have not always been recognized as such. However, illustrations from several sites leave no doubt about what these symbols actually represent (fig. 29). Vulva symbols can occur in various forms while still referring to the same general concepts. The basic forms are triangles (fig. 30), bisected ovals, and circles with dots. Symbolic meaning of these forms has been suggested by Marija Gimbutas: " . . . the vulva is portrayed either as a supernatural triangle associated with aquatic symbolism, as a seed and sprout, or as an oval vulva swollen as in preparation for birth. Each category has its own meaning: the first is the cosmic womb of the Goddess, the source of the waters of life; the second is the sprouting of life; the third is the giving of birth" (Gimbutas 1989, 99).

It is interesting to note, however, that the vulva symbol's latent power was not always perceived in similar ways. In some cultures the vulva apparently represented a potent and dangerous shamanistic symbol

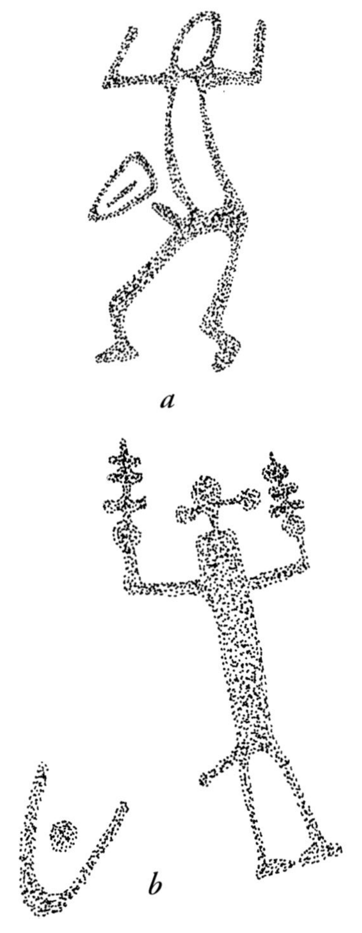

fig. 29. Petroglyphs depicting phallic males in association with vulva symbols: a. Galisteo Basin, New Mexico; b. Petrified Forest National Park, Arizona.

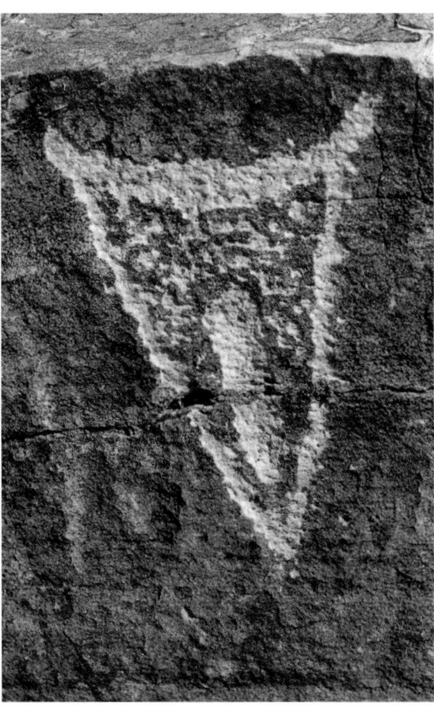

fig. 30. Petroglyph of a vulva symbol, Jemez Mountains, New Mexico.

perhaps pertaining to sorcery. This is illustrated by a Northern Paiute account that the worst form of sorcery a man could experience was a twitching vulva during intercourse—because the female's orgasm represented uncontrolled sexual (supernatural) power. Even the sight of a vulva was considered a perilous circumstance (Whitley 1996, 82).[24]

Rock art images of vulvas have been recorded throughout the continental United States, in Mexico, Canada, South America, and Hawaii. They are frequent and widespread in the Southwest (fig. 31), sometimes occurring as isolated or scattered images among various designs at rock art sites, other times in concentrations at particular sites that apparently had special fertility significance. A few examples of such places are given here, while others are described in the section "Fertility Shrines and Rites."

A "vulva colony" of more than one hundred petroglyph images occurs on tuff cliffs at the Chalfont site in Owens Valley, California (fig. 32). This rock art is thought to have been created by Paiute Indians, and many of the vulva images are bisected circles, some of which are made by incorporating natural holes and other rock features to create sculptural vulvas (see the section "Fertility Shrines and Rites" for more on this site).

Similarly, hundreds of vulvas are carved and deeply incised into a naturally porous cliff face known as Mother Rock, on sacred Corn Mountain near Zuni Pueblo in New Mexico. Here, prayers and offerings were made by expectant couples who desired a girl baby (Stevenson 1904, 294). Moreover, vulva petroglyphs are the most common elements engraved in the rock shelters in central Baja California's Comondu Great Mural region. About this area, author Harry Crosby writes:

> The cave is engraved with hundreds of oval devices virtually identical to others created all over the world during the past 20,000 years. . . . It has been suggested that they were created during fertility ceremonies, girls' puberty rites, or as calendrical notations, making use

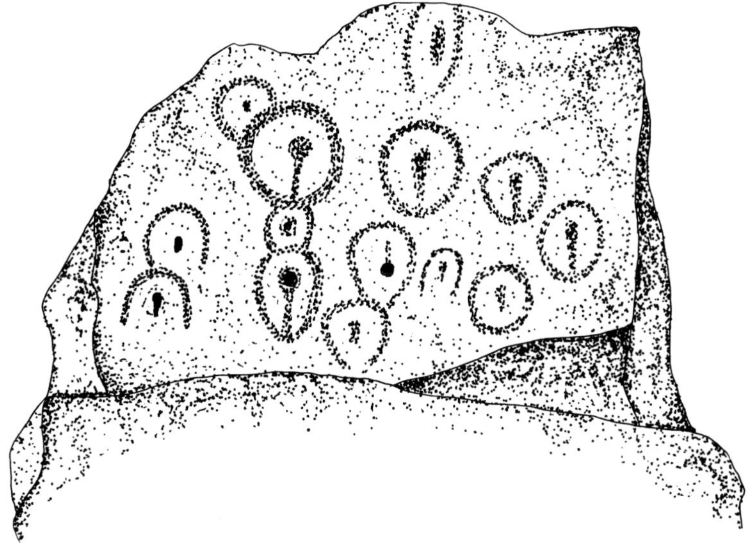

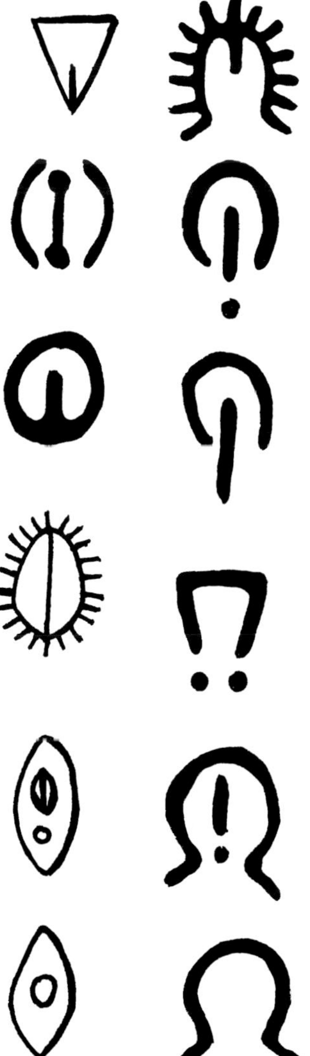

of the regularity of the menstrual cycle and its similarity to the lunar month. Whatever the reason, they are the commonest symbols found engraved in the soft rock shelters in the Comondu Great Mural region (Crosby 1984, 134–35).

fig.31. (left) Variations of vulva symbols in southwestern rock art (after Warner 1991, 163).

fig. 32.(top) Petroglyph panel of vulva symbols, Chalfont, California.

Further north, in the Anza-Borrego Desert of southern California, giant versions of the vulva symbol, known as yoni rocks (fig. 33), are so abundant that the term Vulva Valley has been applied to the area (Begole 1984, 4).

In some depictions of females, the vulva is greatly emphasized presumably to stress the significance of sexual and creative power (fig. 34). In fig. 35 the bodies of the two females themselves resemble giant vulvas, with deeply pecked holes between the legs. Furthermore, the two females in fig. 36 have nondescript torsos attached to enormous vulvas, as do the Ute petroglyphs shown previously in fig. 15.

Baskets have been linked to vagina symbolism as well. Usually made by women, they are considered female objects. In myths, supernatural beings and sometimes all of creation are born out of baskets (Whitley 1994, 23). Certain rock art motifs have been linked to basketry designs. Ethnography suggests the two have influenced each othe, and that for some cultures rock art sites and baskets correlate to symbolic vaginas.

fig. 33. (right) Large vulva-form (yoni formation), a natural formation that has been enhanced by grinding, Anza-Borrego State Park, California.

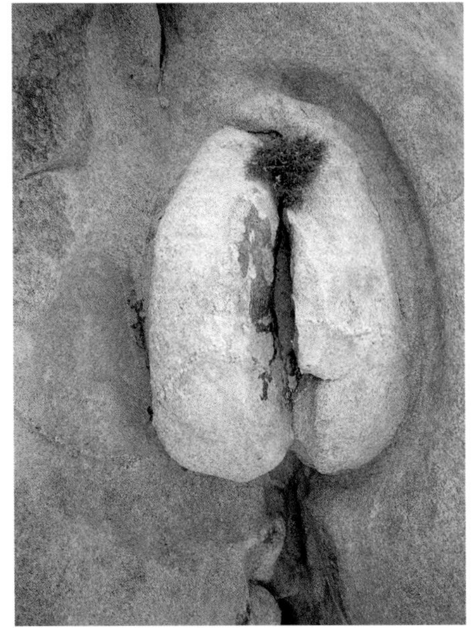

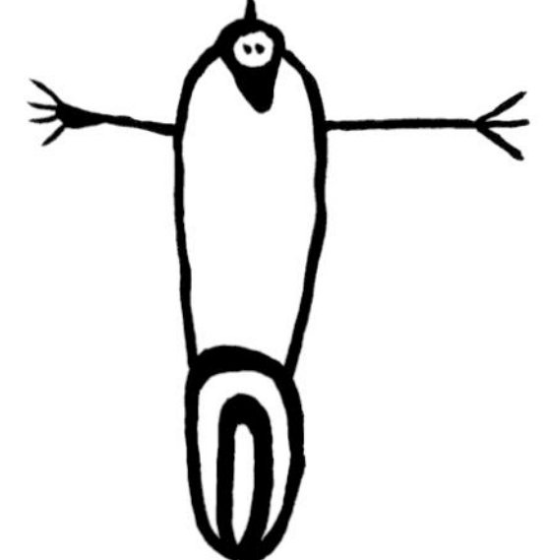

fig. 34.(below) Petroglyph of vulva, Ute Mountain Tribal Park, Colorado; photo: Chris Larsen.

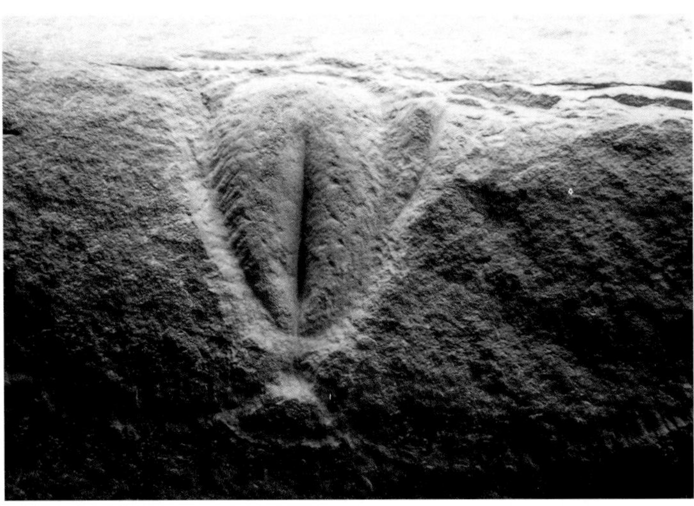

fig. 36. (above) Petroglyphs of two females with exaggerated vulvas that are deeply abraded, probably from ritual activity, White River Narrows, Nevada (after photo by James Duffield).

fig. 35. (right) Petroglyphs of vulva-shaped anthropomorphs with deeply abraded holes at genitals, Kane Creek, Moab, Utah.

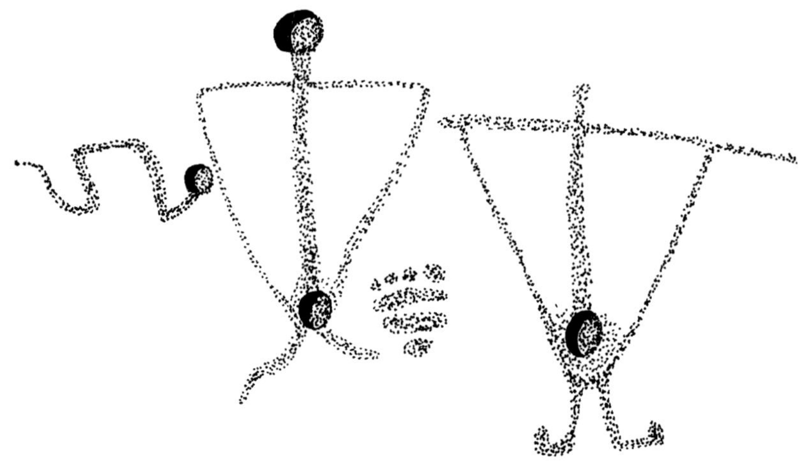

REFLECTIONS OF SEX AND PROCREATION

In examining rock art portrayals of sexual activities, it is necessary to keep in mind that concepts of obscenity and pornography are European inventions and did not exist in prehistoric cultures of the Southwest. Graphic sexual scenes are not as rare as early scholars would have us believe—more than sixty have been documented throughout the region in this study. Some were probably created as a joyous celebration of life, love, and pleasure. Others perhaps served symbolic religious and ritual purposes to ensure the continuity of all life, since the complementary principles of male and female are the obvious agents of creation.

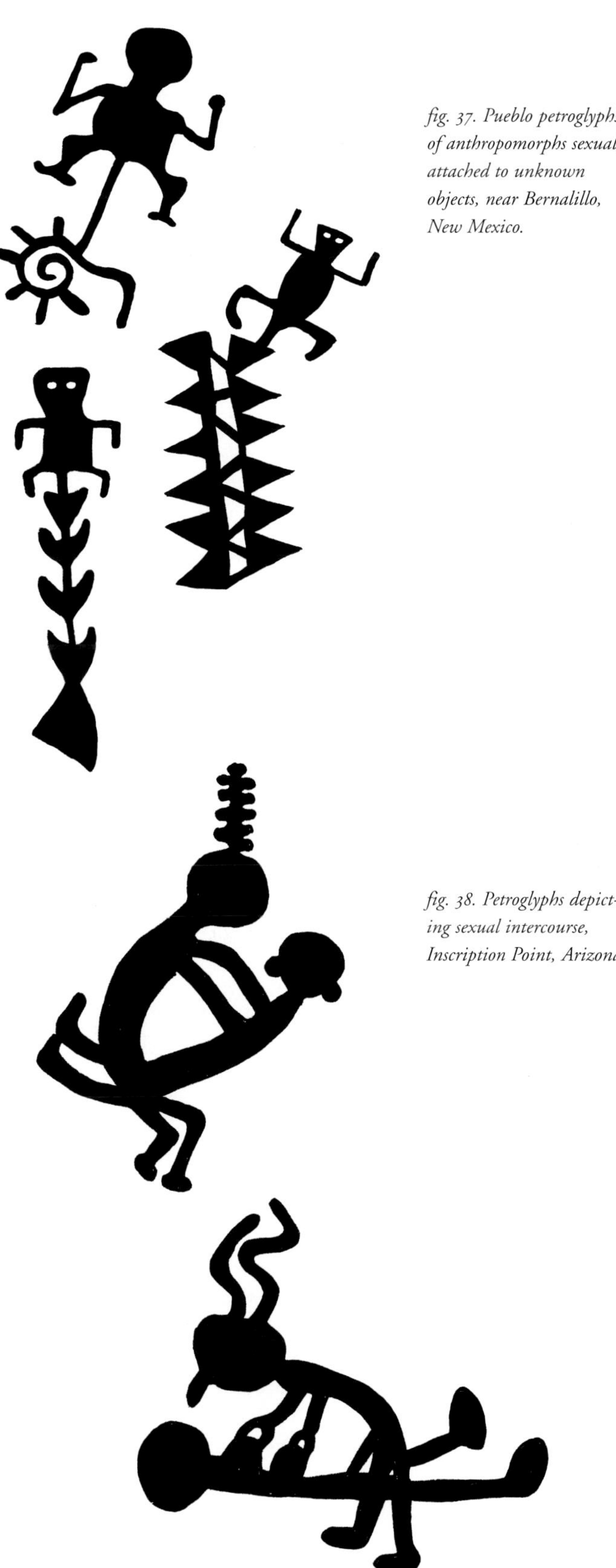

fig. 37. Pueblo petroglyphs of anthropomorphs sexually attached to unknown objects, near Bernalillo, New Mexico.

fig. 38. Petroglyphs depicting sexual intercourse, Inscription Point, Arizona.

Images of Sexual Intercourse

Coital scenes occur throughout the greater Southwest, primarily in rock art of the Anasazi in the Colorado Plateau and upper Rio Grande, the Fremonts in Utah, the Mogollons in southern New Mexico, the Sinaguas of central Arizona, the Navajos and Apaches in New Mexico and Arizona, and the Plains Indians. Although ways of depicting anthropomorphic figures differ considerably, less variation is employed in depicting the sex act. Certain images indicate symbolic copulation, where phallic males are positioned next to a vulva symbol or a natural hole in the rock (figs. 29 and 70). Phallic males are also shown sexually joined to objects or symbols such as geometric motifs, the sexual significance of which is unknown (fig. 37). Of the more than sixty images of sexual intercourse documented in southwestern rock art in this book, the majority show couples face-to-face (fig. 38); only about ten portray the position that the Spanish priests decried as "bestial" (fig. 39). Occasionally, these images are fairly realistic, but most are simple figures, some of which are stylized to varying degrees.

Scenes of sexual activity were probably created for a number of reasons. Some may simply represent an individual's desire to attract the opposite sex or to

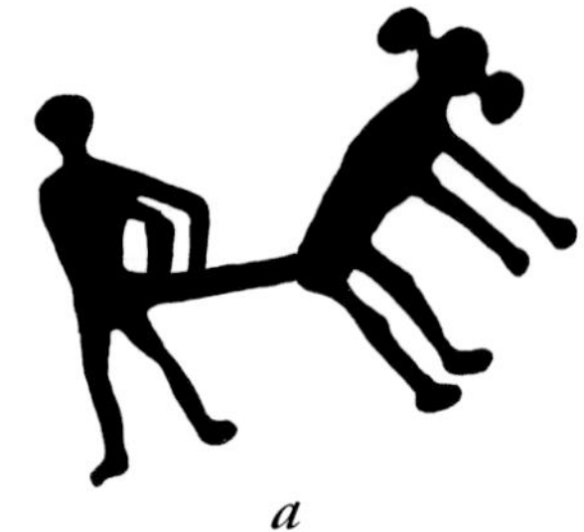

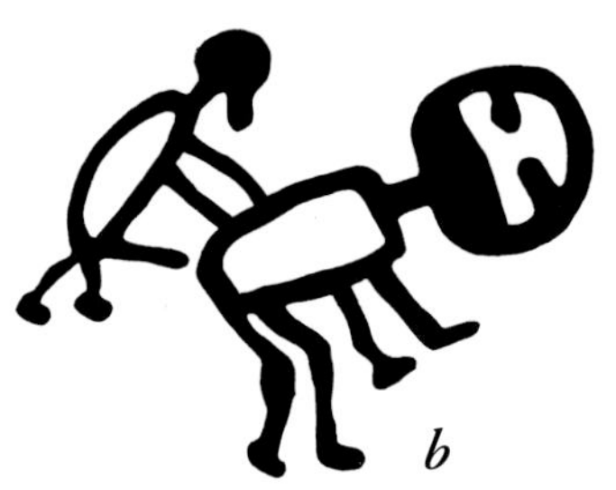

fig. 39 Petroglyphs depicting sexual intercourse: a. Tenabo, near Abo, New Mexico; b. Petrified Forest National Park, Arizona (after McCreery and Malotki 1994, 110).

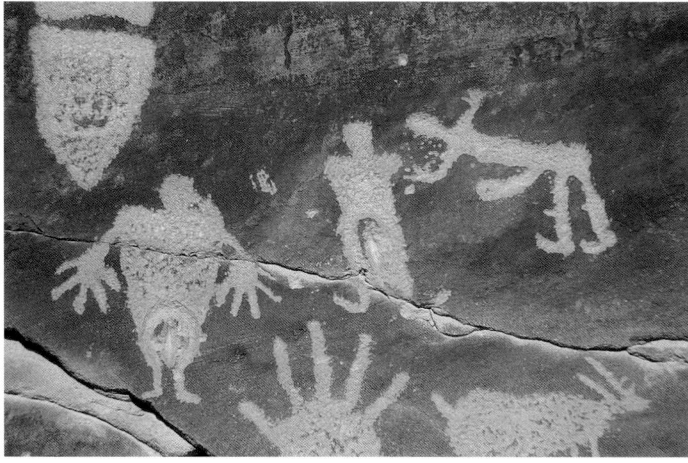

fig. 40. Fremont petroglyphs of a phallic male and women with enhanced vulvas—perhaps representing a courtship or seduction scene, Nine Mile Canyon, Utah.

record success in doing so. For example, the theme of courtship or seduction is suggested by the scene depicted in fig. 40, where an extremely phallic man seems to be bowing towards, or attempting to embrace, two females with enlarged vulvas. Perhaps depictions such as this are explained by the following types of accounts:

> The men joked together and told many stories about sexual intercourse. They drew figures on the rocks representing the sexual organs. I found a carving of this kind near the Buffalo shrine. There was an outline of a vulva with a coyote symbol and eight marks above it; nearby was a drawing of the male organs, and above them the symbol of our Sun shield. I was told it signified that a man of our Sun Clan had had intercourse with eight women of the Coyote Clan. Somebody was boasting. My companions drew similar pictures on other rocks, some with arrows leading to sheltered places suitable for the act (Talayesva 1942, 76).

> Near the village the trail led past a corner formed by two large boulders. On the face of one rock had been carved the pictographs of a reed (*bakap*), gun, vulva, and coyote head. Ned said that these pictographs indicated that at this spot someone had detected a Bakap clansman having intercourse with a Coyote clanswoman (Titiev 1972, 151).

Other images may have originated as part of fertility rites with broader, spiritual connotations, such as the Sacred Marriage alluded to earlier. Still others could have been made by shamans to indicate concepts like "entering the rock" or "penetrating the supernatural"—metaphors for going into the shamanic trance (see the section "Sex and the Shaman"). Additionally, these images may illustrate mythic or supernatural events (" . . . the sun cohabited with the earth, and out of her womb life came . . ."; Benedict 1953, 115). Some of the figures in such scenes do not appear quite human and may represent supernaturals, ancestors, or spiritual beings, or perhaps they are persons wearing masks as part of a ceremony or rite (fig. 39).

The majority of these images are, of course, part of rock art panels and thus associated with other elements. For the sake of clarity, in the drawings used here, only the most adjacent or obviously connected elements have been included. The two most commonly associated motifs accompanying scenes of sexual intercourse

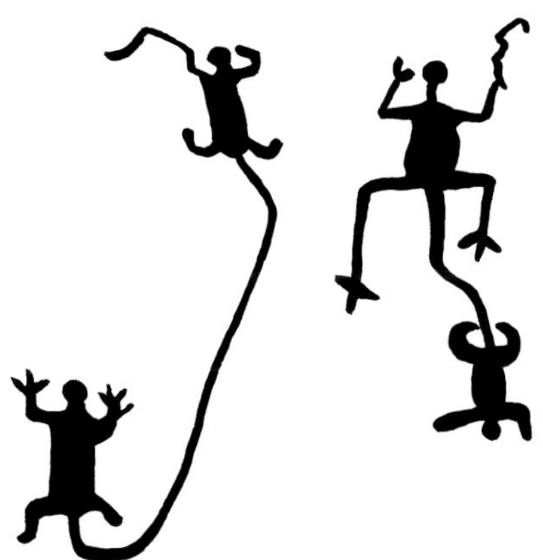

fig. 41. (left) Petroglyphs depicting phallic connections as "power lines," La Cienega, New Mexico.

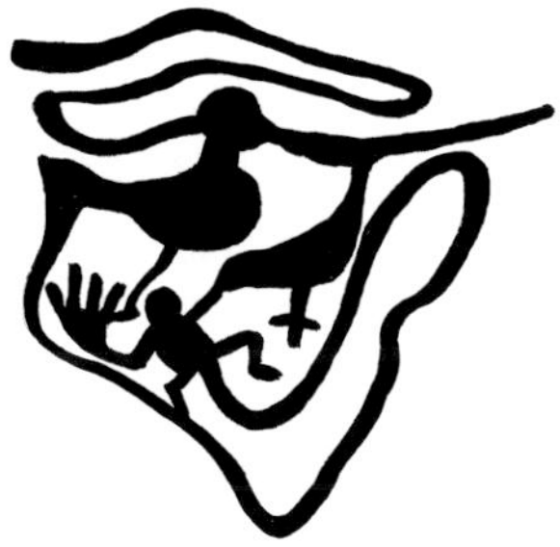

fig. 42. (below) Petroglyphs depicting sexual intercourse; a. Castle Gardens, Wyoming; b. Jemez Mountains, New Mexico; c. Velarde, New Mexico; d. Puerco River, Arizona.

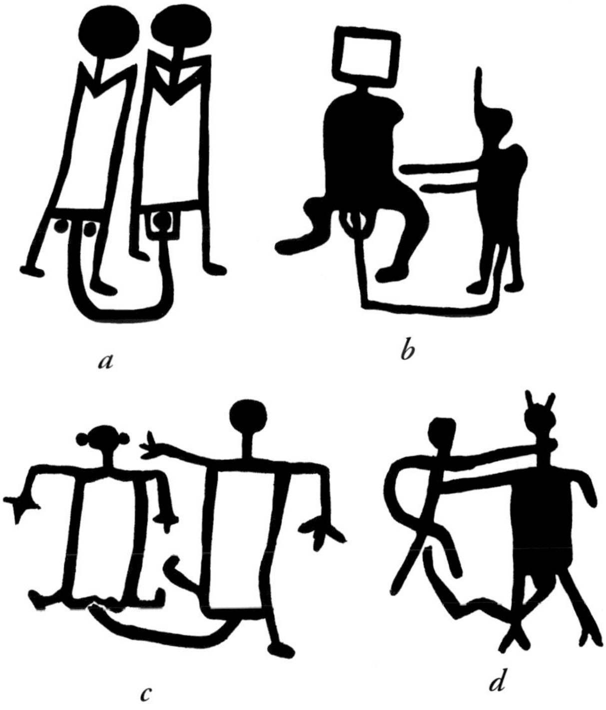

a b c d

are snakes and flute players—both fertility symbols discussed in detail in later sections. Likewise, the relation of certain rock art images to origin myths and fertility rites is further elaborated in subsequent sections. Also see Chapter 5 for more examples of the creative ways sexual intercourse has been depicted in rock art of other cultures worldwide.

Certain images of sexual intercourse seem to be emphasizing power or a spiritual connection between the couple, rather than mere physical union. In these instances, long, curving "power lines" may substitute for a phallic link between somewhat distant partners and objects (fig. 41). By intentionally representing intercommunication in this way, the distortion of the image is probably connoting some abstract concept in addition to copulation. However, without ethnographic substantiation, we can only imagine what is intended here. There is also the possibility that some artists had difficulty depicting complex, three-dimensional subjects and solved this problem by connecting the couple with a greatly enhanced, U-shaped phallus (fig. 42). One possible ethnographic parallel to such an exaggerated petroglyphic image is suggested by a Kokopelli tale from Hopi in which the libidinous flute player inserts his very long penis into a hidden tube of hollow reeds to secretly inseminate an unsuspecting maiden as she relieves herself. A petroglyph that may illustrate this story is shown in fig. 43, and the text of the story is recounted in the section "Myths and Stories about Fertility." Additional exam-

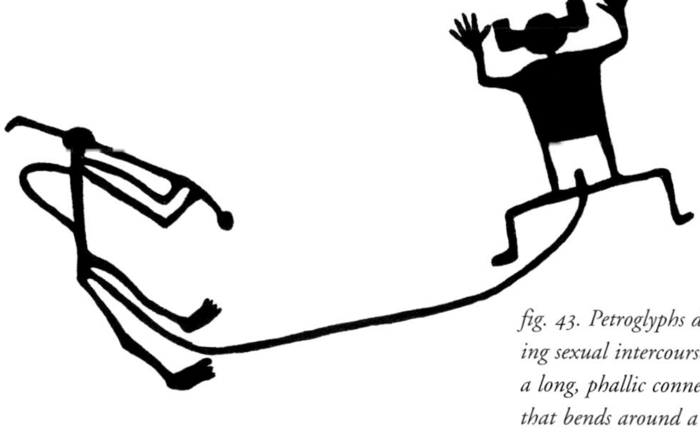

fig. 43. Petroglyphs depicting sexual intercourse with a long, phallic connection that bends around a corner of two rock faces, Jemez Mountains, New Mexico.

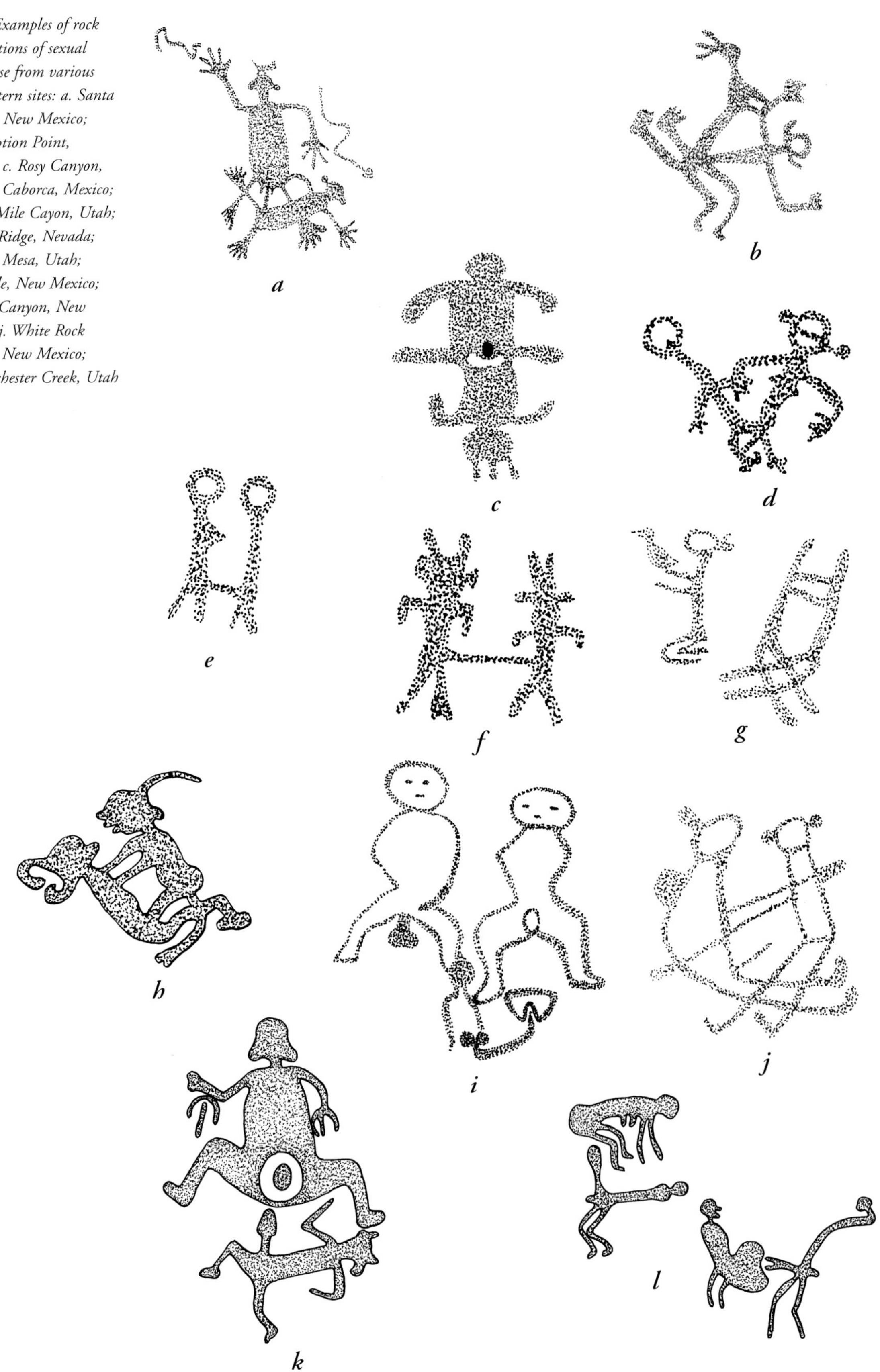

fig. 44. Examples of rock art depictions of sexual intercourse from various southwestern sites: a. Santa Fe River, New Mexico; b. Inscription Point, Arizona; c. Rosy Canyon, Utah; d. Caborca, Mexico; e. Nine Mile Cayon, Utah; f. Bitter Ridge, Nevada; g. Cedar Mesa, Utah; h. Velarde, New Mexico; i. Tapia Canyon, New Mexico; j. White Rock Canyon, New Mexico; k.–l. Rochester Creek, Utah (cont.).

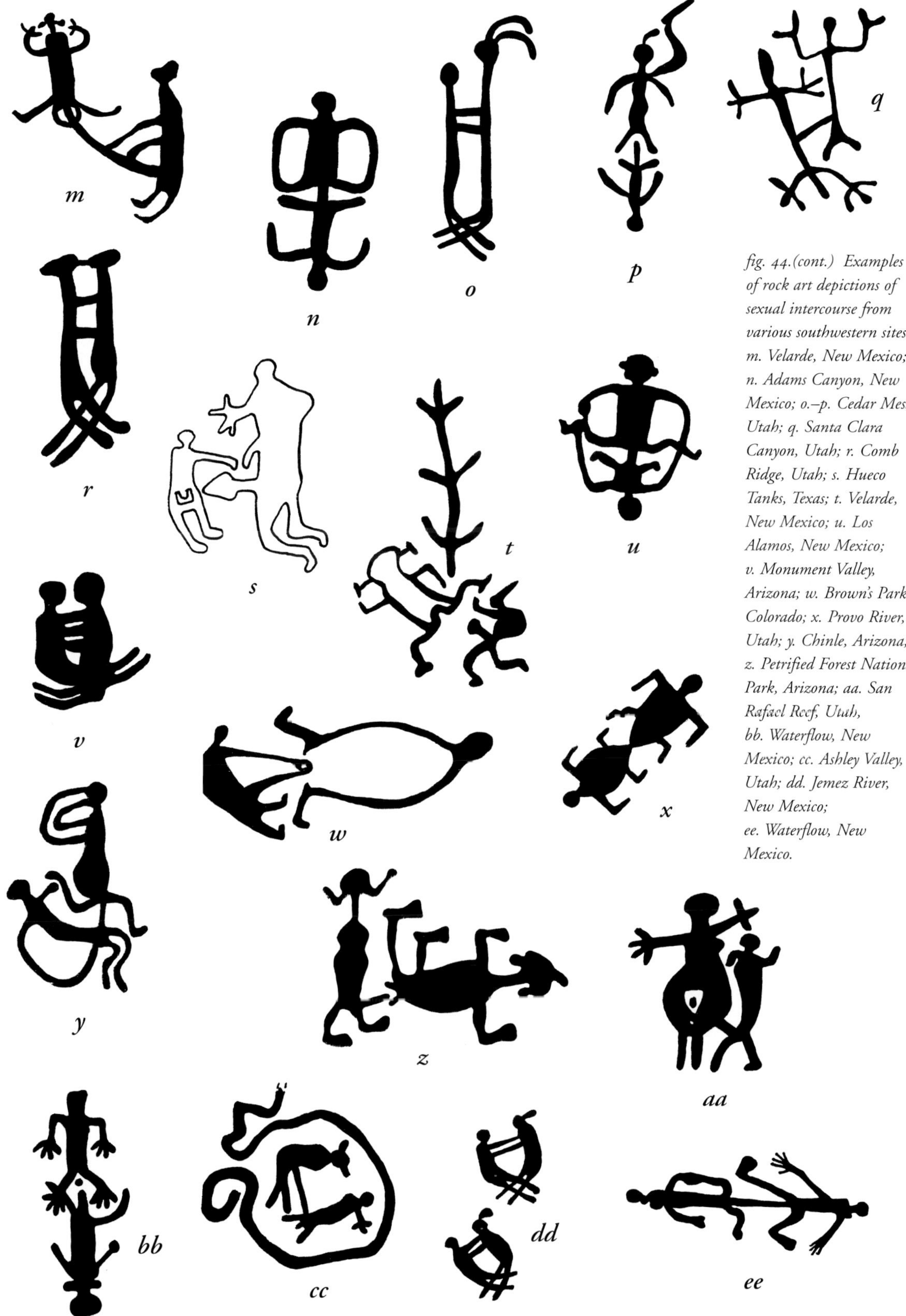

fig. 44.(cont.) Examples of rock art depictions of sexual intercourse from various southwestern sites: m. Velarde, New Mexico; n. Adams Canyon, New Mexico; o.–p. Cedar Mesa, Utah; q. Santa Clara Canyon, Utah; r. Comb Ridge, Utah; s. Hueco Tanks, Texas; t. Velarde, New Mexico; u. Los Alamos, New Mexico; v. Monument Valley, Arizona; w. Brown's Park, Colorado; x. Provo River, Utah; y. Chinle, Arizona; z. Petrified Forest National Park, Arizona; aa. San Rafael Reef, Utah, bb. Waterflow, New Mexico; cc. Ashley Valley, Utah; dd. Jemez River, New Mexico; ee. Waterflow, New Mexico.

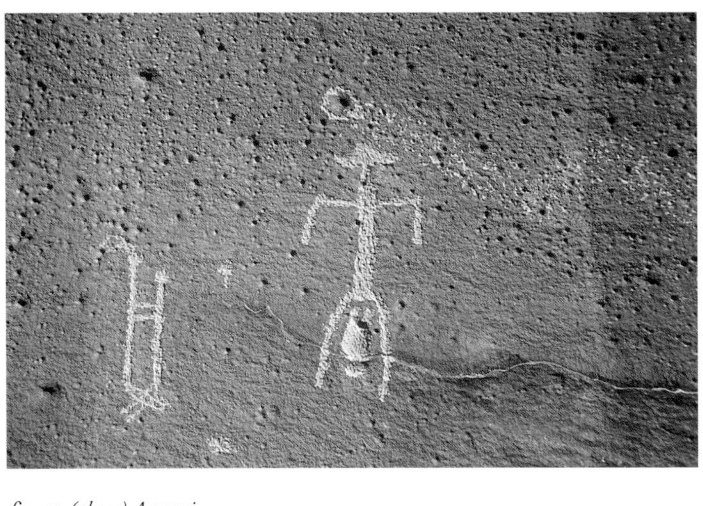

fig. 45. (above) Anasazi petroglyphs depicting a copulation and birthing scene, Cedar Mesa, Utah.

fig. 47. Petroglyphs of a mother and child, Little Colorado River, Arizona.

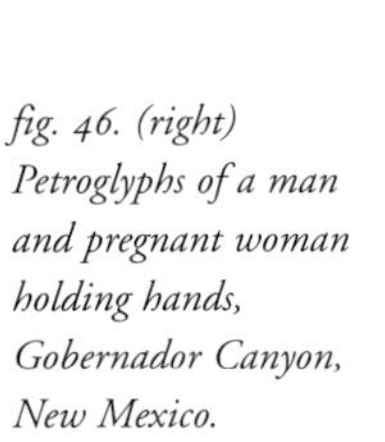

fig. 46. (right) Petroglyphs of a man and pregnant woman holding hands, Gobernador Canyon, New Mexico.

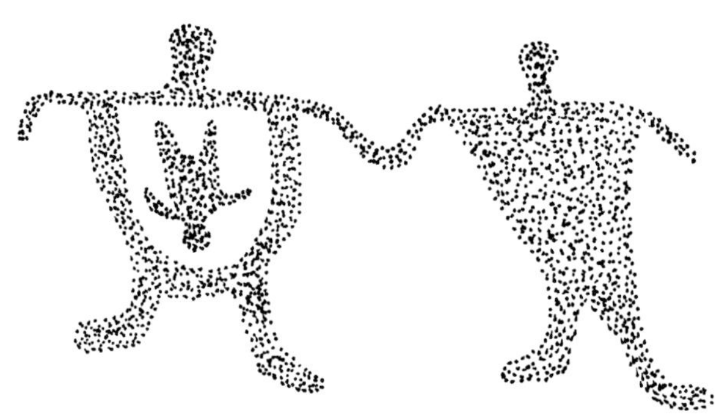

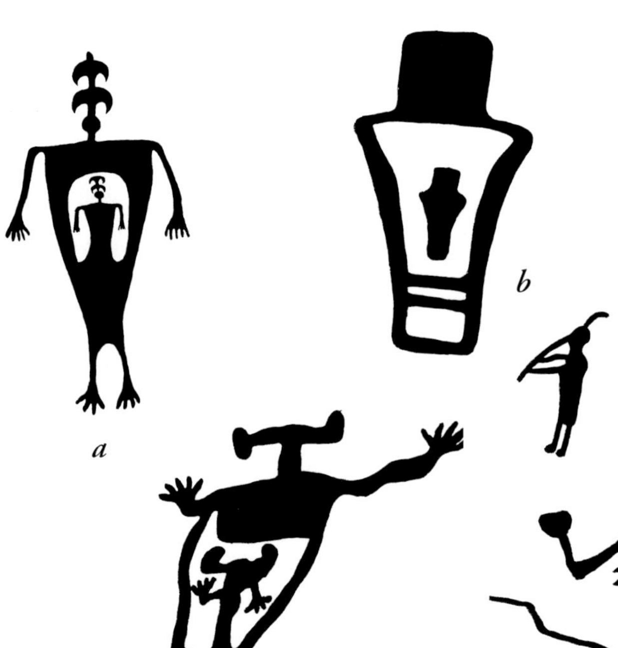

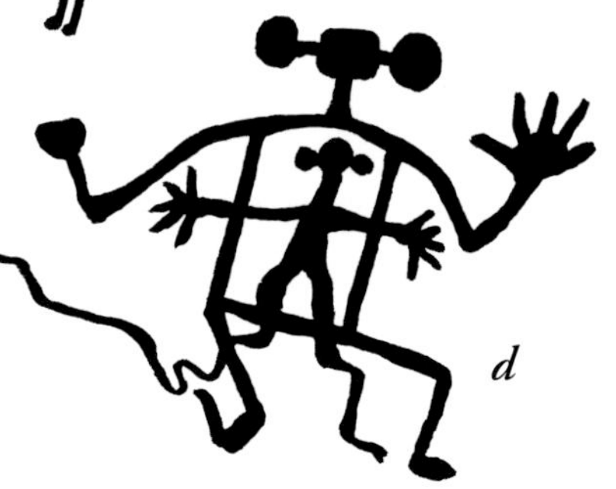

fig. 48. Examples of rock art portraying pregnancy from various sites: a. Yellowjacket Canyon, Colorado; b. Indian Creek, Utah; c. Legend Rock, Wyoming; d. Velarde, New Mexico (cont.).

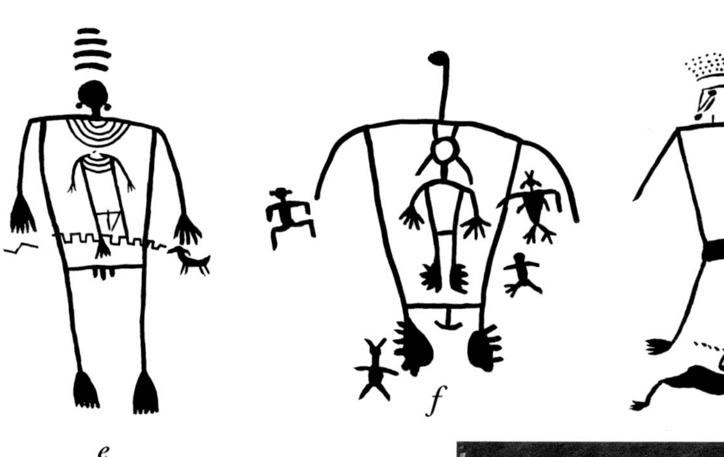

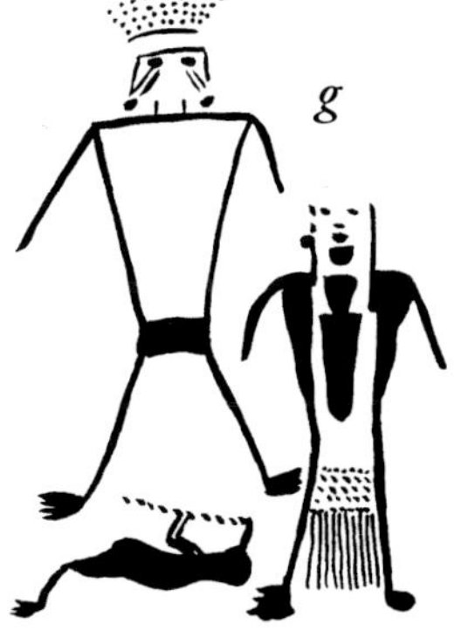

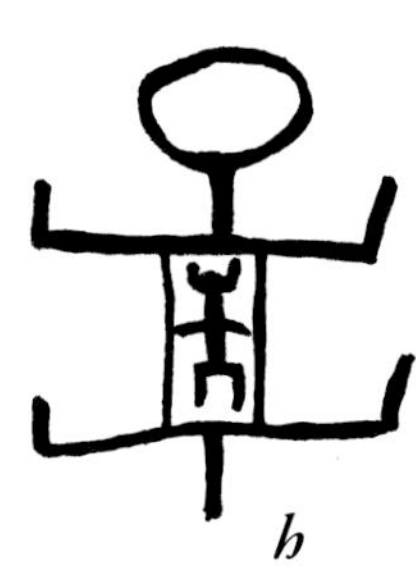

fig. 48. (above) Examples of rock art portraying pregnancy from various sites: e. San Juan River, Utah; f. Poncha House Ruin, Arizona; g. Dry Fork Valley, Utah; h. Sand Canyon, New Mexico.

ples of sexual intercourse depicted in southwestern rock art are presented in fig. 44 on the following pages.

Images of Pregnancy and Birth

An obvious result of copulation was pregnancy and birth. That this was a desirable outcome is attested to in rock art, where images of pregnancy and birthing are not only widespread but more common than depictions of coitus. Rarely are these themes combined in the same scene, proving that the connection between sex and birth was well known (fig. 45). The numerous reasons for making these images are probably the same as those given above, and consequently a wide range of depictions of pregnancy and birth occurs in rock art. Some include poignant family scenes with hand-holding, expectant couples (fig. 46), or proud mother with child (fig. 47).

In many portrayals of pregnant females, there is a small anthropomorphic figure inside the female's body, a convention occurring in various rock art styles of different cultures (figs. 48), no doubt in many cases depicting pregnancy, although in some instances smaller figures inside anthropomorphs perhaps do not portray pregnancy but instead represent the concept of an individual's spirit, or perhaps even possession by another spirit. In some depictions of pregnancy, it seems that

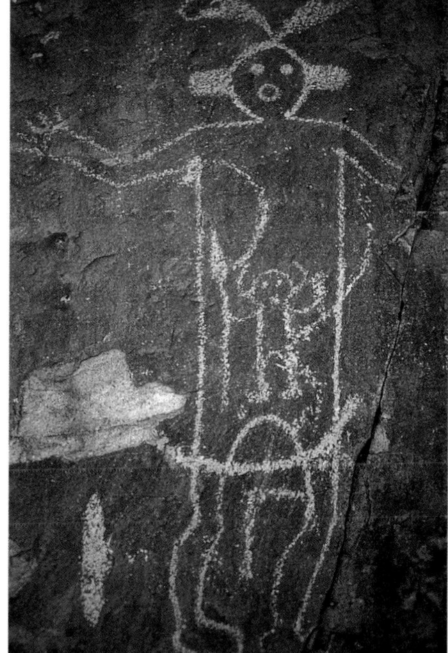

fig. 49. (left) Southern Tewa petroglyphs of an anthropomorph with a small warrior-baby or a spirit inside, Galisteo Basin, New Mexico.

wished-for attributes of the unborn child are indicated—such as the little horned warrior holding weapons inside the womb in fig. 49. Symbols of warfare dominate the iconography at this site, and perhaps the unborn child symbolizes the importance of producing plenty of fierce warriors to defend the tribe. Further, sometimes pregnancy is implied by either profile or frontal views of figures with swollen abdomens (fig. 50).Occasionally, natural rock features such as bumps or protuberances incorporated into an image depict a swollen abdomen.

The act of giving birth is also portrayed in various ways. Sometimes the

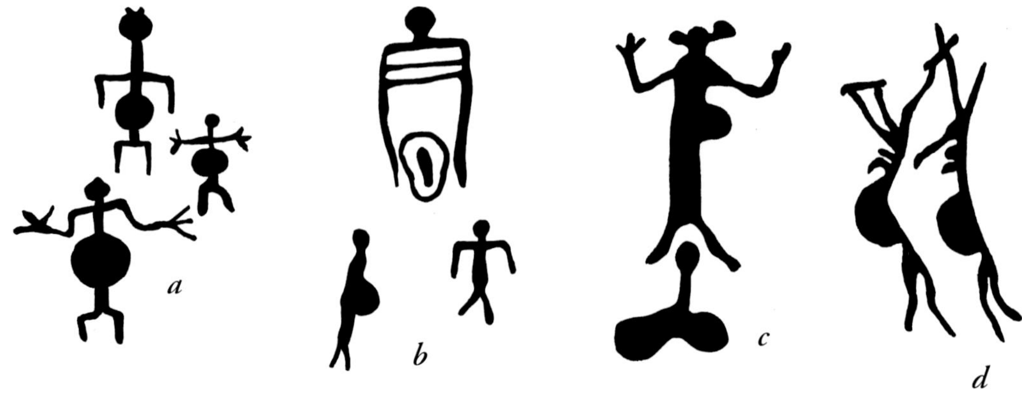

fig. 50. Examples of rock art depicting pregnant females: a. Comb Ridge, Utah; b. Cedar Point, Utah; c. Petrified Forest National Park, Arizona; d. Seminole Canyon State Park, Texas.

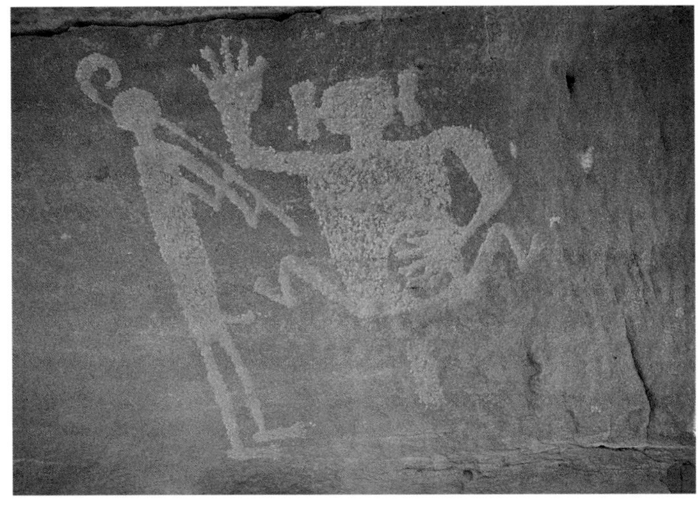

fig. 51. (right and below) Petroglyphs showing a phallic flute player and a female who has given birth, near Quemado, New Mexico.

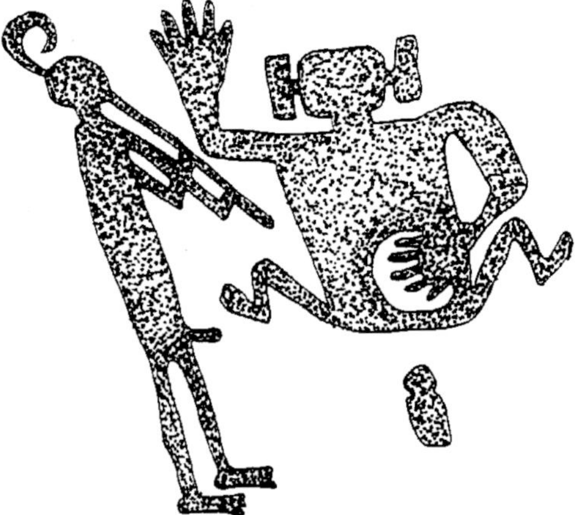

female has a prominent hollow womb, with little emphasis on the baby itself, which is shown as a small, amorphous blob (fig. 51). However, more typically a small anthropomorphic figure can be seen emerging from between the legs of a female squatting to give birth. In other birthing scenes, though, the baby is less recognizably human and may represent some mythic or supernatural birthing (figs. 53 and 54). There are possible depictions of the umbilical

fig. 52. (right) Petroglyph of a birthing scene, Clay Hills, Utah.

fig. 53. (below left) Petroglyph of a birthing scene, Kane Creek, Moab, Utah.

fig. 54. (below right) Petroglyph of a birthing scene, Monument Valley, Utah.

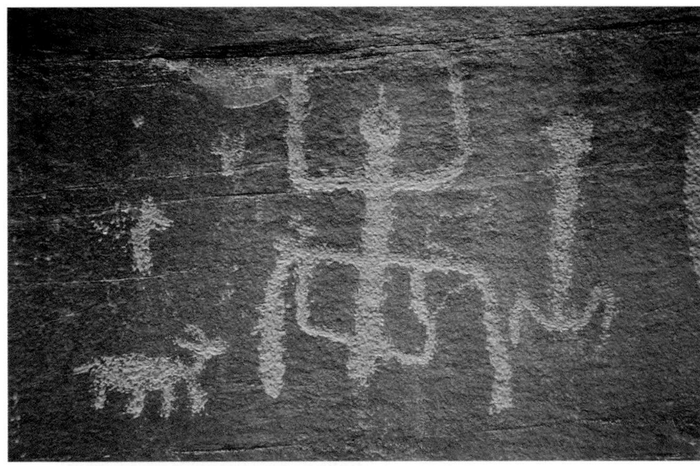

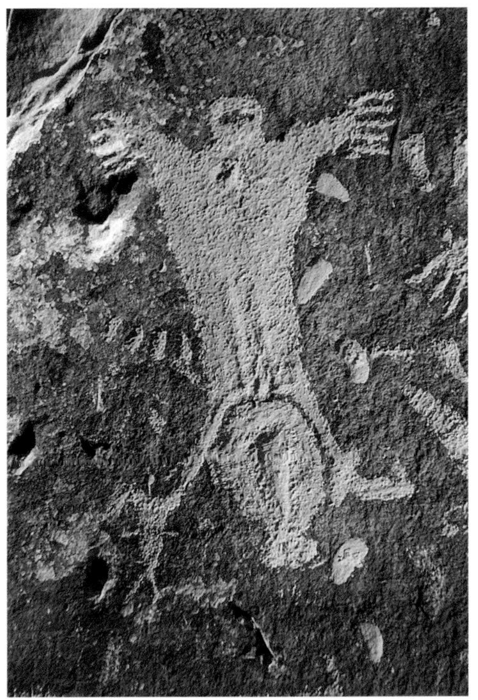

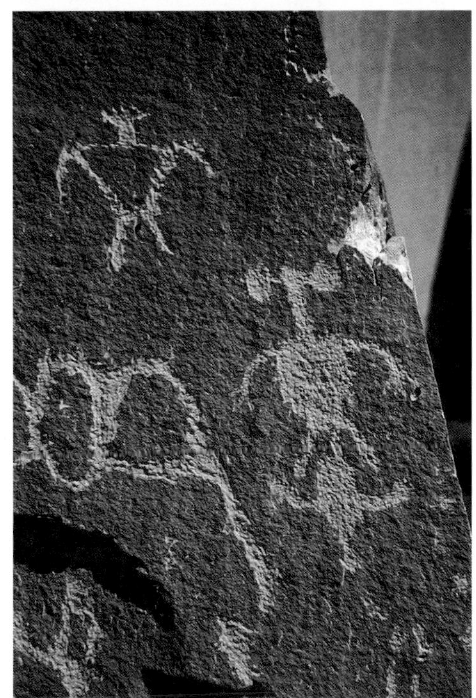

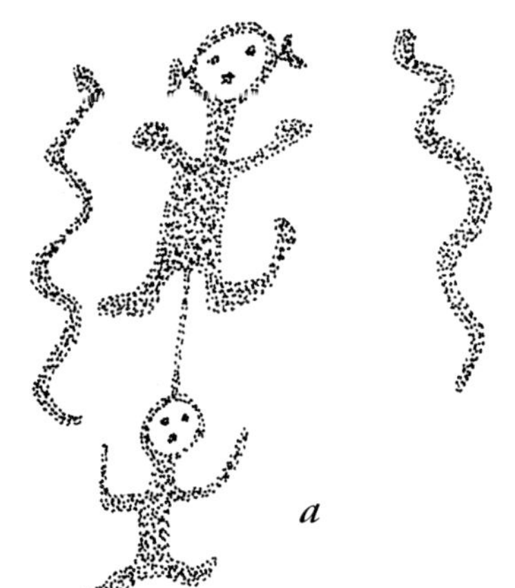

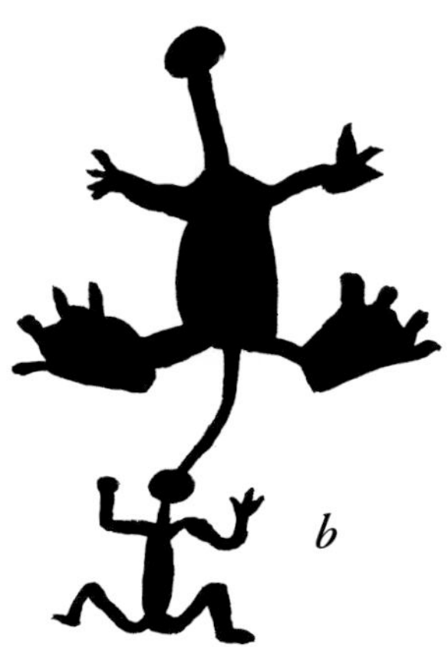

fig. 55. (left) Petroglyphs of birthing scenes showing umbilical cord attachment: a. White Rock Canyon, New Mexico (after Schaafsma 1975, 11); b. Carrizo Wash, near Quemado, New Mexico.

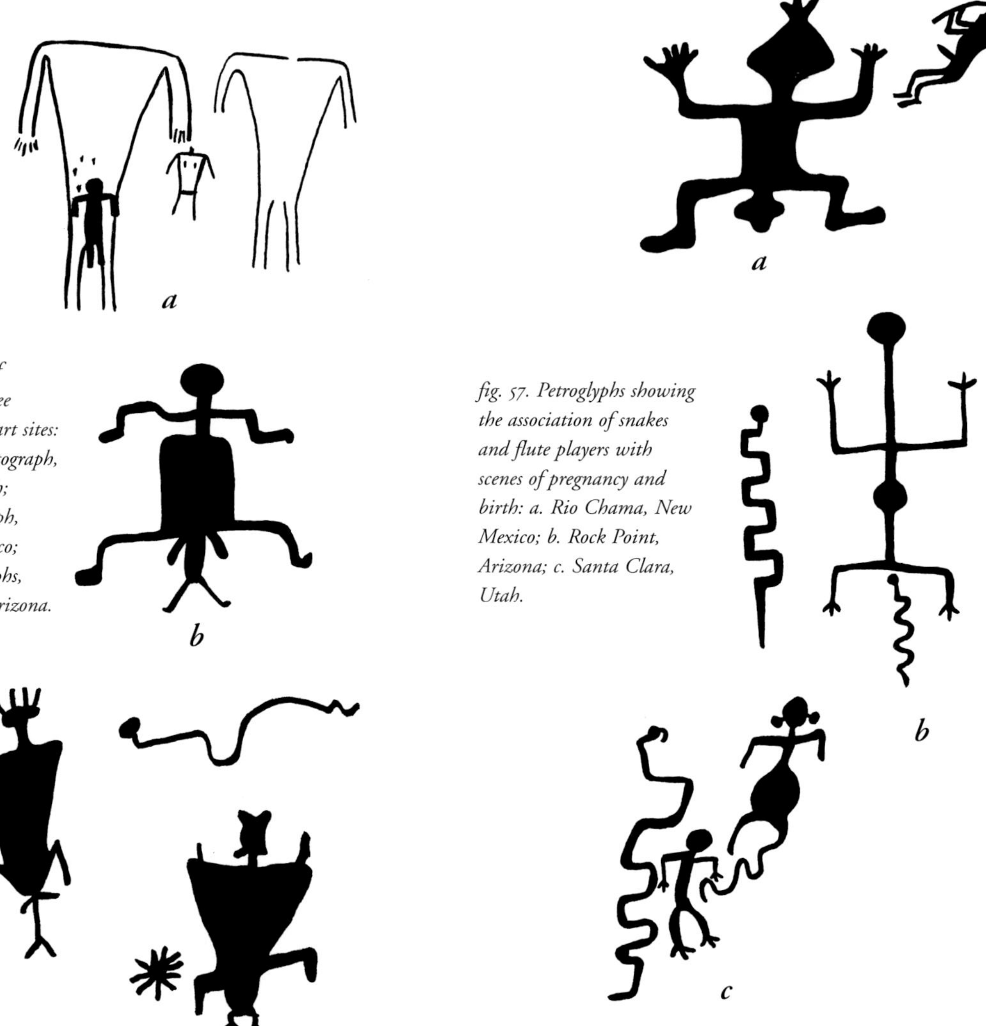

fig. 56. Depiction of breech births at three Southwestern rock art sites: a. Basketmaker pictograph, Grand Gulch, Utah; b. Anasazi petroglyph, Lupton, New Mexico; c. Anasazi petroglyphs, Dinnebito Wash, Arizona.

fig. 57. Petroglyphs showing the association of snakes and flute players with scenes of pregnancy and birth: a. Rio Chama, New Mexico; b. Rock Point, Arizona; c. Santa Clara, Utah.

cord connecting mother and child as well (fig. 55). Portrayals of apparent breech births (feet first) also exist at several sites in Arizona, New Mexico, and Utah (fig. 56). Moreover, as with the depictions of sexual intercourse, snakes and flute players are often seen next to scenes showing pregnancy and birth (fig. 57).

As clearly demonstrated in world mythology, giving birth was the true mark of divinity in nearly all primitive belief systems. The first gods, if they were to claim any supremacy, had to give birth and bring about creation. Ethnographic examples of birth and origin beliefs from the Southwest are discussed in the sections "Myths and Stories about Fertility" and "Fertility Shrines and Rites." Here more rock art depictions of pregnancy, birth, and child rearing are presented from the Southwest (figs. 58 to 60); others from different parts of the world are given in Chapter 5.

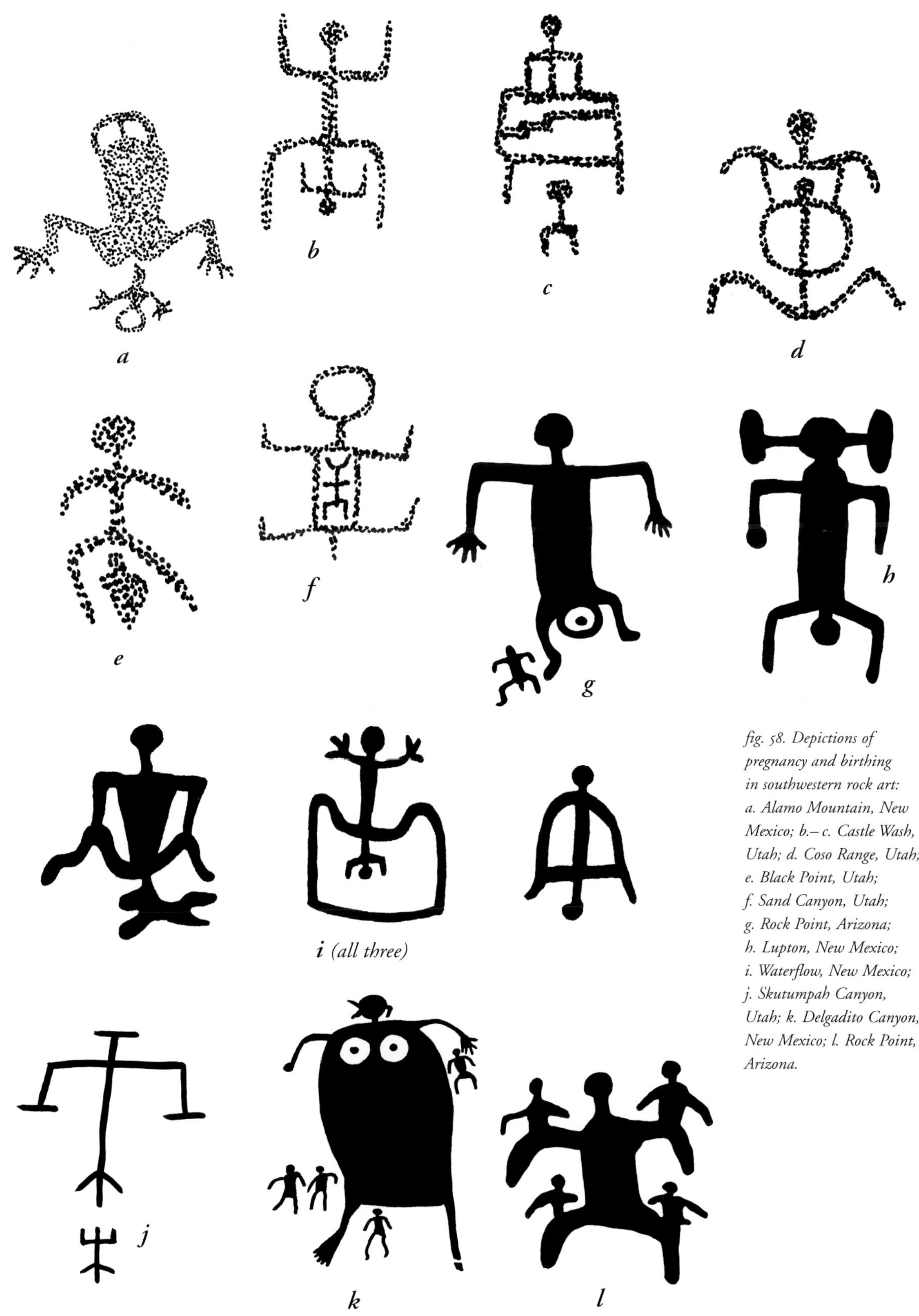

fig. 58. Depictions of pregnancy and birthing in southwestern rock art: a. Alamo Mountain, New Mexico; b.– c. Castle Wash, Utah; d. Coso Range, Utah; e. Black Point, Utah; f. Sand Canyon, Utah; g. Rock Point, Arizona; h. Lupton, New Mexico; i. Waterflow, New Mexico; j. Skutumpah Canyon, Utah; k. Delgadito Canyon, New Mexico; l. Rock Point, Arizona.

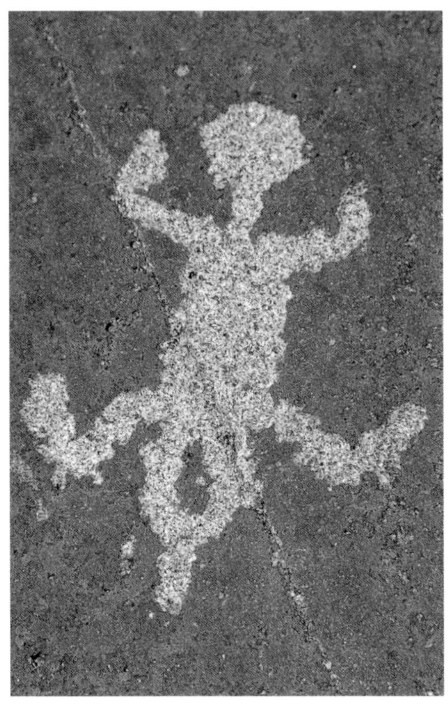

fig. 59. Petroglyph of a possible birthing scene, Anderson Pass, Arizona; photo James Duffield.

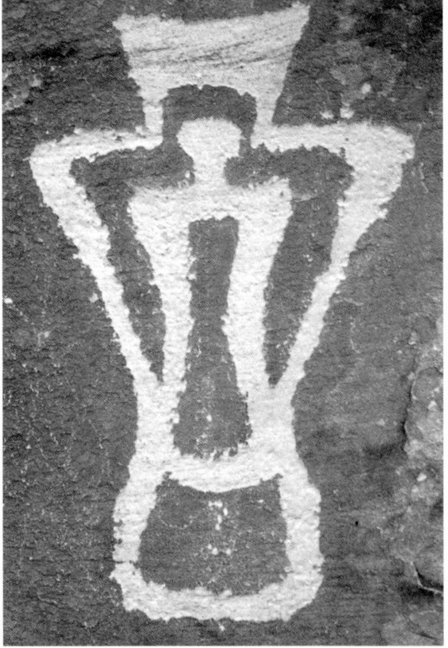

fig. 60. Petroglyph of a possible pregnancy, Indian Creek, Utah

Menstrual Blood

Ever since the Paleolithic era, blood has been a significant part of ritual and worship:

> From the earliest human cultures, the mysterious magic of creation was thought to reside in the blood women gave forth in apparent harmony with the moon, and which was sometimes retained in the womb to "coagulate" into a baby. Men regarded this blood with holy dread, as the life essence, inexplicably shed without pain, wholly foreign to male experience (Walker 1983, 635).

Among certain groups of Indians in South America, it was said that all humans were made of "moon blood" in the beginning. In ancient Mesopotamia, the goddess created mankind from clay, infusing it with her "blood of life" and teaching women to make clay dolls smeared with menstrual blood as fertility magic. This is behind the feminine form of the biblical name Adam—Adamah, meaning "bloody clay," more delicately translated as "red earth" (Walker 1983, 635). Further, an Egyptian hieroglyphic sign for the holy blood of Isis was essentially the same as the vulva symbol, and was painted red. In many ancient cultures the color red is symbolic of rebirth. Some societies have used red ochre to paint their bodies and ritual objects red to simulate the sacred, regenerative power of menstrual blood. For example, bones covered with red ochre have been found in ancient tombs nearly everywhere. Moreover, an Australian Aboriginal ceremony links rebirth with the red blood of the womb. Performed at a symbolic "vulva of the earth," the chants emphasized redness:

> A straight track is gaping open before me. An underground hollow is gaping before me. A cavernous pathway is gaping before me. An underground pathway is gaping before me. Red I am like the heart of a flame of fire. Red, too, is the

hollow in which I am resting
(Walker 1983, 639).

Even in medieval times, peasants in Europe thought menstrual blood had the power to heal and nourish. Some thought a crop could be protected if a menstruating woman walked around the field or exposed her genitals in it. Women carried seed to the fields in rags stained with their menstrual blood (Walker 1983, 644). Further, in today's Christian cultures the symbolic drinking of Christ's blood is a central sacrament of Communion.

As with cultures worldwide, many Native American cultures perceived blood as a powerful essence. Ritual bloodletting activities among some Native American groups had important fertility implications and were used to summon and provide offerings for the gods. Similarly, women's menstrual bleeding received special attention in religious and ceremonial practices. Because it was believed that significant activities which depended on spiritual help, such as hunts or raids, could be influenced by the power inherent in blood, such events were timed to placate the spirits involved. In some groups certain "manly hearted women" elected to participate in warfare, but they were almost always postmenopausal for this reason (Williams 1992, 243).

Many cultures have menstruation taboos (taboo means both sacred and unclean), which probably originated in the human tendency to turn any flowing of blood into some form of sacrament. A woman's ability to bleed regularly and in relation to lunar cycles undoubtedly inspired awe. It may also have led to the proliferation of myths and male fears about a powerful, castrating *vagina dentata*, or vagina with teeth (see the section "Myths and Stories about Fertility"). Although commonly the subject of taboos, menstruation among Native Americans was treated more often as something powerful than shameful or unclean.[25] Typically a girl's first period was celebrated with special puberty rites. One author has written: "Women are perceived to be possessed of a singular power, most vital during menstruation. . . . Indians do not perceive signs of womanness as contamination; rather they view them as so powerful that other medicines may be canceled by the very presence of that power" (Williams 1992, 243–44). Among some cultures where shamans were nearly always men (such as the Great Basin and southern California), the primary impediment to women becoming shamans was their menstrual blood, which was considered inimical to supernatural power. For this reason, women were prohibited from attending or participating in rituals during their periods. Only after they reached menopause could women become shamans, and even then they were probably seen as oddities when selected for this calling by spirits in visions (Whitley 1996, 122-23).

In rock art some images apparently depict menstrual blood and may be examples of native views on this subject. The use of red ochre (naturally occurring iron oxide minerals used for pigment) in making pictographs and for painting objects, including the human body, has been an ancient and universal practice. It has been suggested that mankind's first "art" may have been body decorations; red ochre has been documented in archaeological contexts from graves in Africa dating back to 130,000 B.C., after which its use became very widespread (Taylor 1996, 99). In some instances red ochre has been used to simulate blood and its power. Red ochre on ancient human remains indicates it was used to simulate blood and hence the monthly renewal of female fertility and life. It has also been proposed that red ochre may have been used by females in sham menstruation, although the exact purpose of doing so has not been established.

The flow of menstrual blood seems to be suggested by the application of red pigment to the lines drawn between the legs of a stylized female figure in an Archaic, Barrier Canyon Style petroglyph in Utah (fig. 61). This may also be the intent of the petroglyph shown in fig. 62, where a female has been pecked around a natural hole in the rock, from which lines indicate the flow of liquid, to perhaps represent the life-nurturing fluids of blood, *fig. 61. (right) Barrier Canyon Style petroglyph/pictograph with possible menstrual blood symbolism, Dirty Devil River, Utah.*

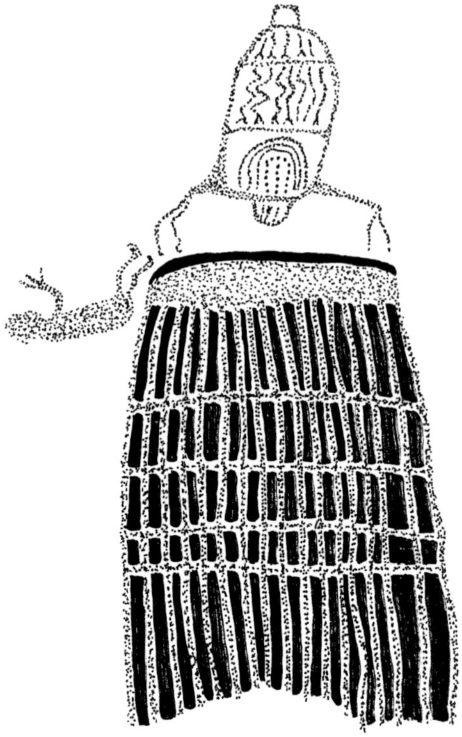

water, or milk. This also may be symbolic of the connection between the body of Mother Earth and water that issues from her dark recesses as springs or pools. World mythology is full of metaphors linking water and female generative powers with earth symbolism. For example, in Navajo sand paintings of Mother Earth there is a circle on her abdomen that symbolizes the lake at the center of the world, from which the first people emerged into the sunlight (Krupp 1997, 99).

At an Anasazi petroglyph site along the San Juan River in northwestern New Mexico, naturally occurring iron oxide concretions that cause red, blood-like stains to form on the cliff walls have been incorporated into fertility-related designs that indicate these features were seen as symbolic vulvas with menstrual blood (Warner 1983). Here at least eight circular cavities with red pigment stains have been intentionally pecked—sometimes the rim of the concretion (fig. 63), and sometimes the red stain on the sandstone itself. It has been suggested that this represents an effort to ritually stop symbolic menstrual flows, necessary for conception to occur. There are several human female figures depicted by incorporating a concretion in the genital area, and a phallic male is shown penetrating a concretion as a symbolic vulva (fig. 64). This petroglyph site was probably an important fertility location for the reasons given; it also contains other obvious fertility-related symbols such as several copulating figures and birthing scenes (fig. 58 i), anthropomorphs shown in a family context, flute players, possible sprouting seeds, and blanket-like designs that could suggest consummation (at Hopi and other pueblos, the marriage blanket has ritual significance in this regard, as in the act of having symbolic intercourse beneath a wedding blanket with the Salt Woman Shrine).

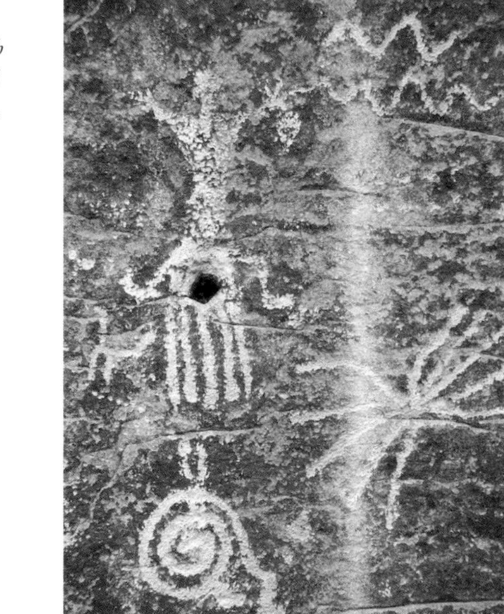

fig. 62. Basketmaker Anasazi petroglyphs with possible menstrual blood symbolism, Cedar Point, Utah.

Other examples of rock art that relate to the significance of menstrual blood are found in Basketmaker Anasazi images from the San Juan River region in southeastern Utah. At a petroglyph site in a narrow canyon on Comb Ridge, there are stylized depictions of females wearing belts with possible aprons or menstrual pads (fig. 65) in association with other obvious fertility images such as a flute

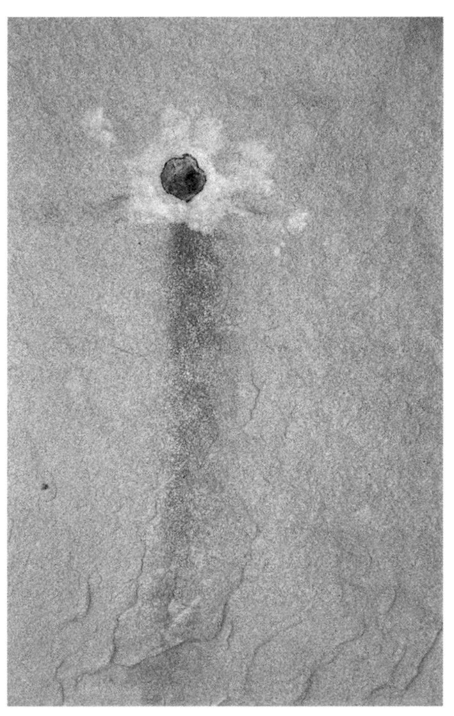

fig. 63. (left) Natural concretion and iron oxide stain that may have represented menstrual blood, with the rim of the concretion pecked, Waterflow, New Mexico.

fig. 64. (left & above) Petroglyphs with fertility symbolism incorporating natural concretions with iron oxide stain that may have represented vulvas and menstrual blood, Waterflow, New Mexico (after Warner 1983).

fig. 65. (left) Basketmaker Anasazi petroglyphs depicting stylized females wearing possible menstrual aprons, Butler Wash, Utah.

player, copulating couple, a phallic humpbacked figure holding a crook-necked staff, lobed circle motifs, and a stylized yucca plant with seedpods or flowers. Similar diaper-like clothing has been observed on Basketmaker female figurines of unfired clay (fig. 66) and on vegetal female effigies. These supposedly functioned as fertility fetishes (Cole 1989, 66). Basketmaker women apparently wore such aprons with fiber menstrual pads. Archaeological excavations of Basketmaker sites in northeastern Arizona have uncovered a number of such items, described as follows:

> Nearly all of the aprons were stained in the central portions of their length, indicating their use by women during their menstrual period. Most of them were subsequently folded and tied into a neat bundle so that the stain was hidden (Morris 1980, 104).

A pictograph in Canyon de Chelly, Arizona, shows a female wearing a similar

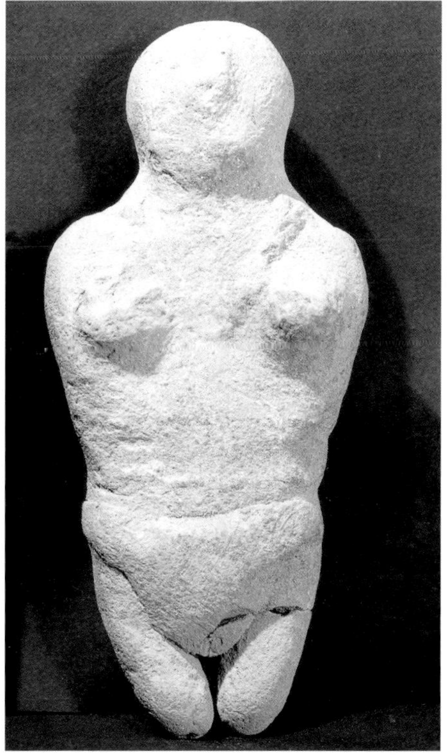

fig. 66. Basketmaker II clay figurine of a female wearing a possible menstrual apron and representing a fertility fetish, southeastern Utah (courtesy American Museum of Natural History Library, negative no. 124089; photo by A. J. Rota).

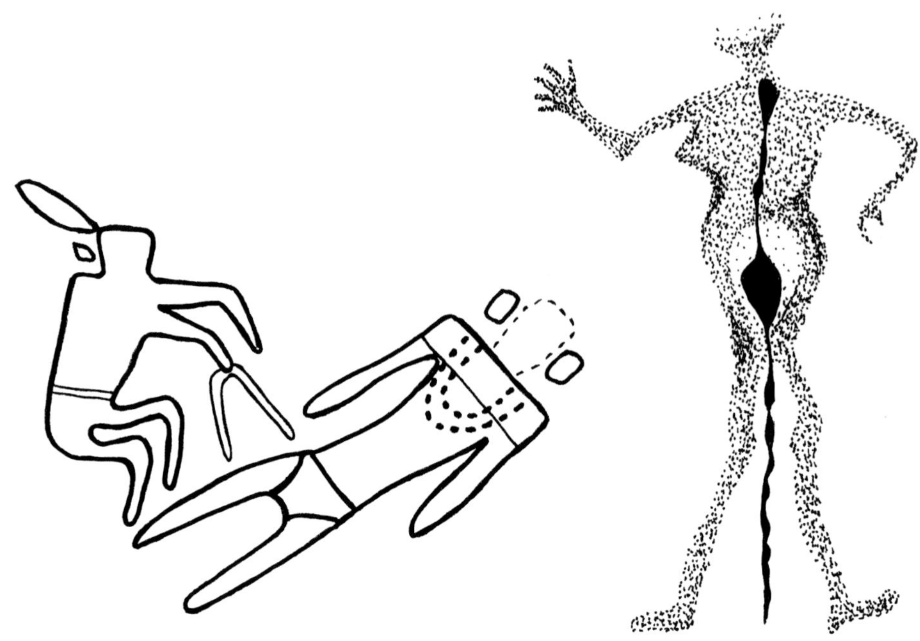

fig. 67. (left) Basketmaker Anasazi pictographs that may represent a shaman in a curing or fertility ritual with a reclining female wearing a possible menstrual apron, Canyon de Chelly, Arizona (after Grant 1978, 185).

fig. 68. (right) Petroglyph of a female incorporating a natural rock fissure with red iron oxide representing a natural vulva and menstrual blood, Peterborough, Ontario (after Vastokas 1973).

apron or diaper-like article; she appears to be a patient being attended to by a shaman, who holds an object over her pelvic region in a possible curing ritual related to fertility (fig. 67).

Although not located in the greater Southwest, an image at the Peterborough, Ontario, petroglyph site is worth mentioning here. An imposing, nearly life-sized female figure has been pecked on a limestone slab with her length along a natural rock fissure (fig. 68). Her genital area is a natural widening of the fissure, which contains a reddish-brown iron oxide compound (symbolic menstrual blood). The rendering of the image was certainly inspired by the red seam in the rock (Vastokas and Vastokas 1973, 80). This site is thought to have been a sacred fertility locale because of this image and many others with sexual connotations found there (see Chapter 5).

Another fascinating example of the veneration of female creative power as symbolized by menstrual blood occurs in a temple in Assam, India, which honors the vulva of the goddess Sati:

> Inside the temple, the yoni is represented by a cleft rock, kept moist by a natural underground spring which runs red with iron-oxide once a year, at the onset of the monsoon. This annual "menstruation" is interpreted by worshipers as nature's way of confirming the veneration of the female vulva and the processes to which it is subject, and as proof that the Goddess is the earth (Husain 1997, 97).

FERTILITY SHRINES AND RITES

> *The sacred place acts as an inexhaustible source of power and sacredness and enables man, simply by entering it, to have a share in the power, to hold communion with the sacredness. Moreover, this holy place is "never" chosen by man; it is merely discovered by him: in other words the sacred place in some way or another reveals itself to him.* [26]
>
> —Mircea Eliade
> *Patterns in Comparative Religion*

> *The women, each holding in one hand cornmeal and in the other hand three prayer feathers, follow a*

trail along the mesa top, pausing for prayer at certain shrines, then proceed down the rocky face of the cliff to a huge volcanic boulder whose top is covered with small brown nodules surrounded by curious whorls, which are taken to represent the embryo within the fetal membranes of the womb. The maiden members rub their hands over these whorls, offerings are left at the shrine below the boulder, and the company files up the cliff to prepare for the public ceremony.[27]

—Joseph Campbell
The Way of the Seeded Earth

Many ceremonial activities related to fertility were integrally tied to a sacred location or connected with a certain landscape feature. Indigenous cultures have found powers of fecundity in the concept of Mother Earth and through divine rites carried out at select sites found assurance of the continuance of all life. These primal places were imbued with spiritual potency and possess some special quality or feature that distinguishes them. Towering stone outcrops probably suggested symbolic phalli, certain hills resembled breasts, and caves or rock clefts symbolized vulvas and the earth's womb. Such landscape features were charged with the power of creation and used to harness that power through rituals as described by the following:

> certain landscapes and geological formations and, in fact, "all the remarkable spots in the country" were considered the favorite haunt of the spirits, especially "rocky cliffs" and "the clefts of craggy mounts," while waterfalls were thought to be their "sporting scenes." Rocky hills were particularly charged with holiness and the most appropriate places to seek visions. . . . Boulders, rocky hills, and outcroppings with unusual dimensions or character, such as clefts, holes, or crevices, were especially charged with *manitou* and often conceived as the dwelling-places of mythological creatures (Vastokas and Vastokas 1973, 47–48).

In some locales, if such features did not exist naturally they were created by carving vulva forms, deep grooves, and cup marks in the rock surface to represent fertility.

Humanity has always had a mystical relationship with rock, which was recognized as a living being, the home of spirits, the sacred womb of Mother Earth, and a source of physical and spiritual security. Caves, especially, are places of creation and power, used by Stone Age people for shelter or sacred rituals. Usually associated with female sexuality, caves, graves, and other womb-like openings have fostered human interaction with the spirit of Mother Earth. As mysterious, dark, interior spaces, they were seen as places of power and the territory of spirits. As the source of underground waters that sustained life, they were linked through birth imagery to the navel of Mother Earth. In some cultures, caves are seen not only as places of creation but as a destination for the dead and a source of rebirth. The cave is the heart of the world—the center of the cosmos (Krupp 1997, 110–11).

These symbolic concepts linking fertility rites to specific landscape features are evident at many sites throughout the Southwest. For example, the Cave of Creation, a rock shelter with pictographs in the Tehachapi Mountains of California's Mojave Desert sacred to the Numic-speaking Kawaiisu Indians, is the locale where the First People were created and ancestors' spirits still reside in large boulders. The Cave of Creation resembles a huge vulva with a forty-foot cleft in the rock down which a seasonal waterfall flows. The Kawaiisu people say the world emerged from a bedrock mortar here—another symbolic vagina (Krupp 1997, 101).

A further example of sexual symbolism in the correspondence between landscape features and the human body has been documented in connection with the sacred Kumeyaay mountain Cuchama in southern California. This mountain, where there is a ten-foot-high rock monolith that resembles both female and male genitals when viewed from different directions, was a source of power for shamans: "It is a formidable monument symbolizing creative male generative power within which is contained female fertility" (Staniford 1977, 34, quoted in McGowan 1982, 17). At a similar fertility shrine in southern California, a large, natural, phallic-shaped rock formation contains pictographic elements (fig. 69).

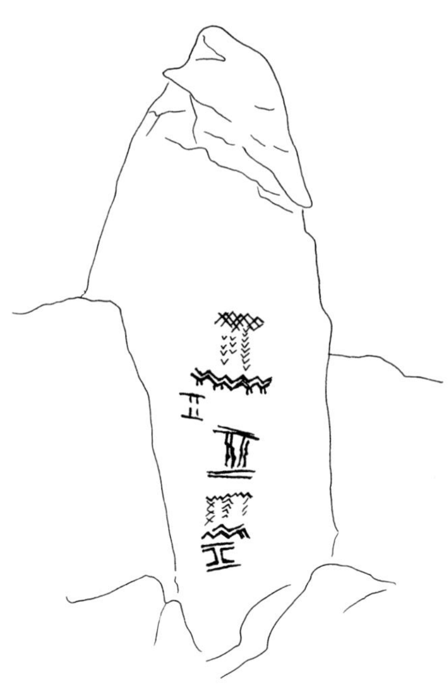

fig. 69. Pictographs on a phallic rock formation, Riverside County, California (after Smith and Freers 1994, 73).

In the Cave of Life in Arizona's Painted Desert, Anasazi petroglyphs portray a fertility ritual that has been interpreted as an enactment of the Sacred Marriage rite known to exist in some historic Native American cultures (Hunger 1982; Faris 1986). Far from being pornographic, the scene depicts a profound religious ritual. Here a copulating couple is linked to a group of animals and other elements, including an outlined cross as the focal point of the composition (fig. 26 and Plate 19). An ancient symbol of uncertain meaning, the cross could represent the four cardinal directions, therefore the universe, lending credence to the sacred nature of the pictured ceremony. It has also been proposed that the cross represents a star; a shaft of sunlight from a solar marker strikes it on certain dates near the winter solstice. These dates may be similar to those of the Hopi Wuwuchim ceremonies, which focus on phases of creation and the germination of all forms of life on earth. Above the composition stands a phallic male figure holding two staffs—probably a shaman. The couple likely represents two people (not necessarily married) symbolic of the forces of life and creation in this sacrament, which is designed to restore harmony and well-being to the community. The sole purpose of this ritual coitus is to re-create the world and rejuvenate life.

Ritual coitus in the context of the Sun Dance among the Southern Arapahos was recorded in 1902 as follows:

> Her husband was also present when she, still inside the Medicine Lodge, removed her clothing under a robe gathered around her. Her husband saw when the two celebrants, in an air of intense emotion, left the lodge, making a sunwise circuit as they passed out . . . stepping over the rising incense. Outside they circumambulate in conformity with the four cardinal points of the sky. At the final Point . . . is spread the buffalo robe of the woman (to lie down, thus exposing her naked body to the moon). And here the intercourse takes place, the woman facing the moon. This act represents intercourse between the sun and the moon, bringing strength to the people and increase to the tribe, for thus were created the beings of the world. After having duly consummated their ritual coition, it is the woman who leads their return to the Medicine Lodge, and as they enter she addresses her husband, saying "I have returned, having performed the holy act which was commanded" (Dorsey 1902, 172–78).

Another form of ritual coitus—between men and a rock formation known as the Salt Woman—took place at a shrine in the Grand Canyon as part of a traditional Hopi salt-gathering expedition. This symbolic sexual intercourse was performed in connection with rituals for safe travel into the canyon and was associated with fertility—not just for individuals but for the survival of the entire Hopi community and to ensure rain and bountiful crops. The following is a description of this rite at the Salt Woman Shrine during a 1912 expedition as told by the Hopi Don Talayesva in his autobiography *Sun Chief*:

> We journeyed to a sacred spring, placed prayer offerings by it, and prayed to the spirits who live there to send rain upon our crops . . . . We followed an old riverbed . . . and entered a narrow gorge . . . the War Chief took out a white wedding blanket. Glancing at me, he smiled and said, "This is the shrine of the Salt Woman. We will have intercourse with her." He stepped to a white, slightly elevated sandstone about two feet wide and six feet long, and covered it with the wedding garment. Removing his trousers and loincloth, he took a prayer feather and some corn meal in his hand, crawled under the cover, and went through the motions of copulation. At the same time he named a woman whom we all knew. Then he arose, expressed thanks for the pleasure, and dressed. After my father had gone through the same performance, I was told to do likewise. . . . I obeyed, stepped to the stone, raised the cover, and looked. Embedded in the center of the smooth, white surface was a small, black stone shaped like a vulva. . . . At the bottom lay the prayer feathers and the sacred corn meal of the War Chief and my father.
>
> I arose, thanked the Salt Woman, dressed, and said, "Well, fathers, I would like to know the meaning of this." The War Chief replied: "When the Spider Woman, who owns the salt, was making a trail for the Hopi to Salt Canyon . . . she turned herself into this stone so that she could guide the Hopi to salt. Whenever we have intercourse with her, we are doing it to increase our children and improve our health. This is not a "dirty trick," as the Christians have called it, neither is it the worship of a stone image, for we know that the Salt Woman is a living goddess, and that intercourse with her means life" (Talayesva 1942, 235–37).

Although rock art specific to the Salt Woman is not known to have been created as part of this rite, Hopi members of the salt expeditions made petroglyphs of their clan symbols along the way to record their passing (Talayesva 1942, 235),[28] and elsewhere in the Southwest there is rock art that shows phallic figures inserting their penises into natural holes in rock (fig. 70). On their return from the salt source, the Hopi men left offerings to the Salt Woman:

> The War Chief took a large lump of salt, stepped up to the image, and said, "My Mother god, I have brought you a fine piece of salt. It will last you a long time." We all prayed and placed our salt on the "vulva" of the goddess. . . . I had learned a great lesson and now knew that the ceremonies handed down by our fathers meant life and security, both now and hereafter (Talayesva 1942, 178).

Certain shrines show a connection between fertility and cosmic order associated with seasonal cycles. Some sites probably functioned as solstice markers or observatories; the winter solstice particularly is a crucial time of transformation. This is why vulva symbols, emblems of fertility and birth, can occur at a solstice shrine where the return of the sun heralds the rebirth of world order. For example, at several solstice shrines in southern California and the Great Basin, there is a congruence of vulva symbols, womb-like topography, and solar interaction with various features, including rock art ele-

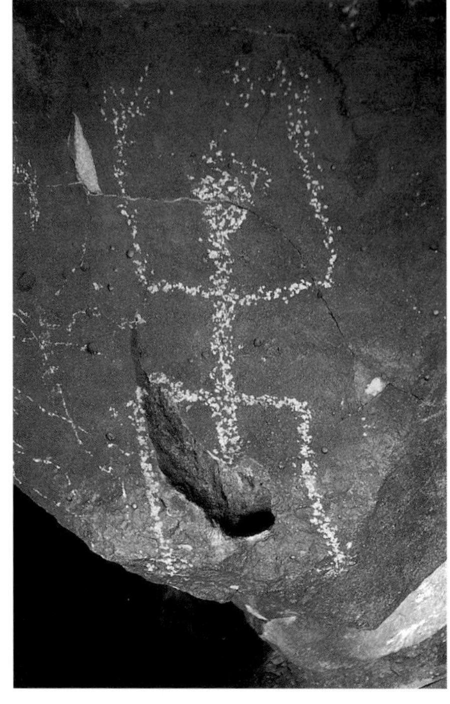

fig. 70. Petroglyph of a phallic anthropomorph incorporating a natural hole in the rock as a vulva, Gila River at Gillespie Dam, Arizona.

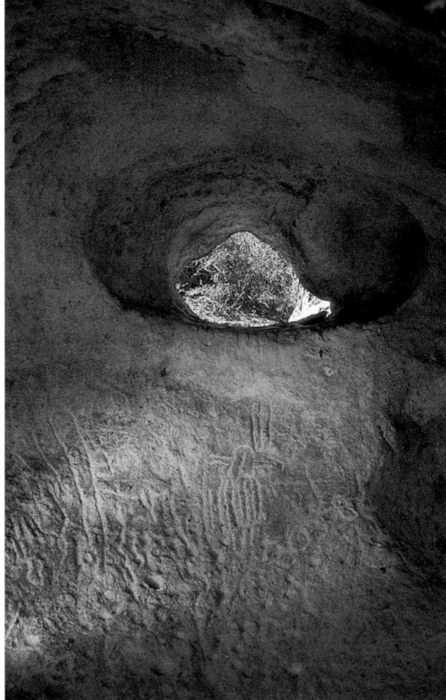

fig. 71. Womb Rock, a natural birth tunnel that may have been used in puberty initiations or other fertility rites, Providence Mountains, California.

ments (Krupp 1983, 42–43; Krupp 1997, 100–10).[29] Here sunlight penetrates into womb-like chambers, suggesting the fertilization of a woman's womb and marking the birth of a new year.

This relationship between rock art, myths about fertility and human sexuality, and the cosmos is especially evident at Womb Rock, a fertility shrine in the Providence Mountains of California's Mojave Desert (Rafter 1982 and Krupp 1983, 43). Womb Rock is one of several large boulders fallen from a cliff and sculpted into organic shapes by erosion. Petroglyphs and pictographs occur on a number of these boulders, but the aptly named Womb Rock is most evocative of a large, natural birth canal that opens to the east (fig. 71). The tunnel through the boulder is large enough to crawl through, and its smoothly polished floor indicates that many people have done this—probably in conjunction with some ritual. On its east face, Womb Rock is decorated with many petroglyphs, some of which resemble male and female genitalia. Foremost is a vulva symbol (bisected oval) with seven lines issuing from it and two appendages on the side. These, and other elements, may echo a Chemehuevi myth about a Woman of the Cave who became pregnant by the rays of the rising sun (Laird 1976, 204-9). Womb Rock may thus symbolize earth (Woman of the Cave) becoming fertile from the sun. Symbolic reenactment of birth in shamanic initiation rituals could have taken place here in connection with seasonal observations.

The Chemehuevis are a Southern Paiute group who recognize east as symbolic of beginnings and birth. Although it is not known if these petroglyphs are Chemehuevi in origin, they seem to illustrate the myth about the Woman of the Cave, and since there are variations of this story throughout the greater Southwest, the rock art of this site may reflect this myth regardless of who created it. In this story, the Woman of the Cave would emerge each morning, lie down, and open her thighs to the sun. She was impregnated by the sun's rays—described as the sun's "seven whiskers" (perhaps portrayed

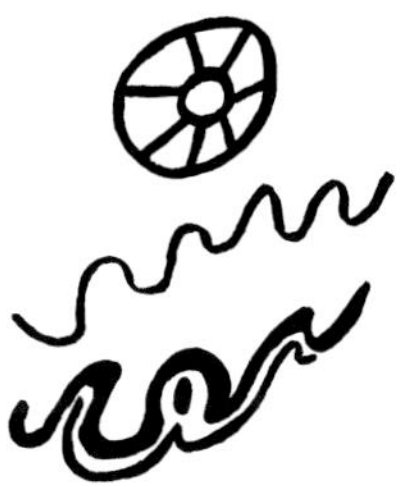

fig. 72. (left) Petroglyphs at Womb Rock that may depict parts of a myth about the sun impregnating the Earth Woman with his fertilizing rays, Providence Mountains, California.

by the seven lines attached to the prominent vulva petroglyph, with the two side appendages representing the woman's legs). She gave birth to the Twin Sons of the Sun. As further corroboration of this interpretation, other petroglyphs on a nearby boulder show a seven-rayed sun disk above a wavy line that could represent the mountainous horizon, below which appears to be a vulva between two legs spread wide (fig. 72). About this site, one researcher has written:

> Shamans may have passed through the birth canal of Womb Rock as part of a seasonal effort to renew the world. Youth on the edge of adulthood may have crossed the frontier with the passport of rebirth. Womb Rock may also have been a portal for the symbolic transformation of shamanic candidates into genuine dreamers. We can see what kind of power is transferred from these wombs of Mother Earth even if we can't be certain who were the beneficiaries (Krupp 1997, 109).

This idea of a masculine sun fertilizing a feminine earth has analogues on other continents as well. Among the Neolithic ruins of western Europe and the British Isles there are numerous tombs (passage graves) in the form of earth mounds constructed to resemble female anatomy, with vulva-like entrances to womb-like chambers, some of which are oriented to allow a shaft of sunlight to penetrate on the winter solstice. Newgrange is one of some three hundred in Ireland (Krupp 1997, 134–35). The male force (as embodied by the sun) entering these symbolic wombs is intended to resurrect the bodies of the dead, just as the year itself is resurrected in midwinter at the solstice.

Perhaps the ultimate symbolic earth wombs in the greater Southwest are the large vulvas known as yonis found on granitic boulders in the desert foothills of the Peninsular Range in southern California. The term yoni has been applied to them because it is a Sanskrit word for the female organ of generation and has been widely used in studies of religion, mythology, and art (McGowan 1982). These unique geological formations bear a marked resemblance to the human vulva but on a large scale (fig. 73). They formed as a result of differential erosion along fractures and resistant rock features,

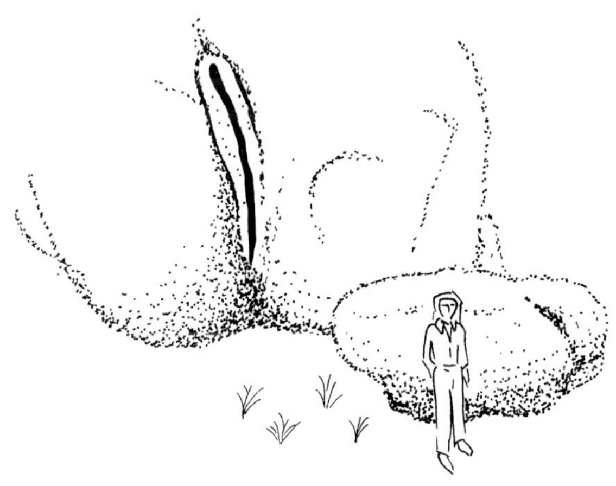

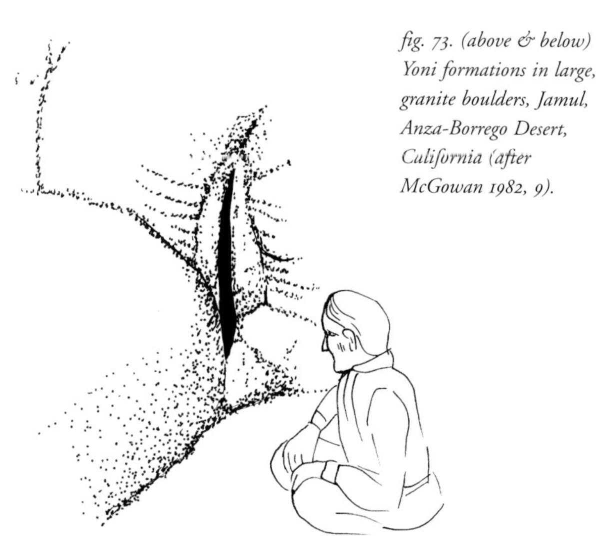

fig. 73. (above & below) Yoni formations in large, granite boulders, Jamul, Anza-Borrego Desert, California (after McGowan 1982, 9).

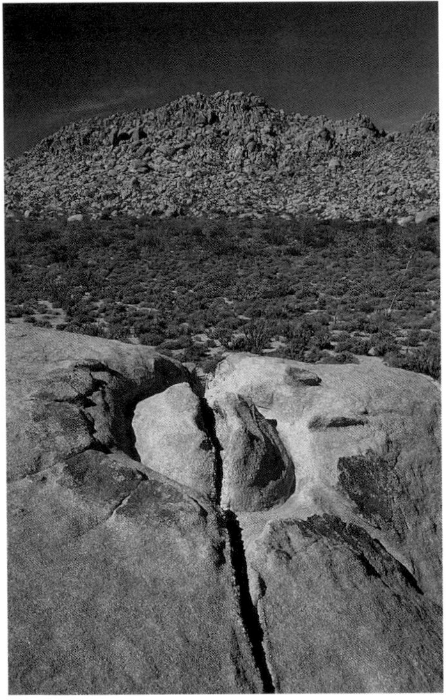

fig. 74. Large yoni formation near a painted cave at Indian Hill, Anza-Borrego State Park, California.

but in many cases they have been enhanced by prehistoric people who carved and abraded them to more closely resemble vulvas (fig. 74). They frequently occur in association with archaeological sites, further indicating that early inhabitants of the area recognized the sexual symbolism and special powers associated with these features.

Yoni formations are numerous in southern San Diego County and extend southward into Baja California. In southern California, they occur in the former territory of the Kumeyaay (Southern Diegueno) and Luiseno tribes. Among the Luiseno Indians, rock art is associated with puberty rites for girls, but there is no record of rock art connected with Kumeyaay puberty rituals. Apparently the yonis stand alone as symbolic earth vulvas, recognized for their special power and used accordingly for fertility shrines. An old Kumeyaay shaman told a local rancher in 1935 that "when a young girl acquired a man and she didn't have any children right away, they would take them up there and show them the magic stones" (McGowan 1982, vi). After certain rites were performed, the women were able to have children. In a 1906 description of the elaborate Kumeyaay puberty ritual, it was stated the girls " . . . were led away to a hillside where they were shown the sacred stone . . . it was said to symbolize or have reference to the female organ of generation." Although the yonis were prominent features of these fertility rites, the Kumeyaay Indians also used smaller, crescent-shaped stones that were heated and placed on the girls' abdomens to aid future childbirth. There is abundant evidence that this tribe performed elaborate female fertility rituals focusing on the yonis.

In the Luiseno territory to the northwest, yonis have also been observed, and there are ethnographic accounts linking the creation of rock art to girls' puberty initiation rituals (Whitley 1996, 180–81). Girls' puberty rites are common to many cultures throughout the world and were a prominent ritual aspect of Native American life. The making of pictographs as part of such rites has been reported in connection with various tribes, including the Nez Perce in the Northwest and the Salish and Thompson River Indians of British Columbia (Grant 1967, 29–31). Typical aspects of these ceremonies included teaching, seclusion, visions, and recording of the visions in rock art.

Among Native American tribes of California, puberty rites for both boys and girls were a major public event and time of transformation. Although the ceremonies differed for the sexes, both made rock art as part of the activities, with girls painting with red and boys with black. The girls' sites are quite common in southern California, while boys' sites, for unknown reasons, are less so. Takic-speaking groups (Luisenos, Cahuillas, and Gabrielinos) shared cultural traditions in this area, and all made rock art. Most often, the girls' red pictographs consist of zigzag and diamond-chain motifs—universally identified as symbols of the supernatural rattlesnake that was the female's spirit helper and guarded the vagina (Whitley 1996, 186). The use of red pigment was also symbolic of female menstrual blood. Some of these pictographs seem to have been placed on rocks in association with naturally occurring reddish stains that may have represented menstrual blood (Plate 14).

Girls' puberty initiation ceremonies were similar for these groups and involved isolation in a warmed pit for a period of days to simulate the immobility of childbirth, ingestion of hallucinogens to promote a supernatural vision, a race, and painting designs on rocks to represent the visions received during the experience. Details of the rituals, referred to by early Spanish padres as the "roasting of the girls," were recorded by several observers early in the century:

> The initiation ceremony took place in the *wamkic*, or ceremonial enclosure, and started with a purifying tobacco drink. The girl's face was painted black and her head was covered with a basket cap and garlands. She was handed a scratching stick and laid face down in the "roasting pit."
>
> This episode of the ceremony, generally referred to as the "roasting of the girls," was the central theme of the initiation rite and lasted four days and three nights. During the nights old men and old women danced around the "roasting pit" and sang songs taught to them by the goddess of the moon when she dwelled among the Cahuilla. In these songs she (Moon) instructed girls how to care for themselves during their menstrual periods.
>
> While she was lying in the pit, two warm stones were placed on her abdomen or between her legs. The stones were considered to help in later years to ease the pain of giving birth or during menstrual periods. The "roasting pit" also played a major role later in a woman's life. She was placed in a warmed pit after having given birth to a child, and warmed stones were placed on her abdomen to ease the pain (Knaak 1988, 69).

After further ceremonies in which a ground painting was used, the girls had a race to a certain rock. Here relatives of the girls stood to give them red paint when they arrived, and they painted diamond-shaped designs, representing the rattlesnake, on the rock (McGowan 1982, 15).

Even though in southern California there is less rock art made by boys during puberty initiation rituals, we know something about these rites, which were more arduous than corresponding rites for girls. They drank toloache, a strong hallucinogenic concoction made with jimsonweed (datura); were laid on the hills of stinging ants and then brushed with nettles; were shown sand paintings; and participated in sacred songs and dances, including a great fire dance, at which shamans jumped into the fire and handled the hot embers (Knaak 1988, 71–72).

A major, ancient, type of fertility-related rock art found in nearly all rock art regions of the greater Southwest is known as cupules or in a related form known as pit and grooves. In some areas, these simple cup-like depressions in rock surfaces are ubiquitous (fig. 75). They occur on boulders as well as rocky outcrops and cliffs. Cupules are thought to be some of the earliest rock art and are found throughout the world. In the Great Basin, cupules are believed to be 5,000 to 7,000 years old (Heizer and Baumhoff 1962, 234–35). In Europe, they have been dated from the age of Neanderthal man—at least 35,000 years ago. Cupules in European rock art settings have been described as metaphors for supernatural eyes in the rock, and where they occur on horizontal surfaces and collect rainwater they may represent fertility and the healing power of water—in all cases they were symbols of the Earth Goddess's life force (Gimbutas 1989, 61).

Most cupule rock art sites are believed to have been associated with fertility in a general sense, and sometimes quite specifically. Pit and groove rock art, consisting of cup-like depressions accompanied by deeply-incised grooves, is considered a related form, and has a specific fertility context based on Pomo ethnography from California, where these types of sites are known as "Baby Rocks." Interpretation of cupules varies, including that they are

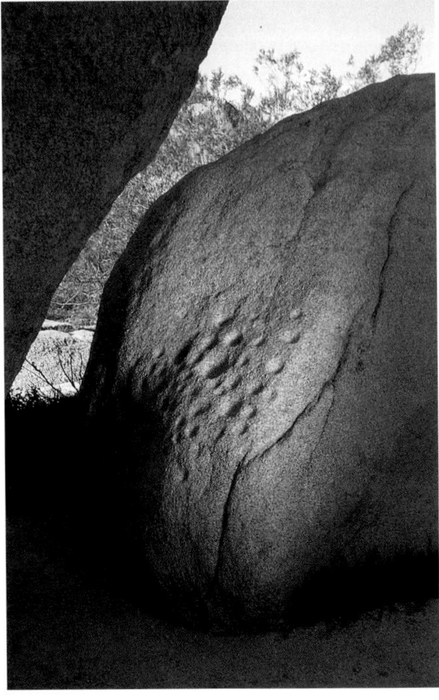

fig. 75. Cupules on granite boulder at a site of girls' puberty rites, Anza-Borrego State Park, California.

symbolic of vulvas and were used for curing sterility, that they were created during puberty initiations, that they were used as score-keeping or notation devices, for weather control, as stone drums, and that they were symbolic "work rocks" representing mortars for milling plants. Even where ethnographic information is lacking, it is usually assumed that cupules were made for ritual purposes and that they had something to do with beliefs about the rock itself—perhaps that the rock surface was the entrance to the supernatural world and that grinding or pecking cupules into it provided access to supernatural power.

Among the Pomo Indians of north-central California, boulders covered with pit and groove elements were known as "Baby Rocks" and were used in rituals to cure sterility (fig. 76). Couples who could not conceive conducted rituals at these sites, where they would grind off some of the rock and make a paste, which was then utilized to paint designs on the woman's abdomen and was inserted into her vagina. Sexual intercourse followed, with the hope that the woman would get pregnant as a result of the magic contained in the rock (McGowan 1982, 14).

Among the North Pomos, women desiring a child could go to one of these rocks or to certain trees, although the rocks were preferable. Such a rock was called *kawi kabe* (Child Rock), and when a woman went there she put her arms around it and her body against it as if it were a man, and prayed *kudi homto kawi* (good bring-me child) (Loeb 1924, 248). The Pomos believed the spirits of future children lived in the rocks and would be born to parents who followed the proper ritual. Additionally, sterile women were given a clay female effigy called Earth Woman to ensure conception (Parkman 1996, 25). Believing that fertility power resided inside the earth, and the spirits of unborn children lived in the Baby Rocks, Pomos may have thought that making petroglyphs on the rocks allowed access to those spirits.

Another Indian Baby Rock exists in Picture Canyon in southeastern Colorado (fig. 77). Although it is spatially and temporally unrelated to the foregoing examples, it is nonetheless an interesting parallel. This was reportedly a place where women went to give birth—and make cupules in the process; it is also said that young couples came here to let blood in order to become fertile (McGlone, Barker, et al. 1994, 62).

Further, a fertility shrine important to Zuni Pueblo in New Mexico is known as

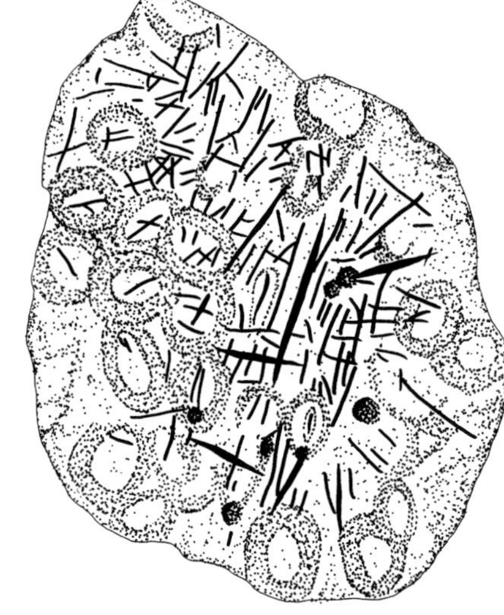

fig. 76. (right) "Baby Rock" petroglyphs, Knight's Valley, California (after Hedges 1983, 14).

Mother Rock. Situated on sacred Corn Mountain, this shrine consists of a cliff face pocked with hundreds of pits and openings resembling vulvas, some of which may be natural but most created by pecking and grooving. In 1904, an anthropologist described the use of this shrine, stating that Zuni couples wishing to have a female child would visit Mother Rock, where pregnant women would scrape off grains of sand from the stone and deposit them in a tiny vase for an offering to be left in one of the cavities at the site (Stevenson 1904, 294). Moreover, there is another shrine nearby in a fissure on the same mountain, where supplicants would go to petition for a male child. There they would sprinkle cornmeal and pray that a son would be born to them and that he would be distinguished in war and after death become great among ancestral gods. These sites also apparently functioned as fertility shrines for childless women. The Zunis believe that the features of these shrines were created by gods: "They belong to the old; they were made by the gods" (Young 1988, 177).

Another fertility shrine that may be a possible Mother Rock occurs in the Rio Grande Gorge near Taos, New Mexico. On a large boulder are a number of Anasazi petroglyphs suggesting the site had a fertility function, including vulvas, many game animals, tracks, a possible birth scene, snakes, and other symbols (fig. 78). The panel is arranged around a natural hole and groove in the rock that suggest vulva symbolism, and one of the animals has a long tail that extends up into the groove as if emerging from the rock. Further, one of the anthropomorphs has a leg that extends to become the tail of another animal. These images may represent a story of emergence of Indian ancestors or creation of the world. In addition, at a nearby petroglyph site is a possible depiction of the Mother of Animals or, in this case, the Deer Mother (Slifer 1998, 67).

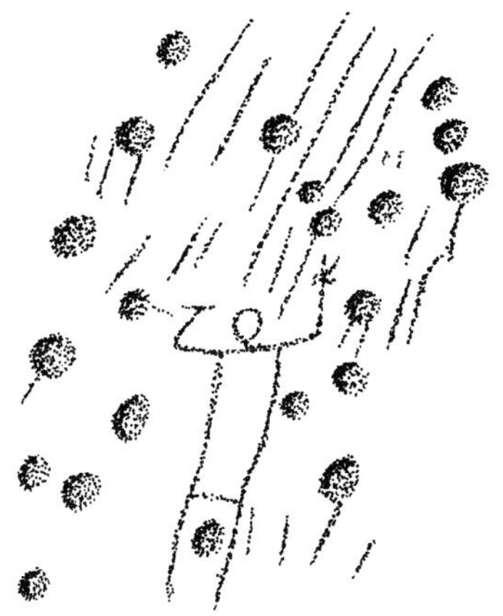

fig. 77. "Indian Baby Rock," Picture Canyon, southeastern Colorado.

Possibly the world's largest symbolic vulva rises from the Carrizo Plain in southern California—a major Chumash pictograph site known as Painted Rock. Many archaeologists and authors have commented on the rock's resemblance to a

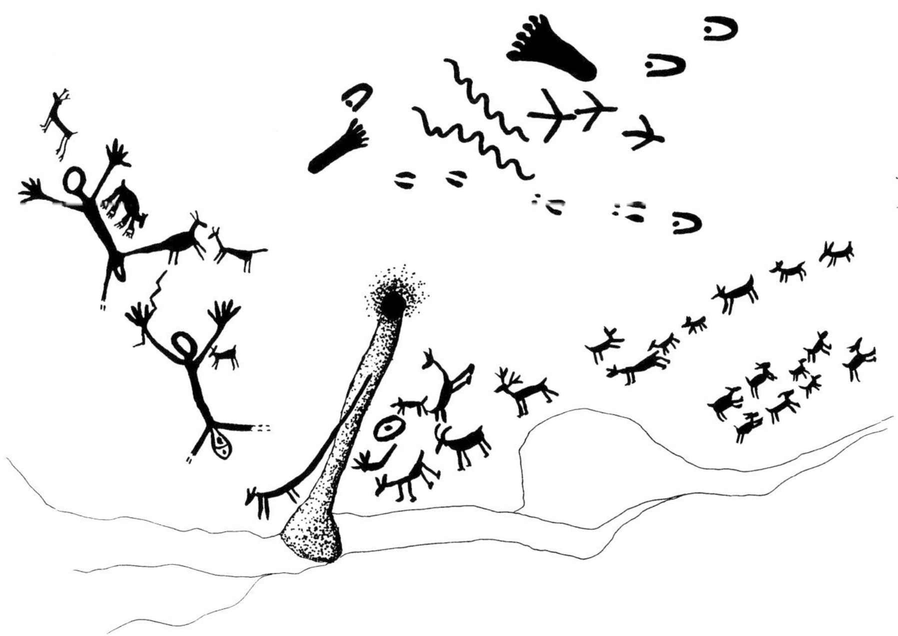

fig. 78. "Mother Rock" petroglyphs, Rio Grande Gorge, Cerro, New Mexico.

giant vulva, and this was no doubt also noticed by the Chumash, who created the panels of rock art in its interior. This massive monolith is a U-shaped sandstone outcrop more than fifty feet high, with an entry on one end. Painted Rock once contained the largest and most elaborate collection of Chumash polychrome paintings, but much of that was destroyed by shameful vandalism (target shooting and graffiti) in the early twentieth century. Despite this tragic loss of a national treasure, there is still plenty to see, and the setting itself is impressive in its sexual symbolism. The amphitheater, which is shaped like a uterus, probably served as a sacred place for rituals and public ceremonies, and the Chumash may have regarded it as a fertility shrine or perhaps a place of creation.

Much Chumash rock art was created by shamans, whose access to the supernatural in a trance state has been likened to "entering the rock," a sexual metaphor. Penetrating into the interior of this giant vulva-shaped rock outcrop can be regarded as ritual intercourse. In addition, the Chumash also had another metaphor for sexual intercourse—"entering the canoe" (Whitley 1996, 166). Among the images depicted at Painted Rock is a painting of four men standing in a Chumash plank canoe.

The symbolism of canoes as vaginas is also found in the mythic imagery of other cultures. For example, according to the elaborate origin myth of the Tukano Indians of the Amazon, the first males were brought to this earth in a live snake canoe named "Fermentation Placenta."

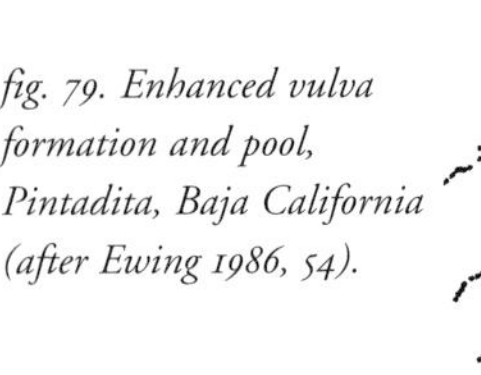

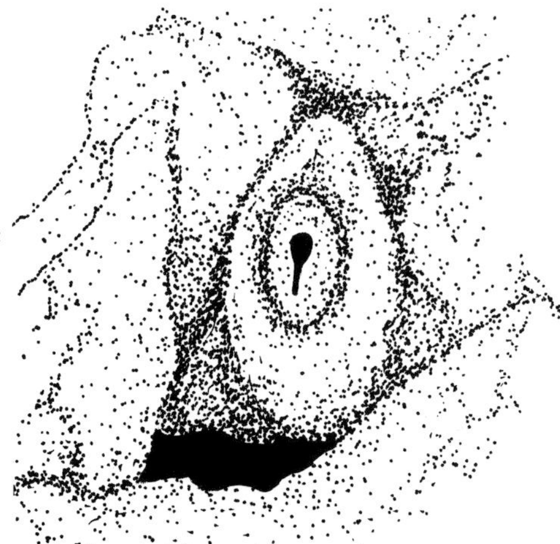

fig. 79. Enhanced vulva formation and pool, Pintadita, Baja California (after Ewing 1986, 54).

While traveling down the "River of Milk" with a spiritual guide named "Flowing Forth (Ejaculating) Man," the canoe struck a "perforated rock" (a feminine sexual symbol), and the men gushed forth like white bubbles from a hole in the front of the canoe—sexual imagery of coitus, ejaculation, and birth (Reichel-Dolmatoff 1971, 57). For the Tukanos, all humans are connected by an invisible umbilical cord to the cosmic womb in the River of Milk, and a snake canoe is the symbol of that connection.

As shown by the canoe metaphors, at some shrines there is a strong connection between fertility and water. Throughout the arid Southwest, water and moisture are a major component of fertility, as all life depends on it. In some areas, water sources such as springs, lakes, and caves were synonymous with the birth of natural and supernatural forces and were places where the First People emerged from the underworld, which was considered to be a very fertile place. One of the shrines of the Four World Quarters in the ancient Tewa Pueblo territory was a mountain in northern New Mexico called Lake Peak that was consecrated to fertility. At its sacred lake, "mating ceremonies of the most secret and sacred sort were held" (Hewett 1953, 130).[30] The Tewas also believe their ancestors emerged from the underworld through a lake, located in what is now Colorado's San Luis Valley.

In most regions of the greater Southwest, the majority of rock art sites are located close to water, such as rivers, springs, or bedrock pools (tinajas). One of the best examples linking rock art, water, and fertility symbolism occurs at the Pintadita site in the Sierra de San Luis, Baja California. In this harsh desert environment, not far from a pictograph site with fertility components, is a tinaja that holds a pool of precious water in conjunction with an obvious yoni (fig. 79). Unnaturally smoothed rock surfaces at this location suggest it was the site of a fertility rite (Ewing 1986, 54). As mentioned previously, vulva symbols are the most common petroglyph element at rock art sites throughout the central Baja California region, implying a major con-

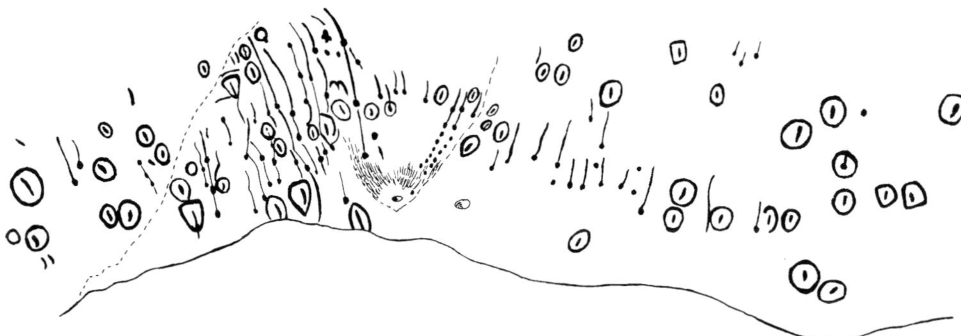

fig. 80. Petroglyphs of vulvas and a natural "seat" at fertility shrine site, Cave Valley, Chihuahua, Mexico (after Davis 1978).

cern with female fertility by the prehistoric inhabitants of the area.

Another female fertility shrine in Mexico occurs in Cave Valley, on the banks of the Rio Piedras Verdes in northern Chihuahua (fig. 80). This unusual petroglyph site contains dozens of incised vulva symbols, along with grooves terminating in small holes, somewhat similar to the pit and groove rock art noted much further north (such as the Pomo "Baby Rocks"). This panel covers approximately ten feet of rock surface in a small rock shelter. A unique feature here is a natural seat-like depression in the floor at the center of the panel, a convenient place for a person to sit. In the center of this natural chair has been carved a cupule two inches in diameter. It is probable that this feature figured prominently in the use of the site as a fertility shrine and that women seeking fertility magic sat here (Davis 1978, 43). All the elements here relate to fertility—the petroglyphs of vulvas as well as the grooved lines and pits, which may represent symbolic penes or semen.

A female fertility shrine equally charged with power is the Chalfont site in the Owens Valley of California. At this Paiute site, more than one hundred vulva symbols dominate the petroglyphs carved into a tuff cliff over a distance of six hundred yards (fig. 32). Some of these vulvas were created around natural holes in the rock, while others were sculpted into three-dimensional designs. There are no ethnographic records among the Numic peoples of the Great Basin to suggest this rock art was made in connection with girls' puberty ceremonies, but there are indications that the sexual symbolism at Chalfont is associated with shamanism. As recounted in the section "Sex and the Shaman," among the Paiutes the vulva

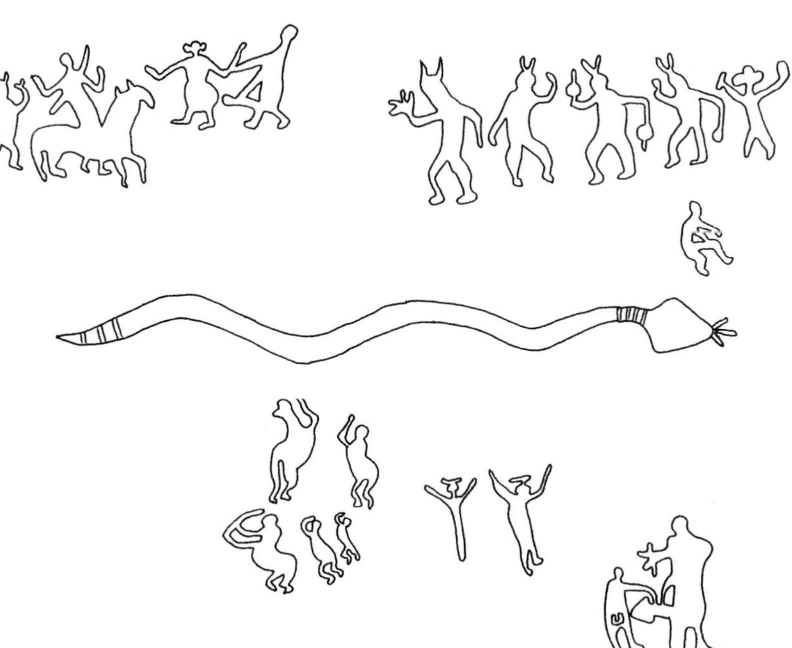

fig. 81. Pictographs of an Apache Victory Dance or fertility ritual, Comanche Cave, Hueco Tanks State Park, Texas.

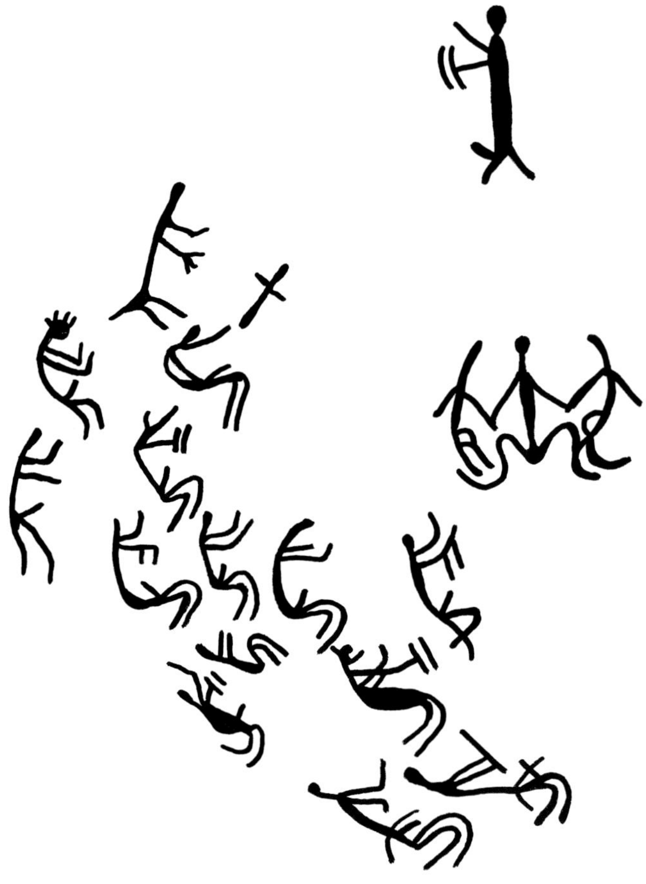

fig. 82. Pictographs in the Archaic, Red Linear Style, depicting a possible fertility ritual, Pressa Canyon, Texas (after Kirkland and Newcomb 1967, 94).

was a potent and dangerous symbol of supernatural power. At Chalfont, these symbols were probably made by male shamans following their vision quests and could represent their "entry into the rock" during a trance or pertain to sorcery due to the vulva's association with supernatural power (Whitley 1996, 80–82). The vulva colony at Chalfont is somewhat unique for the area—at none of the other nearby petroglyph sites does this motif dominate the images as it does here.

Images depicting fertility ceremonies and apparent sexual license are also portrayed in Apache pictographs at Hueco Tanks, Texas (fig. 81). Although famous as a major Jornada Mogollon rock art locale, the Apaches are known to have frequented Hueco Tanks in historic times, and it is thought that they created the large panels of white pictographs found in Comanche Cave. These painted figures probably represent a fertility ritual or a victory dance (also a time for loosening restrictions on sexual behavior), and include men on horses, lively dancing figures (some of which are pot-bellied and may be pregnant), copulating couples, and large snakes (ten to fifteen feet long) with spear-shaped heads. Several of the men sport an exaggerated penis with a spear-shaped head that bears an uncanny resemblance to the snakes. Despite the distorted scale of the phalli, the stylistic links between the various elements on this panel suggest it was created as a unit and that it is probably a realistic depiction of actual fertility dances. Moreover, the fact that one of the phallic men at Comanche Cave is humpbacked is a further indication that fertility is the main theme of this panel (see the section "The Flute Player" for more discussion about humpbacked anthropomorphs as fertility symbols). The association between male fertility and snakes, as phallic symbols, is fairly explicit here. That these Apache images show a strong concern with the forces that control human fertility and procreation is also evident in the setting of Comanche Cave. It is a deep shelter (symbolic vulva) and contains one of the largest freshwater reservoirs (water as the source of life) for which Hueco Tanks is named (*hueco* is Spanish for tank or natural cistern that catches and stores rainfall runoff). The Apaches believed that mountain caves were the abode of spirits known as *Gahe*, who are the sources of supernatural power. They probably perceived Comanche Cave as such a spiritual source, and used it accordingly as a shrine for fertility rites.

Another Texas rock art site at which fertility is the principal theme is located in the lower Pecos River region. An unusual panel of red pictographs, which is probably Archaic, contains a scene with sixteen, mostly phallic, small human figures. The majority of them have bent legs and are facing toward a squatting figure, which is probably a male holding hands with two flanking females (fig. 82). The researchers who originally recorded this scene surmised that "this group of murals was drawn at a sacred spot or at one where highly important, perhaps secret ceremonies having to do with fertility and reproduction were held" (Kirkland and Newcomb 1967, 95).

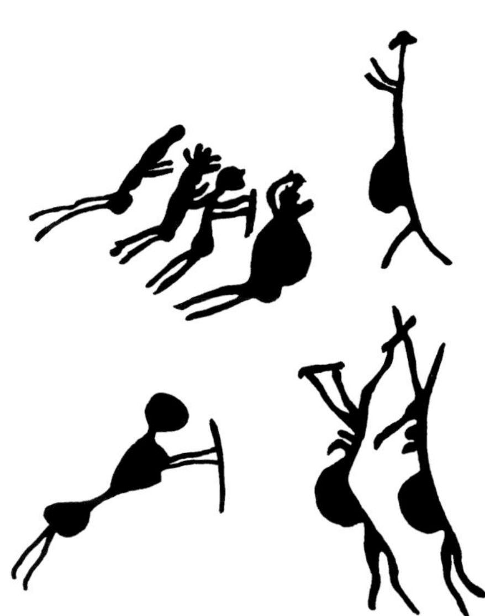

fig. 83. (left) Pictographs in the Archaic, Red Linear Style, depicting pregnant females and possible fertility rituals, Fate Bell Shelter, Seminole Canyon State Park, Texas (after Turpin 1990, 104).

Pictographs of this type have been ascribed to the Red Linear Style and dated to the Middle Archaic age (about 4,000 to 3,000 years ago); they have been described as "miniature figures engaged in highly mobile group activities [that] brim with vivacious energy" (Turpin 1990, 103). The location of most of these scenes suggests ritual painting that may have been part of puberty or initiation rites. In the rock art of the lower Pecos region, Red Linear Style is unique in its depiction of gender and human reproduction. The males are phallic, and the women, which are sometimes shown with breasts or with circles in the pubic region, are occasionally pregnant (fig. 83).

Concerns with fertility and sex are also evident at two other sites in the Southwest where unusual numbers of phallic flute players are depicted. The Pueblo petroglyphs at the La Cieneguilla site near Santa Fe, New Mexico, and at Dinnebito Wash in northeastern Arizona each contain more than one hundred flute player images in various fertility contexts, including scenes with copulation, birth, hunting, snakes, corn, and rain-bringing activities. Both large sites with thousands of petroglyphs, it is not known why the flute player figure is emphasized to such an extent at these locations (figs. 84 and 116).

Overlooking the Little Colorado River in Arizona, Inscription Point undoubtedly functioned as a fertility shrine also. Among the petroglyphs here, numerous images of copulating humans and animals were arranged together, along with depictions of snakes and flute players (fig. 9). It seems apparent that concerns with human fertility were linked with similar concerns for the fecundity of animals and the natural world, and that rituals to this effect were probably carried out here. Tragically, the majority of these fascinating images were intentionally destroyed sometime in the 1980s, reputedly by a fundamentalist minister who was offended by their overt sexual nature (fig. 8). Fortunately, they were recorded prior to this attack, and not all of the scenes depicting sexual activity were found and destroyed—a few hidden ones remain (fig. 85).

In the San Juan River drainage of southeastern Utah, there are a number of Basketmaker Anasazi rock art sites which exhibit pervasive themes of shamanism and fertility and which probably functioned as fertility shrines. For example, a petroglyph panel in Butler Wash contains such images associated with fertility,

fig. 84. (below) Anasazi petroglyphs depicting flute players and a copulation scene, Dinnebito Wash, Arizona.

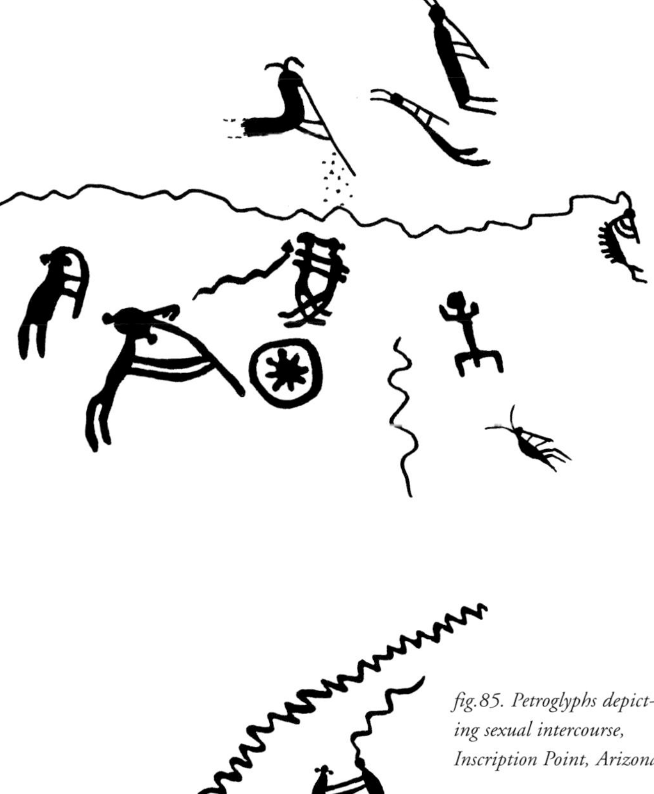

fig.85. Petroglyphs depicting sexual intercourse, Inscription Point, Arizona.

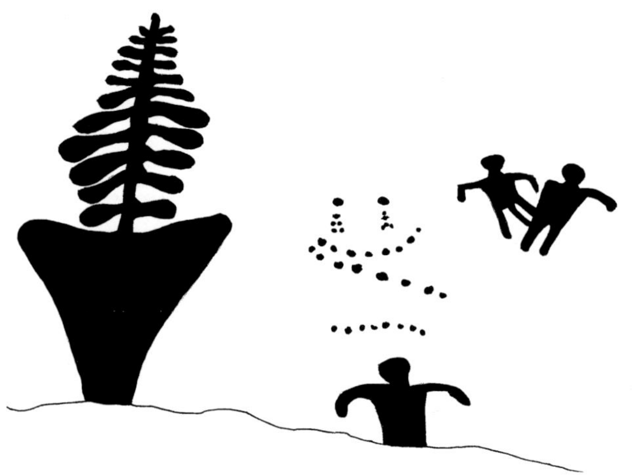

fig. 86. Basketmaker Anasazi petroglyphs representing fertility with a sex scene and a flowering yucca plant, Butler Wash, Utah.

human sexuality, and ritual (Cole 1989, 77; Manning 1992, 159), including a copulation scene, flute player, stylized females wearing menstrual pads, crook-necked staffs, lobed circles, a possible birth scene, and a fruiting yucca plant with possible baskets for harvesting (fig. 86).

Finally, there is an impressive Basketmaker Anasazi petroglyph site in Monument Valley, Utah, that radiates the power of ancient fertility magic (fig. 87). On a large boulder are many well-crafted images relating to fertility, including two copulating couples, birth scenes, flute players, vulva symbolism, snakes, a crook-necked staff, abundant game and plants, water (symbolized by a woman carrying a jug), and symbols of twins and multiple births expressed as pairs of objects. On a separate boulder at the foot of the main panel, next to an inverted figure holding a crook, is the compelling image in fig. 166, which apparently depicts simultaneous copulation and birth. This may represent a shaman in trance—suggesting the shaman's role in securing fertility and supernatural power for the benefit of his group. It is difficult to imagine a more inclusive or compelling presentation of fertility symbolism at a single rock art site.

MYTHS AND STORIES ABOUT FERTILITY

The American Southwest, where archaeological and ethnologic research overlap, provides opportunities to interpret some rock art through the myths, rituals, and stories of native peoples. Despite the fact that a great deal has been written about the mythology of Native Americans, and much of that lore pertains to themes of origin, birth, and fertility, there is relatively little information linking these myths and stories to specific rock art images. Although it is beyond the scope of this book to comprehensively review Native American mythology, the following is a summary and some examples relating to sex and fertility as they are expressed in southwestern rock art.

Myths describe a belief system for a particular group of people. As human consciousness and society developed, mythology grew more complex. Stories of mythic figures serve as role models for coping with major life events such as puberty, marriage, birth, and death. Thus the images in myths are archetypes of human behavior and perception. Further, in attempting to understand the forces of nature, all cultures have produced creation myths which contain inherent sexual elements. Proper sexual behavior and the appropriate taboos are thus defined by each culture to fit its particular needs.

It is known that some historic cultures in the Southwest portrayed mythic events and beings in their rock art, while others did not (Whitley 1996, 16–18).[31] Nonetheless, there are major geographical areas and prehistoric cultural traditions in the greater Southwest about which little is known regarding the expression of mythic subjects in rock art. Consequently, it is likely that some rock art depictions of mythic themes do occur but are not recognized as such. Entire myths or tales could not be "told" in the limited medium of rock, but key elements could be represented—perhaps as mnemonic devices to facilitate ritual retellings or as metaphors to symbolize certain attributes of characters or events. Although this is an area of much speculation in interpreting rock art, it deserves attention here.

Creation and Emergence Myths

The sexual union of male and female is a common metaphor for creation in many mythologies, and the earth is usually female—reflecting the link between the fecundity of nature and the fertility of women. The mythologies of the Southwest are primarily those of agriculturalists—that is, they reflect "the way of the seeded earth" (Campbell 1988, I:2:241). Although there are a few exceptions to this, such as the nomadic Numic and Athabaskan groups who assumed an agricultural life-style late, the majority of southwestern cultures share aspects of mythologies of the emergence of the First People from the womb of the earth. Such emergence myths of the Southwest often feature the birth of twins to a mysterious virgin mother following the emergence of the First People. Joseph Campbell sees these myths as "the pouring of living creatures from the fertile body of a primal female power and presence . . . " and recounts a 1934 version of the emergence myth from the Jicarilla Apaches (who by then had adopted certain Puebloan agricultural ideas), which includes this phrase: "The earth they made in the form of a living woman; sky in the form of a living man. He faces downward; she upward. They are our mother and our father" (Campbell 1988, I:2:241).

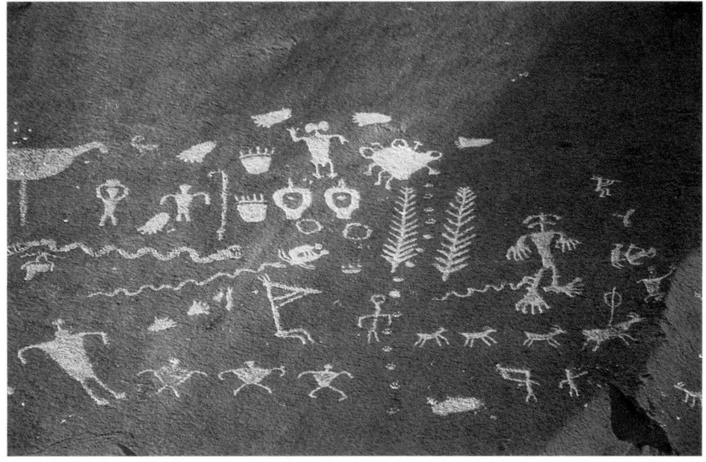

Among the various Pueblo Indians, there is similarity in origin myths, which involve a female creator and the emergence of the First People from a dark, wet underworld. It has been recorded that the "lizard-man figures" so prevalent in the rock art of the Colorado Plateau, Little Colorado River drainage, and the Zuni–Cibola region may in some cases represent figures from origin myths. Zunis have identified such petroglyphs as "the way the Zunis looked at the time of the beginning . . . when we still had tails." It is possible that this fairly widespread rock art image may be analogous to the Zunis' mythic "moss-people," or unformed humans before they emerged from the dark, wet underworld (Young 1988, 122). That emergence myth goes on to tell of how the Sun Father sent his sons the Twin War Gods to lead the First People to the

fig. 87. (above & below) Basketmaker Anasazi petroglyph panel with fertility symbolism, Monument Valley, Utah.

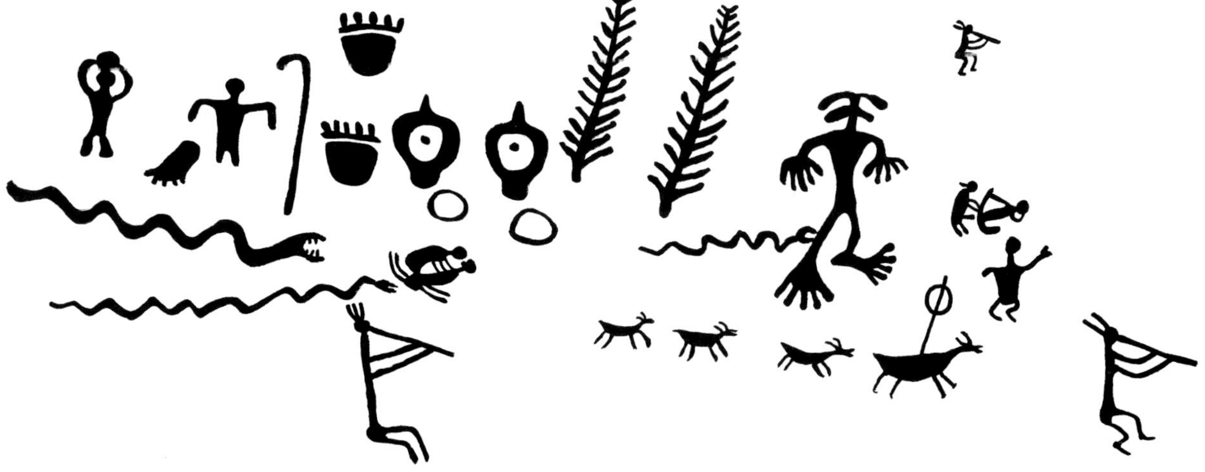

surface of the earth (see the section "Twins" for further discussion of this symbolism). Another rock art symbol common in the Southwest that may have some relevance to the mythic theme of emergence is the spiral, which is sometimes said to represent the principles of emergence, birth, and life force. (For further discussion of the spiral motif as a fertility symbol, see the section "Spirals.")

From other regions of the Southwest, there are cosmogonic myths of sexual intercourse. For instance, the Yuman tribes believed "the sun cohabited with the earth, and out of her womb life came— the inanimate objects men use, as well as men and animals" (Benedict 1953, 115). The metaphor of the sun's fertilizing rays as semen impregnating the earth or a female deity, and the possible expression of this mythic theme in rock art, has been previously discussed in the section "Fertility Shrines and Rites." Examples of several sites from southern California were given, but there may be more such examples of this concept in southwestern rock art that are yet to be recognized.

The invocation of cosmogonic principles through sacred rites involving sexual intercourse has long been recognized throughout the world, and it has been suggested that expressions of the Sacred Marriage rite are depicted in southwestern rock art. One such example may be the Cave of Life in Arizona (fig. 26 and Plate 19). Further, picturing the re-creation of life through images of ritual coitus also may be the intent behind such scenes. In a petroglyph panel from the Uinta Basin of northeast Utah (fig. 88), which may portray a cosmogonic myth with a copulating couple contained in a sacred circle or hoop, a sinuous "power line" connects them to an anthropomorph with a very large, upraised hand—perhaps an expression of divine or creative power. The connecting line is suggestive of a snake, an image frequently depicted in fertility scenes in world mythology and rock art, including the Southwest.

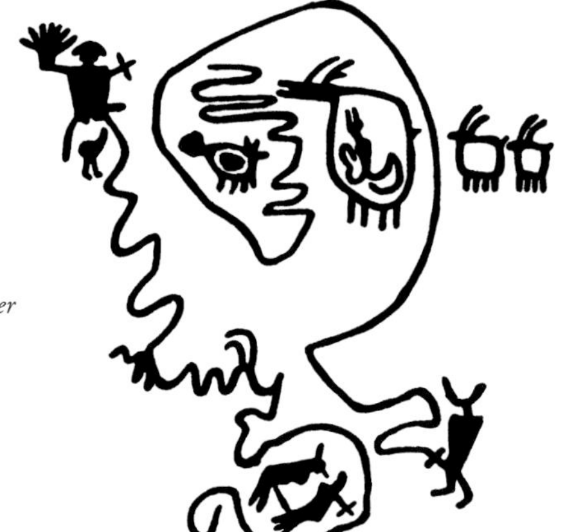

fig. 88. Petroglyphs that may depict elements of a cosmogonic myth, Ashley Creek, Utah (after Warner 1982, 116).

Horned Serpent

In mythology worldwide, the serpent is a common metaphor for fertility and sexual activity, including the act of creation. Snake images can be seen in much of the rock art illustrated in this book, and it is likely that in some contexts it is related to mythic events. The snake is the most powerful of the beast-gods and has always been a potent symbol for fertility and other attributes (see the section "Other Symbols of Sex and Fertility" for further discussion of this topic).

In some Native American origin myths, the masculine principle is symbolized as the liquid, conceptive, serpent energy of the universe and is seen in the night sky as the Milky Way (Getty 1990, 7). More commonly, serpent images related to fertility are found in the many portrayals of the horned or plumed serpent in Anasazi and Mogollon rock art (fig. 89). Also known as the Horned Water Serpent, this powerful beast-god, whose horn is symbolic of spiritual powers, is in charge of water. Further, among many Pueblos he is associated with fertility and longevity and at times may be invoked to overcome sterility. In addition to his power to bring rain, this mythic creature guards springs and underground waters and may impregnate bathing women (Hultkrantz 1987, 47). Since water and fertility are practically synonymous to Pueblo peoples, it is clear why this creature embodies both concepts.

The Horned Serpent, or Horned Water Serpent, is described as a gigantic serpent inside the earth presiding over all the waters and nourishing the lifeblood of animals and the sap of vegetation (Tyler 1964, 225). The Horned Serpent of the southwestern Pueblos is the god of waters and associated with fertility and longevity. He may be related to the plumed serpent of ancient Mexico—Quetzalcoatl, another snake god. His name varies in different tribes but generally translates as Water Serpent. The Hopi name is Paluukong; at Zuni he is known as Kolowisi; and among some eastern Pueblos he is Awanyu. Although the names and rituals vary, this creature represents the same basic concepts about water and fertility. According to a story from Hopi, traveling clans carried a small vessel containing herbs, stones, shells, prayer sticks, and a small water serpent, which they used to create springs as needed (Geertz and Lomatuway'ma 1987, 178–79, in Schaafsma 1999, 184).

Certain aspects of the Horned Serpent are illustrated by effigy puppets at Hopi and Zuni pueblos which have goggle eyes filled with corn kernels and seeds of important plants—indicating that this figure also has a significant role in agricultural fertility (Young 1994, 115). Ethnographic accounts record varied rituals centered around this creature. For instance, the Hopis have a special fertility ceremony called Palulukonti in the spring, in which effigies of the Horned Water Serpent figure prominently. In kivas filled with artificial cornfields, the heads of six serpents emerge from sun symbols and engage in activities related to fertility, including entry into the underworld with all the seeds necessary to make the earth bountiful, and symbolic nursing by a snake mother:

> The central and largest serpent is equipped with eight mammae which are made of skin stuffed with all seeds. "Cotton, melon, watermelon, gourd, sweet corn, seeds of all these and corn kernels are in the paps of the effigy of the mother Pa'lulukonuh . . . " (Stephen 1936, 300). On either side of her are two small ones which are referred to as babies, and beyond them are three effigies of male serpents. The fertility mimetically invoked here seems to be that of the earth (Tyler 1964, 246).

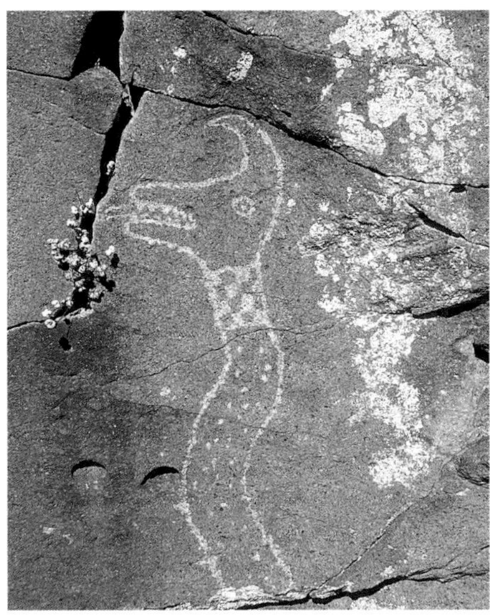

fig. 89. Horned Serpent petroglyph, Galisteo Basin, New Mexico.

Kokopelli Stories

Some of the most interesting fertility-related stories involve Kokopelli and other flute-playing figures from the various pueblos. Although the Hopis are the source of the Kokopelli Kachina and most of our information about him, there are counterparts for the Kokopelli Kachina from other pueblos, notably Acoma and Zuni. Kachinas are benevolent supernaturals, revered ancestor spirits associated with clouds, rain, and fertility. They bring rain and well-being to the people and are personified in the masked dancers at the pueblos. Rock art studies indicate the kachina cult arrived in the Pueblo area in the fourteenth century from the Jornada Mogollon region to the south.

The following is an interesting story about Kokopelli from the Hopi mesas:

> At the time when Oraibi was first inhabited, the katcina Kokopele was living nearby with his grandmother. Within the village there dwelt a good-looking girl who was so vain (qwivi) that she rejected the advances of all the young men. . . . Kokopele confided to his grandmother that he meant to try his luck with this pretty girl, but his grandmother laughed at him because he was humpbacked and far homelier than many of the

> Oraibi boys. . . . Kokopele had noticed that . . . the girl was in the habit of going to a particular spot at the edge of the mesa to perform her natural functions. . . . His first step was to dig a trench leading from his house to the exact spot which the girl was accustomed to visit. Then he cut and hollowed out a number of reeds, fashioned them into a continuous pipe, and laid it in the ditch . . . he filled in the trench and smoothed it over . . . the next day the girl came to the spot. . . . Hardly had she finished than she felt something stirring under her, and enjoying the sensation, made no effort to investigate. It was the penis of Kokopele that she felt, for so cleverly had he arranged his hollow tube that on inserting his organ into it at home he was enabled, thanks to its unusual length, to direct it into the girl's vagina. From then on Kokopele never failed to take advantage of his device nor did the girl abandon her customary visits to this spot. At last she found herself pregnant, but neither she nor any of the people in the village had the slightest idea of her lover's identity . . . when in due time a boy was born to her, his paternity was as much a mystery as ever (Titiev 1939, 91–94).

The question of the child's paternity was resolved that spring when the village held a footrace for all the men and boys. They all picked and ran with a bouquet of flowers, which each presented to the baby as he finished the race. The baby would accept flowers only from the runner who was his father. The baby would not take the flowers from any of the runners until Kokopelli, who finished the race last, offered his bouquet. When the child accepted Kokopelli's flowers, the village knew he was the father. The villagers told the girl to take the kachina home and keep him for her husband. This she was happy to do, for as a kachina, Kokopelli was a good provider and brought lots of rain. The critical portion of this myth (the act of impregnation) is apparently depicted in a petroglyph from the Jemez Mountains of New Mexico, which depicts a humpbacked flute player and a female joined in sexual intercourse by an unnaturally long penis that wraps around the corner of two rock faces (fig. 43).

A similar version of this Kokopelli story is recorded from Acoma Pueblo:

> A long time ago two Dapopo brothers lived at Acoma near the house of Masewi, the elder of the twin war gods. The younger Dapopo asked the War Chief's daughter to let him sleep with her but she refused. Then the older Dapopo asked her the same thing but was also refused. In fact, the chief's daughter rejected the advances of all the boys at Acoma. The Dapopos were angry and kept thinking of how they could get the girl. At last the older brother advised the younger to dig a hole in the ground at the side of the mesa and hide there until the girl came to relieve herself in the evening. In this way the Dapopo got his girl. She did not realize exactly what had happened, but she liked the sensation so much that she repeatedly returned to the same spot. Then the older brother hid and he too got the girl.
>
> Soon the Acoma people noticed that she was going to have a baby. . . . When the time came two babies were born, one for each of the Dapopo. The War Chief decided to find out who had fathered his daughter's children so he announced a test. All the young men and boys of the village went out and gathered bunches of flowers. Then they lined up and offered them to the babies but they would not accept them. Finally the Dapopos, who were last in line, presented their flowers and the children took them, thus acknowledging the Dapopos for their fathers (Titiev 1939, 94–95).

A flute-playing hero and fertility symbolism is also celebrated in the rich oral tradition at Zuni Pueblo, where some narrative poems have been recorded and translated (Tedlock 1972, 118–131). One performance, lasting forty minutes, relates a story about the flute-playing Nepayatamu (Payatamu) and his medicine society kin. He is brought back to life by singing and drumming after being wrongly killed, and then leads his brothers in revenge on his wrongdoers. When he blows on his flute, a big swallowtail butterfly comes out of it, and when he sucks on his flute the swallowtail goes back into it (butterfly and moth are fertility symbols here, and in many other Indian traditions, as discussed in the section "Other Symbols of Sex and Fertility"). He sends the butterfly to his enemies, who are certain women, one of whom was responsible for his death. The swallowtail sprinkles the women with his wing powder when they try to catch him in order to use his pattern in their basketry. This makes the women go crazy, and he leads them to Nepayatamu, who is perched up in a cottonwood tree. The women try to catch the butterfly by throwing their clothes at him until eventually they are naked. When they lie down to rest in the shadow of the cottonwood tree, Nepayatamu spits on them, and they go to sleep. Nepayatamu then summons his grandfathers (ancestors), who come out of hiding and have pleasure with the sleeping women. When they awake, they find Nepayatamu still sitting in the tree with his legs dangling down. He sucks the swallowtail back into his flute. He throws down leaves, and these become blankets, in which the women dress themselves. Then Nepayatamu leads the women to his house, where they are fed, and then takes them towards the place where the sun comes out. But they get tired and keep falling down. When Nepayatamu sucks on his flute, the elder sister, the killer, goes inside it. Then he blows, and a group of white moths comes out. The woman becomes a moth and he tells her, "Now, this is the life you will live, so that when spring is near you will be a sign of its coming." Eventually he also turns all the other women into moths. Then Nepayatamu goes on to meet his father, the sun, who praises his way of getting revenge on the women. In this way the Clown Society was created long ago. Although they may not be specifically related to this story, there are two petroglyph panels in northern New Mexico that seem to contain its symbolic essence, since they combine the elements of moth or butterfly with flute player (fig. 90, from White Rock Canyon) and vulvas (fig. 91, in the Galisteo Basin).

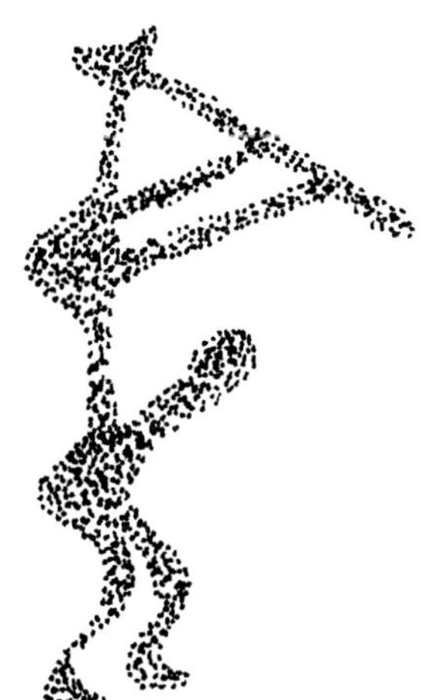

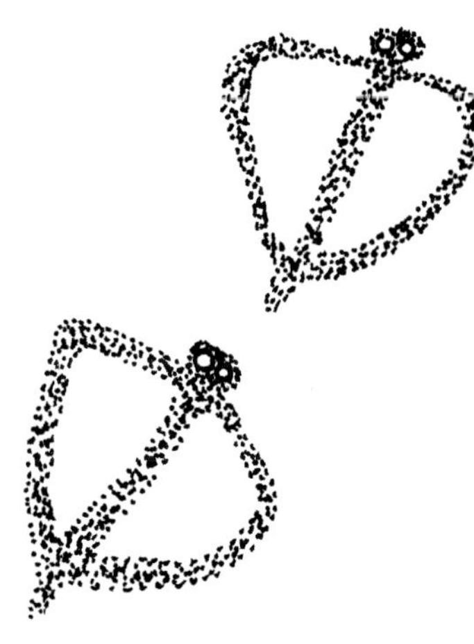

fig. 90. Petroglyphs of a phallic flute player and moths or butterflies, White Rock Canyon, New Mexico.

The transformation of the flute player into an insect-like being occurs in both rock art and in ethnographic records. The flute player has been identified with the locust, a revered insect that is featured in the Hopi emergence myth and is patron of the Hopi Flute Societies. In the emergence myth, Locust is sent up from the lower world to seek an exit for man. When the clouds shoot their bolts through him, he continues playing his flute. The Flute Societies have locust medicine to dream the future, and pieces of

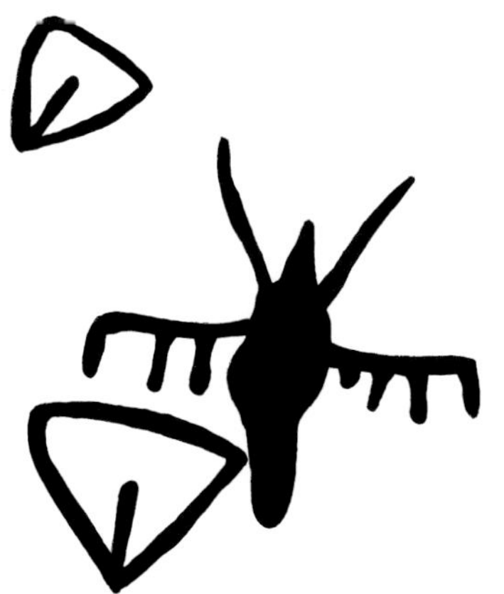

fig. 91. Petroglyphs of a moth and vulva symbols, Galisteo Basin, New Mexico.

locusts are thrown on the fire to hasten the return of warm weather. Locust plays the flute to melt the snow when appealed to by the sun-loving snakes. This may help explain two aspects of the flute player image in rock art—the fact that some of the flute players resemble insects, and the common association of humpbacked flute players with snakes (fig. 92).

Flute players and other fertility symbols in several petroglyph panels at La Cienega, New Mexico (fig. 93), are metaphors that may illustrate the Tewa myth of the "Water Jar Boy" (Patterson-Rudolph 1990, 43–51). This myth from Pueblo oral tradition is about a girl who does not want to marry, a supernatural conception, and a son of virgin birth seeking the identity of his father. In it the girl becomes pregnant when mud gets into her while she mixes it for her mother's pottery. Subsequently, she gives birth to a little water jar that grows into a boy within the jar. Later the boy cracks the confining pot on a rock while rolling down a hill during a rabbit hunt with his grandfather. After emerging he goes on a quest for his father, whom he eventually finds living inside a spring. Eventually, the boy and his mother go to live with his father there.

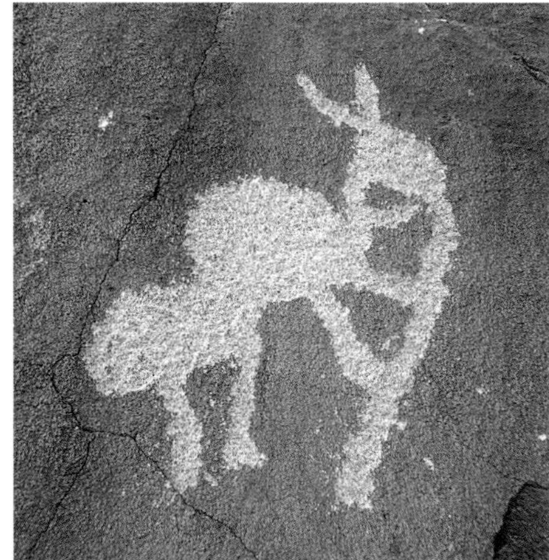

fig. 92. Petroglyph of a flute player resembling an insect, Velarde, New Mexico.

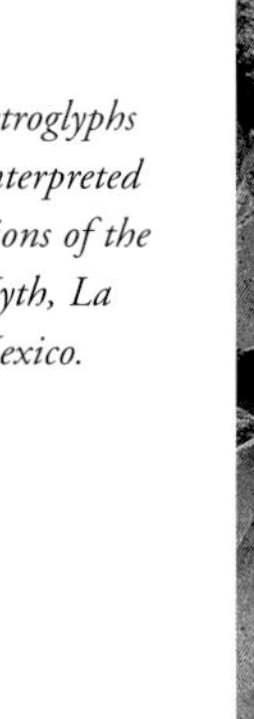

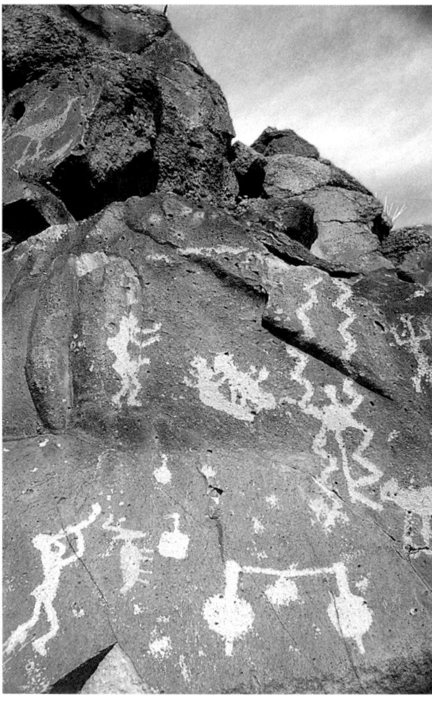

fig. 93. Pueblo petroglyphs that have been interpreted as depicting portions of the Water Jar Boy Myth, La Cienega, New Mexico.

It has been proposed that the panels at La Cienega metaphorically illustrate the events of the "Water Jar Boy" myth. For instance, a row of phallic flute players is explained as young Pueblo men going wife hunting, carrying gifts for brides in their packs and playing flutes to court them. These suitors are all going in the same direction (none returning to suggest having been chosen), indicating that none were responsible for the birth depicted nearby.

The petroglyph panels at La Cienega have also been interpreted as representing the supernatural conception in the myth. Pueblo mythology is known for many stories about pregnancy resulting from supernatural events. In fig. 94 is a copulating couple next to a phallic, humpbacked man and a zigzag design—the basic symbol for movement back and forth (Patterson-Rudolph 1990, 52). The symbolic movement may refer not only to the

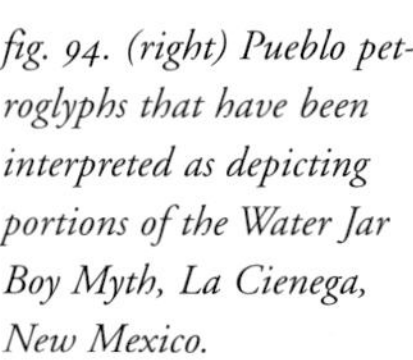

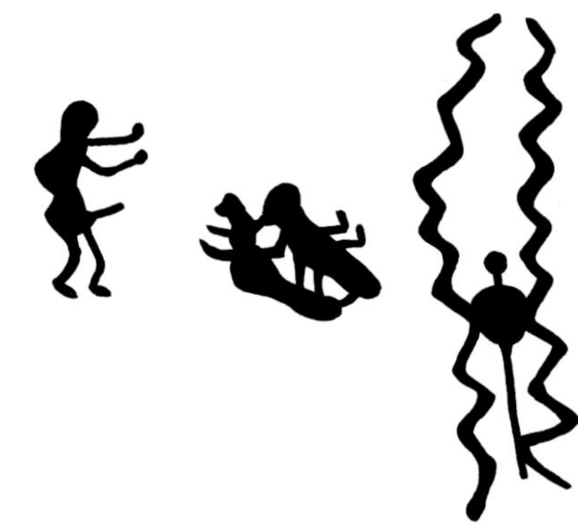

fig. 94. (right) Pueblo petroglyphs that have been interpreted as depicting portions of the Water Jar Boy Myth, La Cienega, New Mexico.

copulation but could also represent the girl's conception from mixing mud.

Toothed-Vagina Stories

Many Native American tribes have stories about a woman with a toothed vagina (*vagina dentata*), a theme that may be archetypal, as it occurs worldwide. It has been theorized that this notion may have developed as a result of male fear of castration in response to the sight of menstruating women (Bishop 1996, 125) and the obvious mouth symbolism of the vulva. The word *mouth* is from the Anglo-Saxon *muth*—the same root as "mother" (Walker 1983, 1035). Moreover, vulvas have labia, lips, and in many male minds teeth lie behind lips. Recognized universally in myth and fantasy, this male fear of being devoured is perhaps akin to experiencing the birth trauma in reverse. In this regard, a Maori myth from New Zealand tells of the trickster hero Maui, who tries to defeat mortality by climbing up into the vagina of a supernatural female—reversing the birth process. However, he is killed by the vagina's snapping, flint edges, which generate sparks and lightning (Husain 1997, 26).

Stories of the devouring mother are common. For example, according to the Yanomamo Indians of the Amazon, one of earth's first beings was a woman whose vagina became a toothed mouth that bit off her partner's penis. Further, in ancient China women's genitals were "executioners of men," and a Moslem saying held that "Three things are insatiable: the desert, the grave, and a woman's vulva" (Husain 1997, 26). Such concepts probably explain why many cultures viewed ejaculation as a loss of man's vital force, which was "eaten" by women. The Greek word *sema*, the root of semen, means both seed and food, and the Yanomamo word for pregnant also means satiated or full-fed and "to copulate" is synonymous with "to eat" (Husain 1997, 26).

Among Native American legends, such as those of the Apache and Navajo that tell of women with deadly toothed vaginas, are some in which these vaginas are even independent creatures. This concept may be behind the petroglyphs shown in fig. 95. Such creatures are usually slain or outwitted by culture heroes such as the War Twins, Coyote, or Spider Woman, and highly sexual imagery is used to describe their defeat. One of the more ferocious is known as Filled Vagina, who mates with cacti and is killed by Monster Slayer when he drives a club into her to break her sharp teeth. In some southwestern groups, this is reenacted with a carved wooden phallus. In other myths, taboos about birth and menstruation are imposed on the vagina-creature. By restricting its bleeding to a monthly cycle, an important aspect of her power is brought under control (Husain 1997, 96).

One Hopi story emphasizes the male need for protection against the *vagina dentata*. Spider Woman warns her grandson to stay away from some beautiful girls because they are dangerous. Then after some flirtation between him and the girls, Spider Woman insists that he must have some protection and helps him fabricate a penis sheath from wild lemonberry dough, telling him, "Now don't let this slip off—perhaps it will set their teeth on edge and wear them down." When he visits the girls, that is exactly what happens. After their teeth are worn down, the brave boy slips out to discard his protective sheath and then returns for his pleasure (Talayesva 1942, 77).

In a similar tale from Hopi, the Jimson Weed Girls (Tsimonmamant) are anthropomorphized jimsonweed plants that represent oversexed unmarried females with toothed vaginas. In the tale's scene of revenge, the offending teeth are defeated with carved wooden penises as the Jimson Weed Girls are copulated to death by the heroes of the story (Malotki 1983).

Similarly, in other regions of the greater Southwest, related mythology may be expressed in rock art, though with greater complexity. In the Great Basin, especially the Coso Range of California, there are many depictions of bighorn sheep being killed (fig. 96). Formerly explained as simple hunting magic, these images are now understood to be much

fig. 95. (below) Anasazi and Ute petroglyphs depicting stylized vulva-creatures: a. Mancos River, Colorado; b. Butler Wash, Utah; c.–f. Courthouse Rock, Utah.

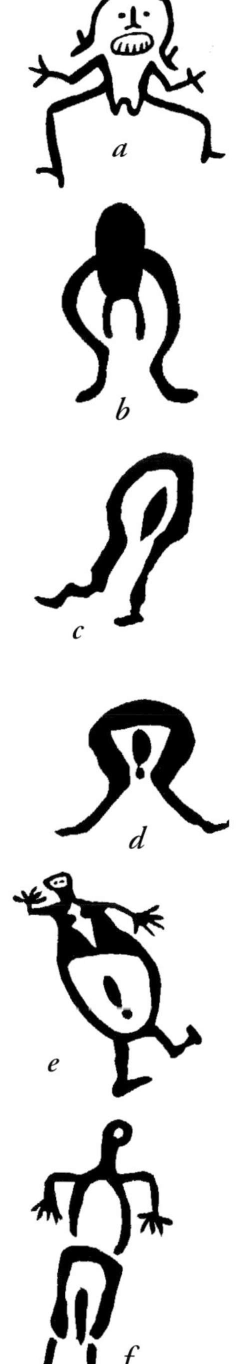

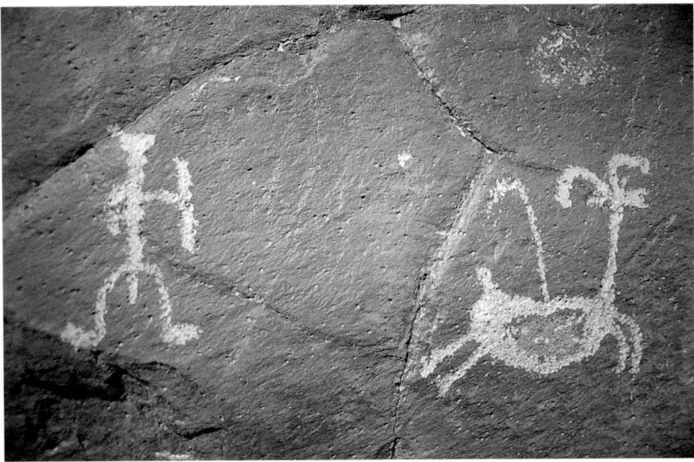

fig. 96.(above) Petroglyphs depicting the killing of a bighorn sheep, Coso Range, California.

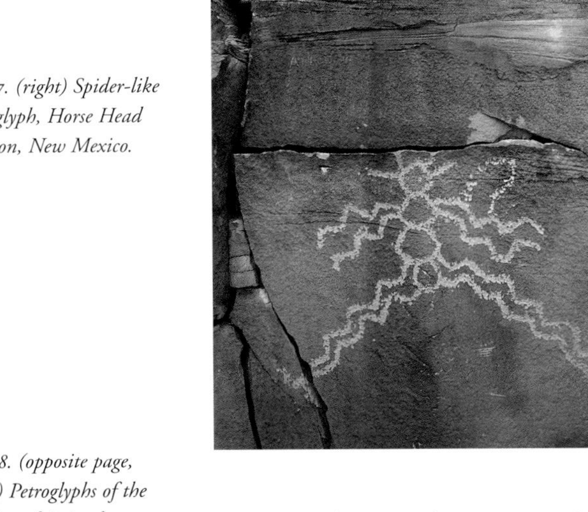

fig. 97. (right) Spider-like petroglyph, Horse Head Canyon, New Mexico.

fig. 98. (opposite page, right) Petroglyphs of the Mother of Animals: a. Paria Canyon, Arizona; b. Rio Grande near Pilar, New Mexico; c. Colorado River at Oak Canyon, Arizona; d. Galisteo, New Mexico; e. Petrified Forest National Park, Arizona.

fig. 99.(opposite page, bottom) Petroglyph of the Mother of Animals, Little Colorado River near Woodruff, Arizona.

more complex metaphors representing a shaman's trance (metaphorical death) as he enters the supernatural realm, in this case for rainmaking power. In Numic mythology of this area, Coyote (trickster and mythic shaman) is frustrated in his efforts to copulate with First Woman due to her toothed vagina. He eventually kills a bighorn sheep and uses its neckbone as a protective penis sheath to impregnate the woman. When he later opens a basket she has presented him, he populates the world. This myth combines several metaphors—killing a sheep (trance as death) and sexual intercourse are both related to shamanic altered states of consciousness, while baskets symbolize wombs or vulvas (Whitley 1994, 23). Thus images of bighorn sheep when interpreted in such mythological contexts could stand for male success in hunting and sexual activities in general.

Spider Woman

Myths and stories about the creator goddess Spider Woman, or Spider Grandmother, are found in a number of southwestern groups, including the Keresan Pueblos, the Hopis, and the Navajos. In these cultures sacred stories of genesis are associated with Spider Woman as a female creator deity who wove the web of creation. Spider Woman represents the equivalent of a female earth deity at Hopi because the spider makes a hole in the ground and lives in the earth. Here she is the goddess of wisdom and can change her shape and cause good or evil. Although each tribe depicts her differently, she is usually not portrayed in a realistic spider form but rather in symbols that reflect her attributes. Her appearance is thus a function of various mythic roles. As a metaphor for something small and intangible yet powerful, she represents spirit, wisdom, and creativity. Iconic images that may portray Spider Woman in rock art of the Four Corners region are thus diverse and subject to imaginative interpretation. However, given the importance of this figure in the traditions of native peoples in this region it is possible that some representational rock art depictions of Spider Woman do exist as, for example, a petroglyph from the Zuni Pueblo area in New Mexico (fig. 97) that is an unambiguous spider-like image.

Mother of Animals

Another mythic female figure from the Southwest related to fertility is the Mother of Game, or Mother of Animals. In the historic Pueblo pantheon, this deity owns the animals and is responsible for their increase. If hunters follow the prescribed rituals, she grants them the right to hunt her children. Although her image differs from tribe to tribe, this concept of a female spirit who owns the animals is ancient and could have shamanic roots originating in Paleolithic times. Her various names include Mother of Animals, Earth Mother, Patroness of the Hunt, Fertility Goddess, Childbirth Water Woman, and Mother of Kachinas. Lore about this figure is most varied at Hopi, where ethnologists have gathered myths for years. One of her names there is Tiikuywuuti, which means "Child-Sticking-Out Woman," referring to a legend about a pregnant woman who dies in childbirth and is transformed into a goddess after giving birth to infant game animals (McCreery and Malotki 1994, 140). Such a scene seems to be depicted in the petroglyph from the Grand Canyon area shown in fig. 98a, where a female gives birth to a small deer-like animal, and in the petroglyph from the Little Colorado River area (fig. 99) that shows a squatting female figure with a small game animal beneath her. It has also been reported that the fertility powers of Mother of Animals extend to humans—she "bestows infants" and "sends infants inside women" (Parsons 1939, 178, 318).

Rock art depictions of the Mother of Animals have been best documented in the Little Colorado River drainage near Petrified Forest National Park in Arizona (McCreery and Malotki 1994, 139–42). In this area she typically is depicted in the same rigid posture with legs spread and arms upraised, often flanked by twin disks (of unknown significance) and surrounded by animals, symbols of hunting, and flute players (fig. 98e). Similar representations have also been observed along the upper Rio Grande near Taos, New Mexico (Slifer 1998, 71–72). Another possible portrayal of the Mother of Animals in the Rio Grande region near Santa Fe, New Mexico, is shown in fig. 98d, where she is in the same posture and has a female hairstyle but also has animal traits, including a tail and three-toed hands and feet. Here she is flanked by two birds and two symmetrical, humpbacked figures, who are copulating with her. Perhaps these squat little humpbacks have replaced the two disks that are usually shown at her side in examples from elsewhere.

Among some Pueblos, the Mother of Animals is dreaded for her ghastly appearance, which terrifies hunters. In his autobiography, Hopi Don Talayesva describes a frightening encounter with her:

> Suddenly a powerful being jumped upon me and caught me around the waist. . . . And she locked my arms in a powerful embrace, my memory faded, my breath weakened, and my body became limp. . . . I tried to roll over and get on top of the spirit, but she was too much for me. As we wrestled, I came on top once, got a glimpse of her face, and discovered that she was the Mother god of wild game such as deer, buffalos, and rabbits. As she swung herself on top again, she turned her face from me and said, "I came to have intercourse with you, but you don't seem to want it. Do you wish to be a good hunter?" "Yes," I replied. . . Finally she looked back at me, sat down, and spun herself round like a top, and disappeared into the

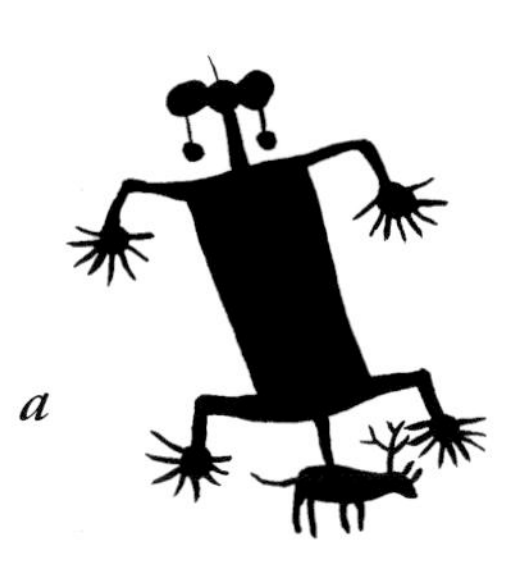
a

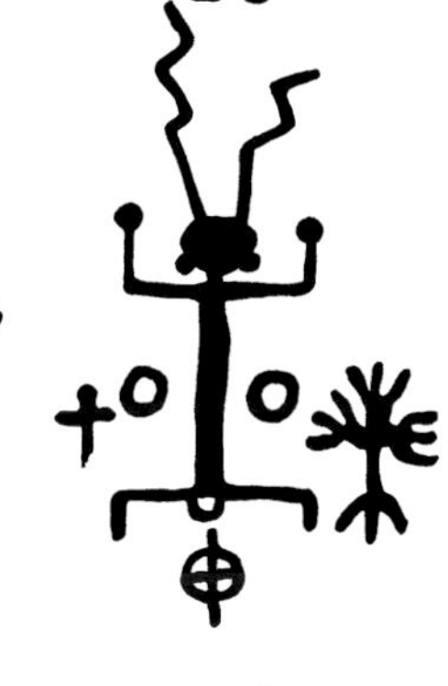
b

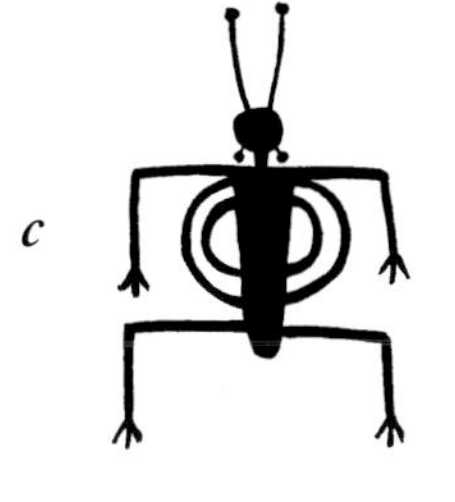
c

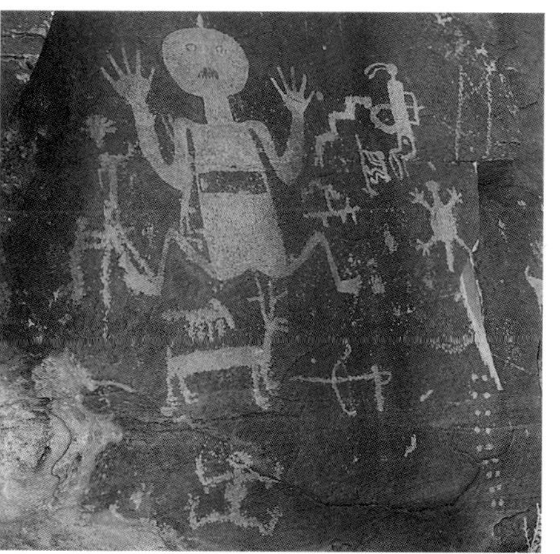

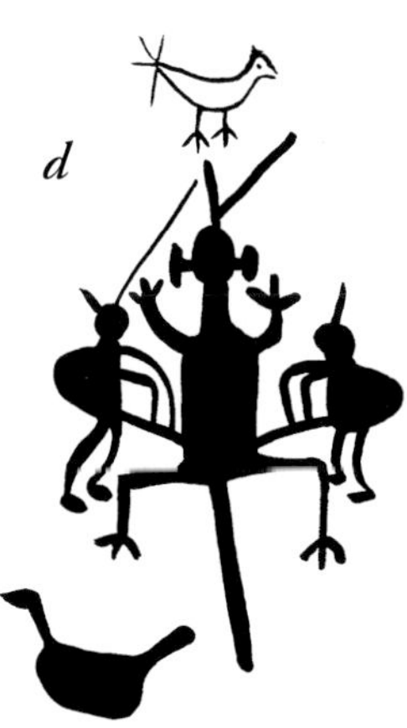
d

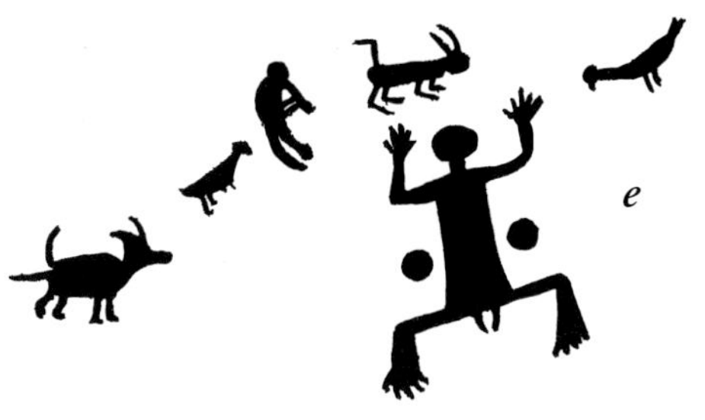
e

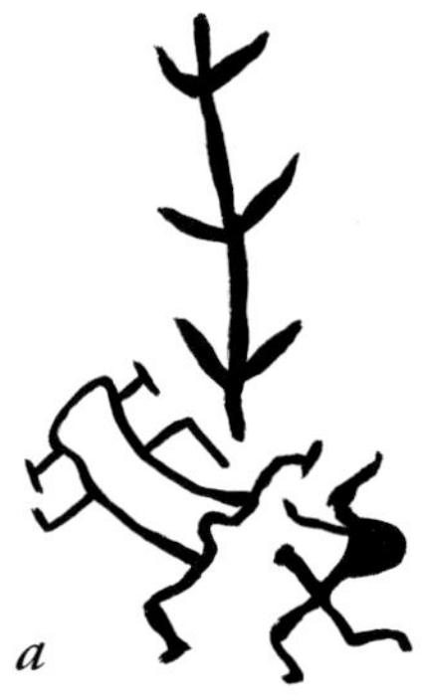

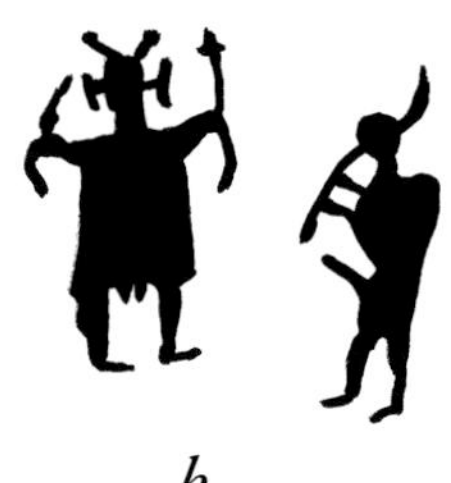

fig. 100. (above & below) Pueblo petroglyphs that may represent the Corn Maidens Myth: a. Velarde, New Mexico; b. La Cienega, New Mexico.

ground. I ran to the spot but saw no hole. There were four dead rabbits nearby, and I heard a voice saying, "Don't be afraid. Take them home with you, for they are your reward." Then I awoke with bells ringing in my ears, found my body wet with sweat, and feared that something was going to happen (Talayesva 1942, 343).

Corn Mother and the Corn Maidens

Other important female fertility deities and mythic figures in the Southwest are Corn Mother and the Corn Maidens. Numerous ethnographic accounts indicate these figures played a prominent role among southwestern peoples. To some Pueblos, such as the Zunis, Corn Mother is a dominant divinity, as might be expected in a matrilineal, agricultural group (Hultkrantz 1987, 96). Corn Mother is known as Iyatiku among the Keres, where she is a powerful intermediary between mankind and creator deities. Her counterpart at Hopi is a male corn god, Muingwu (Tyler 1964, 94). Further, Corn Mother has earthly counterparts—two sisters who plant trees, release animals from their baskets, and serve as mothers for humankind. As a goddess of fertility, Corn Mother also plays a role as a deity of death by receiving the deceased into her underworld realm (Tyler 1964, 121). The Corn Maidens are the main figures in myths that portray the flight of these fertility/vegetation goddesses after being ignored in rituals or insulted by unwelcome sexual advances (the desirable Corn Maidens were often the subject of someone's lust)—thereby causing famine in the land. Various messengers and culture heroes (usually the Warrior Twins) go after the Corn Maidens and lure them back. In one version, the seeker is the flute-playing Payatamu, who taught the people to cultivate corn and who bears the shield of the sun and represents the fertilizing and sexual power of the sun.

Petroglyphs from the upper Rio Grande (fig. 100) may depict aspects of the Corn Maidens or Corn Mother myths. In one image, a phallic, humpbacked figure chases a female beneath a corn plant; in another depiction a phallic, humpbacked flute player (Payatamu?) plays to a female from whose arms vegetation seems to sprout. Although these two scenes are located forty miles apart, they may be related to a similar myth. Both females have hair whorls indicating unmarried Pueblo girls, and both flute players wear a conical hat. It has been suggested that these images may be associated with similar images from kiva murals at Kuaua ruin near Albuquerque, and be connected to an elaborate Pueblo myth which explains how Nepayatamu (Payatamu) brought the Corn Maidens to earth—the female figure may represent the Yellow Corn Maiden, Shiwanokia (Boyd and Ferguson 1988, 67). Flute playing is an important aspect of these myths, as the flute's music was thought to aid germination of seeds and growth of corn as well as generate sexual excitement.

Further, in Canyon de Chelly, Arizona, Anasazi rock paintings in Pictograph Cave and Ceremonial Cave have been interpreted as illustrating components of the Corn Maidens myth, as well as the related War Twins myth (Harris 1993, 123–32). Part of the elaborate panel from Ceremonial Cave is shown in fig. 101. Here a row of six slender anthropomorphs may represent the Corn Maidens moving toward the east (returning to Itiwana—the place they had abandoned near Zuni). The number six usually symbolizes the six directions of the world. Although the number of Corn Maidens varies, six of them represent the corn of the colors of the six directions, with a seventh and eighth sometimes included to represent sweet corn and squash (Tyler 1964, 144).They are being led by a small figure with a disk—these could represent Payatamu and his sun shield. Above them stand two figures painted in contrasting patterns, suggesting these are the mythic War Twins (with opposite natures) who were sent after the fugitive Corn Maidens. The Twins are flanked by two white birds resembling ducks. In one version of the myth, the Corn Maidens are concealed by Mother

Duck and Father Duck. Both ducks are looking in the same direction the Corn Maidens are traveling. Behind the six Corn Maidens and the small figure leading them, all of which are painted in red, are ghostlike doubles painted in white. These may represent the spirits that travel and dance behind the kachina impersonators of supernaturals such as the Corn Maidens and Payatamu. The Corn Maidens agree to send their spirits to dance behind their masked kachina impersonators:

> The Corn Maidens left us because one man desired them and wished to lay hands on them. We are their flesh and they give us themselves to eat. If they give it to us again and we plant in the spring for the rain to water we shall be fed again with their flesh. They will be our mothers and we shall be their children. If at any time we think evil thoughts or are unhappy they will go away from us again and we shall have nothing. When we dance the Corn Dance we shall carry their flesh in our hands. We shall not see them but they will be there in spirit (Tyler 1964, 146).

Also from Ceremonial Cave are pictographs of two slender figures holding ears of corn in their hands—probably representing the Twins, the Corns Maidens, or their ritual impersonators in a Corn Dance (fig. 102). For the Corn Maidens to return, the people of Itiwana had to show respect by dancing with ears of corn. Some Pueblos represent the Corn Mother by perfect corn fetishes. This sacred object represents Earth Mother, rain, vegetation, and all that nourishes mankind (Tyler 1964, 123).

From Pictograph Cave is a related scene showing two flute players beneath the Great White Duck (fig. 103). In their search for the Corn Maidens, the War Twins received directions from this wise, protective motherly figure who knew all the trails and never got lost. Corn Maidens may also be represented by the two slender female figures holding onto a

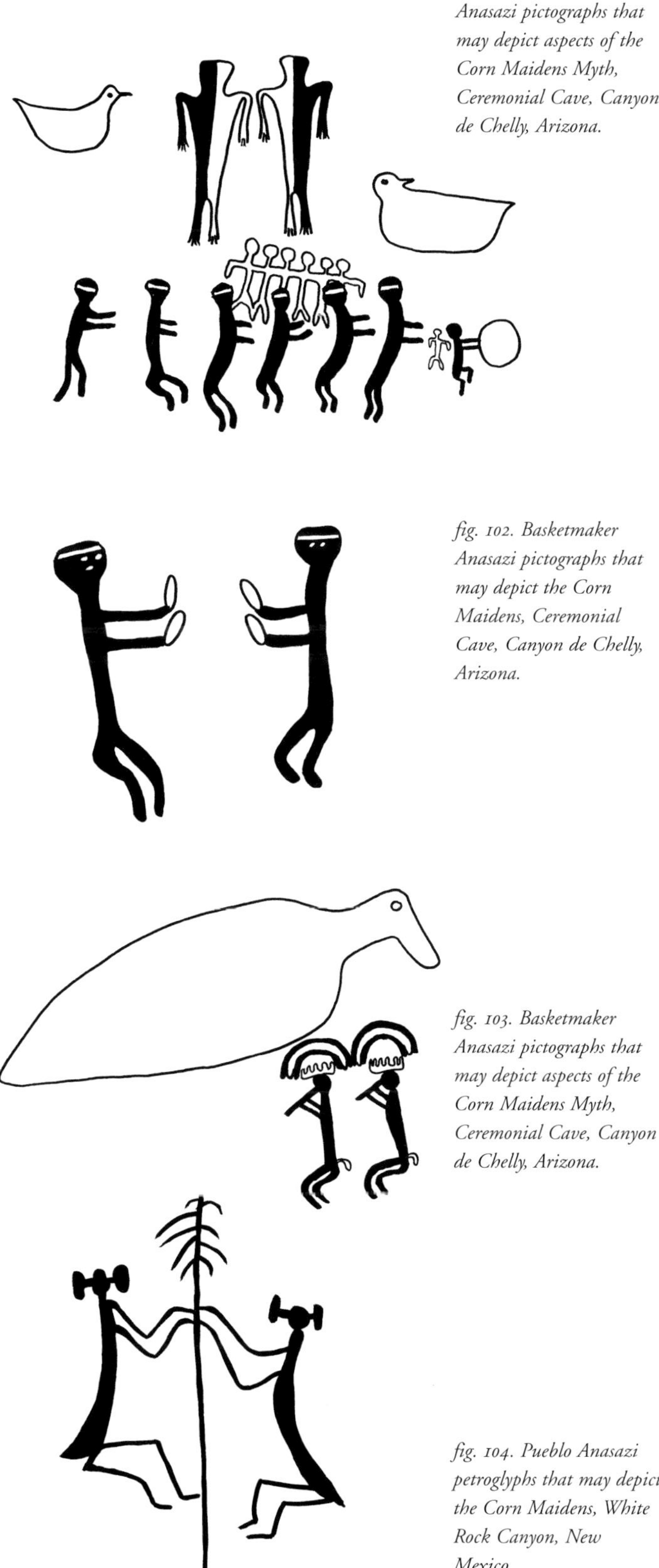

fig. 101. Basketmaker Anasazi pictographs that may depict aspects of the Corn Maidens Myth, Ceremonial Cave, Canyon de Chelly, Arizona.

fig. 102. Basketmaker Anasazi pictographs that may depict the Corn Maidens, Ceremonial Cave, Canyon de Chelly, Arizona.

fig. 103. Basketmaker Anasazi pictographs that may depict aspects of the Corn Maidens Myth, Ceremonial Cave, Canyon de Chelly, Arizona.

fig. 104. Pueblo Anasazi petroglyphs that may depict the Corn Maidens, White Rock Canyon, New Mexico.

corn plant in a petroglyph from White Rock Canyon, New Mexico (fig. 104). In summary, the Corn Maidens represent the staple of life and basic food crops, and their flight is a myth of the cycle of the seasons. Where the Corn Maidens breathe, "warmth, health, and fertility shall follow" (Cushing 1896, 442).

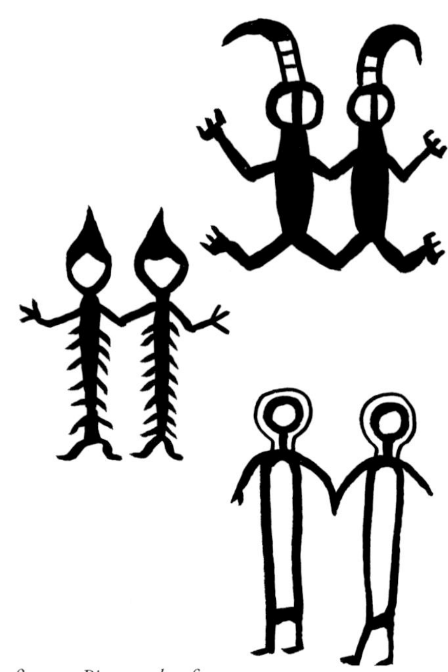

fig. 105. Pictographs of twins, Columbia River area, Washington (after Keyser 1992, 78).

Twins

Twins are important not only in the Southwest but are fertility symbols in mythology and ancient art throughout the world (fig. 105). In addition to the auspicious nature of multiple births, twins are often accorded special powers by native peoples (Keyser 1992, 77–78). Twins inherently represent duality and symbolize opposing principles, a basic tenet of most religions. Throughout all mythologies the same pair occur—twins of light and darkness, born from the Great Mother or primordial womb. In the Americas, myths of the Hero Twins or Warrior Twins are especially prolific, appearing in many guises, such as in cosmogonic myths as the sun and moon (Campbell 1989, II:III: 314). Although they are war gods, they are at the same time intrinsically associated with fertilization—such duality is common in many Native American cultures, and the image of twins represents this concept. The Hero Twins epic has been described as the basic myth in North America, and among southwestern Indian cultures the Warrior Twins Myth is nearly universal. One group of such myths indicates they are powerful sons of the sun; another group tells of their exploits leading the First People and protecting them at the time of emergence from the underworld; a third group describes the twins as crafty hunters who use magic to lure their prey. Because of the special nature of twins and the prominence of twin culture heroes and supernaturals in southwestern mythologies, it is reasonable to assume that these figures are found in rock art.

Among the southwestern Pueblos, there is a great variety of stories about the Warrior Twins, or Twins of the Sun as they are sometimes called. Details differ, but the twins are prominent in stories about emergence and creation, and their conception by a supernatural woman is usually miraculous and is associated with the idea of the fertilization of the earth by the sun and water:

> The impregnation of the mother of these gods was miraculous. Often she conceives when a ray of the sun falls upon her as she sleeps, or when a drop of water splashes on her from a waterfall. Sometimes both events conspire, and one accounts for the elder brother, and the second for the younger twin. Sometimes the miracle is complete and they are born of the Sun's rays on mist (Tyler 1964, 213–14).

In some accounts, the Warrior Twins' grandmother is Spider Woman or Salt Woman. One of the creators of humans, Spider Woman created people in pairs (Tyler 1964, 95). Rock art images suggesting twins and associated mythology occur as pairs of similar anthropomorphs as well as pairs of symbolic elements. This ancient theme is apparently expressed in rock art at least as old as that of the Basketmaker Anasazi. Occurring in the San Juan River area are, for example, Basketmaker depictions of twinned flute players and mysterious objects known as lobed circles that are associated with fertility (fig. 106; Manning 1992, 159–210). The fertility context of the lobed circles motif is further discussed in the section "Lobed Circles."

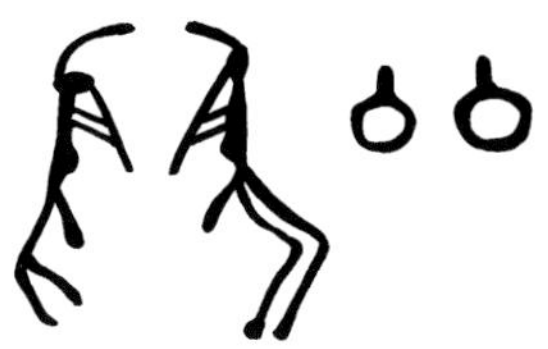

fig. 106. (above) Basketmaker Anasazi petroglyphs depicting twin flute players and paired lobed circles, Sand Island, Utah.

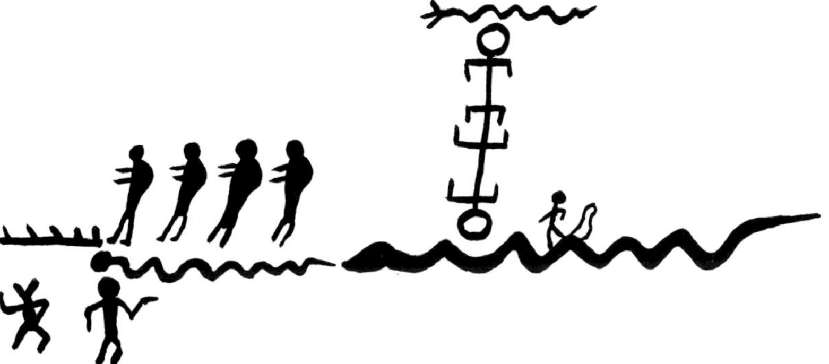

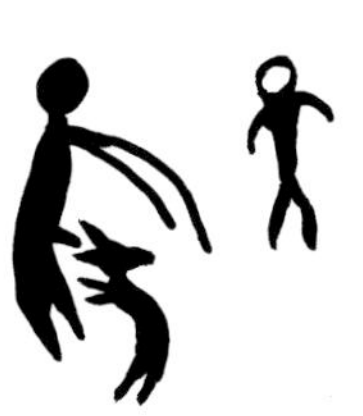

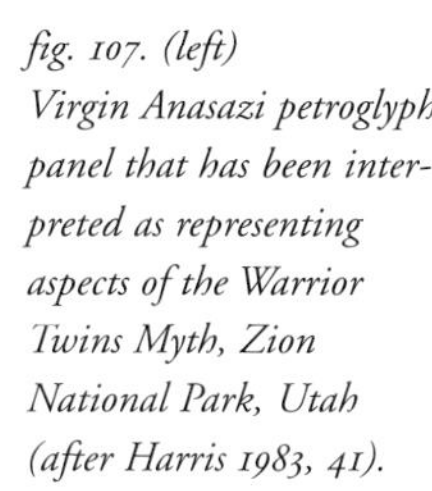

fig. 107. (left) Virgin Anasazi petroglyph panel that has been interpreted as representing aspects of the Warrior Twins Myth, Zion National Park, Utah (after Harris 1983, 41).

fig. 108. (right) Basketmaker Anasazi petroglyph panel that has been interpreted as representing aspects of the Warrior Twins Myth, Natural Bridges National Monument, Utah.

Several petroglyph panels in southern Utah have been interpreted as representing the Warrior Twins emergence myth (Harris 1982, 1983). The images in fig. 107 are a portion of a larger panel of petroglyphs that contains twin figures and seems to show spheres of activity representing different mythic events on rock strata separated by natural divisions. These divisions may be a means of depicting emergence from the first to the fourth worlds. Interpretation of the entire panel in this mythological context is beyond the scope of this discussion, but the images in fig. 107 seem to be the focal point (Harris 1983, 40–47). The two stick-figure anthropomorphs might depict copulation by the First Man and First Woman or show the birth of twins—in this case born of the serpents representing water and sun. The opposite nature of the twins may be indicated here, beginning at birth—the eldest born correctly and the youngest born backward. In the lower left of this panel are two anthropomorphs that may also represent the twins gesturing in opposite directions. The serpents in this scene may depict the Serpent of the Heavens and the Great Mother of Serpents, who here provides seeds from her ovaries that are used

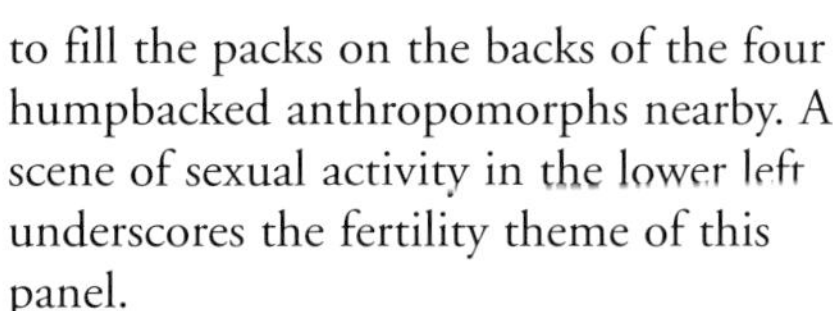

to fill the packs on the backs of the four humpbacked anthropomorphs nearby. A scene of sexual activity in the lower left underscores the fertility theme of this panel.

Depictions of the Warrior Twins are even more apparent in another Anasazi petroglyph panel from Natural Bridges National Monument in southeastern Utah (Harris 1982). In this large, complex panel, curious images of twin anthropomorphs occur at least five times in a variety of settings (fig. 108). Although these petroglyphs are Basketmaker Anasazi and thus predate historic ethnography by more than a thousand years, the repeated *fig. 109. (opposite page, top) Anasazi petroglyphs depicting aspects of twins or "opposite nature": a. La Cienega, New Mexico; b. La Bajada, New Mexico; c. Colorado City, Arizona; d. Galisteo Basin, New Mexico.*

fig. 110. (opposite page, bottom) Jornada Style petroglyphs depicting a coyote and jackrabbit, Carrizo Mountain, New Mexico.

emphasis on twin figures suggests that cultural roots for twin mythology are ancient. As seen above, the Warrior Twins also figure prominently in myths about the Corn Maidens, and there appear to be ancient (Basketmaker) roots for this myth as well.

Portrayals of the mythic Warrior Twins also occur in more recent rock art of the Navajos. Born of the sun and Changing Woman, the twins are major Navajo deities. The elder twin is often called Monster Slayer, while the younger is named Born-for-Water. In Navajo rock art, they are depicted in various ways that express their power (Schaafsma 1980, 315). Born-for-Water is symbolized by an hourglass-like design that represents the scalp-knot, whereas Monster Slayer is represented by the bow. In the monster slaying tales, the bow is used by Monster Slayer to kill the creature, and Born-for-Water scalps it.

An interesting aspect of myths about twins is the notion that twins were originally united in the womb but were forced apart at birth; thus constituting a single person they belong together, and it is necessary, though difficult, to reunite them. In this regard, they represent the two sides of human nature, such as masculine/feminine, introvert/extrovert, and dynamic/acquiescent. This polarity has been expressed in stories that relate to the nature of the soul and to sexuality. Like the special powers ascribed to hermaphroditic individuals, berdaches, and transvestite shamans, twins also have a spiritual nature, as explained by the Lakota shaman Lame Deer:

> They were not like other men, but the Great Spirit made them *winktes* and we accepted them as such. . . . We think that if a woman has two little ones growing inside her, if she is going to have twins, sometimes instead of giving birth to two babies they have formed up in her womb into just one, into a half-man/half-woman kind of being. . . . To us a man is what nature, or his dreams, make him. We accept him for what he wants to be (Fire and Erdoes 1972, 117, 149).

The same idea is expressed by Hopi Don Talayesva in his autobiography *Sun Chief.* He first tells how he had been twins in his mother's womb, but since she only wanted one child, with the help of a medicine man, she willed the twins to twist themselves together into one being. Then he describes the reactions of his family after he was born:

> Sure enough, I was twins twisted into one. They could see that I was an oversize baby, that my hair curled itself into two little whorls instead of one at the back of my head, and that in front of my body I was a boy but at the back there was the sure trace of a girl—the imprint of a little vulva that slowly disappeared. They have told me time after time that I was twice lucky—lucky to be born twins and lucky to just miss becoming a girl (Talayesva 1942, 27).

Some of the beliefs about twins can be extended to the various ways in which duality has been expressed among Indian tribes (Wellman 1981). Ideas about the dualistic personality pervade Indian myth and ceremony and derive from ancient, archetypal sources. These are expressed in such ways as the trickster-transformers, hermaphroditic personalities, intratribal divisions, and Clown Societies that do everything backward or abnormally. A common means of visually depicting duality is a face divided and painted in two colors. There are numerous examples in rock art of such expression, like the petroglyph that incorporates a natural black inclusion in the rock as half of a face, the two-sided face looking in two directions, and the two-headed anthropomorph motif (fig. 109).

Coyote

Of all the subjects of Native American myths and stories, the trickster figure

Coyote seems to have the greatest libido and propensity for getting into outrageous sexual situations. In fact, Coyote was widely credited with inventing copulation as well as other sexual acts and taboos, and among some cultures he even had three penes. Throughout the Southwest, and elsewhere in North America, this sacred clown is the amusing subject of countless stories involving courtship and seduction. An example was given in Chapter 2 of a story in which he tries to fool some girls picking berries into believing that the tip of his penis is a ripe strawberry. In another story, Coyote is aroused by some mallard duck girls he sees swimming on the other side of the river. Hiding in the bushes, he lengthens his penis and floats it across the river just below the surface of the water with a rock tied to it and then copulates with the oldest girl. When she begins thrashing around, her sisters see what is happening and try to pull the penis out but cannot. Then Coyote calls out, "What is the problem over there?" and tells them to cut the thing off with some wire grass, which they do. When the girl becomes sick, Coyote offers to cure her if they leave him alone with her in the lodge so no one can see his medicine. First he sings, "I will stick it back on, I will stick it back on." Then he copulates again with the mallard duck girl and recovers the end of his penis. She is cured, and everyone says Coyote's medicine is great (Erdoes and Ortiz 1984, 318–19). Depictions in rock art of animals that resemble coyotes are not uncommon, and some of these may represent the mythic Coyote (fig. 110). He is also depicted in ceramic designs such as the Mimbres bowl shown in figure 185 where he is copulating with a bighorn sheep.

Celestial Imagery

Because so many cultures perceived the earth as mother and the sky as father, there is abundant mythical symbolism about the heavens and their connection with fertility. Just as earth's seasonal changes affected life, so did the celestial cycles offer the power of renewal, growth, and creation. Our ancestors learned to watch the sky and predict events such as the solstices and equinoxes, for their survival and well-being depended on knowledge about seasonal changes. Thus ritual, art, and myth reflect a widespread concern with the balance of cosmic forces.

Myths of cosmic order provided our ancestors with a structure for perceiving the world and their place in it. Rock art images related to the seasons and the sky are almost certainly connected with cosmic myths and in many cases are associated with fertility symbolism. Emblems of fertility and birth, such as vulva symbols, can be found at rock art sites that may have also functioned as solstice shrines—places where shamans could participate in the rebirth of the new year as the sun returns. It was the shaman's role to balance cosmic forces, as described in the following:

> By keeping the calendar, by witnessing the sky, and by ritualizing the natural cycle of the cosmos, the shaman enters the celestial realm and siphons off some of its power. . . . In every round of the seasonal cycle, the Indians sensed there was a time of danger for the world's harmony and for the continued well-being of living things. . . . This

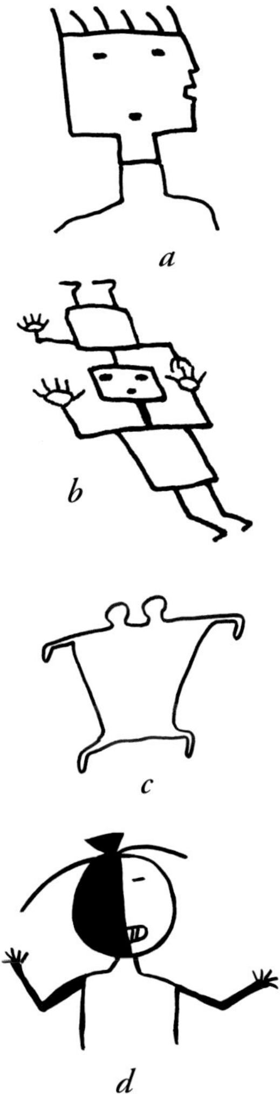

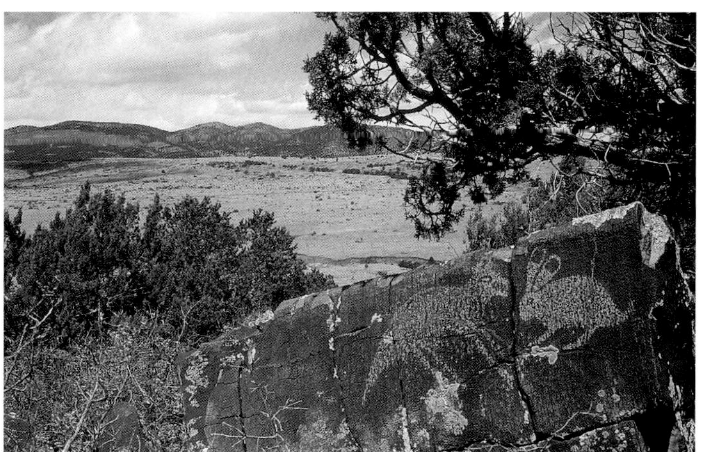

excursion of the sun was, of course, just a metaphor for the threat to cosmic balance, and the shaman's ceremonies symbolized the celestial power that stabilized and oriented the world (Krupp 1983, 40).

fig. 111. Pueblo petroglyphs depicting the sun with rays shaped like vulvas, Jemez Mountains, New Mexico.

The sky has always inspired religious awe and provided the basis for religious expression in primitive societies. Among Native Americans, the womb-like forms of caves and rock fissures were adapted to mythically represent the fertilization of Mother Earth by the rays of Father Sky, resulting in the birth of creative forces of the universe as well as mankind. Such views are foundations of many of the world's great religions, as explained in the following: "It took little effort of the imagination to recognize that sexual intercourse was the human equivalent of interaction between the cosmic forces of yin and yang" (Tannahill 1980, 164). The shaman's mystical flight into the sky is one of the earliest forms of religious experience. Birds, common elements in rock art, are often symbolic of mystical flight or celestial ascent. Black Elk said, "Birds make their nests in circles, for theirs is the same religion as ours" (Neihardt 1961).

As a result of these associations, at certain rock art sites in the Southwest there are connections, sometimes explicit, between the cosmos and human sexuality/fertility. For example, the petroglyphs in fig. 111 portray the sun with four rays that resemble vulvas, symbolizing the sun's power to fertilize the earth and promote fecundity. Such fertility imagery is, in effect, an invocation to the cosmic order and a recognition of the power inherent in seasonal and cosmic processes that affect mankind. Sacred knowledge of this nature is sometimes expressed as the interplay of sun and shadow at diverse sites that functioned as astronomical calendars, star charts, places for puberty initiation or shamanic vision quests, fertility shrines, and numinous mythic locales.

Another rock art site that appears to represent the relationship between sexuality/fertility and celestial elements is the Cave of Life in the Little Colorado River area of northern Arizona, a site previously discussed in the section "Fertility Shrines and Rites" (fig. 26). The copulating couple may represent the rite of Sacred Marriage, with other aspects of the panel suggesting a journey toward the sky (Thomas 1982, 34). The panel is oriented vertically toward a phallic, shamanic figure at the top, and it is located beneath a natural skylight in the ceiling of the cave (opening to the sky); there are also many bird images in the upper part of the cave, as well as on the shaman's staff. This site has also been interpreted as a winter solstice observatory that may be related to the Hopi *Wuwuchim* ceremonies which portray phases of creation and the germination of all forms of life (Faris 1986).

An equally impressive site that combines elements of the cosmos and fertility, and which has been interpreted in a mythic context, is Womb Rock in the Providence Mountains of southern California (see fig. 71). Womb Rock is named for its large, east-facing cavity resembling a birth canal through which puberty initiates or shamans crawled in rituals that probably symbolized rebirth. Looking through the tunnel, one can witness the sun rising from a prominent notch on the horizon on the first day of spring. Petroglyphs on the rock depict vulvas and sun symbols that seem to echo an ancient myth of the Chemehuevi people about Earth Woman, or Lone Woman of the Cave, who becomes impregnated by the sun's rays:

> A lone woman who lived in a cave went out one morning into the mountain to urinate. Each morning she would do this spreading her legs wide to urinate. One day as she did this, the rising Sun penetrated her with his rays and she became pregnant. After that she no longer went there to urinate. In the fullness of time, she gave birth to twin boys, Twin Sons of the Sun (Laird 1984, 204).

Further, it has been observed that other sites in the Mojave Desert region have similar functions, where caves or even bedrock mortars represent the Earth Woman's vagina and are penetrated by shafts of sunlight (the sun's phallus) at the beginning of spring—the season when earth becomes fertile (Rafter 1995, 31–37).

Moreover, themes of fertility and celestial events are found at rock art sites in the Central Desert of Baja California. At certain painted caves the interplay of sun and shadow appears to be related to fertility and the solstice:

> Here sacred power manifests itself in the form of dramatic patterns of light and shadow at a time of great ritual importance. The rock art is placed to show the shaman's interaction with the sacred, and serves to reinforce cosmic order each year as the cycle is repeated (Hedges 1986, 25).

These sites also seemingly incorporate diamond-chain patterns that may represent concepts of vertical paths or ladders to the sky, suggesting shamanic access to celestial realms. This vertical motif is bisected by a sunlight/shadow line on the summer solstice—the shaft of sunlight is said to resemble an erect phallus (Ewing and Robin 1987, 120). A basic element of shamanic practice worldwide involves climbing ladders or poles for ecstatic journeys to worlds above earth (Eliade 1964, 487–93). From the same region, an elderly Kiliwa Indian concluded a story like this: "The next morning, he took a ladder, leaned it on the sky and climbed up to heaven, his footsteps thundering as he climbed to the top of the sky" (Mixco 1984, 222).

If shamanic ascent is indicated by the vertical diamond-chain motif and the phallic shaft of sunlight, this is supported by some of the sexual components of shamanism. Shamans can have dreams and visions of intercourse with spirits, some of which bring increased sexual vigor to the community and renewal of all life. This is illustrated by a report about initiation rites of a Siberian shaman: "When his shamanic instruction is finished, his soul meets his future celestial wife in the sky; with her too his soul has sexual relations. . . ." The initiatory ceremony ". . . includes an ascent to the sky and is followed by a three-day feast of somewhat licentious nature" (Eliade 1964, 75, in Ewing and Robin 1987, 121).

The connection between fertility and celestial realms is further illustrated at additional rock art sites. A Chumash pictograph from a cave in the Coast Range of southern California (fig. 112) depicts a mythological event where a supernatural female is giving birth to the stars, perhaps representing a creation myth or some aspect of seasonal renewal. The equally intriguing anthropomorph in fig. 113, an Anasazi petroglyph from the upper Rio Grande near Taos, New Mexico, may be a deity who brings rain—suggested by a fringe falling from the loins. A similar anthropomorph is shown in fig. 114; this Anasazi petroglyph occurs in Indian Creek in southeastern Utah—250 miles from the Rio Grande image, indicating

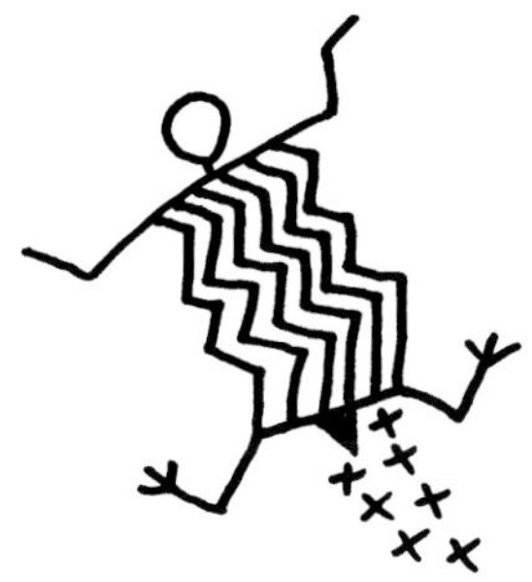

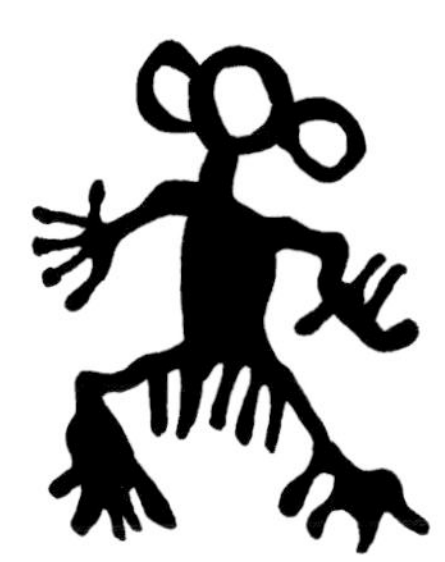

fig. 112. (top left) Chumash pictograph of a supernatural or deity giving birth to the stars, Los Padres National Forest, California (after Krupp 1997, 48).

fig. 113. (top right) Petroglyph of an anthropomorph with possible rain symbolism, Rio Grande Gorge near Cerro, New Mexico.

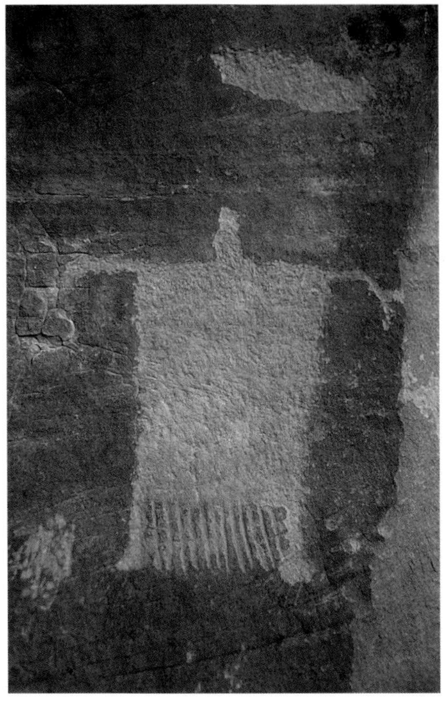

fig. 114. Petroglyph of an anthropomorph with possible rain symbolism, Indian Creek, Utah.

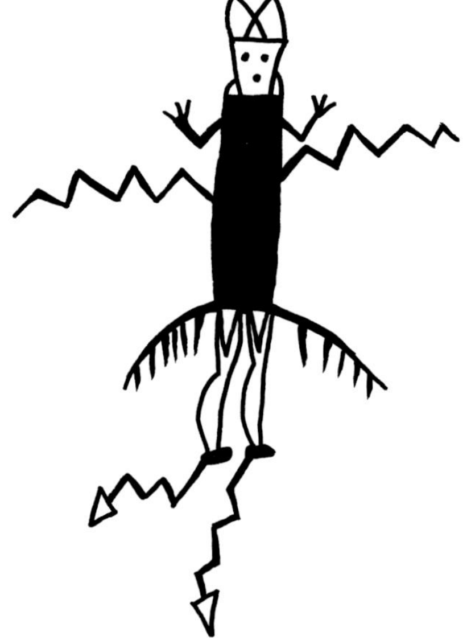

fig. 115. Petroglyph of a Navajo rain deity, Tapia Canyon, New Mexico.

that this mythic theme was widespread. In the petroglyph depiction of a Navajo rain deity shown in fig. 115, a fringe of rain falls from the hips and bolts of lightning emerge from the feet. The myths that inspired such images have mostly disappeared—as rain evaporates in the desert.

THE FLUTE PLAYER: PREEMINENT FERTILITY SYMBOL IN THE SOUTHWEST

A common figure in rock art of the Four Corners region is the flute player, which is portrayed usually in contexts related to fertility and abundance.[32] Often phallic, sometimes humpbacked, these curious images occur in prehistoric rock art, ceramics, and kiva murals over a large area of the American Southwest that includes the Anasazi/Pueblo culture areas of the Colorado Plateau and upper Rio Grande, as well as the Mogollon, Hohokam, and Fremont areas. That this symbol was prevalent within such a large region and for more than a thousand years suggests that the flute player character was very important in prehistoric times. In recent years this figure has become an extremely popular icon of the Southwest and is known erroneously by the name of Kokopelli—a Hopi kachina. Since the Hopi kachina Kokopelli has a humped back, sometimes plays a flute, and is notorious for his libido, the flute player depicted in rock art is usually associated with him. While this connection may be appropriate for some rock art images, it does not apply to all. The true flute player is probably a complex merging of various myths, deities, and traits that evolved over a period of at least a thousand years in the Anasazi world. The Hopis never identify the flute player figure in rock art as Kokopelli, preferring the traditional term *Maahu* (Locust) or *Lahlanhoya*, a clan symbol (McCreery and Malotki 1994, 156). Kokopelli, the Hopi kachina ("respected spirit"), is associated with fertility and rain and has a hump, a long snout (but no flute), and was originally phallic. It is likely that the modern Kokopelli kachina has evolved from the prehistoric lineage of diverse flute players portrayed in rock art and pottery throughout the Southwest.

There is something archetypal and universally appealing about this character. The widely held beliefs that he was a fertility symbol, roving minstrel or trader, rain priest, shaman, hunting magician, trickster, and seducer of maidens have contributed to his popularity. He is one of the few prehistoric deities to have survived in recognizable form from Anasazi times to the present. There are thousands of flute player images found at hundreds of rock art sites throughout the Southwest, ranging from crude stick figures to elaborately rendered designs. Further, this figure occurs alone, in pairs, or in groups and is shown standing, sitting, recumbent, kneeling, dancing to his flute music, being carried, hunting, or making love (fig. 116).

Exactly when they first appear is uncertain, but flute players without humps are present in Anasazi Basketmaker III rock art dating to at least A.D. 700 (Schaafsma 1980, 136). After A.D. 1000 they occur with a hump and flute in Anasazi rock art, pottery, and wall paintings. They also occur on ceramics of the Hohokam and Mimbres in southern Arizona and New Mexico around A.D. 1000 to 1150. These images share a number of interrelated attributes. The flute player has been interpreted as a deity, clan symbol, shaman or medicine man, trader, insect– or animal-like being, and as an individual with a spinal deformity. He often has feathers or antenna-like appendages on his head and may appear as a flute-playing insect or animal. In many cultures, the flute is used in sacred rituals as well as for courtship and evidently had a special role in Anasazi culture, since flutes made of bone and wood have been found among their artifacts.

In many Native American cultures, as well as in other parts of the world, flute lore was associated with sex and fertility. The flute was seen as stimulating growth, abundance, and reproductive energy (fig. 117). Among agricultural societies it is frequently played to encourage the healthy growth of crops. Further, in many tribes the flute was used by young men for courting (Bierhorst 1979, 78). There are tales of men whose flute melodies were so powerful that women could not resist the call and would come to them. Usually, each young man created his own special courting song to be used for love magic. Often such melodies were haunting and

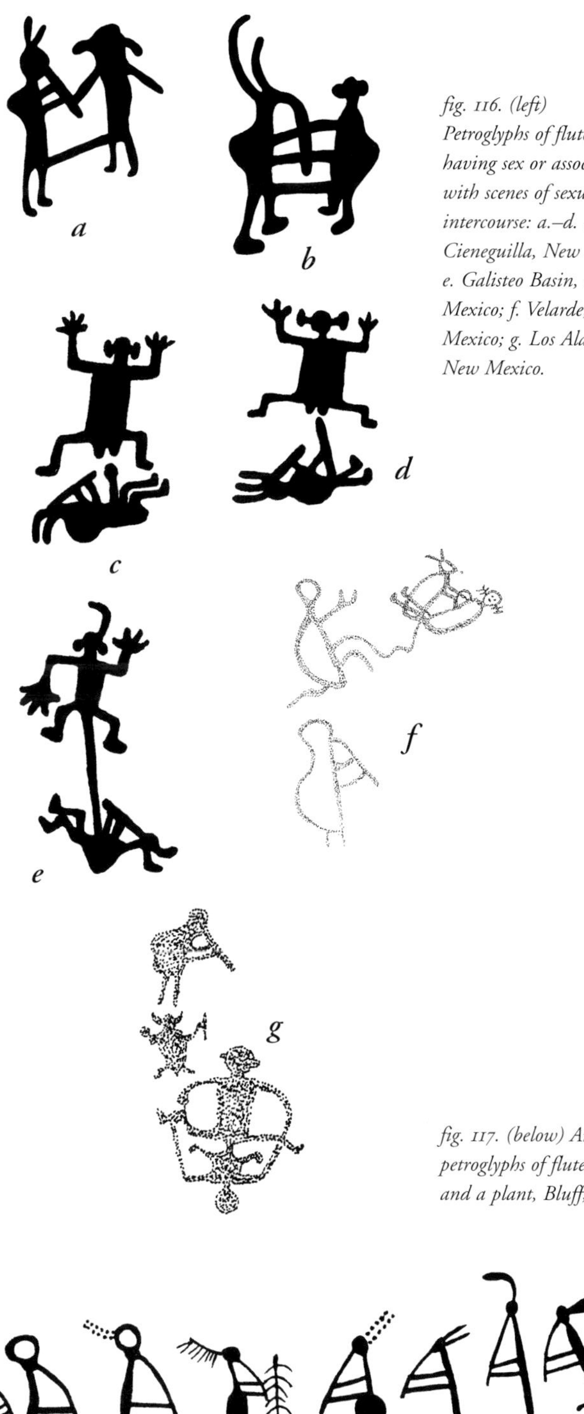

fig. 116. (left) Petroglyphs of flute players having sex or associated with scenes of sexual intercourse: a.–d. La Cieneguilla, New Mexico; e. Galisteo Basin, New Mexico; f. Velarde, New Mexico; g. Los Alamos, New Mexico.

fig. 117. (below) Anasazi petroglyphs of flute players and a plant, Bluff, Utah.

sad, for the purpose of making the courted woman feel lonely. While the flute sounds sometimes resembled an elk's call, other times courting songs imitated crying. The player of a Yuchi flute melody exclaimed: "Oh, if some girls were only here! When they hear that, they cry, and then you can fondle them. It makes them feel lonesome. I wish some were here now. I feel badly myself" (Bierhorst 1979, 82). A Pima song that imitated the sound of a flute with a hypnotic quality was intended to induce a sort of trance—to shake the woman's heart as the song blooms. Among the Hopis, there were magic songs by which a woman could be drawn to a man, even against her will (Talayesva 1942, 77).[33] Some tribes made special courting flutes which were carved with animals and birds known for their showy courtship dances and displays. Some rock art depictions show flutes with animals and birds attached.

In addition, flutes were used for even more powerful applications dealing with the supernatural activities of the shaman. The altered state of consciousness that shamans experience in a trance often begins with aural hallucinations before proceeding to mental and visual ones. In the ethnography of far western North America, these aural hallucinations are often described as whistling, buzzing, whirring, and ringing, and were, therefore, often related to the sounds of flutes and bull-roarers, instruments used by shamans at the start of rituals to transition to sacred time (Whitley 1994, 12). The flute, then, was used to open the portal to the supernatural and to lure the rattlesnake (often a spirit guardian of the supernatural realm) out of his supernatural lair. Like the buzzing of the rattlesnake, the whirring sound made by a covey of quail simulates the aural hallucinations of the shaman. Thus quails were said to play the flute to open the supernatural portal for Yokuts shamans in southern California (Whitley 1994, 27).

Preserved in the Ice Age caves of Europe, flutes, along with bull-roarers and heel marks in clay, suggest that instruments had considerable ceremonial importance in ancient times—perhaps in ritualized, sacred dancing related to the regenerative magic of the cave paintings. In fact, the flute is probably the world's oldest musical instrument—archaeologists have found an 82,000-year-old flute made from the thigh bone of a bear in a Neanderthal cave in Slovenia (Miles and Norwich 1997, 8). Moreover, recent excavation of an early Neolithic site in China uncovered six remarkably well-preserved flutes made from wing bones of cranes. Dated between 7,000 and 9,000 years old, some are in perfect condition and can still be played; their tone scale is similar to the Western eight-note scale that begins "do, re, mi," suggesting that ancient musicians of the seventh century B.C. could play not just single notes but music.[34]

A further example of the nearly universal importance of the flute and its sexual or fertility context is the mythical background for an important ceremony of the Desana people in the Amazon (Reichel-Dolmatoff 1971, 169–70), who recognize male and female flutes, with different sounds and erotic meanings. According to the myth, when the Sun Father's incestual sin of violating his daughter was witnessed by a mantis-like insect, the creature transformed into a person and used a flute to publicly denounce the crime. On the rocks where this happened can still be seen petroglyphs symbolizing these mythic events: a spiral marking the spot where he put the mouthpiece of the flute, as well as an impression of the girl's buttocks, spots of blood, and small holes where she urinated. This instrument produced a sad sound and smelled like the *bari* fruit, having the odor of the genitals of the Daughter of the Sun. This introduced flutes and their ceremonial playing to the Desana people. Afterward, some women observed where the men hid their flutes. After handling the flutes, the women's bodies suddenly grew hair on their pubis and armpits. When the men returned, the women seduced them, even though they belonged to the same family groups. Finally, order was restored after supernatural punishments took place. This myth illustrates how chaos ensues as a result of forbidden sexual acts, and how flutes are played as a reminder of these sins.

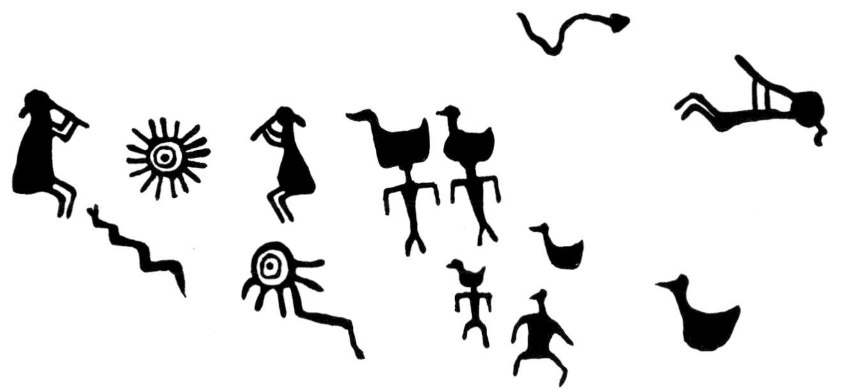

fig. 118. Anasazi petroglyphs of flute players with sun and snake symbols, Moss Back Butte, Utah (after photo by Morris Wolf).

The origins of the southwestern flute player are not known, but some believe the tradition may have come north from ancient Mexico or South America with itinerant traders carrying their goods in sacks (humps) on their backs. These southern traders, known as *pochtecas*, were from an Aztec merchant guild that operated at Casas Grandes (Sonora, Mexico) and throughout the Chihuahua Desert from about A.D. 1200 to 1400 and were at the nexus of relationships between the Southwest and ancient Mexico, helping to spread religious and cultural ideas. In addition to packs, these traders carried walking sticks or canes which they venerated. Canes and crook-necked staffs are portrayed in rock art of the Mogollon, Hohokam, and Anasazi peoples, and also figure prominently in modern Pueblo ceremonies as badges of office, prayer stick bundles, and altar pieces. In many contexts they symbolize fertility and long life (for further discussion of crook-necked staffs as fertility symbolism, see the section "Crook-Necked Staffs"). In the Andes of South America, medicine men still wander between villages with flutes and sacks of corn (Grant 1967, 60). The ancient flute player prototype may have been responsible for carrying maize to the American Southwest and introducing it to the local cultures. Such a prototype could have been Ek Chuah, a prehistoric Mayan deity who wears a backpack, carries a staff, and is patron of hunters, traveling merchants, and beekeepers (Miller 1975, 375).

In addition, the flute player figure has been interpreted as a rain priest who with his flute calls the clouds and melts the snow and warms up the earth when appealed to by the sun-loving snakes (fig. 118). He is often depicted with snakes in rock art scenes (fig. 119). The Flute Societies at Hopi play the flute over springs to bring rain. Further, gourds for carrying water are sometimes attached to the ends of the Hopi flutes; some rock art depictions show a bulbous shape at the end of the flute. In rock art the flute player is portrayed along with moisture-loving creatures such as toads, lizards, and insects. The Zunis claim this association attracts moisture to that locale. Moreover, the flute player figure has been associated with the locust, a patron of the Hopi Flute Societies, and with the gray desert-robber fly, which is known for its frequent mating (Parsons 1938, 337–38).

The flute player's fertility role extended to the animal world and ensured fecundity of game animals in particular. One scene in the lower Santa Fe River Canyon contains about twenty flute players depicting a ceremony, dance, or hunting scene in which a dozen figures carry bows rather than flutes. In rock art images elsewhere, the flute player is portrayed as an indeterminate creature, perhaps suggesting shamanistic activities whereby the shapes of various animal or spirit-helpers are assumed by the flute player as shaman (fig. 92). Among the lore of various Pueblo groups, the flute's magical power could transform creatures from one shape to another, such as a man to a butterfly or an ear of corn into a beautiful maiden (Tyler 1964, 83, 126, 143, 147; Cushing 1979, 360). Whatever label we may attach to this figure—deity, priest, shaman, medicine man, healer, or magician—the flute

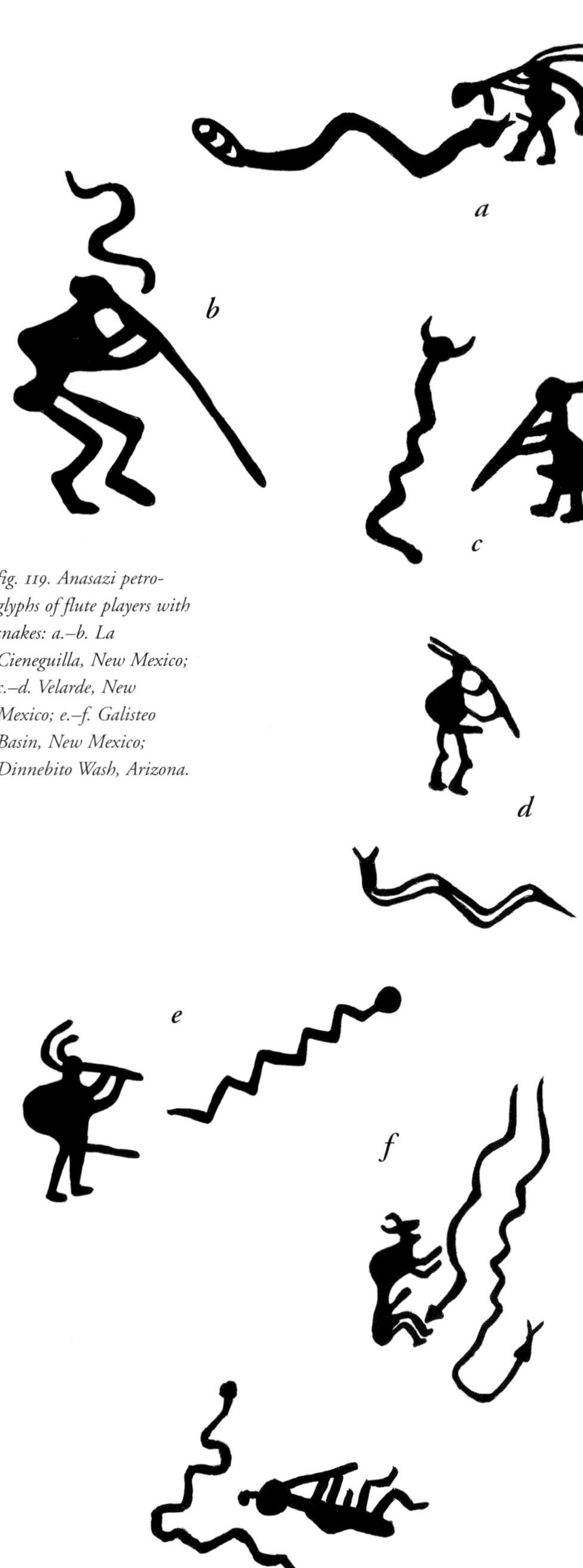

fig. 119. Anasazi petroglyphs of flute players with snakes: a.–b. La Cieneguilla, New Mexico; c.–d. Velarde, New Mexico; e.–f. Galisteo Basin, New Mexico; Dinnebito Wash, Arizona.

player's function was undoubtedly interrelated with creatures of the natural and supernatural worlds.

Further, the hump itself of such figures has various possible meanings. The humpbacked personage is widely associated with supernatural qualities in native myths and religions. The Mesoamerican god-kings Quetzalcoatl, Montezuma, and Xochiquetzal included humpbacks in their courts, where they provided religious consultation as well as entertainment. They were also in great demand as favored sacrificial subjects (Linne 1943, 170). Moreover, humpbacks appear in the architecture, sculpture, and ceramics of ancient Mesoamerica as individuals of apparent important social status.

In addition, the hump on the flute player's back can be interpreted as a burden basket, an object employed throughout northern Mexico and at Hopi, where it was secured by a forehead strap. The burden basket was typically used by women for mundane purposes, but it is also associated with many kachinas and mythic beings. At the Tewa village of Hano at Hopi, the flute player's hump was thought to be filled with buckskin for shirts and moccasins to barter for brides. The flute player depicted in fig. 120 is clearly a man carrying a pack on his back.

Some researchers contend that the flute player's hump is indicative of an individual suffering a spinal deformity such as that caused by Pott's disease (Wellman 1970, 1678–82). A type of tuberculosis, Pott's disease produces kyphosis, an exaggerated convexity of the spine. The existence of tuberculosis in prehistoric America has been demonstrated at a number of sites. Rock art scholars with medical backgrounds have examined paleopathological evidence along with the flute player's traits to suggest this theory. In some rock art portrayals, he also seems to possess a clubfoot and misshaped or paralyzed legs, and is shown lying on his back playing the flute. His erect phallus is further explained as priapism, another symptom of Pott's disease whereby spinal cord damage results in permanent engorgement of the penis. Since priapism

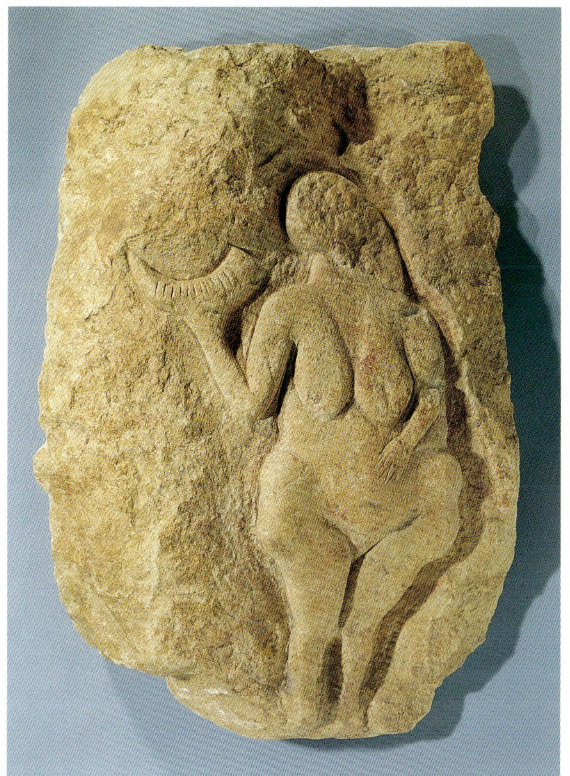

***Plate 1.** The Venus of Laussel, carved on a stone slab in a Paleolithic rock shelter near Laussel, France, dates to approximately 20,000 B.C. This female form may represent the Great Goddess—she holds a horn or crescent object with thirteen marks, the number of lunar cycles in a year. Her other hand seems to point to her womb, perhaps indicating awareness of the link between lunar cycles and female menstruation and fertility (with permission Musee d'Aquitaine de Bordeaux, France; photo: Jean-Michel Arnaud).*

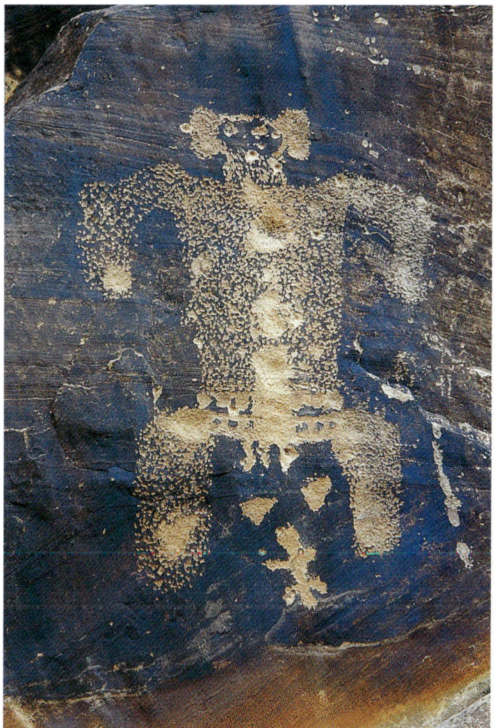

***Plate 2.** This petroglyph of a woman giving birth may have served as a fertility shrine. There are a number of abraded depressions in the body of this figure which may have resulted from repeated ritual activities. Perhaps the spirit within the rock at this locale was thus contacted by supplicants seeking fertility or easy delivery. At some fertility shrines, powder secured from abrading the rock was ingested by sterile women or used to make a paste that was placed on their abdomens in order to foster conception. Chevelon Creek, Arizona; photo by Clay Martin.*

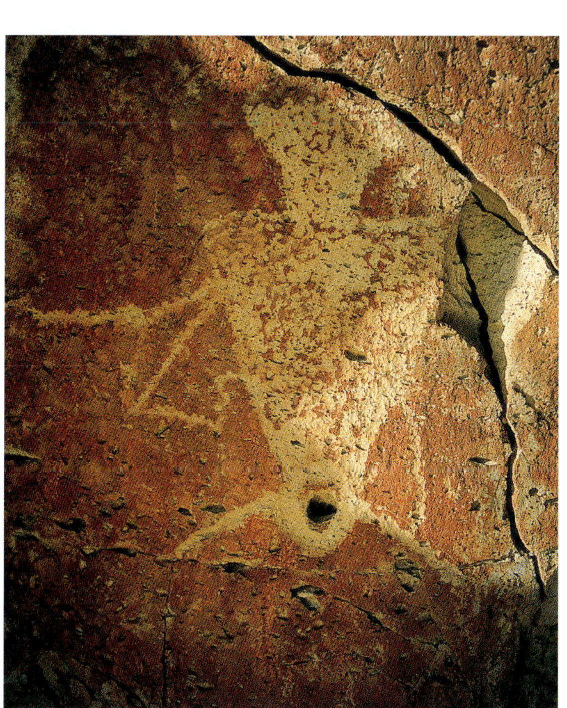

***Plate 3.** Rock art images pertaining to fertility or sexuality sometimes incorporate natural holes or crevices in the rock to suggest vulvas, as expressed in this Fremont petroglyph in Clear Creek Canyon, Utah.*

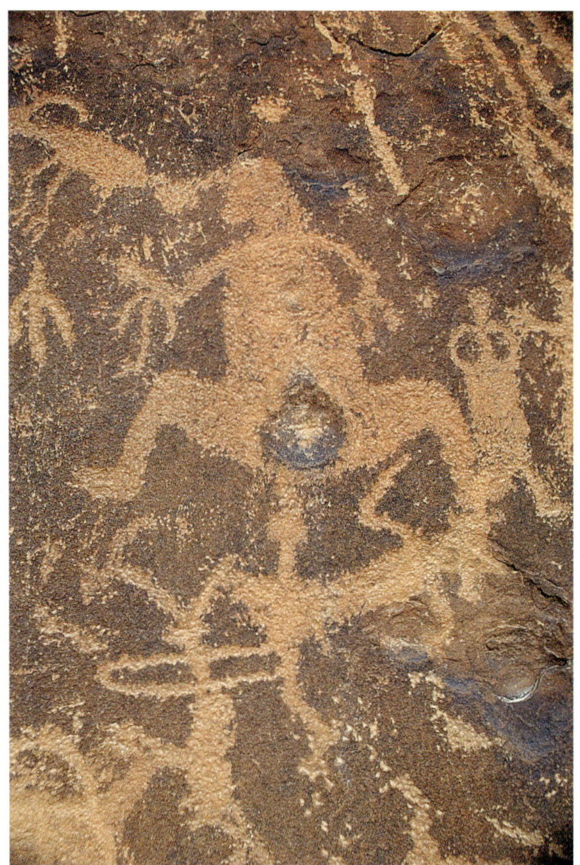

Plate 4. *Another example of the use of natural rock features to suggest wombs or vulvas is illustrated in this petroglyph depicting sexual intercourse. The female figure was made by incorporating a natural depression in the rock. This scene may represent the primal couple or creator deities who bring about creation, or perhaps a sacred marriage ceremony that reenacts creation of the world in their union—they are at the center of a large panel of images representing many creatures, all encompassed by an over-arching rainbow. Rochester Creek, Utah.*

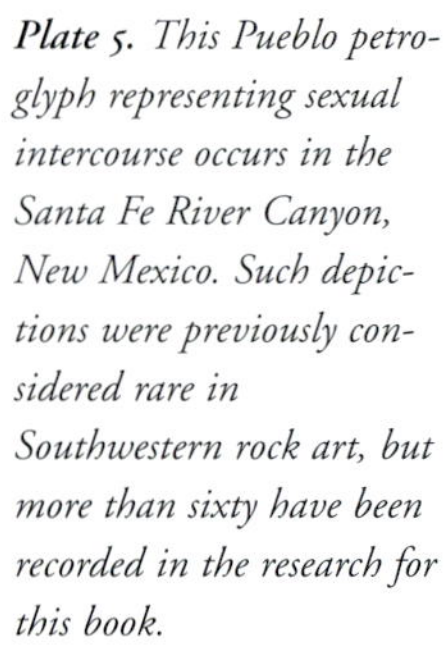

Plate 5. *This Pueblo petroglyph representing sexual intercourse occurs in the Santa Fe River Canyon, New Mexico. Such depictions were previously considered rare in Southwestern rock art, but more than sixty have been recorded in the research for this book.*

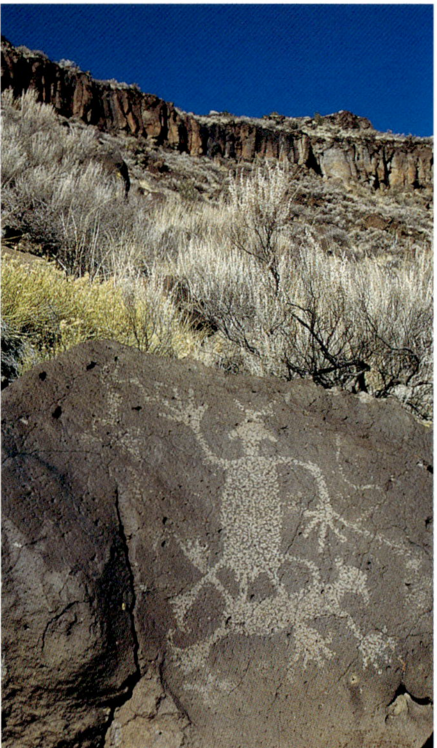

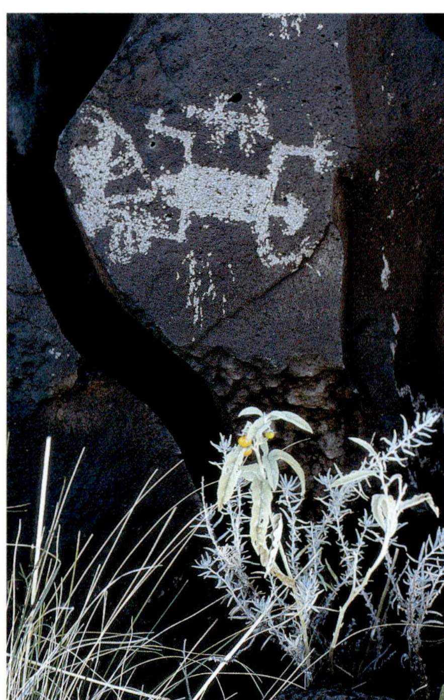

Plate 6. *The humpbacked flute player is a major fertility symbol in rock art of the Four Corners region and along the Rio Grande. Often portrayed as a wanton seducer, here he is shown copulating with a woman while playing his flute. La Cieneguilla, New Mexico.*

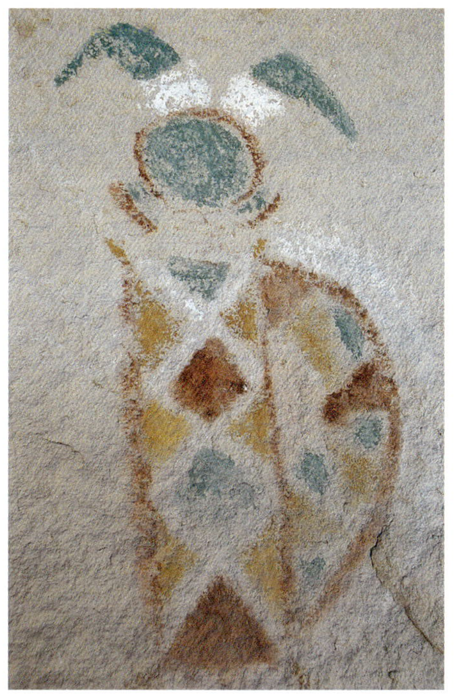

Plate 7. *A Navajo Ye'i (supernatural) who shares traits with the humpbacked flute player is known as Ghanaskidi. His hump contains mist and seeds of all the plants, thus representing concerns about the fecundity of vegetation. Largo Canyon, New Mexico.*

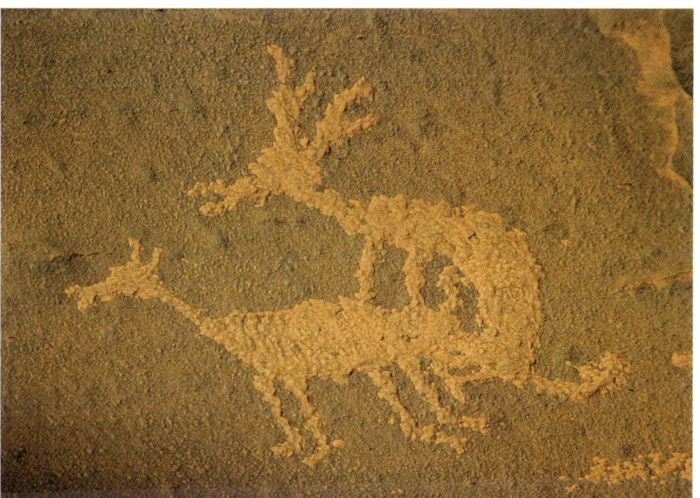

Plate 8. *In addition to concerns with human reproduction and the fruitfulness of plants, other fertility themes in rock art express a desire for abundant animals. In this petroglyph from Inscription Point, Arizona, two deer-like creatures are shown copulating. At this important fertility shrine are numerous depictions of copulating animals and humans, along with abundant serpents and other fertility symbols.*

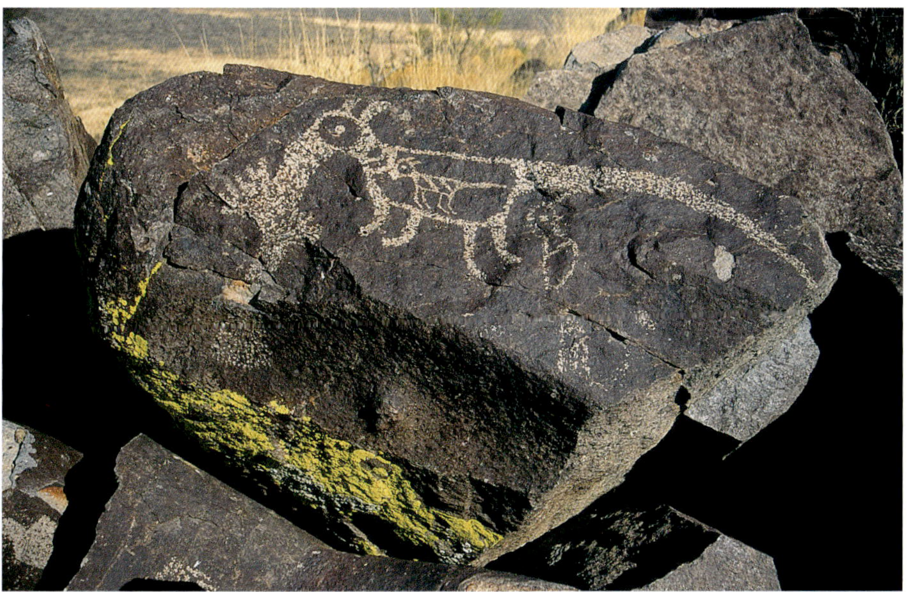

Plate 9. *Concern with fertility of animals is expressed in portrayal of pregnant creatures, such as in this Jornada Style petroglyph at Three Rivers, New Mexico.*

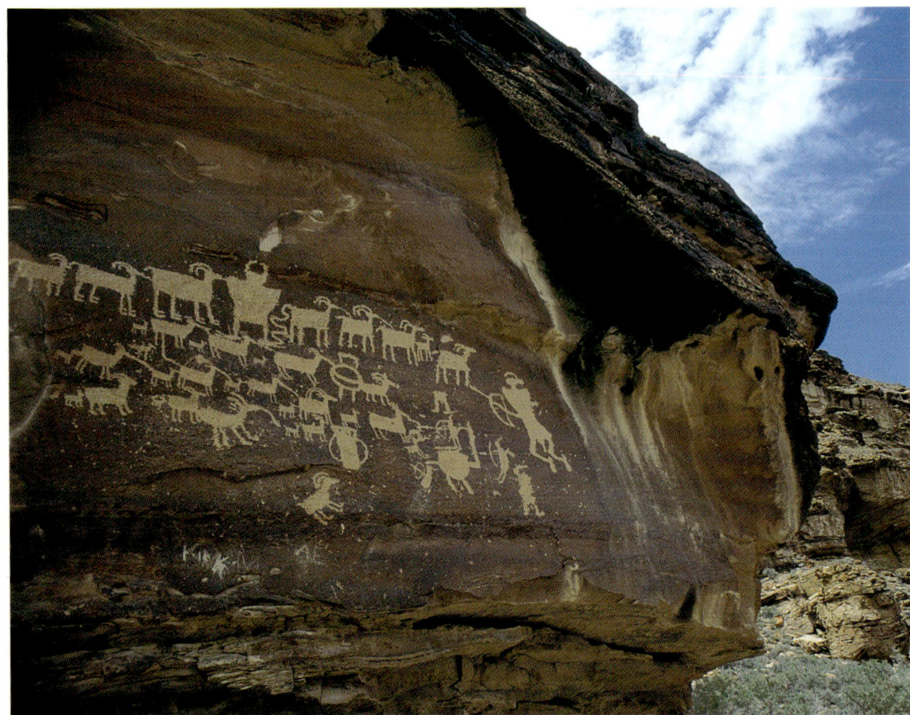

Plate 10. *Abundant game animals seems to be the theme in this Fremont petroglyph panel in Nine Mile Canyon, Utah. Several hunters with bows are present; the largest bow hunter is phallic, perhaps symbolizing the importance of fertility in the relationship between the hunter and the animals he kills.*

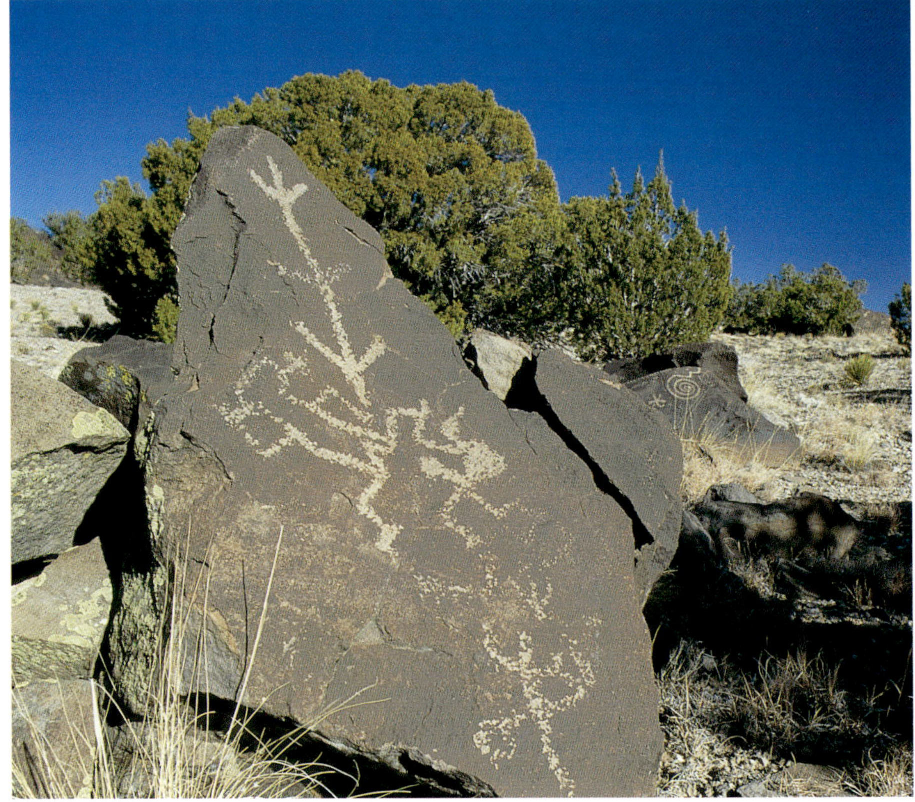

Plate 11. *A phallic, humpbacked figure appears to chase or sexually approach a female in this Pueblo petroglyph along the Rio Grande north of Espanola, New Mexico. This scene also includes a plant which may represent corn, and may be portraying a mythic Corn Maiden and the associated culture hero Payatamu—figures linked to fertility and abundance in many Pueblo stories.*

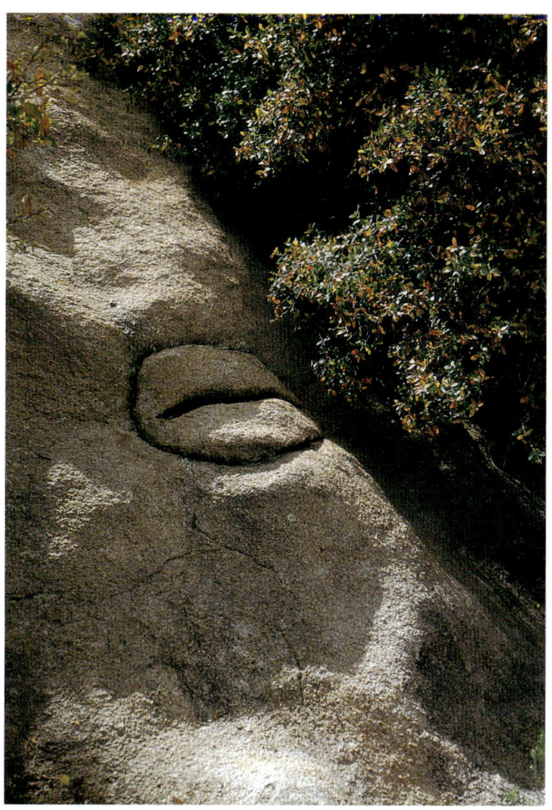

Plate 12. *A large vulva symbol, or yoni formation, occurs on a boulder near some bedrock mortars in the Dos Cabezas Mountains, Arizona. Features like this sometimes have natural origins but in many cases have been enhanced by grinding or pecking to even more closely resemble vulvas and to represent the earth's womb and generative power.*

Plate 13. *The largest yoni formations and vulva symbols are found on granite boulders in southern California's Anza-Borrego Desert. These striking symbols can be several feet in diameter, and were used in ancient fertility rituals such as girls' puberty initiations by the Kumeyaay and Luiseno peoples who inhabited the area.*

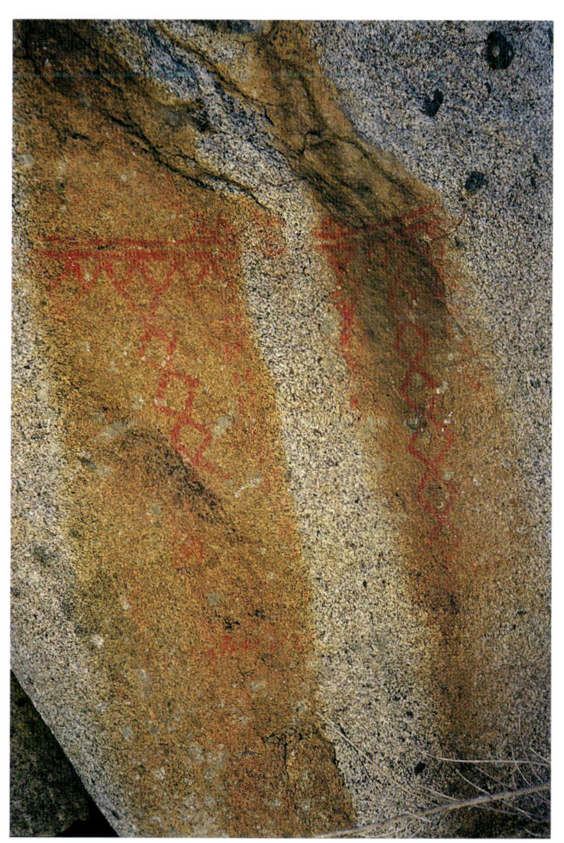

Plate 14. *Among certain tribes in southern California, girls made red pictographs of diamond-chain designs as part of their puberty rites. This motif symbolizes the rattlesnake—women's guardian spirit. Although somewhat faded, these pictographs are painted on naturally occurring reddish stains of iron oxide which streak the rock surface and which may have been perceived as representing menstrual blood and female fertility. Mockingbird Canyon, Riverside, California.*

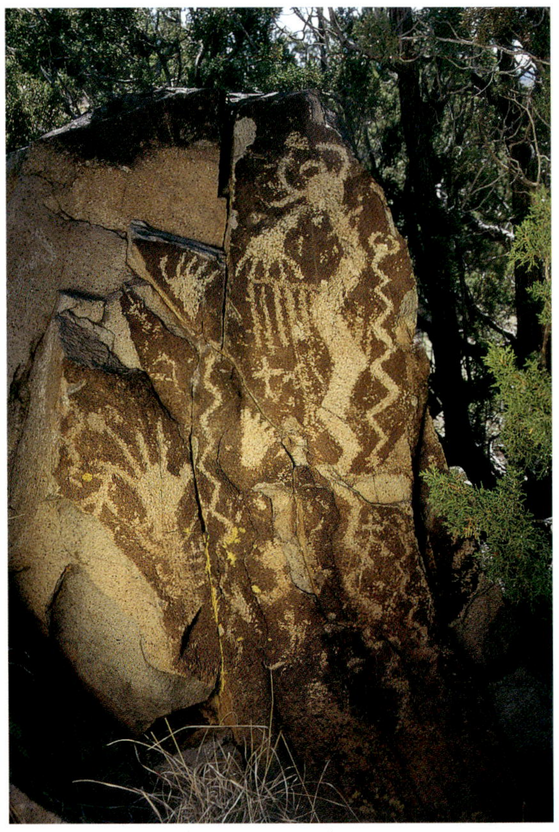

Plate 15. *Snakes are one of the most prevalent images associated with fertility symbolism in Southwestern rock art as well as world-wide. In a large area of the Southwest, the Horned Water Serpent is a powerful supernatural being connected with subterranean water and fertility. Galisteo Basin, New Mexico.*

Plate 16. *Colorful yarn paintings by Mexico's Huichol Indians sometimes contain fertility symbolism similar to rock art images, such as this depiction of Tacutsi, Goddess of Life, who gives birth to every living thing and is another example of the Great Mother archetype (yarn painting by Jacinta Lopez, courtesy of Alan and Mary Wreyford, Line Camp Gallery, Pojoaque, New Mexico).*

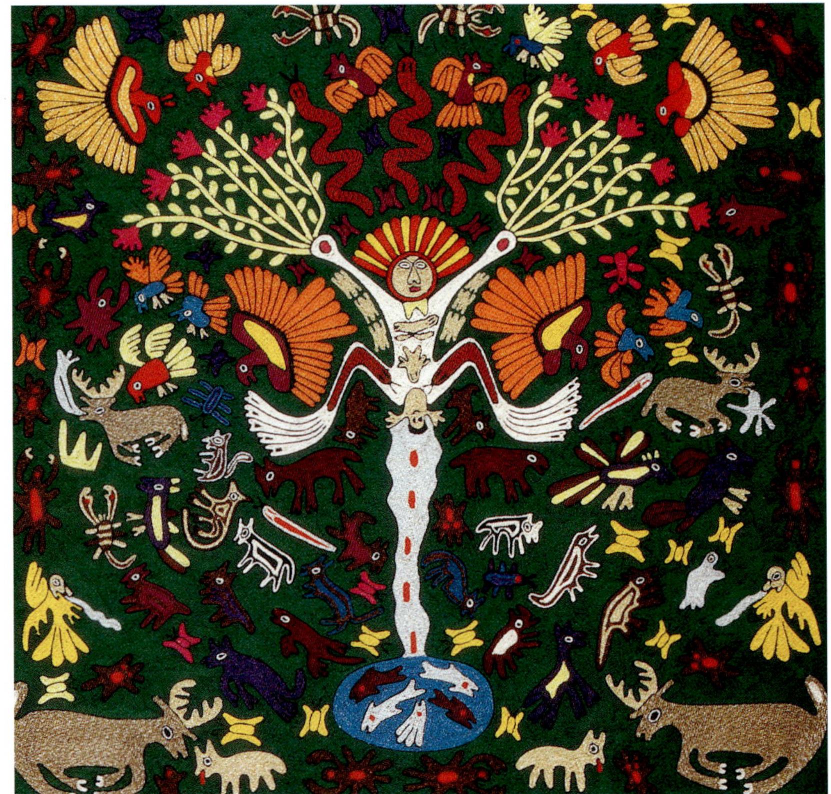

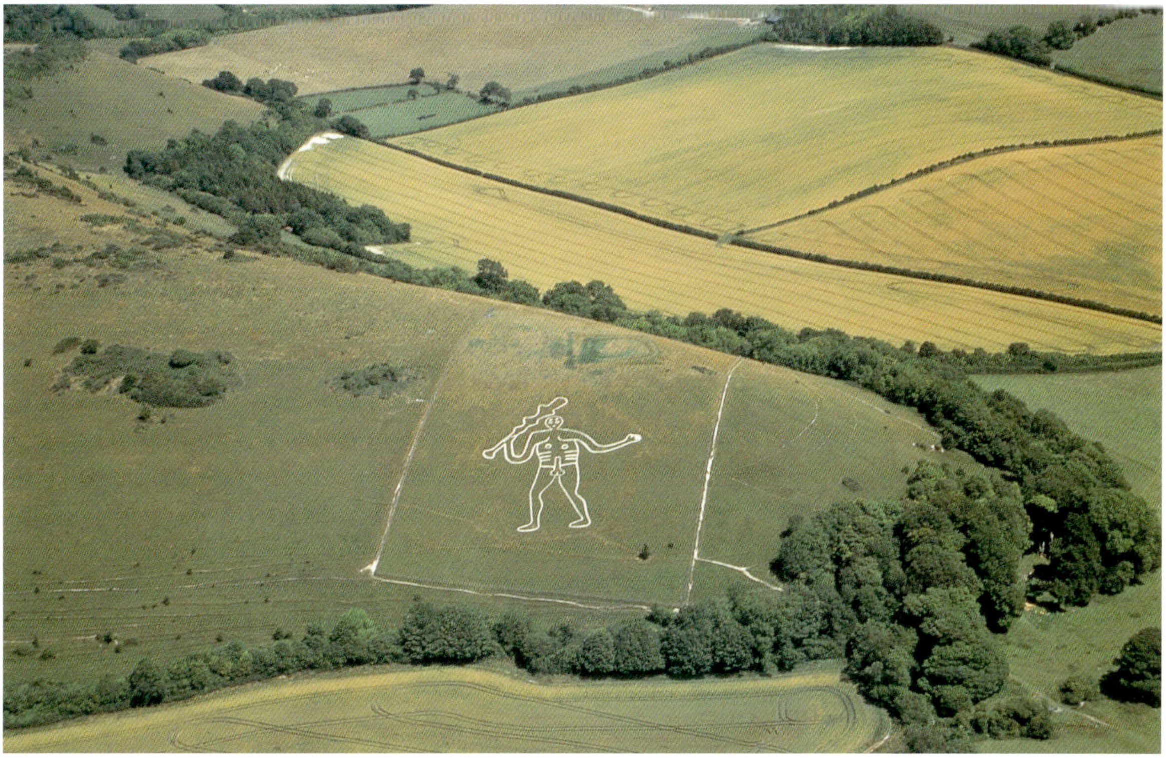

Plate 17. *Geoglyphs are large-scale examples of rock art images created on the earth's surface, and can also exhibit fertility themes. The Cerne Abbas Giant pictured here in an aerial view, is a 150-foot-long figure of a phallic man carved in chalk on a hillside in Dorset County, England. This ancient fertility symbol has long served a prominent role in local folk ritual; women desiring to get pregnant would spend the night sleeping on the giant's penis (courtesy S. P. Wallis and Dorset County Council Archaeology Service).*

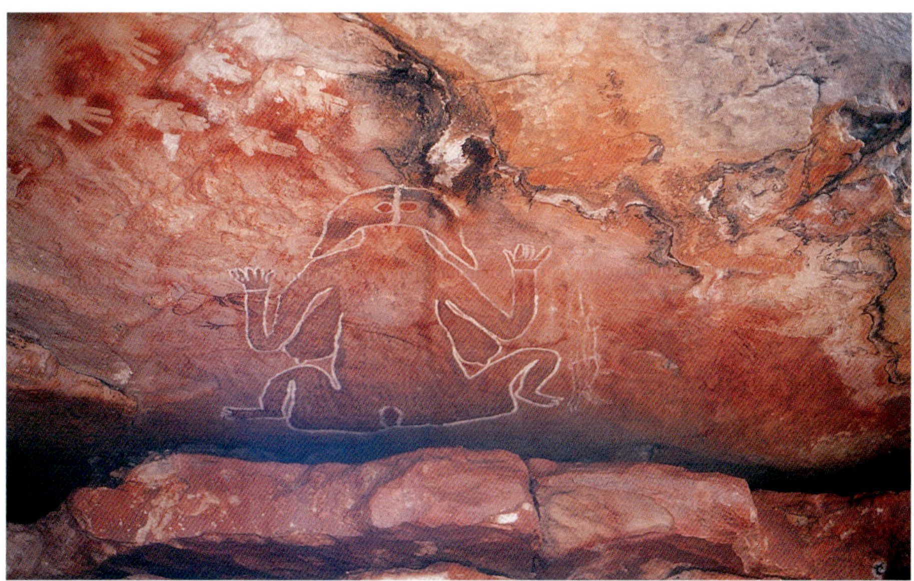

Plate 18. *Rock art on all continents contains themes of fertility and sexuality, as illustrated by this Aboriginal pictograph from Australia. This female figure with pendulous breasts and vulva is shown in a typical birth-giving position, and is painted in a rock shelter near an important water hole (Manyallaluk, Arnhem Land, Australia; photo by Burt Alpert).*

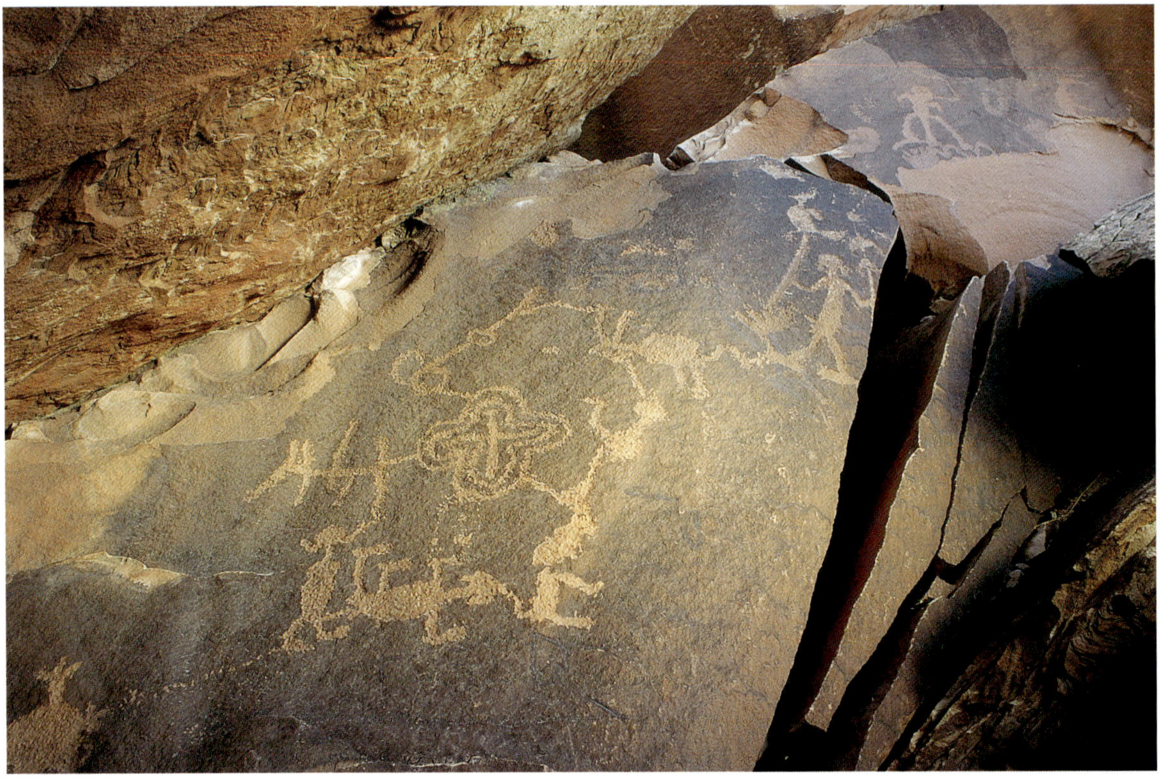

Plate 19. *The Cave of Life, a probable Anasazi fertility shrine, contains images including a couple having sexual intercourse (likely ritual coitus related to the Sacred Marriage Ceremony); a presiding, phallic, priest-like figure holding a staff; an enclosed cross which may have functioned as a solar calendrical marker for denoting seasonal ritual times; and other symbols (Petrified Forest National Park, Arizona; photo by Ekkerhart Malotki).*

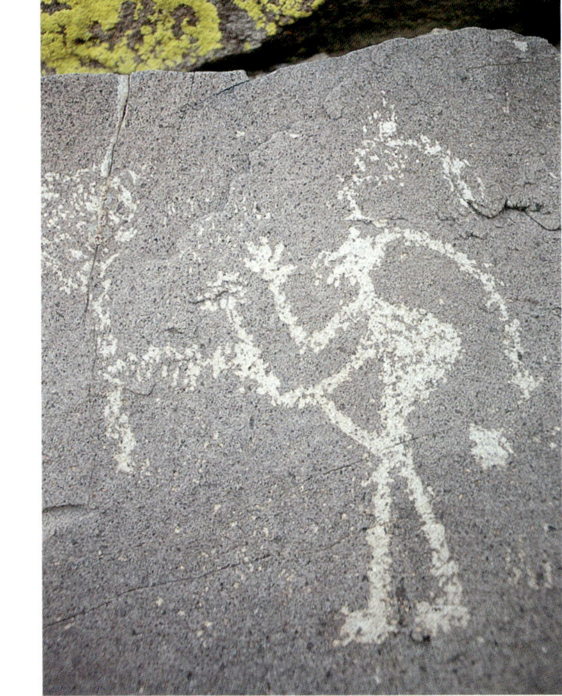

Plate 20. *Phallic, humpbacked figures are important fertility symbols throughout a large area of the Southwest. Usually depicted playing a flute, the humped back and emphatically erect penis are characteristics associated with great fertility and sexual potency in rock art images throughout the upper Rio Grande and Four Corners region. Galisteo Basin, New Mexico.*

creates the appearance of sexual prowess and supports the legendary connection with a fertility role, it is plausible that such individuals could have been considered special.

There are several characters related to the flute player figure in the iconography of groups such as the Hohokam, Navajo, and Mogollon people. Common among the design motifs of Hohokam ceramics are flute players and figures carrying burden baskets on their backs. The exact relationship between Hohokam flute players and those of the Anasazi is unclear, but some researchers postulate that the theme was diffused from Mexican origins to the Hohokam people and eventually to the Anasazi by the Pueblo I Period—about A.D. 700 (Haury 1976, 239). The theme apparently no longer existed among the Hohokam Indians by A.D. 1200.

Ghanaskidi (Ghaan'ask'idii, or Ya ackidi) is a humpbacked Navajo god, or Ye'i, of harvest, abundance, and mist (Reichard 1950, 443). He wears horns, carries a staff, and often has a humpback from which feathers radiate (fig. 121). The hump is said to be made of a rainbow and contain mist or clouds and seeds of all kinds.

In the Mogollon culture region, related forms consist of humpbacked and sometimes phallic figures in rock art and ceramics, but none are playing flutes. An interesting feature of some of these depictions is the crook-necked staff which is held. While some staffs probably represent ceremonial objects or symbols of rank similar to the scepter, the crook-necked staff is thought to have fertility connotations and may sometimes represent a planting stick.

In Pueblo myths, the flute player carries in his hump seeds, babies, and blankets to offer maidens he seduces. In the upper Rio Grande pueblos, he wanders between villages with a bag of songs on his back. As a fertility symbol he was welcome during corn-planting season, and was sought after by barren wives while avoided by shy maidens. Examples of flute players associated with females—some pregnant or giving birth—are shown in fig. 122.

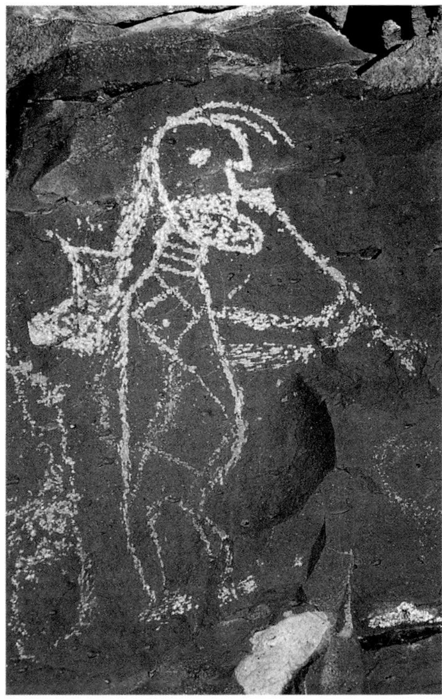

fig. 120. Pueblo petroglyph of an anthropomorphic flute player carrying a pack on his back, Caja del Rio, New Mexico.

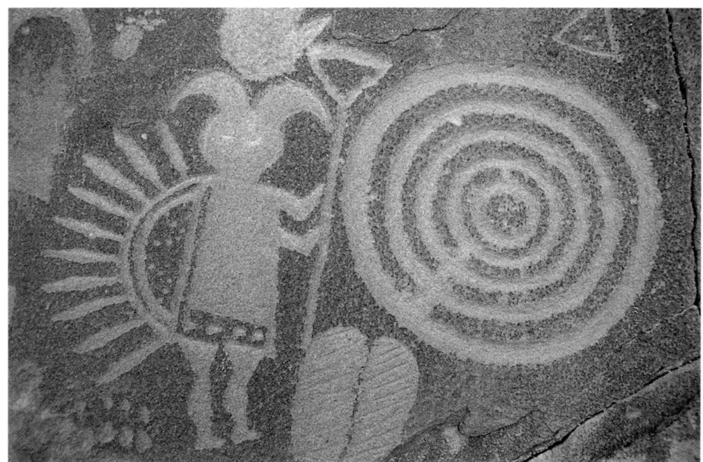

fig. 121.(above) Navajo petroglyph of a humpbacked Ye'i known as Ghanaskidi, Crow Canyon, New Mexico.

As a Hopi kachina, Kokopelli varies somewhat in appearance between villages. However, he is always concerned with increase and fertility among people, animals, and plants. His rainmaking ensures good crops of corn and other food. When he appears in dances, usually in the spring, he wears a black mask with a white stripe, has a long snout, and is erotic (Hawley 1937, 644–46). At dances in the past, he displayed his genitals, but this

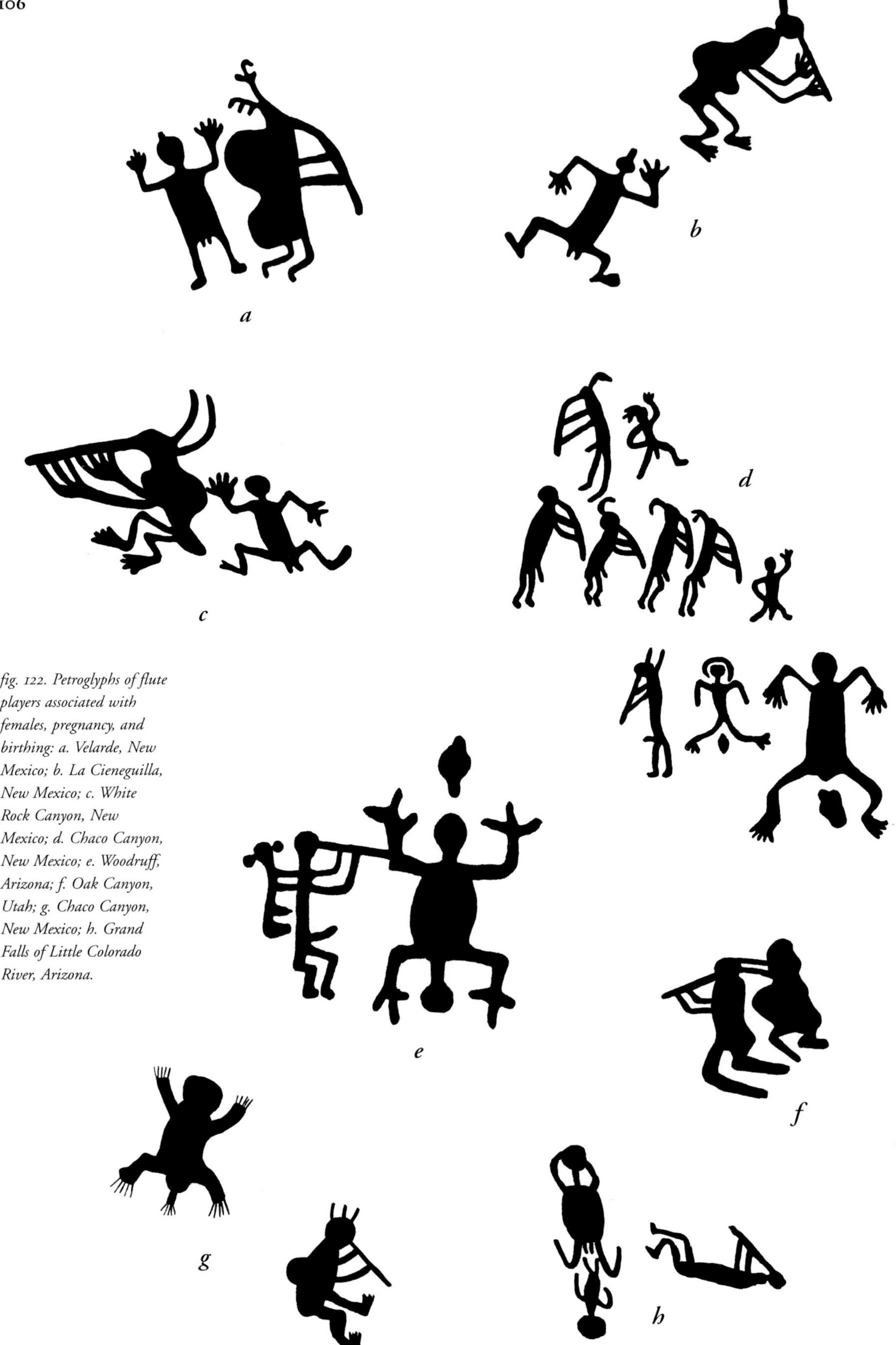

fig. 122. Petroglyphs of flute players associated with females, pregnancy, and birthing: a. Velarde, New Mexico; b. La Cieneguilla, New Mexico; c. White Rock Canyon, New Mexico; d. Chaco Canyon, New Mexico; e. Woodruff, Arizona; f. Oak Canyon, Utah; g. Chaco Canyon, New Mexico; h. Grand Falls of Little Colorado River, Arizona.

evolved into a costume featuring an exaggerated false penis constructed from a gourd (this may be represented in the image from Petroglyph National Monument, New Mexico, shown in fig. 17). He carries no flute, but it is believed his long snout represents a nose whistle. He has a humped back or wears a bag on his back and may carry a stick and rattle. His habit of chasing females, simulating copulation, and "humping" spectators was frowned upon as obscene by early anthropologists, tourists, and priests, but the Hopis do not view his behavior as lewd. Kokopelli used to figure more prominently in Hopi dances but is seen infrequently now, apparently having been suppressed for his ribald routine. An observer in 1939 commented, "The antics of the performers were lewd and obscene, and notoriously obnoxious to prudish white observers" (Titiev 1939, 91–98). The following is a description of a Kokopelli kachina dance in a kiva at Hopi in 1934:

> There were six Kokopele dancers. They wore dark gray masks, and suits of long underwear with a woman's belt tied at the back. Every performer had a hump fixed on his shoulders, and a large red "penis" (of gourd?) strapped in position over the underwear. Each dancer carried a rattle in one hand and held his "penis" with the other throughout the performance. As they entered the kiva the kachinas lunged at the spectators, particularly at the women. They sang and danced facing the audience, advancing in unison occasionally and singing a slow song. The spectators laughed hilariously. Afterwards a Hopi man told Dr. Eggan one should be friends with the Kokopele as they were the ones who sent babies (Titiev 1939, 95).

Hopi kachinas are sometimes represented in both male and female forms with the female counterpart to Kokopelli called Kokopelmana. The role is played by strong runners who chase male spectators and simulate copulation with those who are caught. The following is a description of Kokopelmana at a 1934 Hopi ceremonial:

> Kokopelmana . . . appeared barefooted and barelegged, wearing a ragged manta, a shabby ata'u (small ceremonial blanket worn by women), and a mask comparable to that of Kokopeltiyo. As soon as this impersonator emerged from the kiva, all the men and boys in the vicinity began to scatter. At first the Kokopelmana merely feinted running after them, but suddenly "she" caught up with an unwary man, raised him high in "her" arms and pretended to copulate with him from behind. This done, "she" released him and handed him a few packets of somiviki (cornmeal cakes). From then on "she" ran far and wide in quest of "lovers," pretended to lure men out of their houses, and argued in vigorous pantomime with all women and girls who tried to keep men away from "her" . . . the Oraibi people said that a man was "spoiled" (that is, rendered undesirable to other girls) if the Kokopelmana "got into him" (Titiev 1939, 96).

Certain Zuni kachinas have similarities to the Hopi Kokopelli kachina and the humpbacked flute players depicted in rock art of the Zuni area. Payatamu is a flute-playing culture hero who, although not humpbacked, is, like Kokopelli, associated with fertility and rain. The Owiwi kachina is described by the Zunis as humpbacked or carrying a pack of fetishes on his back. In Zuni culture, there is also a phallic kachina without a hump, known as Ololowishkya. He is the central figure in a ceremony with flute playing and corn grinding by men dressed as women. This ceremony has been described as follows by contemporary Zunis:

> It's embarrassing, but it was for religious doings. Some males dressed like females and stretched out with grinding stones. There were flute players and rain dancers.

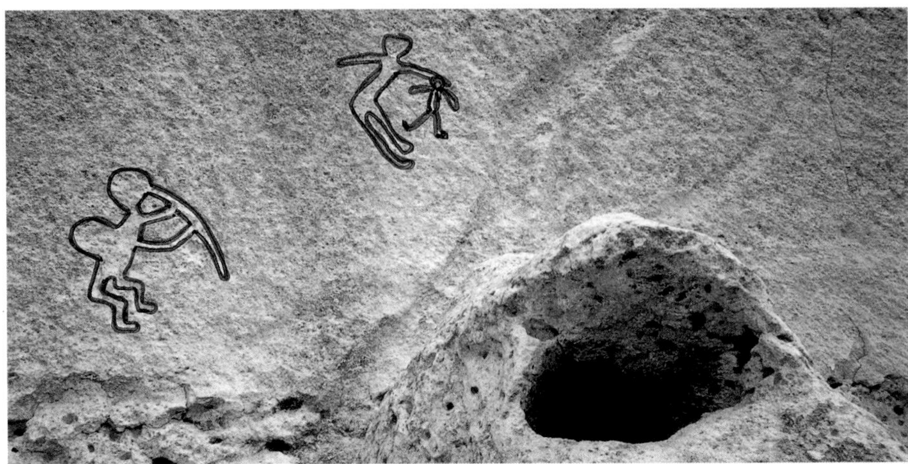

fig. 123. Pueblo petroglyphs associating fertility and birth with a natural womb-like rock feature (images enhanced on photograph), Pajarito Plateau, Los Alamos, New Mexico.

> Ololowishkya had a dingaling made out of a gourd. He peed a sweet syrup into a big pot that had sweet corn in it. He peed to the directions of the earth six times. He made balls of the juice and corn and gave it to everyone. It tasted good. This ceremony was done so there wouldn't be any problem with men's urine. We don't do this now because white people watch (Young 1988, 142).

Another association between Zuni and Hopi religious figures is suggested by the form Kokopelli takes at the Hopi village of Hano, where he appears as the big black man Nepokwa'i who carries a buckskin bag on his back. Even the kachina dolls of this figure are painted black. Nepokwa'i may be based on the Negro Esteban who accompanied Marcos de Niza's 1539 expedition and was stoned to death for molesting women at Zuni. The Tewa people of Hano had lived with the Zunis prior to settling in the Hopi region.

In his many guises, the flute player figure has been seen as a southwestern manifestation of the universal trickster archetype. In this role he shares traits with many characters from other Native American regions: Wakdjunkaga and Hare, the buffoon and culture hero of the Winnebago tribe, Wisaka of the Fox Indians, Sitconski of the Assiniboines, Ishtinike of the Poncas, Nixant of the Gros Ventres, Iktomi (Spider) of the Oglala-Sioux, Nanabozho or Glooscap of the Algonkians, and Raven of the Northwest coast tribes (Wellman 1974, 6). Tricksters are transformers and appear in animal disguise (Raven, Coyote, Hare, Spider). Similarly, the humpbacked flute player has been depicted in rock art of the Southwest in the form of various creatures.

A comparison of Kokopelli with the Winnebago trickster Wakdjunkaga, for example, illustrates many parallels (Wellman 1974a, 6). Both are notorious for their sexuality, as symbolized in each by a large phallus. Wakdjunkaga seduces the chief's daughter, and Kokopelli cleverly impregnates the most sought after girl in the village. Wakdjunkaga carries his penis coiled up in a box on his back, whereas Kokopelli (and Ghanaskidi) carries seeds in his hump. In some accounts both characters are said to carry songs in their backpacks. Further, Wakdjunkaga can change into a woman, while the Kokopelli kachina has the female counterpart Kokopelmana.

In addition to the numerous variations of such figures among North American Indian tribes, they have similarities to other such figures in world mythology. Scholars, including Carl Jung, have compared the North American Indian trickster to manifestations elsewhere in the world, and the southwestern humpbacked flute player is perhaps also related to other musical fertility figures such as Pan and Orpheus. Such archetypes survive from the early stages of human consciousness and may predate the shaman. One scholar states that Kokopelli "may be compared with the universal Trickster archetype, who, in spite of his unrestrained sexuality, in his roles as hunting magician and rain priest changes from an unprincipled amoral force into a creator who brings order and security into the chaos of the world" (Wellman 1974a, 6).

OTHER SYMBOLS OF SEX AND FERTILITY

As seen in the preceding discussion, fertility symbolism in rock art is diverse and interconnected. The following explores some of the many other ways fertility has been represented, including such symbols as snakes, cloud terraces, dragonflies and butterflies, heads and scalps, crook-necked staffs, spirals, lobed circles, blanket scenes, turtles, hummingbirds, and enclosed crosses as well as symbolism of landscape features associated with rock art.

Rock Art Site Symbolism

Because caves and rock fissures can be symbolic of earth wombs or vulvas, the placement of rock art elements near such features can have implicit meaning in terms of fertility or sexuality (fig. 123). For example, images of certain animals such as snakes and lizards are sometimes created near cracks or holes in rock because these creatures have access to the underworld and serve as spirit messengers between worlds. It is possible that such rock features could also sometimes represent the *sipapu*—the place of emergence in mythical times, described as follows: "The traditional opening through which, in ancient times, the people came to the earth's surface, and is associated in the Indian mind with that opening through which individuals as well as races are born" (Jesse Fewkes, quoted in Laeberlin 1916).

The idea of a hole in the earth as a pathway of spirits probably originated with shamanic concepts and is often embodied in religious architecture. Yakut shamans in Siberia could descend to the underworld to visit the spirits through a symbolic opening in the earth. Even the Delphic Oracle of ancient Greece, in the innermost recess of the temple of Apollo, was located above a cave in which a sacred spring flowed and to which the prophetess would listen for spirit messages from the underworld. Such a rock crevice with flowing underground water occurs at a major petroglyph site on the Canadian Shield that has abundant fertility symbolism incorporating vulva-like features of the rock (see the Peterborough, Ontario, petroglyph site described in Chapter 5.) The idea that underground water sources such as springs, caves, and wells have a fertility connection is also present in many archaic religions of Europe, where they were perceived as female symbols and considered passages to the underground womb. In northern Europe they were associated with Mother Hel, whose name gave rise to "healing" and "holy" (Walker 1983, 1067). The sacred springs of pagans thus represented Mother Hel's water-womb, the source of all children.

Similarly, features such as bedrock mortars can represent fertility as symbolic vaginas (fig. 124; Whitley 1994, 22–24). Further, in some cultures of the Far West, such as the Yokuts, Northern Paiute, and Shoshone, bedrock mortars were said to have originated in mythic times when Coyote had intercourse with a rock (Whitley 1994, 22). Some ceremonial pestles were exaggeratedly phallic, and in one myth such a pestle was used by Coyote's aunt for masturbation. The symbolism seems clear—pestle represents penis, while mortar represents vagina. Moreover, ritual intercourse with the rock also has shamanic overtones as a metaphor for the shaman's entrance into an altered state of consciousness as he goes into a trance. An analogy is perhaps the ritual use of sites known as Baby Rocks by Pomo women in California, who would grind small cupules into the rocks and insert the *fig. 124. (left) Bedrock mortars as symbolic vulvas in the vulva-like entrance to a cave, Council Rock, Dragoon Mountains, Arizona.*

fig. 125. (right) Sharpening grooves for stone hoes associated with Faces Anthropomorphic Style pictographs at a site which was probably used for crop fertility rites, Davis Canyon, Utah.

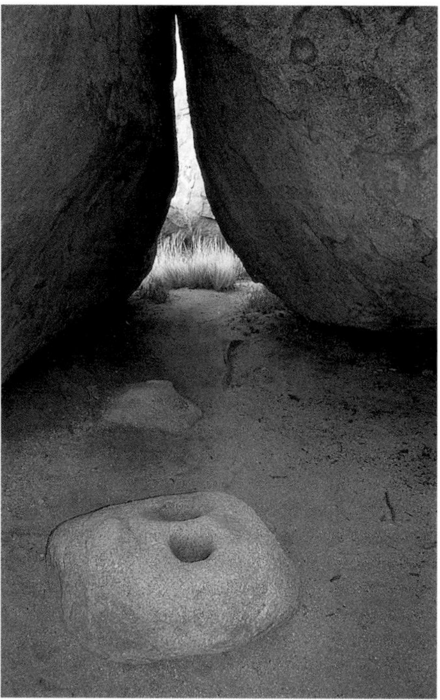

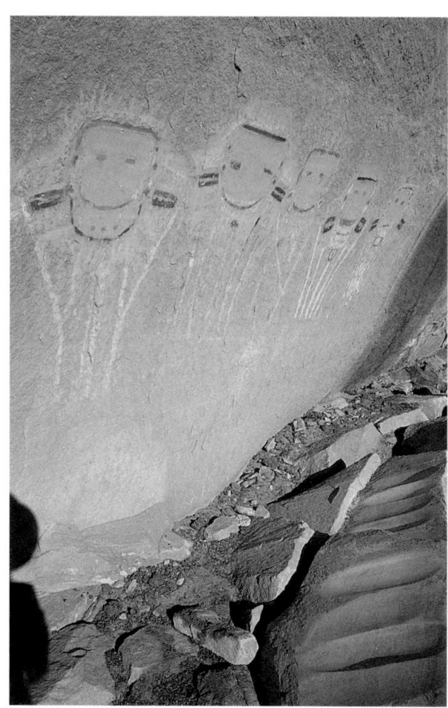

resulting powder into their vaginas as a means of empowering conception—thus having ritual intercourse with a rock.

Another rock feature that has been linked to fertility rituals at some rock art sites is grooves or abraded depressions (such as cupules) that have been ground into the rock surface. In the canyons of southeastern Utah, such features are commonly associated with the unusual Faces Motif Style of Anasazi origin (fig. 125). Thought to be places where stone hoes, or *tcamahias*, were sharpened, these grooves and the accompanying rock art figures are usually found near prehistoric farmlands and granaries and may have been used as part of crop fertility rituals (Noxon and Marcus 1985, 51–52). Moreover, the Faces Motif Style anthropomorphs resemble elaborate clay figurines recovered from sites in the area. It has been speculated that such figurines were connected with human and agricultural increase cults, and that the Faces Motif Style figures may therefore represent related, costumed male figures involved with crop fertility rituals.

Since some rock art sites can perhaps be seen as entrances to the supernatural, features of the rock itself—such as caves, pits, or fissures—are the most significant symbols of such sites and the rituals with which they are associated. The fact that shamans were said to enter the rock at these sites during their trance supports the interpretation of some sites as symbolic earth vaginas that shamans penetrated when they went into the supernatural realm. In Chemehuevi lore, the shaman knocked on the rock with his *poro* (ritual staff), breaking it open and allowing the earth vagina to release its life and fecundity (Laird 1976, 159).

In summary, far western sexual symbolism is typically more related to the site itself than to particular symbols in the rock art. The sites sometimes have an inherent sexual symbolism related to the shaman's altered state of consciousness or to obvious physical characteristics of the site.

Snakes

Images of snakes are one of the most common rock art symbols, and are especially linked to concepts of fertility and sexuality. In addition to the Horned

Water Serpent deity described previously, the Pueblos as well as most other southwestern groups attributed supernatural powers to snakes. Images of snakes are ancient symbols in these cultures, as well as worldwide. By the dawn of history, the snake was widely worshiped as a supernatural power, and had become a profound symbol in mythology. The universality of this symbol is reflected in diverse manifestations in mythology, art, and religion. The snake cult is probably one of man's earliest—serpentine depictions in European caves appear in the Paleolithic period 20,000 to 30,000 years ago.

The snake has been a major symbol of fertility, as well as health, longevity, immortality, wisdom, and power; it embodies the life force and is associated with water, fertility, regeneration, and procreation. Paradoxically, in some cultures it has also represented such qualities as evil, sin, death, disease, duplicity, and temptation.

The profound role this symbol has played in global mythology, religion, and psychology has been explored in detail by many.[35] For example, the significance of the snake in archaeomythology has been eloquently described by noted scholars Marija Gimbutas and Joseph Campbell:

> The snake is life force, a seminal symbol, epitome of the worship of life on this earth. It is not the body of the snake that was sacred, but the energy exuded by this spiraling or coiling creature which transcends its boundaries and influences the surrounding world. The same energy is in spirals, vines, growing trees, phalluses, and stalagmites, but it is especially concentrated in the snake, and therefore more powerful. The snake was something more primordial and mysterious, coming from the depths of the waters where life begins. Its seasonal renewal in sloughing off its old skin and hibernating made it a symbol of the continuity of life and of the link with the underworld (Gimbutas 1989, 121).
>
> The prominence of the serpent [in mythology] . . . is a mystery of profound psychological and sociological import. Repeatedly shedding its skin to be born again, the serpent—like the moon that sheds its shadow in rebirth—typifies life-energy and consciousness locked within temporal space, delivering and suffering births and deaths. Fluent in movement as the waters flowing over and fertilizing the earth, yet with their fiery forked tongues flashing tirelessly as lightning from a storm-laden sky, serpents appear to incarnate the elementary mystery of life, wherein apparent opposites are conjoined (Campbell 1989 II (3), 254).

Every mythology has some form of Great Serpent. From the Bible's serpent in the Garden of Eden to the Hermetic or Gnostic serpent encircling the World Egg he was a basic Indo-European religious symbol. Although it is beyond the scope of this discussion to review the extensive body of knowledge pertaining to snakes and human societies, a discussion of some of the more interesting aspects of this association follows.

Snake worship and symbolism were very prominent in the religions of early Old World civilizations and the culture area known as the Fertile Crescent, the region along the Euphrates River in the eastern Mediterranean. In this ancient realm, the serpent was originally identified with the Great Goddess. In some myths, the male serpent deity became the consort of the Great Goddess, fertilizing her and helping create the world. Perhaps a similar concept is represented in the petroglyph image from New Mexico that seems to depict a female being penetrated by—or giving birth to—a serpent (fig. 126). There are even myths and beliefs that explain the phenomenon of menstruation as being the result of copulation with a supernatural snake. Ancient Persian religious beliefs incorporated the common

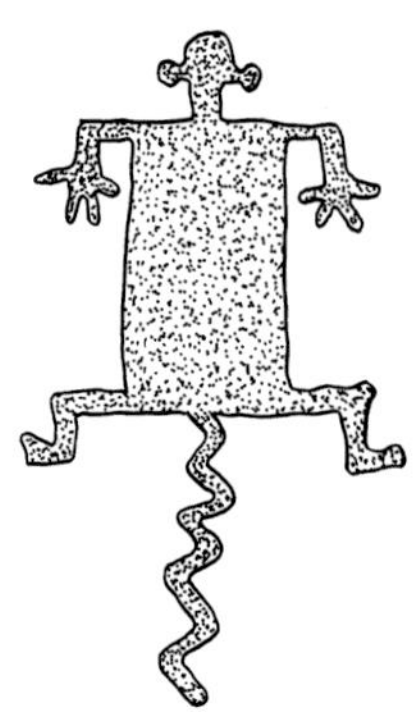

fig. 126. Petroglyph depicting a female and snake-like symbol, Galisteo Basin, New Mexico.

primitive idea that a woman's first menstruation was caused by copulation with a supernatural snake. Ritual vessels used in Minoan Crete resembled a vagina with a snake crawling inside. According to early rabbinical tradition Eve's menstruation began after copulating with the serpent in Eden, and her firstborn son, Cain, was begotten by the serpent, not Adam. Beliefs associating snakes with pregnancy and menstruation continued into modern times; until recently peasant folklore in European countries still held that women could be impregnated by snakes (Walker 1983, 642).

Further, immortality was implied in the union of the skin-shedding serpent and the Goddess. In ancient traditions, the Great Serpent was sometimes identified with the earth's intestines, and it has also been suggested that the association of serpents with the Great Goddess may be derived from the resemblance of the umbilical cord to intertwined serpents. According to the Vedas, the snake was the phallic god who stirred the uterine abyss at creation. The serpent was also kundalini—the inner female soul of humans in serpent shape, coiled in the pelvis and induced through yoga techniques to climb the spinal chakras toward the head for achieving enlightenment. Both India and Egypt portrayed the first serpent as totemic forms of the Great Goddess. Egyptian queens, including Cleopatra, were called "Serpent of the Nile"; they represented the Goddess embracing the king. Egyptians connected the snake with fecundity and the Nile on which their whole economy depended—for them the snake was also closely associated with the daily death and rebirth of the sun.

The use of snake symbolism in religion was also conspicuous in ancient Mesopotamia. The Babylonians worshiped the generative forces of nature by symbolizing the earth's fertility as a snake. In Assyria, the great Mother Goddess Ishtar, queen of sexual love, was characterized by a snake symbol. Like the Nile in Egypt, the Euphrates River in Mesopotamia was called the river of the snake, and its fertilizing waters were imagined as a male serpent.

Snakes were very sacred creatures to the Greeks and Romans as well. As the spirit of life and reincarnation, the snake stood for the perennial renewal of life through death. Romans had snake guardians, who were fed and encouraged to reside in the house. This cult of the household snake became widespread in Europe, especially the Slav countries, where snakes were virtually household gods and were not to be killed under any circumstances. The primitive gods of Greece were various snake deities—even the precursor of Zeus. Ancient fertility festivals were still practiced in classical Greece, where snakes were part of sacred rituals. In a ceremony to promote fertility of women and crops, sacred fetishes in the shapes of snakes and phalli were made from paste and carried about—a custom that persisted in modern Europe. Moreover, during initiation rites, a golden snake was lowered into initiates' laps and drawn out below, symbolizing the snake god fertilizing and spiritualizing the faithful in a sexual and mystical union. Sacred snakes were also used during orgies related to Bacchus and Dionysus. Greek artists portrayed the frenzied women attendants known as Maenads, or "mad ones," brandishing serpents. Such ancient ceremonies involving snake gods provided early Christian fathers with excuses for suppression of rites related to fertility, for snake worship was considered to be the epitome of pagan depravity. Indeed, Christianity was responsible for suppressing snake cults throughout much of the world since snakes were venerated and connected with fertility and sexuality on other continents as well, particularly Africa and Australia. Examples of snake lore and mythology from those areas are presented along with rock art images in Chapter 5.

Similarly, Native peoples throughout the Americas revered the serpent and depicted it extensively in art. Probably nowhere else in the world are so many snakes illustrated in art and architecture as in the Mayan, Aztec, and Toltec area of Mesoamerica. Likewise, throughout the Southwest snake images are one of the most common motifs in rock art. According to ethnography, in the

Southwest snakes were regarded as powerful, sacred creatures for the same reasons as in other parts of the world. The primary attributes of the snake which make it such a potent fertility symbol include its association with water, rain/lightning, and the underworld; its ability to shed skin and appear to be immortal; its phallic form; and its power to kill or to heal. The dynamic energy of the snake as a symbol of regeneration is probably the main reason so many snake images accompany fertility-related rock art.

In the desert Southwest, the symbolic association of serpents and water is of primary importance. Because water and fertility are so intertwined in Native American cultures, and because the snake moves like water and is often seen near water, the symbolic connection is strong. This is illustrated by the petroglyph of a coiled snake in fig. 127 that has been placed to show the creature moving toward an adjacent natural rock bowl that catches rainwater. In addition to rainmaking rituals, snakes have also been used ceremonially to maintain the vitality of springs and rivers. The Hopi Snake Ceremony, still held in August to bring rain, is perhaps the best-known example of snake rituals in the Southwest. The Hopi Snake Men collect dozens of snakes, including rattlesnakes, and after ritual bathing of the snakes and other preparations in the kivas, hold a dance in the plaza where they handle the snakes and release them on the ground. The dancers' bodies are painted with symbols of snakes and lightning—the ceremony is primarily to bring rain but also involves prayers for the fertilizing powers of lightning that strikes their fields. After the ceremonies the writhing snakes are collected and returned to the four cardinal directions as a means of petitioning the spirits to send rain. Similar snake ceremonies once existed elsewhere in the region; a petroglyph site near the Santa Fe River may be a depiction of ritual activities with snakes (fig. 128). Here a man stands amid many snakes, holding one in his hand and another in his mouth.

Further, in Pueblo fertility rituals snakes were lightning symbols that brought summer thunderclouds and rain. People could see the celestial serpents (lightning strikes) come to earth with the rain. For Pueblo people, lightning could be either good or bad, and good lightning could be either male or female (Tyler 1964, 235). A further distinction was made between lightning that blasted and lightning that fertilized the fields. During the Hopi Snake Ceremony, a bull-roarer is used "to divert the influence of bad clouds; it is to call [ask for] the good lightning to strike a place that has been

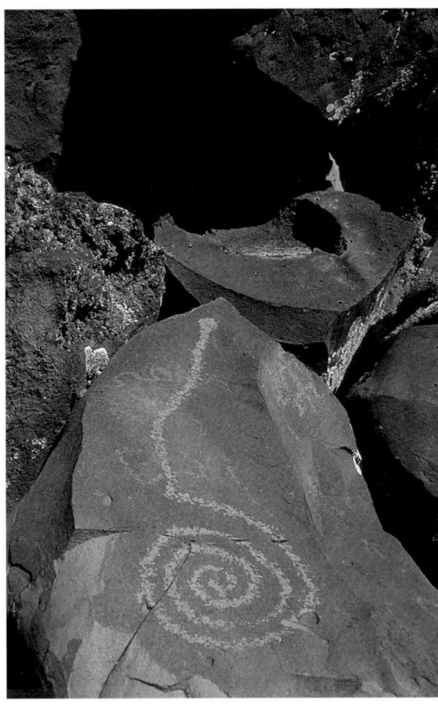

fig. 127. Petroglyph of a coiled snake next to a natural rock basin that catches rainwater, Nampaweap, Arizona.

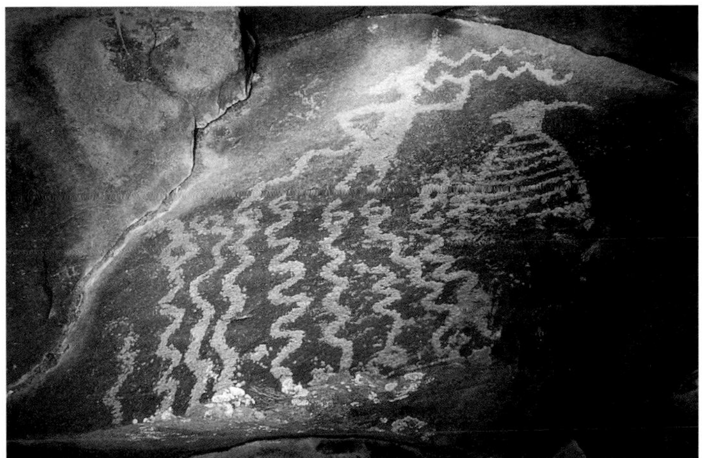

fig. 128. Petroglyph panel that may represent a Snake Ceremony or Snake Dance, Caja del Rio, New Mexico.

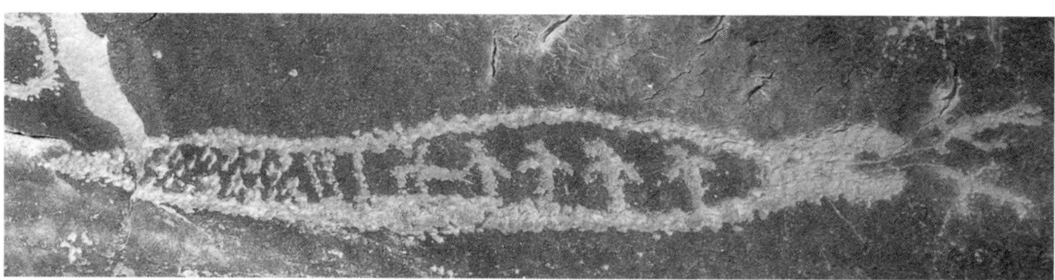

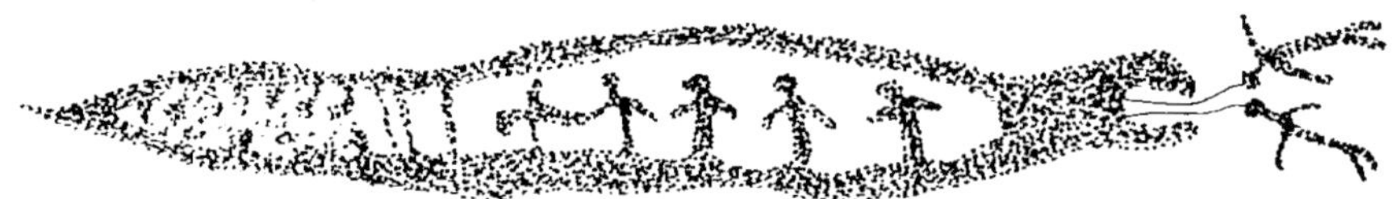

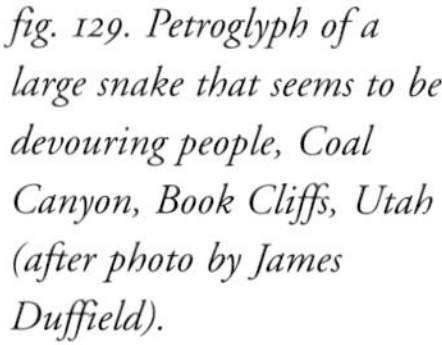

fig. 129. Petroglyph of a large snake that seems to be devouring people, Coal Canyon, Book Cliffs, Utah (after photo by James Duffield).

blasted by bad clouds, a place made barren by them. When good lightning strikes such a spot in the valley, it drives away the bad cloud's influence. Afterwards this place is planted and becomes very fertile" (Stephen 1936, 637–38). By contrast, bad lightning was associated with war, and so the dangerous, swift-striking power of the snake came to represent prowess in war.

Snake Societies played a significant role in Pueblo concepts of fertility, curing, weather control, warfare, and continued well-being of the people. Fertility and the perpetuation of the people were invoked at some pueblos by the ceremonial keeping of snakes:

> Apparently, each Tewa Pueblo has two or more sacred snakes, and two "Snake Mothers" who sacrifice all their children to the snakes. The Snake Mothers have charge of the *Sa-Jiu*, or Frog Water, a liquid for snake bites, while the "Keeper of the Snake" actually takes care of the serpents. The snakes are fed bread cakes with snake symbols on them, and when the snakes grow old they are taken away and others are provided. The theory behind all this is that if the snakes are not properly cared for the people will die (Switzer 1972, 26).

The fact that snakes were kept for ritual purposes is also substantiated by other ethnographic accounts. One states that the eastern Pueblos claimed that "the Pecos adored, and the Jemez and Taos still adore, an enormous rattlesnake, which they keep alive in some inaccessible and hidden mountain recess" (Bandelier 1890, 305-7). Moreover, a grandson of one of Adolph Bandelier's informants claimed that a snake was kept in an underground room at Pecos and was fed newborn infants (Curtis 1926, 20).

Although the veracity of such statements has not been established, there are additional records that mention human sacrifice in connection with snakes. An early white observer at Pecos Pueblo commented that the bodies of those who died of exhaustion while tending the sacred fire "were carried to the den of a monsterous serpent, which kept itself in excellent condition by feeding on those delicacies. This huge snake was represented as the idol which they worshipped, and as subsisting entirely upon the flesh of his devotees . . . live infants, however, seemed to suit his palate best" (Gregg 1845, 272). Even though such tales of sacrifice to snakes have not been verified, a petroglyph from Utah seems to depict something similar—a large serpent contains what appear to be little humans inside its belly and is about to eat several more (fig. 129).

Whether fact or legend, numerous stories exist about the abandonment of Pecos Pueblo in which a huge, captive snake is featured. In one story, the snake's escape is said to have caused many of the Pecos people to become ill and die. Another tale relates that the Pecos men went out to fight the Comanches and the very few that came back became snakes; when the women were unable to restore the snakes to men, the people abandoned the place (Switzer 1972, 28).

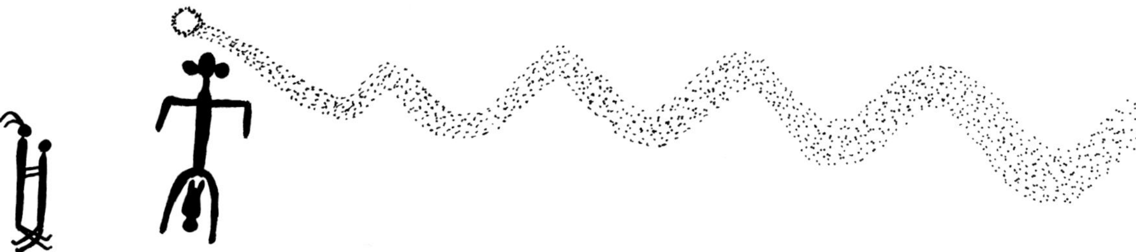

fig. 130. (above) Basketmaker Anasazi petroglyphs depicting a couple having sexual intercourse, a woman giving birth, and a large snake, Cedar Mesa, Utah.

According to a myth, snakes were also kept at Tesuque Pueblo for fertility purposes:

> A handsome youth asked a maiden to be his lover. When she consented, he told her to keep him hidden in a large jar in an unused room of her father's house. When she returned there was no man, but a large snake in the jar. Later she became pregnant and bore two snakes which her father took to the hills and released. He gave them meal and begged them not to harm the people, and today the Tesuques keep snakes in memory of this incident (Curtis 1926, 80).

In some Indian cultures, snakes are also associated with the force of gravity because they are closely connected to the earth and the underworld. It is believed that the destruction of snakes could result in the loss of gravity and the disintegration of the world. Many snake images in rock art probably represent shamanic concepts about these creatures being spirit helpers or messengers to assist in traveling to the underworld or communicating with spirits in the underworld. In myths of the Far West, rattlesnakes guarded the vaginas of supernatural women, bedrock mortars (a symbolic earth vagina), and rock art sites that shamans had to "enter" to gain access to the supernatural realm.

Rattlesnakes are represented at rock art sites in southern and south-central California by diamond-shaped and zigzag motifs in pictographs, some of which are associated with female puberty initiation rites. As spirit helper, the rattlesnake was associated with females throughout the Far West, and the related diamond-chain and zigzag motifs were used as feminine designs. That a masculine, phallic symbol came to represent female elements is thought to be an example of symbolic inversion, expressing the belief that the supernatural realm was the opposite of the mundane natural world. Thus females wishing support for their role in the natural world sought supernatural help from the masculine spirit of the rattlesnake as their guardian (Whitley 1996, 83).

Symbolic associations between the snake, female/vulva, and male/phallus are found throughout the Southwest and are illustrated graphically in rock art from many locations (figs. 132–135). Snake images are commonly associated with scenes of copulation and birth in rock art of the Colorado Plateau and the upper Rio Grande (figs. 130 and 131). An interesting Anasazi petroglyph from southeastern Utah shows an anthropomorph that could be a female being fertilized by a long snake or a male whose phallus becomes a snake (fig. 134). Another example of a symbolic connection between snakes and the phallus is shown in the Jornada Style petroglyph from southern

fig. 131. (below) Petroglyphs of flute players, a couple having sexual intercourse, and a large snake, Ute Mountain Tribal Park, Colorado (after photo by James Duffield).

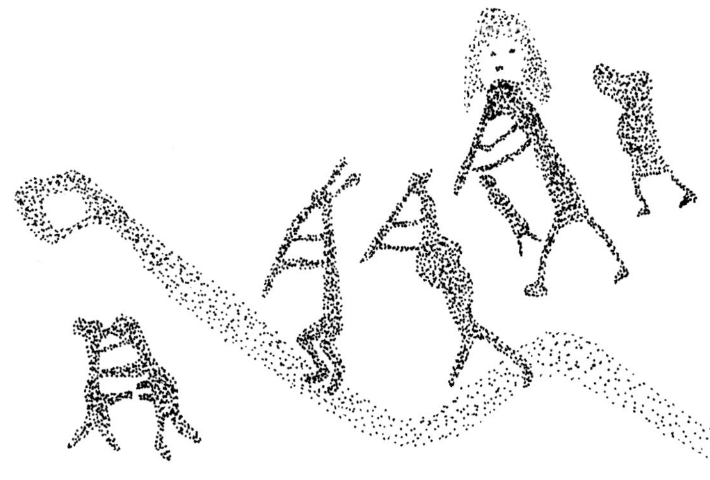

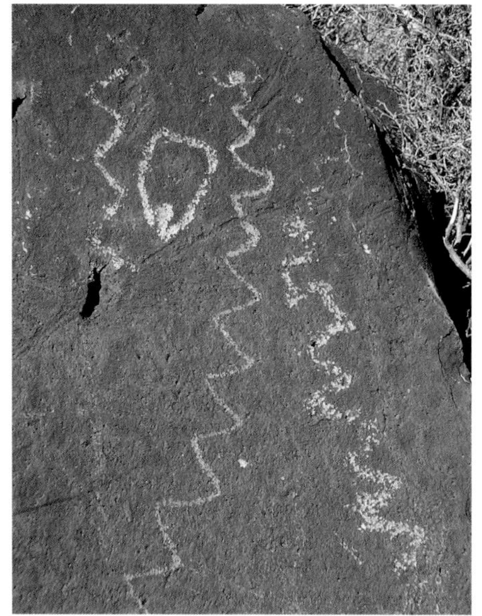

fig.132. (left) Petroglyphs of snakes and a vulva symbol, Santa Fe River Canyon, New Mexico.

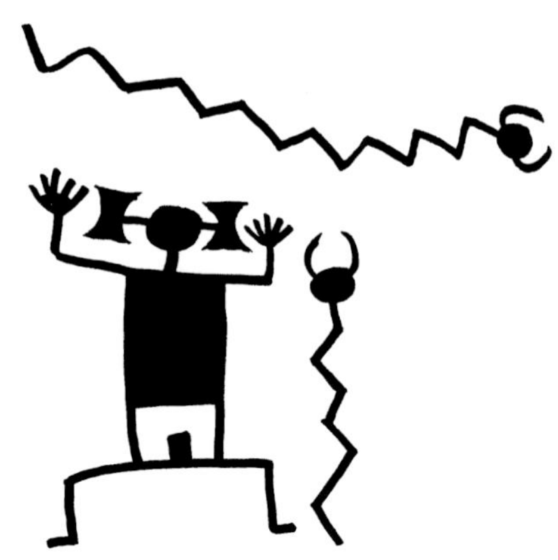

fig. 133. (right) Anasazi petroglyphs of Horned Serpents and a sexually receptive female, Holiday Mesa, Jemez Mountains, New Mexico.

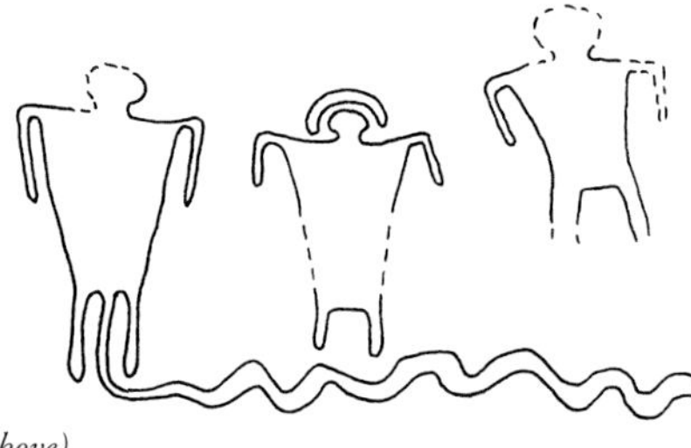

fig. 134. (above) Basketmaker Anasazi petroglyphs showing an anthropomorph with a penis that becomes a long, snake-like design, Lower Deckers, Cottonwood Canyon, Utah.

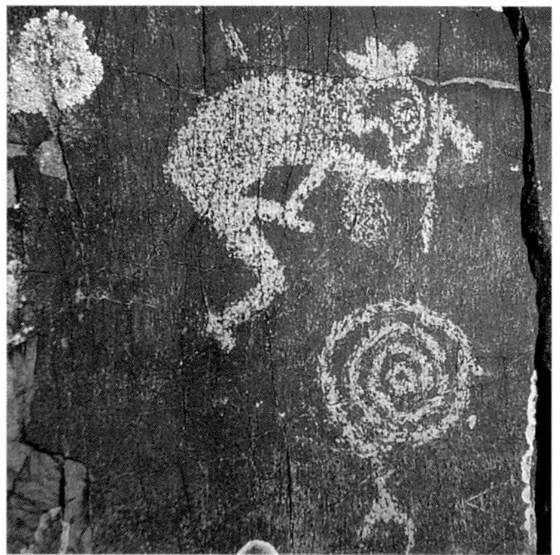

fig. 135. (right) Jornada Style petroglyphs that seem to express an association between male fertility or potency and the snake as a phallic symbol, Carrizo Mountain, New Mexico.

New Mexico shown in fig. 135. In addition, many other examples occur with snake images figuring prominently in scenes involving copulation or birth (fig. 136). The Inscription Point site in northern Arizona is especially significant for its concentration of snake images associated with scenes of sexual activity (fig. 9); see the section "Fertility Shrines and Rites." Snakes are also commonly associated with flute player images (see examples in that section).

One of the more complex examples of snake symbolism and universal fertility themes is found in the Cochimi pictographs at Serpent Cave, in Baja California (Smith 1986b, 27-47). A large, deer-headed serpent with attendant creatures and anthropomorphs are thought to represent mythological concepts at a site where a ceremony to "call upon the fruits to ripen" was performed by the shaman (fig. 137). Serpent Cave may also have functioned as a ritual calendar indicating the seasonal/ritual significance of important food sources such as deer and pitahaya cactus. This function is reflected by the open mouth of the deer—representing the deer in rut and therefore symbolizing procreation—and by the forked tail of the serpent that may signify new growth of plants. Cyclical, seasonal aspects may also be portrayed by undulations of the ser-

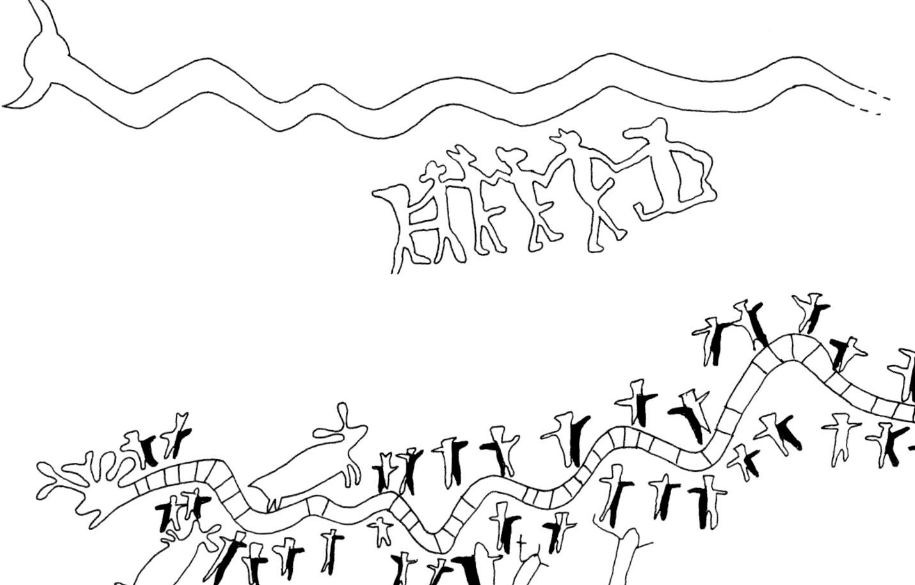

fig. 136. Pueblo petroglyphs in a cave, showing a possible sexual rite beneath a large Horned Serpent, Pajarito Plateau, Los Alamos, New Mexico.

fig. 137. Cochimi pictographs depicting a Horned Serpent and other elements associated with fecundity and seasonal renewal, Cueva de la Serpiente, Baja California, Mexico (after Ewing 1989).

pent's body and its color-coded demarcations. The overall impression is of complex symbolism centered around the serpent, suggesting such an image must have had great spiritual significance for its ancient creators in helping them to sustain the fecundity of their world.

Crook-Necked Staffs

Another interesting rock art symbol found in obvious fertility contexts is the crook-necked staff, or crook, resembling a cane, which is sometimes held by anthropomorphic figures. This symbol occurs both as an isolated motif and in composition with other elements. Crook-necked staffs have been found in archaeological sites throughout the Southwest, including California, Nevada, Arizona, New Mexico, Utah, and the Plains. They still have important symbolic meaning in Pueblo societies. While some probably represent ceremonial objects or symbols of rank, the crook is also a symbol of fertility and may in some cases represent a planting stick. In Anasazi rock art of the Colorado Plateau are portrayals of crook-necked staffs in association with copulating couples (Cole 1989, 79–81), [36] and one petroglyph shows a phallic figure holding both a flute and a crook-necked staff (fig. 138c). There is an obvious fertility aspect to the Mogollon figure from a Mimbres bowl who is holding both crook-necked staff and erect phallus with apparent glee (fig. 139). In addition to the Anasazi and Mogollon examples, there are also Hohokam ceramics and rock art sites showing figures carrying crook-necked staffs and burden baskets, also a symbol of fertility and abundance.

An intriguing petroglyph site in southeastern Utah has long lines of figures which may represent a migration or emergence story; among the figures are ones holding crooks, as if they are leading the people (fig. 140).

As symbols of authority and power among the Pueblos, crook-necked staffs are required possessions of those holding political or ceremonial office (Cole 1989, 81). Moreover, men preparing for a long journey were given such staffs as a prayer for stamina and safe return. The long-distance traders of the Aztecs (known as *pochtecas*) also carried canes with crook-necks, which were venerated with offerings and kept in special shrines between journeys. In the Anasazi trading center of *fig. 138. Rock art depictions of a crook-necked staff at various southwestern sites: a.–b. Butler Wash, Utah; c.–d. San Juan County, Utah; e. Upper Little Colorado River, Arizona; f. Mancos Canyon, Colorado; g. South Mountain, Arizona; h. Deming, New Mexico; i. San Tan Mountain, Arizona; j. Tonopah, Nevada; k. Inscription Point, Arizona; l. southern Arizona.*

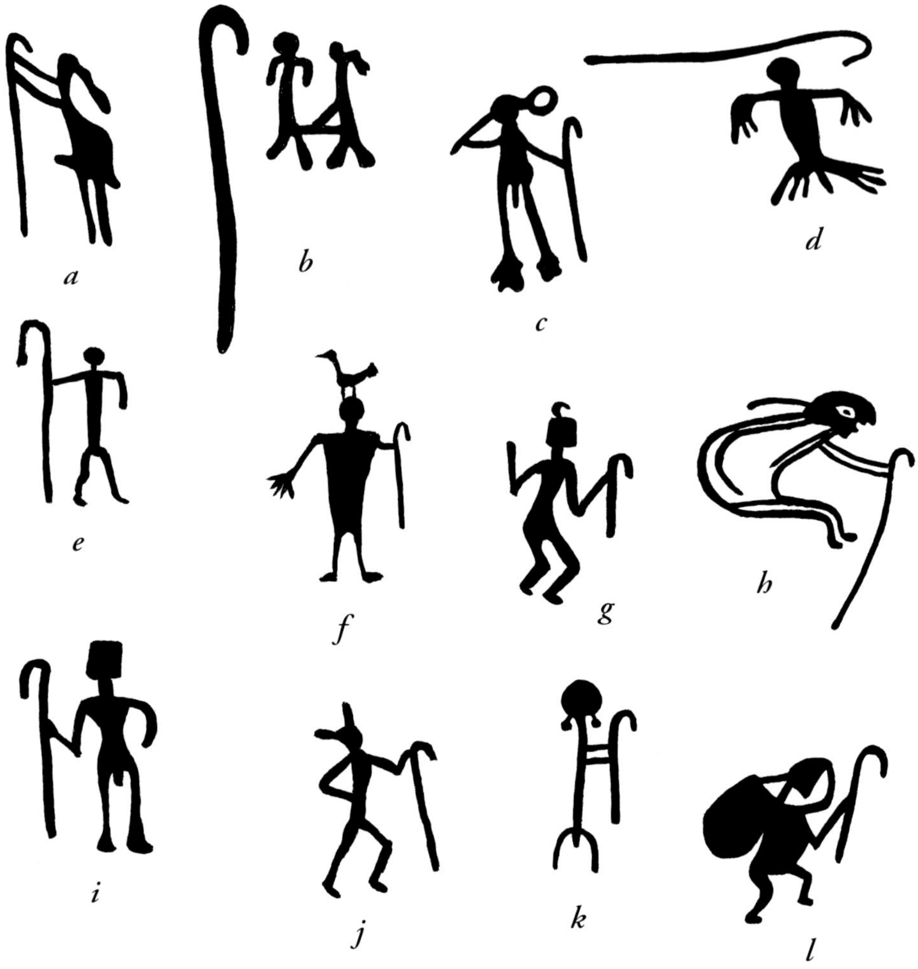

fig. 139. (below) Design painted on Mimbres bowl, Mimbres Valley, New Mexico (after Brody 1977, 150).

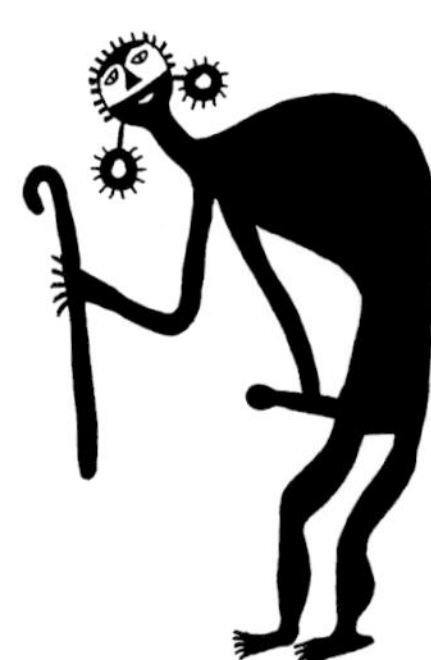

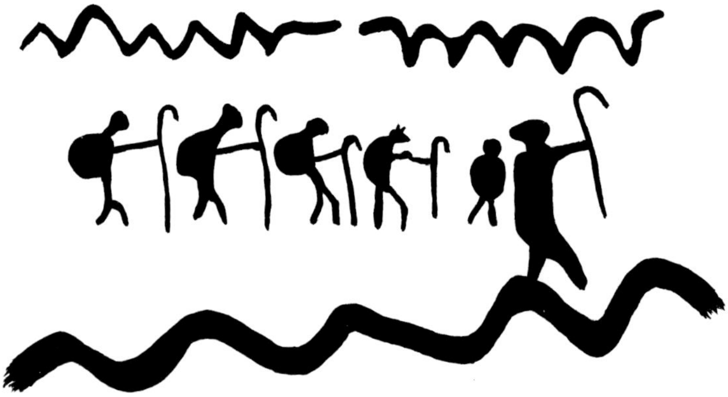

fig. 140. (right) Petroglyphs of humpbacked figures carrying crooks, Comb Ridge, Utah.

Chaco Canyon, excavations have uncovered rooms containing hundreds of such staffs.

In some contexts, the crook-necked staff symbolizes long life, representing an old man with head bent over by age (Fewkes 1914, 30). In addition, anthropologists have recorded the use of crook-necked staffs as sacred paraphernalia in Hopi ceremonies, where they are known

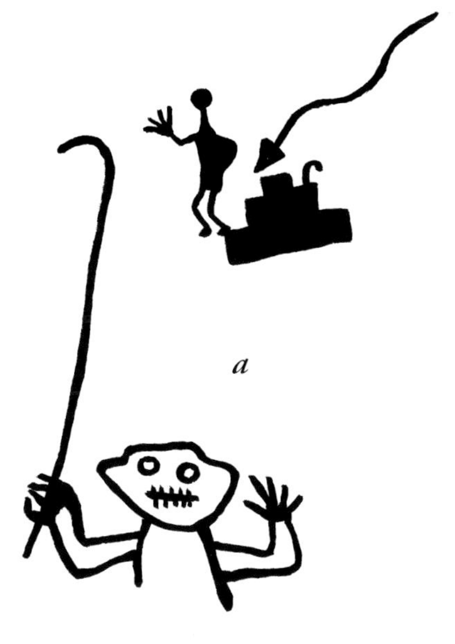

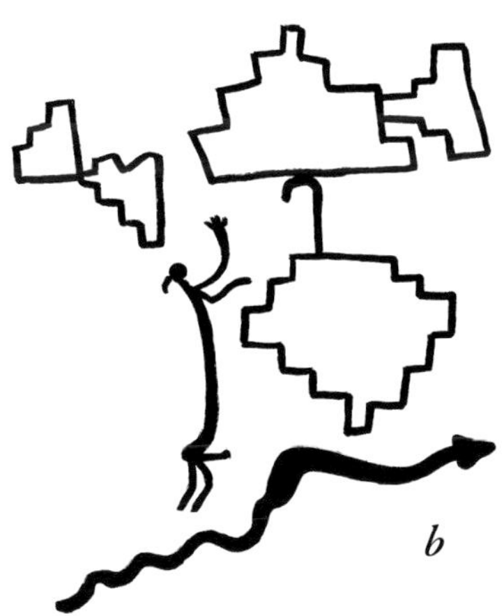

fig. 141. Petroglyphs depicting the association of crook-necked staffs with cloud terraces and other fertility symbols: a. San Cristobal, Galisteo Basin, New Mexico; b. Tenabo, New Mexico.

as *gnelas*. Hopi priests identified these as symbols of ancient weapons (atlatls?) and made them prominent in a number of rituals:

> These crooks or gnelas have been called warrior prayer sticks, and are symbols of ancient weapons. In many folk tales it is stated that warriors overcame their foes by the use of gnelas which would indicate that they had something to do with ancient war implements. Their association with arrows on the Antelope altars adds weight to this conclusion (Fewkes 1914, 28).

In the Hopi Flute Ceremony, a crook-necked staff is used to draw down the clouds when their rain is needed (Fewkes 1914 , 28-29, quoted in Gough 1996, 9).[37] This concept appears to be expressed in the Tewa petroglyphs in the Galisteo Basin, New Mexico (fig. 141a), and by the Tompiro petroglyphs from Tenabo ruin in New Mexico that show a phallic figure gesturing toward cloud terrace symbols that contain a crook-necked staff (fig. 141b).

The crook-necked staff is also associated with Pueblo emergence myths; it was through the use of this object that the people climbed up into the fourth world (Parsons 1939). It is also possible that the depiction in the above figure represents a type of germinator deity similar to Muingwu from Hopi, who has been described as holding a crook-necked staff that represents the stages of life and using a rattle with curved thorns to "hook the clouds" (Tyler 1964, 127).

According to the ethnography of Great Basin peoples the shaman possessed a sacred crook-necked staff, or *poro*, which was a sign of his position and had magical, regenerative powers:

> The Chemehuevi shaman required no feathered headdress, no regalia of any kind, no eagle feathers or down, no sacred bundle, no collection of healing herbs. His one indispensable piece of equipment was his poro (or pooro), a rod shaped like a shepherd's crook. This was an archetypal object of great power. . . . In the myth "How Wolf and Coyote Went Away," it is said that with a single twist of his poro Wolf tunneled through a great mountain and that Coyote used his poro to hook the wind down from its high level so that it might sweep across the surface of the earth. In that ancient, storied time, When the Animals Were People, after all Wolf's or Coyote's warriors had been killed in battle, slaughtered by malevolent beings, or had died of thirst, they were revived by the touch of a poro in the hands of Wolf or some other pre-human

> shaman. The poro was peculiarly the shaman's badge of office. . . . (Laird 1976, 31, quoted in Gough 1996, 2).

Other Chemehuevi myths describe how the *poro* had great power for fertility:

> Cottontail Rabbit pried open the crack with his poro and gave to all the world a plentiful supply of plants bearing edible seeds. Cottontail Rabbit with his poro . . . opens the crack, and an abundance of seeds pours forth. . . .In the Chemehuevi story the dead mother of the orphans is the dead and barren earth; but when the poro opens the crack in the rock (vagina of the Earth Goddess), life and fecundity are restored (Laird 1976, 153, 215, quoted in Gough 1996, 5).

As an important symbol related to fertility, the crook-necked staff occurs in archaeological sites on other continents as well. Among such sites in Europe, where it is a common symbol in the Neolithic Period, is a carved stone in a passage grave in Brittany. The stone represents an abstract image of the Great Goddess, with a central vulva flanked by four rows of "hooks" that are virtually identical to the crooks seen in the Southwest. The hooks are said to be energy symbols that stimulate the life source or represent emanations of its energy (Gimbutas 1989, 289). The crook-necked staff (crozier) is also carried by bishops in the Catholic Church, and as such has a significant tradition in the Old World, where it is primarily a symbol of power but sometimes represents a fertility cult (Crawford 1991, 74–76).

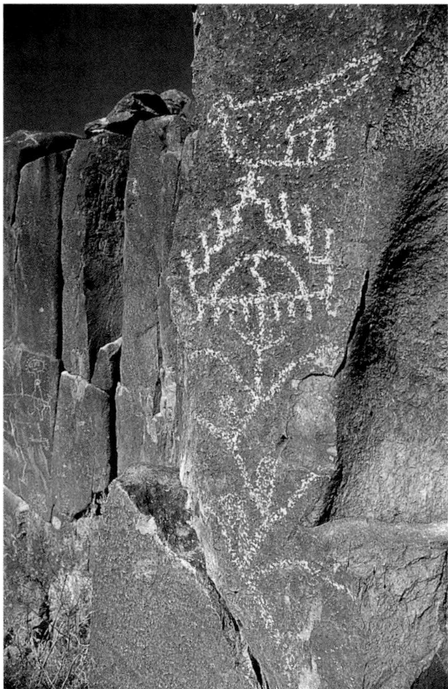

fig. 142. Jornada Style petroglyph of a cloud terrace with rain fringe and corn plant, rainbow, lightning, and bird to carry prayers for rain up to the sky, Three Rivers, New Mexico.

Cloud Terraces

Moisture and the means of attracting it were dominant themes among Indians throughout the desert Southwest. Wherever the water supply was scarce, people ritually summoned rain by some process, and moisture and fertility were closely related concepts in such rituals. Water is the foundation of all life in the Southwest, and the mysterious powers that create moisture are appealed to in rituals for bringing rain. Thus supplications for rain and the well-being of the people are obviously connected with fertility of the land and all its inhabitants.

Depictions of clouds and associated rain and lightning are a common means of symbolizing moisture in the Southwest. In rock art motifs, as well as ceramics, basketry, murals, and other media, the cloud terrace, or rain altar, is a nearly ubiquitous symbol, especially in the Four Corners region. The cloud terrace, which represents the towering thunderheads that bring life-giving rain in the summer, has been drawn in different ways, ranging from geometric, step-like designs to more realistic, rounded, cloud-like renditions. This symbol is clearly very significant, as it occurs over a large area and in relation to a variety of ingenious functions involving symbolism for lightning, rain, growth of corn, and birds carrying prayers for rain up to the sky (fig. 142).

The association of the cloud terrace symbol with fertility is illustrated by the petroglyph in fig. 143 from southern New Mexico. Here a phallic, horned anthropomorph (probably a rain shaman or a supernatural) stands upon a cloud terrace, with another, smaller cloud terrace attached to his penis—perhaps drawing an analogy between the power of rain to fertilize the earth and the power of semen in the fertilization of human life. Some ancient cultures also attributed urine with the same reproductive power as semen, and this beneficial moisture was expressed in art and myth as a fructifying force (Walker 1983, 207).

The connection between fertility and the cloud terrace can also be seen in fig. 144; here a phallic, humpbacked figure blows into a ceremonial cloud-blower to produce two large, symmetrical cloud terraces. Cloud-blowers are pipe-like objects that were used in rainmaking rituals by blowing smoke into the air to simulate rain clouds. The cloud terrace in fig. 145 also connects moisture with fecundity by including plants and another fertility symbol, the moisture-loving dragonfly.

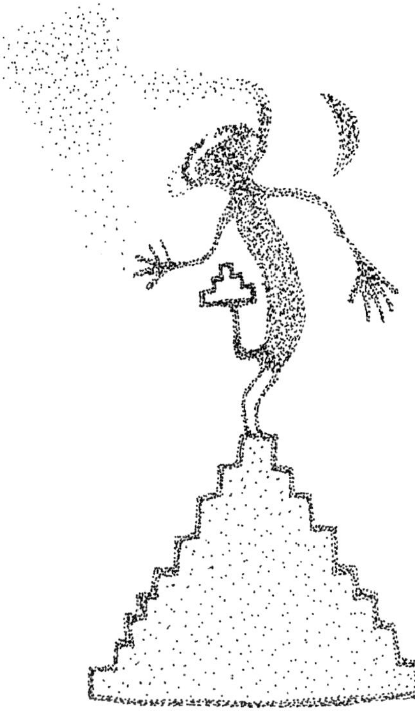

fig. 143. (left) Jornada Style petroglyph of a horned, phallic anthropomorph standing on top of a cloud terrace and with a small cloud terrace on his penis, Carrizo Mountain, New Mexico.

Dragonflies and Butterflies

Depictions of insects, and humans with insect qualities, are sometimes encountered in southwestern rock art, and among the most recognizable are dragonflies and butterflies (fig. 146). What these images may have represented to the prehistoric creators of the rock art is a matter of speculation, but Pueblo myth and lore provide clues to the nature of their fertility symbolism.

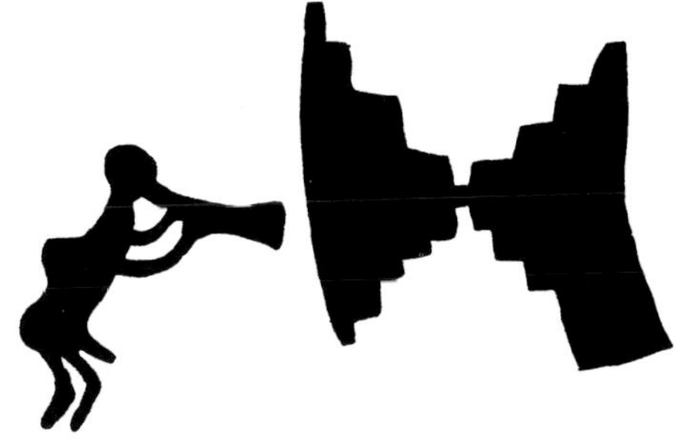

fig. 144. (left) Rio Grande Style petroglyphs of a phallic, humpbacked anthropomorph with a cloud-blower and cloud terraces, La Cieneguilla, New Mexico.

Dragonflies have long been important symbols of water and fertility in the Southwest. Occurring in rock art primarily in New Mexico, Arizona, and Utah, they are sometimes portrayed at Pueblo and Mogollon sites, and occur in certain archaic rock art styles as shamanistic creatures or spirit helpers (Malotki 1997, 57-72). Dragonfly lore from historic Pueblo ethnography, primarily at Hopi and Zuni, is useful for understanding this symbol in

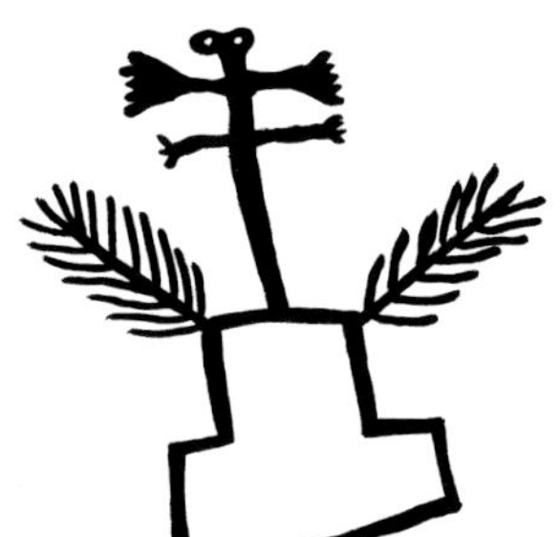

fig. 145. (left) Rio Grande Style petroglyphs of a cloud terrace with plants and a dragonfly, Rio Grande near Bernalillo, New Mexico.

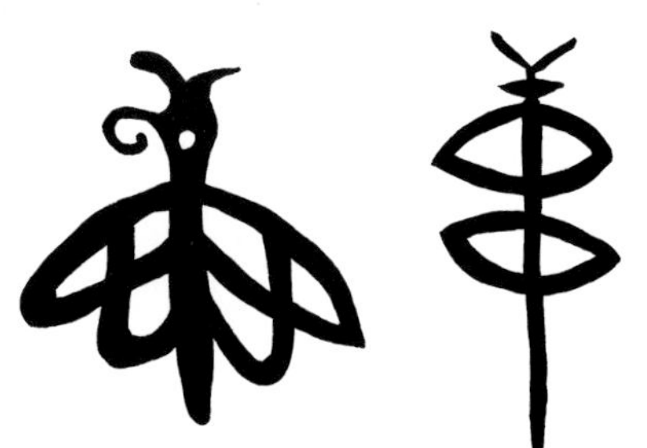

fig. 146. (right) Petroglyphs of butterfly and dragonfly motifs, Hopi Salt Trail, Grand Canyon, Arizona (after Malotki 1997, 62).

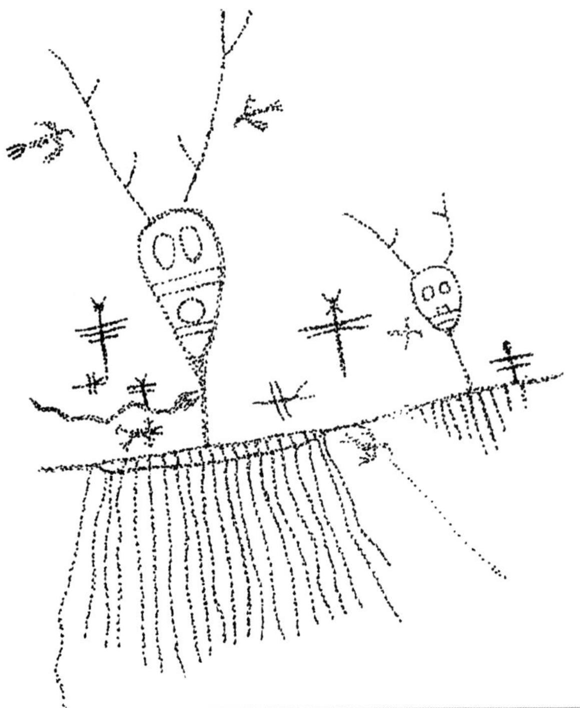

fig. 147. (above) Archaic petroglyphs of shamanic figures with dragonfly spirit helpers, Little Colorado River, Arizona (after Malotki 1997, 68).

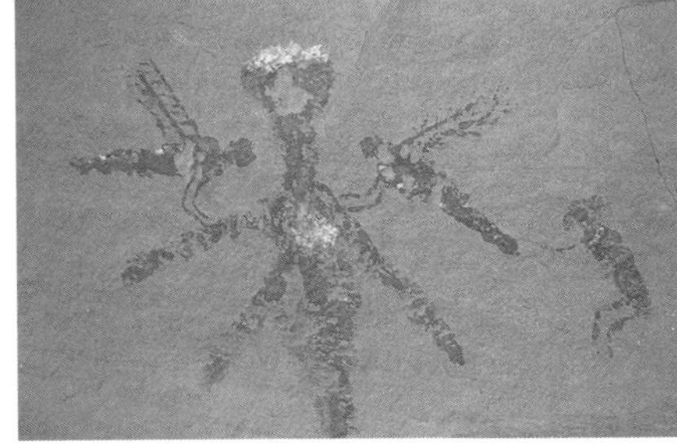

fig. 148. (right) Barrier Canyon Style pictographs of a shaman in the shape of a dragonfly with dragonfly spirit helpers, Moqui Fork Canyon, Utah.

Pueblo and Mogollon rock art, but the ancient roots of these concepts are expressed in Archaic images that are several thousand years older, interpreted as shamanic spirit helpers and metaphors for the shaman's soul-flight to the spirit world. Its use as a power animal by shamans is related to its close association with water and perhaps its iridescent coloring and large eyes, which may have symbolized the hallucinatory visions of the shaman's trance. The dragonfly may have been petitioned in rituals for making rain and worshiped for its role in providing it. These attributes are evident in the millennia-old petroglyphs where dragonflies perch on the shoulders of horned, shamanic figures, along with other spirit helpers such as snakes and birds (fig. 147). These anthropomorphs may be depictions of rain shamans or deities, since their rake-like bodies suggest rain symbolism. Moreover, in millennia-old Barrier Canyon Style pictographs in southeastern Utah, dragonfly images hover realistically at the shoulder of a larger creature that may represent a shaman assuming dragonfly shape in his journey to the spirit world (fig. 148).

Some of the shamanic precepts of Archaic hunter-gatherers continued to survive in later agricultural societies, especially in the role of weather-controlling Pueblo rain priests. Pueblos deified a number of insects for their role in bringing life-sustaining moisture, but the dragonfly was especially important. Apparently the sound of the dragonfly ("tsee, tsee, tsee") resembles the word for water in some Indian languages, which may explain the belief that it is a supernatural with the power of speech and the ability to bring summer rains (Mallery 1893, 704–5). As the servant of the cloud deity Oomaw, the dragonfly could reopen blocked springs and lead people to a new spring (Wade and McChesney 1980, 26).

Further, a Hopi legend tells of a terrible drought which was ended when a young man appeared in the form of a great dragonfly and led rain clouds over the Hopi lands. The youth, who had been sacrificed, "reappeared a long time afterward during a great drought. He was seen for four mornings just before sunrise extended against the eastern sky. On the fourth day a great storm arose and the youth, in the form of a gigantic dragonfly, was seen leading the rain cloud over the land of the Hopitu, and plenteous rains [that] ensued relieved the people of their sufferings" (Wade and McChesney 1980, 26). Moreover, according to another legend, also from the time of a famine at Hopi, dragonflies saved the people. Prayers to the cloud deity Oomaw resulted in a swarm of dragonflies making holes in the ground, in which maize seeds were planted. The dragonflies fanned the growing corn plants for four days, ensuring their maturation and thus saving the Hopis from starvation (Malotki 1997, 60).

Also, in a story recorded at Zuni, the magical dragonfly helps two abandoned children survive and is ultimately responsible for the renewed fecundity of the earth: "That is why we worship the dragonfly, and why no one is allowed to kill it" (Benedict 1969, 1–9). At Zuni, killing a dragonfly was taboo, except for ritual use; the Zunis mixed hearts of dragonflies and butterflies with certain plants to make "sun medicine," which they rubbed on their bodies for psychic purification. This medicine was only used by men, as it was thought to be an aphrodisiac for women (Packard 1974, 22).

In addition to appearing in southwestern rock art (fig. 149), the dragonfly design is also popular in ceramics, jewelry, and ceremonial paraphernalia. This motif is sometimes mistaken for a cross, but it usually has two cross-lines, representing the double wings of the dragonfly, and occasionally the insect's head or large eyes are depicted. At a Jornada Style rock art site in southern New Mexico, there are numerous images of dragonflies being held by humpbacked, sometimes phallic anthropomorphs (fig. 150). The nearby stream must have been associated with wetlands and riparian habitat favored by the dragonfly, but there is also important fertility symbolism conveyed here. Humpbacked, phallic figures in Jornada style rock art, though not usually playing a flute, are thought to be conceptually related to the flute-playing fertility figure so widespread in the Anasazi/Pueblo region. One of the anthropomorphs in fig. 150 appears to be playing a flute-like object. At this same site, another example of the connection between dragonflies and fertility is the phallic man in fig. 151; a large dragonfly is poised over his head, and a snake over his exaggerated penis, which points purposefully at a natural

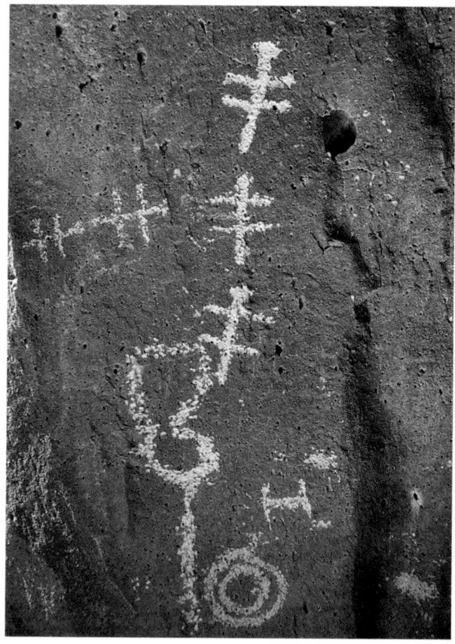

fig. 149. Petroglyphs of dragonflies, Santa Fe River Canyon, New Mexico.

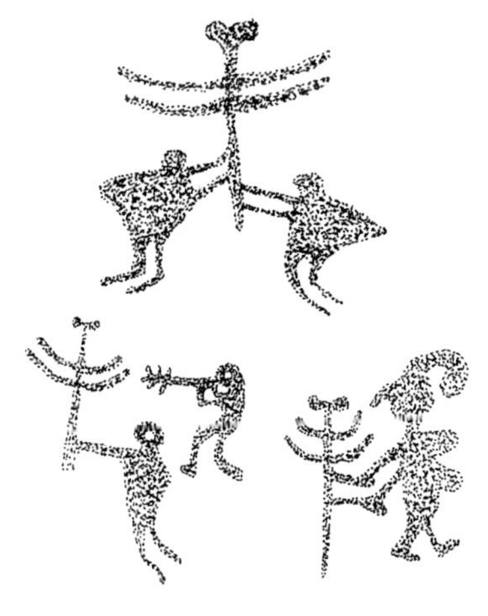

fig. 150. Jornada Style petroglyphs of humpbacked figures and dragonflies, Carrizo Mountain, New Mexico.

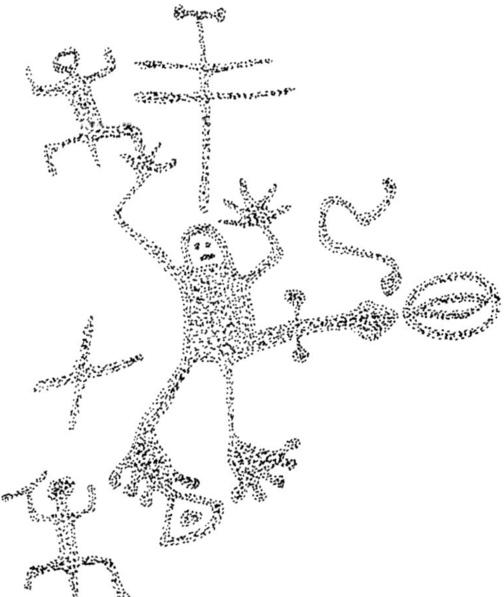

fig. 151. Jornada Style petroglyphs of a phallic figure and vulva symbol associated with a dragonfly, snake, and other symbols, Carrizo Mountain, New Mexico.

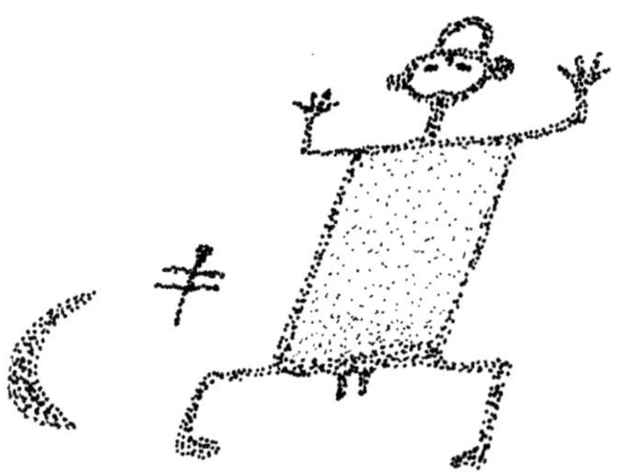

fig. 152. Rio Grande Style petroglyphs depicting a female with dragonfly and crescent moon-like symbol, La Bajada, New Mexico.

vulva-like protuberance on the rock that has been enhanced by selective pecking. Perhaps the boulder on which this scene was placed served as a fertility shrine. Another petroglyph site near Santa Fe, New Mexico, also expresses the symbolic association of dragonfly and fertility (fig. 152). Here the dragonfly is situated between a sexually receptive female and a crescent shape that could represent the moon (associated with feminine aspects such as menstrual cycles) or perhaps a sprouting seed.

Although not a common symbol in southwestern rock art, the butterfly motif also occurs in pottery, jewelry, and other ceremonial applications, such as clan symbols. It is associated with rain, fertility, growth, flowers and pollinating plants, and the well-being of all living things. In some cultures, a butterfly attached to a plume offering sent prayers to supernaturals, and also encouraged an amorous state of mind. In one ritual, sacred clowns carried a drum containing fluttering butterflies, which made people follow them and "go crazy," sexually (Packard and Packard 1974, 23). Some tribes had the same word for butterfly and moth, so these creatures may have served similar symbolic functions. They are sometimes associated with corn, and with the Duck Kachina, because the butterfly is as fond of water as the duck. See the section "Myths and Stories about Fertility" for examples of butterflies and moths in rock art associated with obvious fertility symbols such as vulvas and flute players (figs. 90 and 91).

Heads and Scalps

Seemingly unlikely fertility symbols, heads and scalps are in fact associated with not only warfare but also moisture and fertility. The connection between head-hunting, scalping, and fertility is not limited to the Southwest but is found in numerous other cultures throughout the world. It may have ancient origins in the belief that brain, semen, and bone marrow are all the same life substance. There is fossil evidence that Neanderthals engaged in ritual brain-eating, and the Celts associated taking a man's head with gaining his potency and thus increasing the headhunter's own fertility (Bishop 1996, 41). Even in recent times headhunters in Borneo thought a newly taken head made their women fertile and the forest teem with animals. A decorated head placed between the thighs of an adolescent boy initiated him into manhood because his genitals absorbed the vitality of the head.

In the Southwest, attitudes about heads and scalps seem mainly concerned with fertility through their use as potent rainmaking fetishes. The Scalp Dance was held along with a rain ceremony in some pueblos because the blood of the enemy was, like rain, a fertilizing agent. As an element of warfare, the practice of scalping was widespread in the prehistoric Southwest, and there is evidence that whole heads were taken as well. Historic practices in some pueblos show that scalps are associated with warfare and fertility. Myths and ceremonial uses of scalps by the Zunis and Hopis reveal these associations. At Zuni, the Scalp Chief calls the scalps water beings and seed beings, and at Hopi scalps are cast upon a cloud symbol as part of a ritual (Switzer 1972, 21).

Since scalps were considered inherently dangerous, before they could be used as benign rain fetishes, their power had to be ritually placated. Thus when returning warriors carried scalps into a village, women would greet them and sometimes feign intercourse with the enemy scalps to rob them of their power, after which a Scalp Dance ensued. Scalps were also ritually fed cornmeal—another means of placating their power and incorporating them into the tribe. The Keres Pueblos had the following saying: "We are going to have a little rain, the scalps are crying" (Parsons 1939, 350).

As recounted in a portion of the migration mythology at Zuni, after an important conquest the spirits devised a ceremonial song to be used before returning to battle: "The songs were not for the destruction of the enemy, but were a thanksgiving for the scalps which bring good fellowship between the deceased enemy (ghost self) and the A'shiwi, and therefore much rain" (Stevenson 1904, 34–39).

Further, like those at Zuni, scalps at Hopi symbolized fertility as well as war. The following is a description of a Hopi scalp ceremony:

> Holding the scalps aloft on this stick, the men walked in procession four times around the spring . . . . Coming to the north starting point they threw the scalps into the spring, to take omens and wash them clean. . . . The scalps were taken from the spring, and the party went up the trail to the ledge where the women met them, shook hands with them, sprinkled them with meal and thanked them . . . . The men then entered the kiva and remained inside it for twenty days and nights. "The scalp is dangerous: it and the warrior must be purified because it is like a woman having a baby." . . . They took the scalps to a deep fissure on the mesa edge and, with prayers for rain, threw them in, together with prayer feathers and meal. . . . Each year at Wi'widzim, members of the Kwakwa'ndi society, dressed in full ceremonial costume, fed the scalps by throwing wafer bread into the fissure with prayers for rain (Beaglehole and Beaglehole 1976, 23–24).

Heads and scalps are portrayed in rock art from several regions of the Southwest—the Basketmaker Anasazi area of the San Juan River Basin, the Fremont area of northeastern Utah, and the Pueblo Anasazi area of the upper Rio Grande. The large, shamanic anthropomorphs of Basketmaker rock art are sometimes associated with depictions of heads or scalps, which have been correlated with actual prehistoric scalps recovered from archaeological sites in the region (Cole 1989, 71–76). Full heads are most commonly seen in San Juan Basketmaker rock art, probably representing flayed human head skins with a loop or handle on top for carrying and suspending them. Such a whole-head scalp, or trophy head, was excavated from a Basketmaker II burial site in northern Arizona, where it was found placed around the neck of a young woman with a leather thong attached to the top of the scalp. It was described as follows:

> It is the entire head skin of an adult, with the hair carefully dressed. . . . The face has been colored rather elaborately; the "part" and tonsure are painted with a pasty, greenish-white pigment; up the center of the "part" and across the tonsure runs a narrow streak of yellow. Just under the forehead seam there is a thin, horizontal band of red. From this to a line drawn across the face half an inch below the eyes is a zone of white (Kidder and Guernsey 1919, 190–191).

The pattern of facial painting and the hairstyle of this head closely match a colorful Basketmaker pictograph in Grand Gulch, Utah (Cole 1989, 71), as well as a number of Basketmaker petroglyphs in the region, such as the two mask-like images in fig. 153 that resemble whole-head scalps with carrying loops on top. They are accompanied by a phallic flute player and a receptive female—further supporting a fertility association.

Additionally, comparable representations of whole-head scalps also occur in Fremont rock art of the San Rafael and Classic Vernal Styles in northeastern Utah. These scalps are usually shown being held or carried by ceremonially attired anthropomorphs, and while they are stylistically different from the Basketmaker scalps, they do have handles or loops at the top of the head, hair bobs, and necks and are

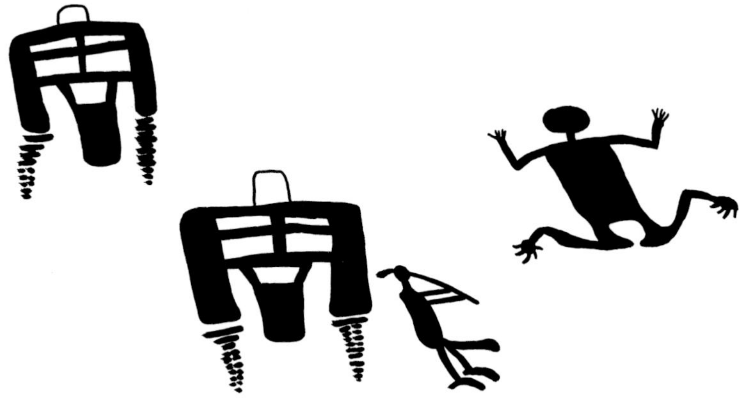

fig. 153. Basketmaker Anasazi petroglyphs representing whole-head scalps with a phallic flute player and a receptive female, Sand Island, Utah.

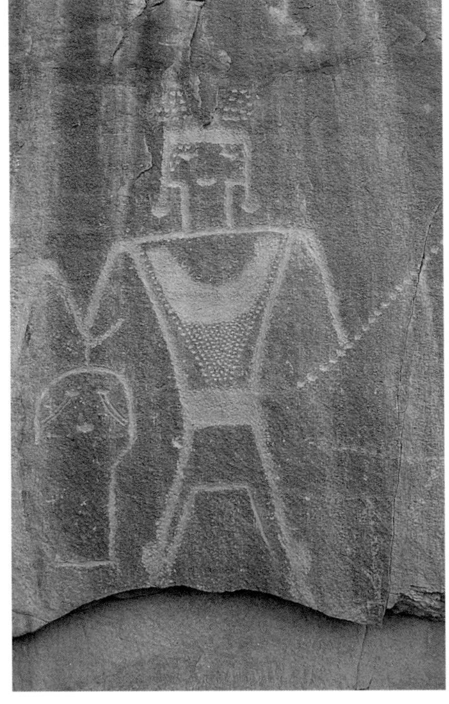

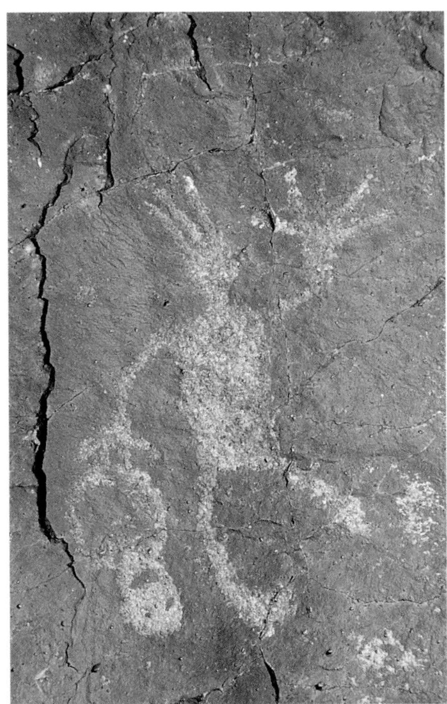

fig. 154. (left) Fremont Style anthropomorph holding a trophy head, Dry Fork Valley, Vernal, Utah.

fig. 155. (right) Petroglyph of an anthropomorph holding a head or mask with a carrying strap, Santa Fe River Canyon, New Mexico.

therefore similar to Basketmaker examples (fig. 154). A possible whole-head scalp from a Pueblo rock art site along the Santa Fe River is shown in fig. 155; less detail is present in this image, and the head appears to be carried upside down in contrast to preceding examples.

Spirals

One of the most ancient and universal signs, the spiral has symbolized energy, renewal, and cycles of time since the Paleolithic era. The life force inherent in the spiral is manifested in nature in many ways—it is associated with serpentine forms (coiled snakes), crescents (curved animal horns and shells), vegetative shapes such as sprouting seeds and twisting vines, and even the serpentine umbilical cord connecting mother and child. Thus spirals are nearly ubiquitous in ancient art (Gimbutas 1989, 278–88).

In the Southwest, the spiral is a very common rock art motif that has been given a variety of meanings by native peoples of the region. It is known as the Life

Way for the Pima and Tohono O'odham peoples of southern Arizona, and presumably was equally significant to the earlier prehistoric Hohokam and Salado peoples, who left many spiral petroglyphs etched on the rocks in that area. For Pueblo people, the spiral represents such varied concepts as wind, water, serpents, and migrations or journeys. At Zuni the spiral is associated with the journey of the people in search of the center, referring to their origin or emergence myth (Young 1988, 136). The Hopis also interpret spirals as signs of their ancestors' journeys, with the direction of the spiral indicating whether they were going or returning.

The significance of the motif seems to lie in the spiral movement, and most fertility aspects relate to this. Cornfields were sometimes planted in a spiral; some Pueblos would begin at the outside and work in to the center, while Navajos would start in the center and move outward in circles. In some Pueblo ceremonies, participants circle the village four times (a sacred number) in a spiral pattern and end in the central plaza at the symbolic *sipapu*—Place of Emergence (Mother Earth Navel), a sacred point that draws the web of life like a centripetal force.

Depictions of the spiral can also represent the life force that animates all things. For Tewa people, this is called *powaha*—the breath of life that flows through all of life's expressions. *Powaha* translates as water-wind-breath, and many rituals are about achieving harmony with this force (Swentzell 1993, 141). A petroglyph from the Santa Fe River area may depict the breath of life symbolized by a spiral on the chest of a virile, phallic male (fig. 156). Sometimes anthropomorphs are shown with the spiral leaving the body, perhaps to suggest the escape of the breath of life in transitional states such as death, shamanic trance, or soul-loss associated with sorcery. Examples of this can be seen in rock art from Keams Canyon, Arizona, which depict the spiral on the chests and coming from the loins of anthropomorphs (fig. 157); further examples are shown in ceramics and wall murals in the section "Sex and Fertility in Other Media." In addition, the life force of the spiral is also frequently expressed in rock art as coiled snakes (fig. 135), and sometimes as sprouting vegetation.

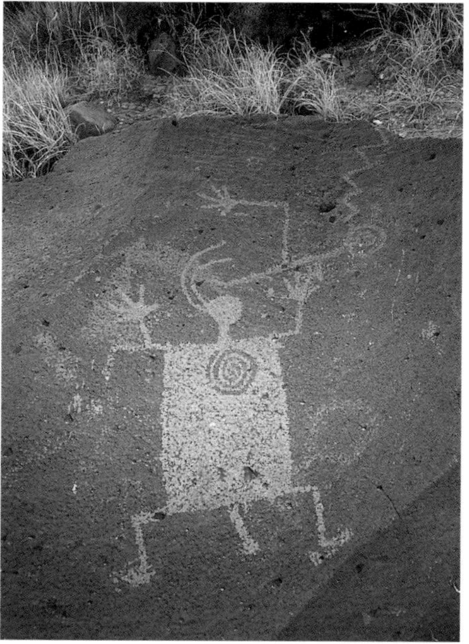

fig. 156. Rio Grande Style anthropomorph with a spiral on his chest, La Bajada, New Mexico.

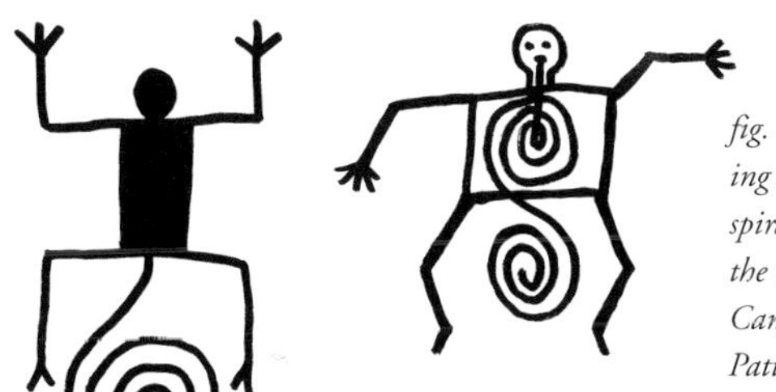

fig. 157. Petroglyphs showing anthropomorphs with spirals perhaps representing the breath of life, Keams Canyon, Arizona (after Patterson 1992, 186).

Moreover, there are shamanic origins for spiral designs. In rock art of the Great Basin of Nevada and southern California, spiral and concentric circle motifs indicate concentrations of supernatural power and are often metaphorically associated with the whirlwind and the shaman's trance. In this area they are one of the few geometric designs that can be interpreted in light of cultural meaning. Throughout this part of the greater Southwest, whirlwinds were thought to contain spirits, and were associated with the shaman's power to fly—a metaphor for entering an altered state of consciousness (Whitley 1996, 75–76).

A Paiute shaman's vision begins when he is sucked up into the sky by a whirlwind. At social gatherings of the Numic people, the Circle Dance also concentrated supernatural power for the benefit of the community by inscribing a series of concentric circles on the landscape, traces of which can still be seen in some places. Petroglyph depictions of Numic shamans often use spirals or concentric circles as stylized heads or faces because the shaman, like the whirlwind, concentrates supernatural power, often using such power in rituals pertaining to fertility and curing.

Spirals and concentric circles that were created in shamanic contexts can be viewed as a specific type of entoptic phenomenon (see the discussion about meaning and function of rock art in Chapter 1). Hallucinatory imagery experienced in an altered state of consciousness (shamanic trance, drug-induced visions, near-death experience) often includes a vortex, portal, or tunnel through which the individual may travel. The spiral or concentric circle motif can in some cases convey this experience of ascending or descending to different physical or spiritual levels.

Finally, spirals are sometimes used as markers for astronomical events such as solstices and equinoxes. As seasonal calendars that indicate important celestial transitions, they are related to fertility through mythic/ritual concepts about the sun's power to fertilize the earth and promote fecundity among all living things.

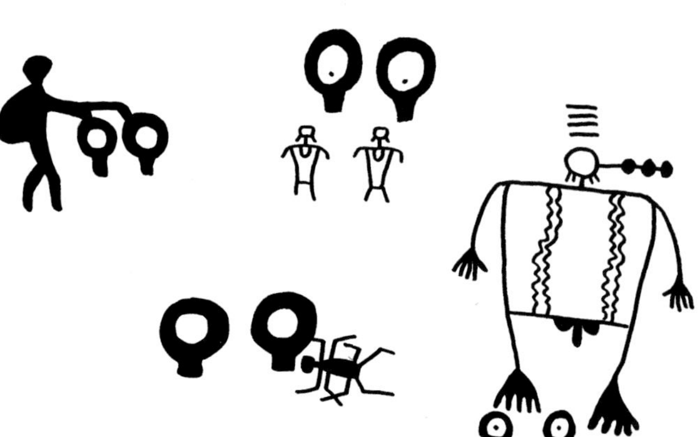

fig. 158. Basketmaker Anasazi petroglyphs depicting pairs of lobed circles, San Juan River drainage in southeastern Utah (after Manning 1990).

Lobed Circles

A unique and enigmatic symbol, the lobed circle motif occurs frequently in San Juan Basketmaker rock art in southeastern Utah, appearing in contexts suggesting fertility symbolism (Manning 1992). These circles with lobe-like extensions often appear in pairs and in association with the imposing shamanic figures of the San Juan Anthropomorphic Style (fig. 158). They are identical in form to an unusual type of Basketmaker artifact that has been found on the chests of Basketmaker burials in northern Arizona—carved wooden pendants, sometimes covered with inlaid turquoise and other stones (Morris 1925, 273). Archaeologists do not yet know what these objects or the rock art images of them represented to the Basketmakers.

Lobed circles often occur in petroglyph panels where the general theme appears to be fertility and human sexuality. One such site, in Butler Wash, Utah, is discussed in the section "Fertility Shrines and Rites." Among the images there are a copulation scene, females wearing menstrual aprons, crook-necked staffs, flute players, and flowering plants. The frequent emphasis on pairs of lobed circles has been interpreted as representing the birth or conception of twins. Such a pair can be seen in a petroglyph panel near Bluff, Utah, where the two lobed circles hover above a row of phallic flute players centered around a plant form as if to hasten its growth. Other examples of such a pair, including some anthropomorphized versions, are in fig. 158. Because of its shape and occasional occurrence in the pelvic area of anthropomorphs, lobed circles have also been seen as representing fertility and reproduction by symbolizing a womb (fig. 159). By analogy, they also seem to mimic the shape of ceremonial chambers known as kivas with their *sipapu* or place of emergence (Manning 1992, 179–99). Although the ideologies behind the creation of the mysterious lobed circle image evolved to incorporate many different forms in Basketmaker culture, the overriding themes are birth, emergence, creation, fecundity, and sexuality.

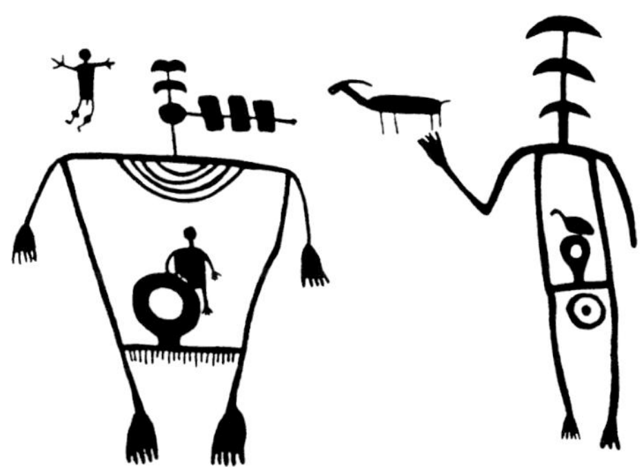

fig. 159. (left) Basketmaker Anasazi petroglyphs depicting lobed circle motifs in anthropomorphs, San Juan River drainage in southeastern Utah (after Manning 1990).

Blanket Scenes

The term blanket scene is used here to describe a series of related images occurring in Pueblo rock art in northern New Mexico. These consist of decorated, rectangular shapes resembling blankets with human heads an d sometimes feet projecting out from beneath (fig. 160). Although the exact meaning of such images is unproven, it has been speculated that they represent concepts or rituals related to fertility as modest scenes of copulation. In one petroglyph of this motif, a pair of heads suggests a man and woman lying under a blanket next to a phallic flute player who seems be serenading them. Other blanket scenes depict as many as five heads, presumably some of each sex. A number of blanket-like motifs containing fertility symbolism in the form of sprout-like designs and cloud symbols occur together with other obvious fertility symbols such as copulation and birth scenes at the Waterflow site near Farmington, New Mexico, suggesting its possible use as a fertility shrine (Warner 1983). The significance of the Pueblo Wedding Blanket, which was discussed earlier in describing ritual coitus with the Hopi Salt Woman Shrine, adds further credence to the interpretation of blanket scenes in a fertility context. Moreover, blanket scenes are not limited to rock art—one decorates a Mimbres ceramic bowl as well (see fig. 180 in the section "Sex and Fertility in Other Media").

Turtles

For some peoples turtles have symbolized fertility, and their images are found in certain rock art styles. In some tribes, turtle charms were worn by girls hoping for children and family life (Grant 1967, 31). Along with other reptiles and amphibians, it was believed that turtles brought rain or were otherwise associated with moisture. Turtles were also associated with the earth—in a dance, the rattle of turtle shells and stamping of feet awakened the earth and send a message for rain (Packard and Packard 1974, 21). In

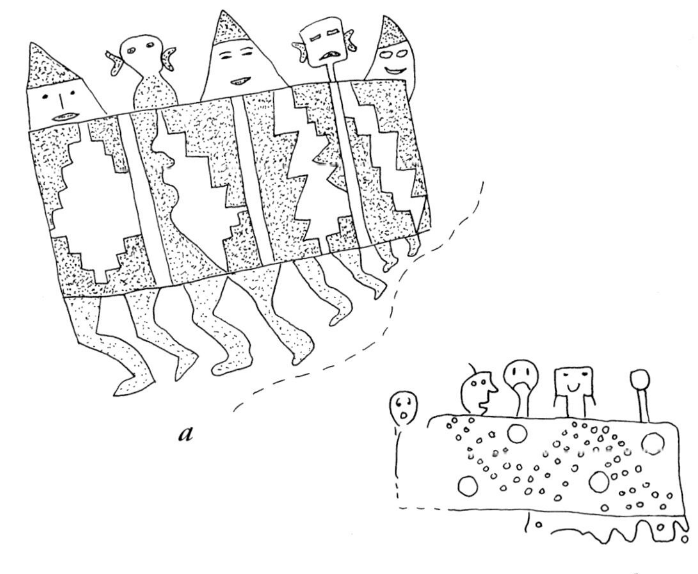

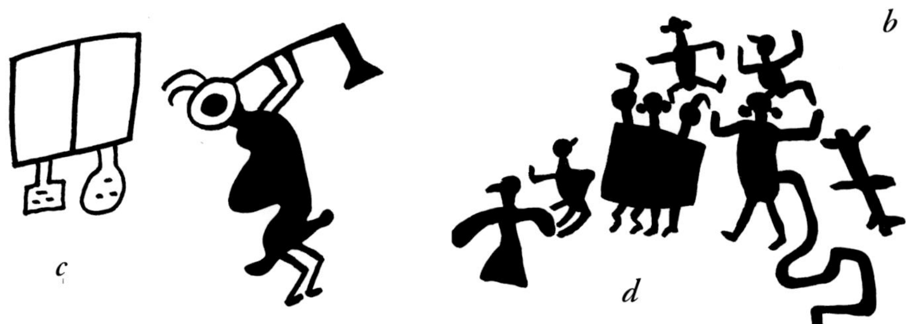

fig. 160. (right) Petroglyphs of blanket scenes: a.–b. White Rock Canyon, New Mexico; c.–d. La Cieneguilla, New Mexico.

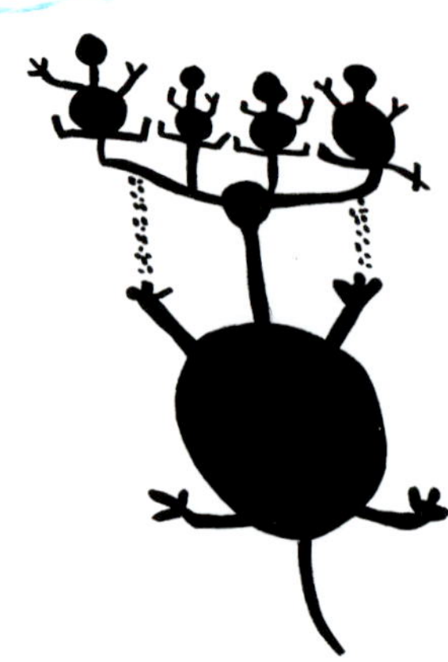

fig. 161. Petroglyph depicting a turtle mother with babies, Rio Grande near Bernalillo, New Mexico.

Algonkian and Ojibwa lore in Ontario, the turtle was a particularly sacred creature, regarded as a symbol of the earth and fertility, and addressed as mother (Vastokas 1973, 107). At one of their petroglyph sites, there are dozens of turtle images—some depicted with eggs, indicating their fecundity (see fig. 288 in Chapter 5). A petroglyph from the Rio Grande near Albuquerque depicts a turtle mother with her children—a possible invocation for fertility (fig. 161). The Zunis believe turtles are beloved ancestors who are associated with clouds and rain, and therefore treat turtles with great respect. It is also sometimes a hunting fetish whose depiction was a prayer for rain to make tracking easier and medicine to assure game moved slowly (Vastokas 1973, 22).

Hummingbirds

Another creature sometimes associated with fertility is the hummingbird. In Pueblo societies, these diminutive birds are said to "spend their time hovering about the flowers that are a sign of fruitfulness" and "have rainbow hues and suck nectar from flowers. Nectar is a quintessential liquid representing all the moist forces in growth and life" (Tyler 1979, 14, 117). These birds are also connected with stillbirth; at Isleta Pueblo, prayer sticks are made with hummingbird feathers at winter solstice for stillborn babies in the belief that they will be born again (Parsons 1974, 299–300). This is related to the role hummingbirds play in rejuvenating the sun as it is reborn at winter solstice, and so may serve the same purpose for stillborn children. A petroglyph from the Dirty Devil River in southeastern Utah appears to depict hummingbirds next to a womb-like design with a small anthropomorph inside (fig. 162). An interesting parallel to these concepts is found among the Tucano Indians of the Amazon, who believe that "the souls of the dead who lived conforming to the norms of their culture are converted into hummingbirds and enter a uterine paradise which is found under the earth" (Reichel-Dolmatoff 1967, 100).

Enclosed Crosses

The enclosed, or circled, cross occurs frequently in southwestern rock art, and in some contexts seems to be related to fertility. The association of the enclosed cross motif with other fertility symbols, such as vulvas or flute players, and its presence at rock art sites of known fertility significance have been used to link these concepts (Gough 1998). There is also ethnographic data from Hopi pottery symbols to support the fertility association. The enclosed cross symbol was used in ceremonies when a girl reached puberty. In relation to puberty, this emblem symbol-

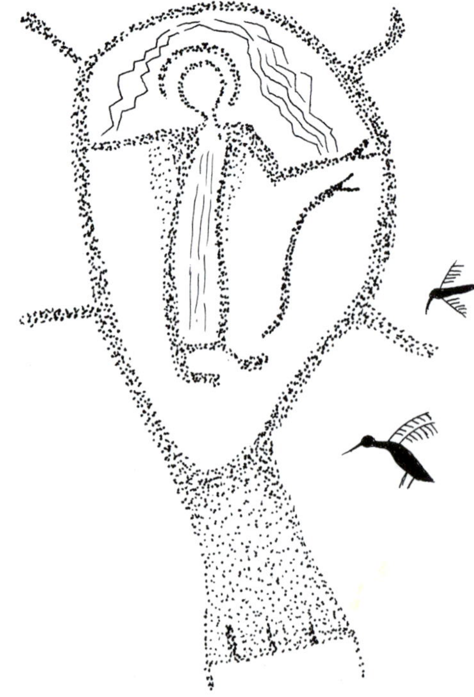

fig. 162. (right) Petroglyph depicting hummingbirds and an anthropomorphic figure enclosed in an oval-shaped object, Dirty Devil River, Utah.

izes the ability to bear fruit—to have a child. Pottery used in such puberty ceremonies had the symbol, and the girl's hair was dressed in such a way to produce the related Maltese cross design that served as an "emblem of fructification" (Patterson 1994, 197).

Further examples of enclosed crosses occur in rock art at well-documented fertility shrines, such as the Apache pictographs at Hueco Tanks, Texas; petroglyphs at Womb Rock in the Providence Mountains of California; the Chalfont petroglyphs in California's Owens Valley; and the Cave of Life in Arizona's Petrified Forest (see the section "Fertility Shrines and Rites"). The panel at the Cave of Life (fig. 26) seems especially to link this motif with fertility concerns since a large enclosed cross is the focal point of the composition, which includes copulating figures and a phallic shamanic figure who presides over the ritual. Moreover, that enclosed cross is the target of a shaft of sunlight about the time of the winter solstice. This feature has been referred to as the sky god's window, which releases germinating elements to descend on the coital scene and facilitate new life. The enclosed cross is also said to be "the eye of Co-tuk-inunwa, who is the sky god looking down through the sky window onto the earth. . . . Through this window Co-tuk-inunwa sends that particular element which causes life. The germs of all living things are formed, created by Muingwa, but Co-tuk-inunwa alone can endow them with vitality" (Alexander M. Stephen, in Patterson 1994, 62).

A final example of this motif in a fertility context can be seen in the Pueblo petroglyph of a possible Mother of Animals deity from the Rio Grande near Taos, New Mexico, where an enclosed cross is directly beneath her vulva, as if she were birthing the symbol (fig. 98b).

Other Fertility Symbols

Additional fertility symbols in rock art can only be mentioned briefly here. First, kachinas and Tlaloc images are both important fertility symbols in that they are related to moisture, rain, and fecundity (Schaafsma 1999). Many images of kachinas appear in Pueblo rock art after A.D. 1400, and images of Tlaloc—an analog of the Mesoamerican storm god linked with the earth, clouds, and rain—are diagnostic of Jornada style rock art of the Mogollon people (fig. 163). Other symbols may accompany them and stand for equivalent concepts of moisture and fertility—such as pots and bowls full of sacred water to symbolize springs or the *sipapu* and access to the underworld; crosshatched net patterns symbolizing clouds, appearing on netted shields and water jars; and stepped-fret designs similar to the cloud terrace which often decorate the torso of Tlaloc images and pots to represent clouds. The complex ideology of kachinas, Tlaloc figures, water containers, clouds, masked effigies, sacred bundles, and ritual paraphernalia all relate to themes of creation, emergence, fertility, rain, and regeneration, and their representation in southwestern rock art embodies these concepts.

Moreover, other symbols can be associated with fertility in particular places by

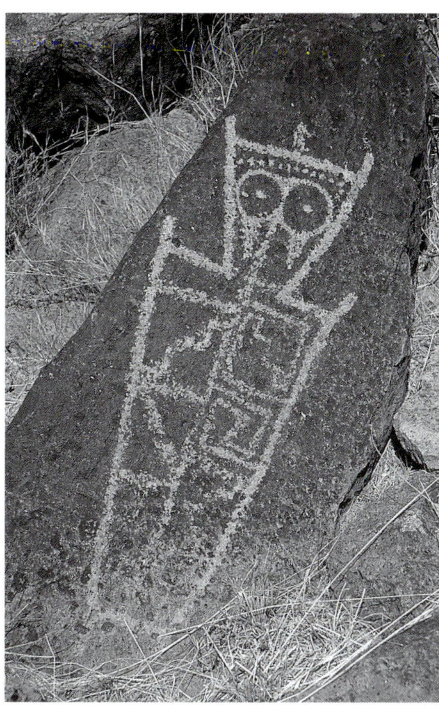

fig. 163. Jornada Style petroglyph of Tlaloc, the rain/storm deity, Three Rivers, New Mexico.

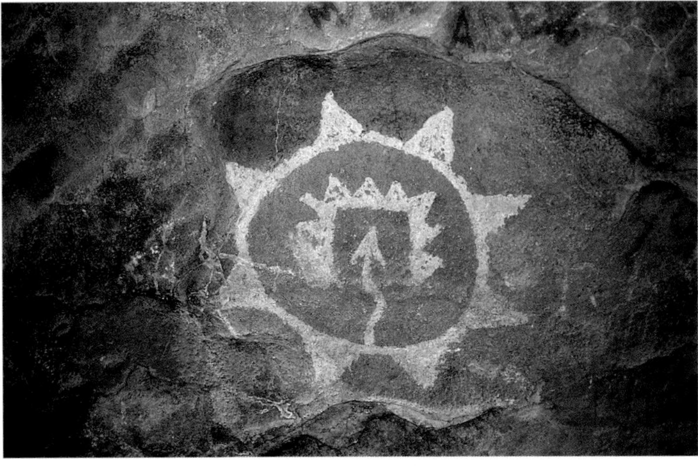

fig. 164. (above) Apache pictograph incorporating images of phallus, vulva, and sun, Comanche Cave, Hueco Tanks State Park, Texas.

certain cultures. Several images involving sun symbolism provide a final example of fertility symbolism in rock art. In a series of petroglyphs from the Jemez Mountains in New Mexico, the sun is depicted as a circular shield or face, to which are attached four "rays" that are shaped like vulvas (fig. 111). Further, in an Apache pictograph from Hueco Tanks, Texas, the rayed sun disk contains a box that symbolizes a vulva, which is being penetrated by a phallic arrow that probably represents the sun's fertilizing rays (fig. 164). Both images probably derive from ancient, archetypal beliefs about the supernatural union of sun and earth, from which all creation flowed.

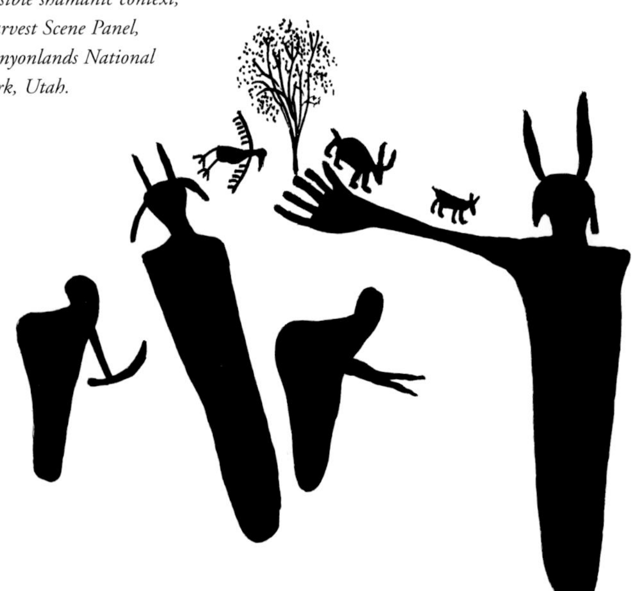

fig. 165. (below) Barrier Canyon Style pictographs representing fecundity of plants and animals in a possible shamanic context, Harvest Scene Panel, Canyonlands National Park, Utah.

SEX AND THE SHAMAN

> *While I stood there I saw more than I could tell and I understood more than I saw; for I was seeing in a sacred manner the shapes of all things in the spirit, and the shape of all shapes as they must live together like one being. . . . and I saw that it was holy.*[38]
>
> —Black Elk, Oglala Sioux

Because shamanism is such a worldwide phenomenon, it is considered by many scholars to be the basis of religion. Many of the symbols employed in shamanic practice by myriad cultures are universal. These persistent, cross-cultural symbols are explained by the fact that all humans are "hardwired" the same way—that is, our nervous systems and bodies have similar physical responses to the altered state of consciousness experienced in trance states. Since experiencing altered states of consciousness, or entering the supernatural realm, is a fundamental aspect of shamanism, the archetypal imagery from these experiences is valuable in understanding the iconography of rock art from cultures with shamanic roots.

The interconnectedness of all things is a basic tenet of the shamanic worldview. With the aid of spirit helpers, the shaman travels to other realms to contact supernatural powers in the interests of healing, fertility and abundance, divining, hunting, and weather control. They played important roles in influencing the health and economic and social well-being of their group.

Depictions that illustrate some of the shaman's roles can be seen in southwestern rock art. A fine example is the Barrier Canyon Style pictograph panel in southeastern Utah known as The Harvest Scene (fig. 165). Here it appears as if vegetation (perhaps Indian rice grass) is sprouting from the extended hand of an imposing, one-armed, horned shamanic figure. Birds and animals hover over his arm, perhaps representing spirit helpers or the abundance of food sources. There are also two humpbacked figures holding implements suggestive of harvesting tools like digging and winnowing sticks. Since humpbacked figures are connected with fertility, these figures may represent persons wearing packs or burden baskets for carrying the harvest. Other rock art examples of shamanic roles relating to fertility include a possible curing ritual with a female patient in a Basketmaker pictograph from Canyon de Chelly, Arizona (fig. 67); an upside-down shaman (in a trance?) with his crook next to a copulating couple giving birth in a Basketmaker petroglyph panel in Monument Valley, Utah (fig. 166); and a scene probably expressing shamanic hunting magic in a Fremont petroglyph panel from Nine Mile Canyon, Utah (Plate 10).

Recent advances in rock art research related to shamanism have resulted from the study of ethnographic sources as well as neuropsychological knowledge (Turpin 1994).[39] There is compelling evidence that much rock art in the Southwest, especially that of hunter-gatherer cultures, was created to depict visions and spirit helpers experienced during altered states of consciousness.[40] In the Great Basin and southern California, ethnographic records link rock art to shamans and puberty initiates, both of whom entered altered states of consciousness to acquire supernatural power. Native words from the region reflect this relationship. Among the Yokuts, terms for rock art sites were *pusin tinliw* (medicine house) and *choishishiu* (shaman's cache or shaman's spirit helper place). Further, Numic people of the Great Basin referred to a rock art site as *pohaghani* (house of supernatural power). Throughout the Far West, rock art reportedly was created by shamans following vision quests, and these sites were considered powerful portals to the supernatural (Whitley 1994, 3–4). Although there are not many ethnographic links for the rock art of the Colorado Plateau and the Lower Pecos River region in Texas, shamanic symbolism in the rock art of these areas is particularly evident, and similar conclusions about its origin and meaning have been drawn (Turpin 1994).

The nature of shamanic symbolism in

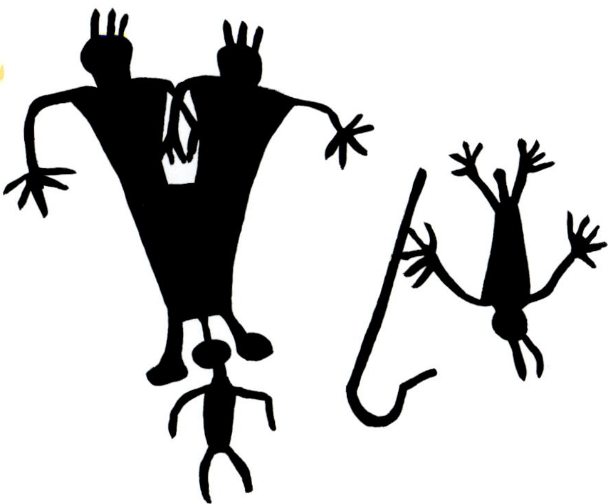

fig. 166. Basketmaker Anasazi petroglyphs of copulation, birth, and possible shamanic trance or fertility ritual, Monument Valley, Utah.

rock art was discussed in previous sections about entoptic phenomena and the neuropsychological model for explaining certain types of abstract rock art, and about the role of the flute as it pertains to aural hallucinations. For representational styles of rock art, there are numerous other models and metaphors for interpreting shamanic themes in rock art (Whitley 1994, 12–24). Some of the major ones are: death (because of the obvious physical similarities between dying and going into a trance); mystical flight (shamans in many regions of the world can "fly" to the supernatural realm, and their art is replete with flight imagery, including birds); drowning or going under water (many of the sensations in an altered state of consciousness simulate this); and sexual intercourse. It is with this last category that we are primarily concerned here.

People in shamanistic societies believed that the supernatural world was intimately connected to the fecundity of the natural world, and that the shaman could manipulate this power to influence the mundane world. Because of these links between sex/fecundity and fecundity/power, it was believed that sexual potency was an expression of supernatural power. The extreme sexual appetites and virility of shamans are emphasized in the ethnographic literature, which abounds with tales of shamans forcing themselves on young women (Whitley 1994, 21). Strongly erotic elements characterize many shamanic rites, which may include wearing of phallic symbols and singing erotic songs to strengthen sexual impulses and increase fertility (Vastokas 1973, 86). It is likely that many phallic figures in rock art originate in shamanic concepts.

As a result, sexual themes are sometimes expressed in rock art related to shamanism. An example of the connection between shamans and sexuality is found in the Southern Paiute term for the shamanic attribute of intelligence/understanding, which translates as "having semen" (Laird 1976, 84). The sexual intercourse metaphor for shamanic trance is illustrated by a number of ethnographic records from the Far West. Hallucinogens were sometimes used by shamans to induce an altered state of consciousness, and certain ones such as tobacco and jimsonweed (datura) can result in sexual arousal. Sexual symbolism in this regard is further expressed by the use of exaggeratedly phallus-shaped pestles for the ritual preparation of such hallucinogens. Moreover, nocturnal emissions, even for non-shamans, were believed to be supernatural experiences of intercourse with spirits from the world of dreams; in the acquisition of power during trance, shamans often have sexual intercourse with spirits.

Because shamans were said to "enter" rock during trance, sites became symbolic vaginas that were penetrated to reach the supernatural realm. The obvious sexual symbolism of caves, yoni formations, and other vulva-like rock features is discussed in Chapter 3. A shaman knocked on the rock with his ritual staff (*poro*) to open the vagina of the earth and release its fecundity (Laird 1976, 216). In a Chumash female initiation ritual where young girls were given jimsonweed, shamans copulated with them during their altered state of consciousness. Further, Numic shamans of the Great Basin sometimes had sexual intercourse with female patients during cures. Among the Numic-speaking Southern Paiutes, the mythic shaman Coyote was said to have three penes and to have invented copulation, as well as other sexual acts and taboos (Whitley 1994, 22). Moreover, during certain rituals in southern California tribes sexual intercourse was permitted for the entire community during a period of sacred time, with which trance states were typically associated. It is therefore likely that many rock art images depicting vulvas, copulation, or powerful, phallic anthropomorphs are related to shamanistic concepts about potency and fertility.

In seeming contradiction to the shaman's customary virility, some cultures occasionally had female shamans, and there are also many records of male shamans who were described as androgynous ("soft men"), or as transvestites or hermaphrodites. Apparently the androgynous nature of some shamans was an important source of power. The female powers of creation and fertility were sought by male shamans to balance spiritual forces within them. Transvestism is found in a majority of ancient priesthoods as well, where it was rooted in the ancient shamanic desire to imitate female magic and power. It is for this reason that berdaches were respected as mediators and seers—because they shared attributes of both sexes, they had "double vision" and could mediate between the psychic and physical, "seeing" more clearly than an individual of single gender (Williams 1992, 41–42). "Soft men" excelled at shamanism in many cultures throughout the world; this tradition has been documented especially in Siberia and much of northeastern Asia in connection with spiritual power, gender variance, and homosexual behavior (Williams 1986, 252–54). This attempt to fuse male and female power within one person (symbolized by the yin/yang concept in the Orient) may be an ancient source of transvestism and gender blending traits in humans.

An example of this strategy by shamans in southern and south-central California is the ritual of painting themselves black and red—the colors representing male and female, respectively. Such shamans were called *Paha*, which is also a name of the California red racer snake—an animal with black and red color phases during its life, which were thought to be male and female snakes. Thus these shamans believed they were combining the power and attributes of both sexes by painting themselves in such a manner (Whitley 1994, 28).

Examples of shamanic rock art with sexual and fertility connotations occur in many other parts of the greater Southwest. The depiction of visions and spirit helpers from the supernatural are common elements throughout North America and many parts of the world. The frequent association of snakes with fertility images has been discussed in Chapter 3. Another example may be the occasional transformation of the flute player figure into animal or insect forms—a process called shape-shifting that is associated with shamanic trance. Depictions of phallic males entering natural openings or symbolic vulvas in the rock are known from rock art sites throughout the region, and may, in some cases, be analogous to the shaman's "entering" the rock as recorded in the Far West (fig. 70). A possible shamanic curing ritual by a phallic figure with a plant and reclining patient is known from a Jornada Mogollon petroglyph site in southern New Mexico (fig. 167). The apparent sexual activity in fig. 168, from a Utah site, seems to depict a man and woman embracing in the presence of another phallic male who watches them in an attitude of supplication. His posture, phallic state, and elaborate headgear suggesting an aura of power indicate he is a shaman performing a ritual for fertility or curing. Moreover, a similar depiction in another southeastern Utah petroglyph (fig. 169) shows a couple embracing next to a kneeling figure who holds a bird—probably an officiating shaman (this panel contains numerous other birds and bird-headed anthropomorphs typical of ancient metaphors for shamans).

Another interesting example of rock art influenced by shamanic concepts relates to the role of power in curing and healing rituals. Power could have either positive or negative applications, such as witchcraft or sorcery, which is a reason why shamans were usually feared. A panel of predominately Basketmaker petroglyphs located on the San Juan River in southeastern Utah was ritually desecrated by Navajos living nearby during the late 1950s, after a Navajo witch was implicated in causing sickness to others by utilizing power taken from the rock art. This is believed to have been accomplished by scraping away some of the sandstone from the images, grinding it into a powder, and blowing it into the flesh of victims with a small tube. The curing rituals which followed determined that harmony and healing could be achieved by destroying the power of the images in the rock art.

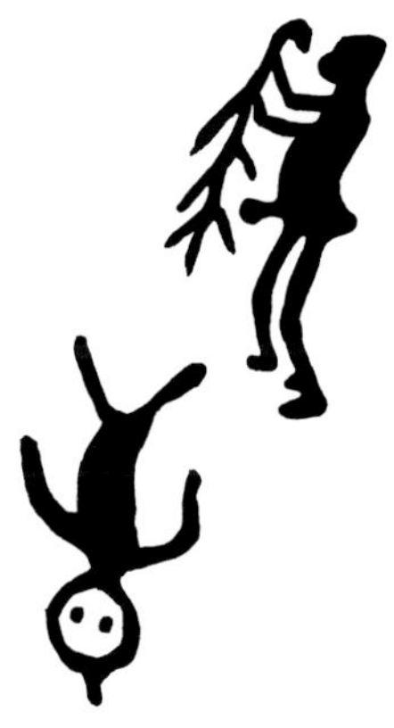

fig. 167. Jornada Style petroglyphs of a possible shamanic curing rite, Three Rivers, New Mexico.

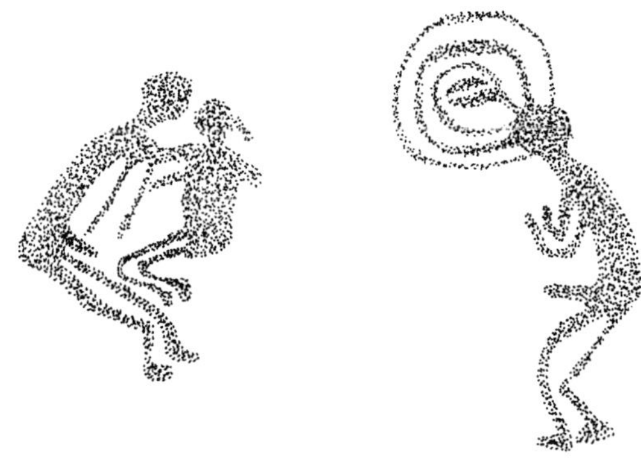

fig. 168. (above) Petroglyphs of a shamanic figure with a couple in a possible fertility rite, Mussentuchit, Utah.

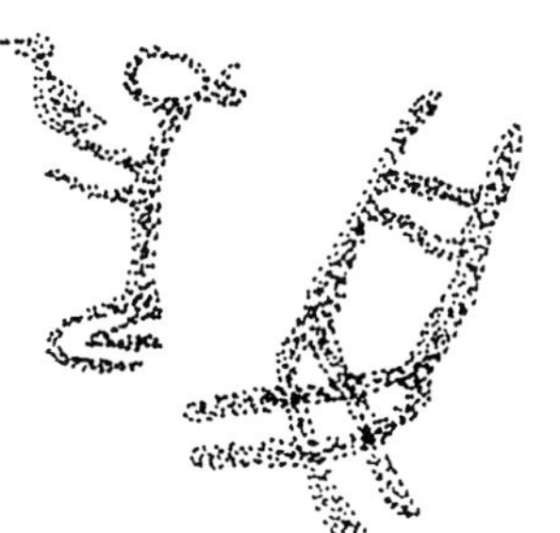

fig. 169. (left) Basketmaker Anasazi petroglyphs of a shamanic figure with a couple in a possible fertility rite, Cedar Mesa, Utah.

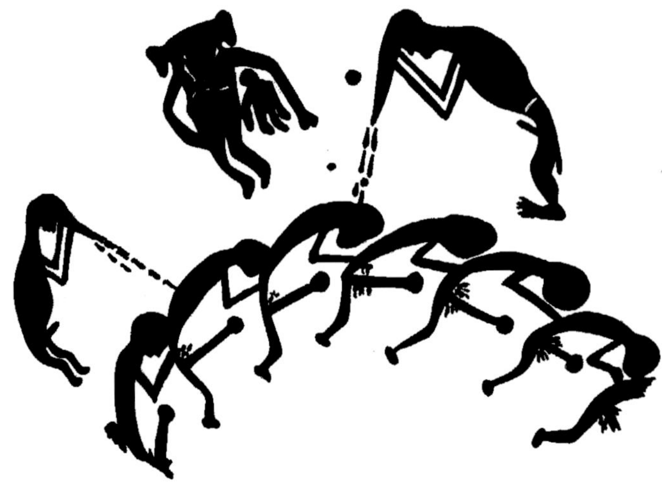

fig. 170. (above) Design in a ceramic bowl depicting a row of phallic dancers with two phallic males who seem to be ritually washing their hair and who flank a female and a child. Keam collection from Awatovi ruins at Hopi, Arizona (after photo A4273, Staatliche Museen zu Berlin–Preubischer Kulturbesitz Ethnologisches Museum, Germany).

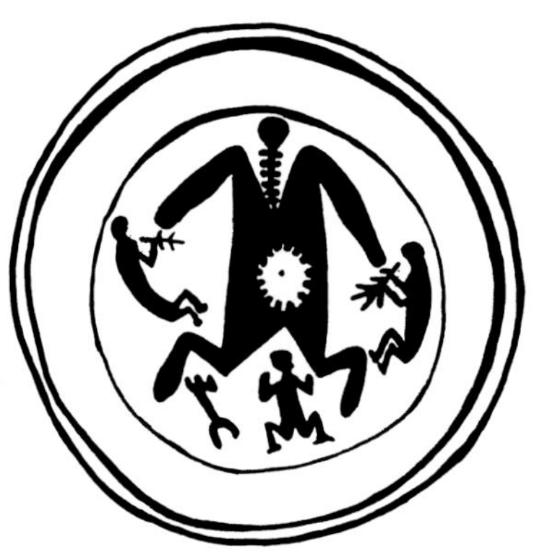

fig. 171. (right) Birth scene on a Pueblo IV bowl (after Hays 1994, 53).

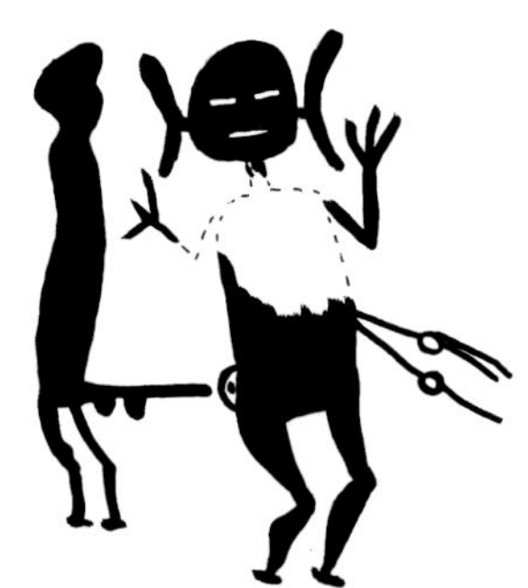

fig. 172. Painted design depicting copulation on a prehistoric Hopi (Sikyatki) bowl (after Fewkes 1919, Plate 29).

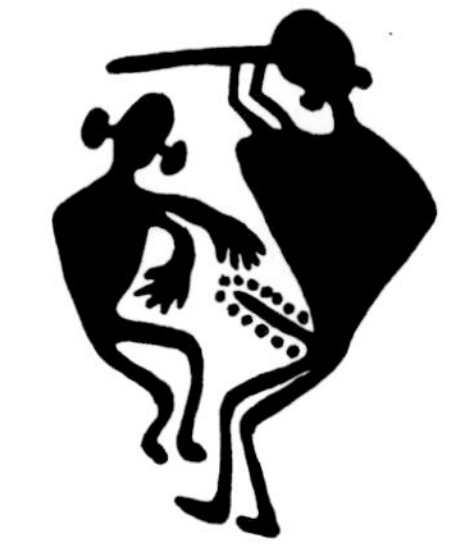

fig. 173. Painted design of a female and phallic, humpbacked flute player on a prehistoric Anasazi bowl in the Chappel Collection, Anasazi Heritage Center, Dolores, Colorado (after Slifer and Duffield, 1994, 111).

Certain figures in this panel, primarily the anthropomorphic images suggestive of Basketmaker shamans, were therefore ritually obliterated with metal tools such as chisels or axes.

SEX AND FERTILITY IN OTHER MEDIA

Although the focus of this book is rock art, southwestern native cultures created many fertility-related images in other media, including ceramics, wall murals, geoglyphs, and yarn paintings. The following are some representative samples for comparison and to provide cultural context for the rock art images. Many of the themes and symbols are the same, but it is important to bear in mind that rock is a relatively limiting medium compared to others, and that the level of detail present in an image can vary accordingly. Most wall paintings, for example, are more highly structured than rock art, suggesting those paintings and the architectural spaces surrounding them may have served more precise ritual objectives (Brody 1991, 139). Moreover, ceramics could have been made to serve utilitarian as well as ceremonial purposes, and their decoration probably reflects this.

In ceramics, images related to fertility and sexuality are quite similar to those observed in rock art, and include scenes of copulation, birth, phallicism, and fecundity of plants and animals. Examples shown here are from prehistoric bowls and pots made by Anasazi/Pueblo peoples in the Four Corners region and by Mimbres peoples in southern New Mexico. Among the Anasazi pieces that date from the Pueblo II to Pueblo IV periods are scenes of birth (fig. 171), copulation (fig. 172), and courtship and seduction between a humpbacked flute player and a female (fig. 173).

Regarding the scene depicted on the bowl in fig. 172, anthropologist Jesse Fewkes has said:

> While the figure of the man is likewise indistinct, the nature of the act in which he is engaged is not

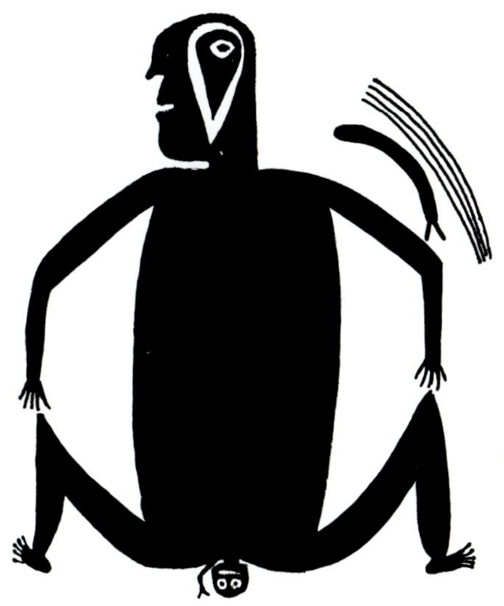

left in doubt. The attitude of the male and female here depicted was not regarded as obscene; on the contrary, to the ancient Sikyatki mind the picture had a deep religious meaning. In Hopi ideas the male is a symbol of active generative power, the female of passive reproduction, and representations of these two form essential elements of the ancient pictorial and graven art of that people (Fewkes 1919, 663).

In addition, numerous other examples of fertility themes in Anasazi pottery exist, such as depictions of snakes, cloud terraces and other symbols for moisture, crook-necked staffs, dragonflies, spirals, and twins. Moreover a substantial number of flute player depictions are known from prehistoric ceramics, a figure nearly always connected with fertility (Slifer and Duffield 1994, 110–15).

Ceramic designs of the Mimbres culture in southern New Mexico (contemporaneous with the Anasazi of Mesa Verde and Chaco Canyon, approximately A.D. 1000 to 1200) are famous for their creativity and sophistication and express belief in the connectedness of all things, as well as the continuity between the living and the dead, the natural and spiritual worlds. Mimbres ceramics have become a symbol of "primitive" sophistication. Rock art motifs of the Jornada Style occurring in southern New Mexico are stylistically similar to the designs on Mimbres ceramics, and both express fertility.

Birth is celebrated on the Mimbres bowl depicted in fig. 174, which shows a squatting female with the baby's head and arm emerging below. By contrast, death seems to be portrayed in fig. 175, which shows an anthropomorph pierced by a large arrow and with a spiral flowing out between the legs to suggest the life force leaving the body. The figure grasps a large centipede, which is often symbolic of death and the underworld. Other Mimbres bowls portray child rearing (fig. 176). In one scene, a woman holds a child on her lap; in the other scene, one of the adults holds an object, possibly a toy or rattle indicating play or a ritual item, representing a shamanic curing ceremony for a sick child. A ceramic effigy bowl from Casas Grandes, Mexico (fig. 177) depicdts a mother nursing her child. Further, a pregnant woman is depicted in fig. 178.

fig. 174. (left) Painted design of a birthing scene on a prehistoric Mimbres bowl, Swartz Ruin, Mimbres Valley, New Mexico (after Zimmerman 1996, 103)

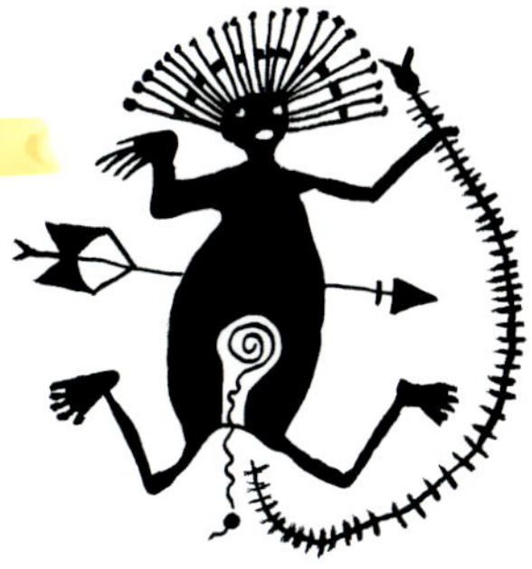

fig. 175. (above) Painted design of a death scene on a prehistoric Mimbres bowl (after Cunkle and Jacquemain 1995, 74).

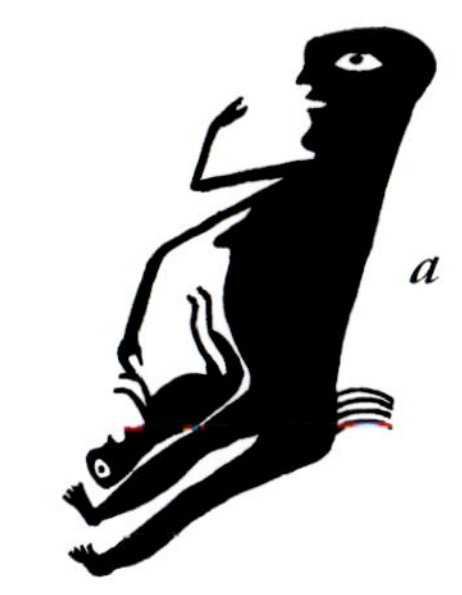

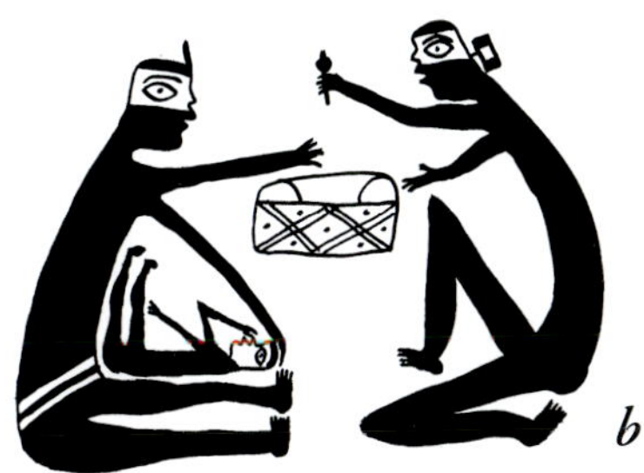

fig. 176. (above) Painted designs on prehistoric Mimbres bowls depicting child care: a. (after Moulard 1984); b. (after Brody 1977, 50).

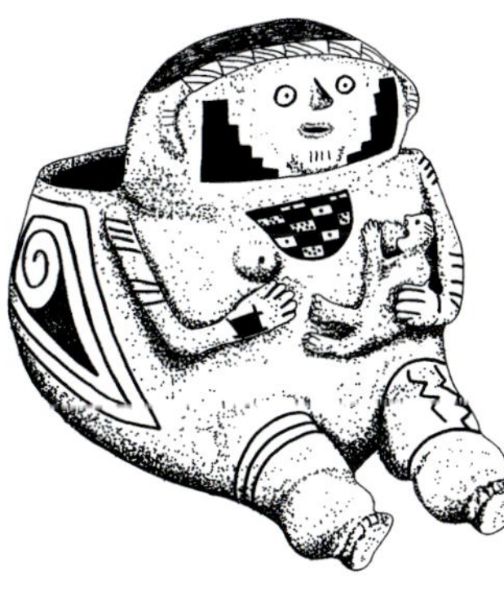

fig. 177. Ramos Polychrome ceramic effigy of a woman nursing a child. The cloud terrace (rain symbol) design on her face, along with the burden basket shape of the vessel and basket-like design on her chest combine to suggest this may represent a supernatural figure symbolizing fertility and abundance in a broad context. Casas Grandes, Mexico.

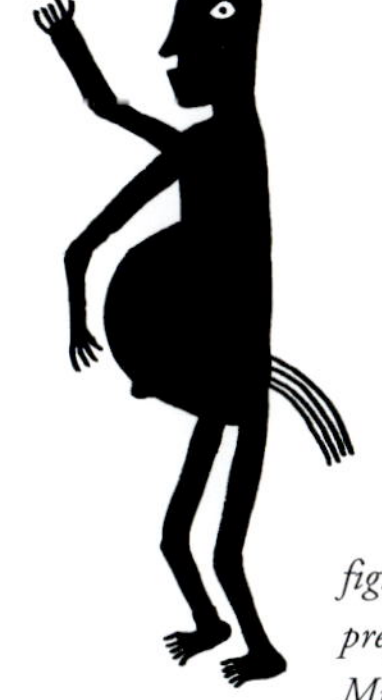

fig. 178. Depiction of a pregnant woman on a Mimbres bowl (after Snodgrass 1975, 8).

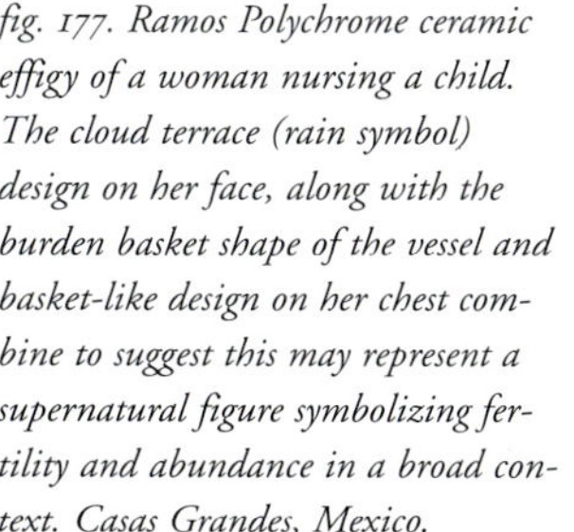

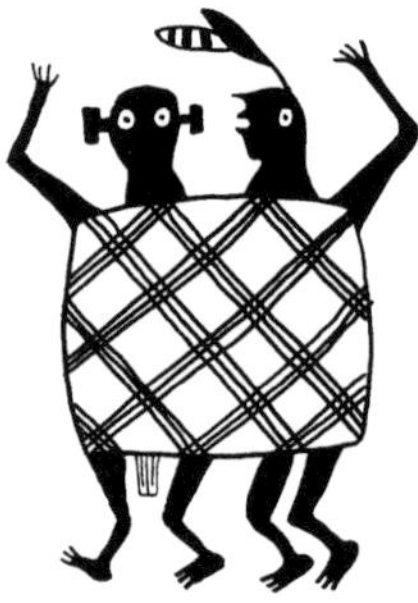

fig. 179. (above) Blanket scene painted on a Mimbres bowl (after Snodgrass 1975, 8).

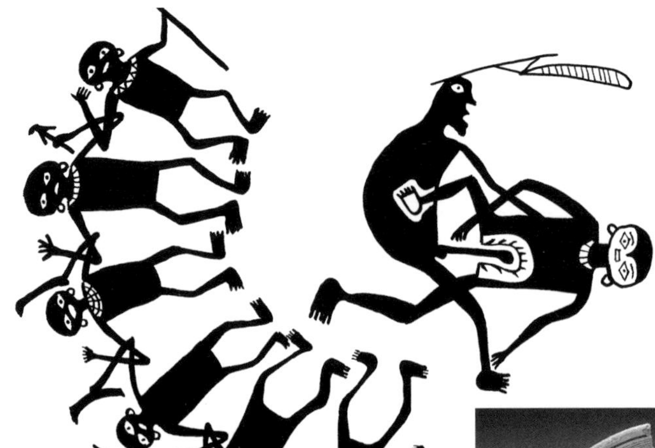

fig. 180. (left) Depiction of ritual coitus on a Mimbres bowl (after Snodgrass 1977, 279).

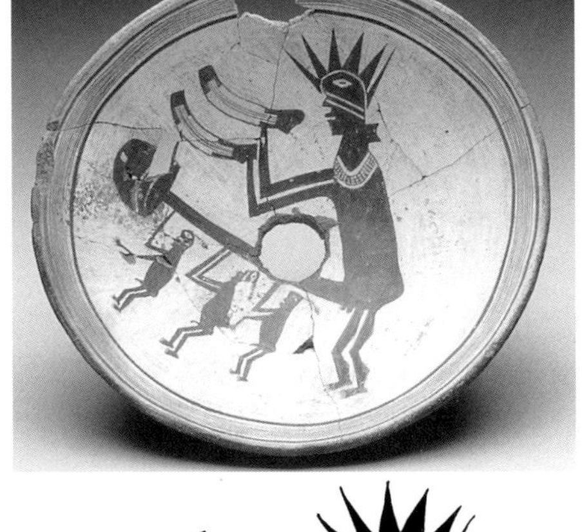

fig. 181. (right) Painted design of an exaggeratedly phallic man and three small assistants on a Mimbres bowl, 1000–1500 A.D.., (collection Frederick R. Weisman Art Museum at the University of Minnesota, Minneapolis. Transfer, Department of Anthropology, University of Minnesota).

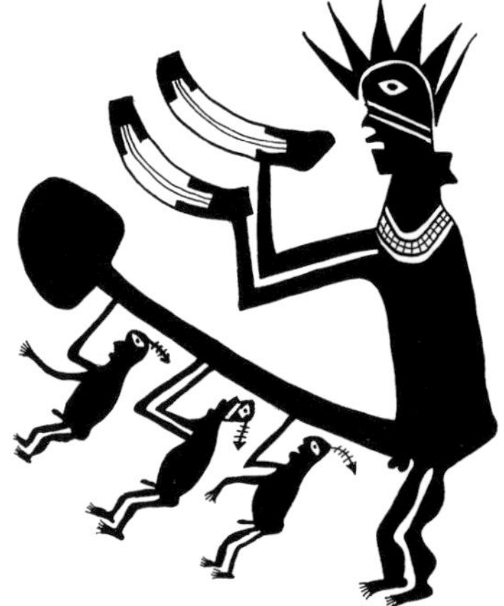

A rare scene of human copulation is depicted on the Mimbres bowl in fig. 180. This is probably a ritual activity since the couple is being closely observed by six figures whose arms are locked together as if in a dance, most of whom are holding prayer-stick-like objects, including a crook-necked staff—an object often associated with fertility or magical powers. A more modest depiction of intercourse may be implied in the blanket scene in fig. 179. A man and woman are shown beneath a blanket with a woven pattern—perhaps representing the Wedding Blanket, to which great ritual significance is given in some Pueblo cultures.

Other images are devoted to the male role in fertility. The anthropomorph in fig. 182 has an object on his back that may be equivalent to the hump on the back of flute players and other fertility figures; its curious shape may be a stylized rendering of a cloud terrace, or rain altar, thereby symbolically connecting male potency with the rain's power to fertilize the earth. Further, the image in fig. 181 shows a man with an outrageously exaggerated penis being supported by three small assistants, and carrying what may be two throwing sticks. There must have been an element of humor involved in creating this design, which has been described as follows:

> This suggests that the Mimbres people were familiar with men who thought themselves bigger than life, or bigger than anybody else, and felt they did not have to carry their own weight. However, the middle small man gapes at the big penis—a reaction suggesting that self-important attitudes were not common in the Mimbres world. The painter of the bowl may have been making fun of men who became too big in any way. In modern Pueblo thinking, any man who thinks himself bigger—that is, better—than others and does not do his own work or

fig. 182. (below) Phallic anthropomorph painted on a Mimbres bowl from the Pruitt Site, New Mexico (from the collection of Western New Mexico University, accession number 73.8.373).

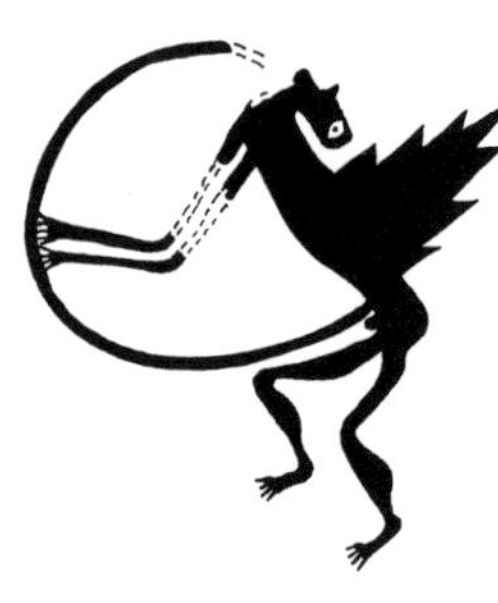

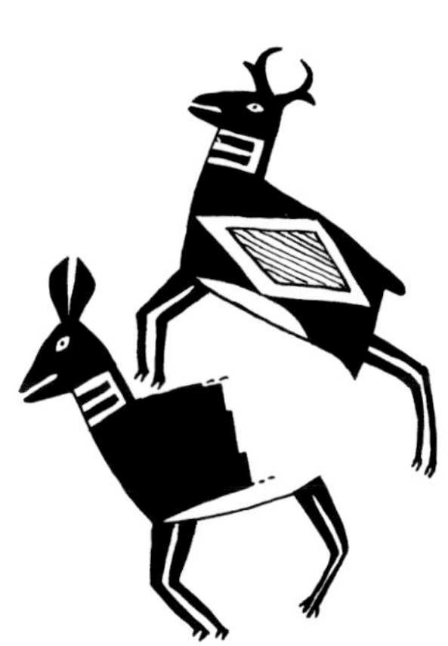

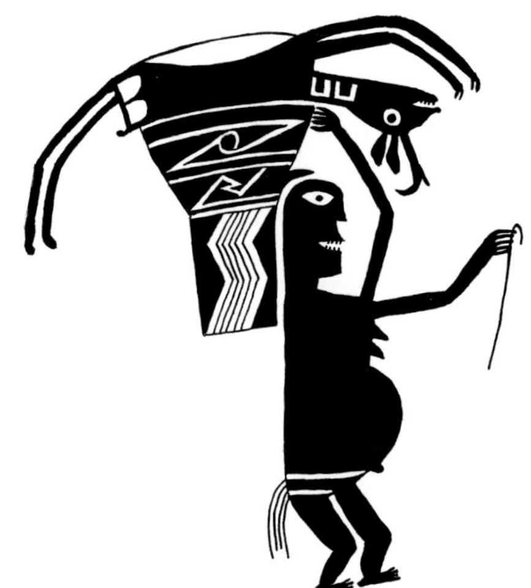

fig. 183. (left) Depiction of a mating antelope on a Mimbres bowl (after Brody 1977, 182).

fig. 184. (right) Painting of a pregnant female carrying an antelope in a burden basket (after Brody 1977, Plate 16).

assume equal responsibility for the welfare of the group is called a *wakusoyo*, a person with a penis that is too big. This is among the most derogatory terms in the Tewa language (Brody and Swentzell 1996, 35).

Fecundity of the natural world and an abundance of game animals are themes of some Mimbres ceramic designs. The scene in fig. 183 depicts two antelopes mating, while fig. 184 shows a pregnant woman carrying a dead antelope in her burden basket. She also holds a tiny crook-necked staff that is too small for use as a walking cane, suggesting it is a ritual object related to fertility (see discussion about these objects as fertility symbols in Chapter 3). Intercourse between a bighorn sheep and a coyote or dog is shown in fig. 185, which is an unusual depiction of interspecies mating that probably is a mythic encounter. Another supernatural sexual encounter, between a deer and two anthropomorphs, is depicted in fig. 186. Finally, agricultural fertility is implied in fig. 187, which shows two people working with curved planting or digging sticks in a garden or field full of growing plants—probably corn.

An unusual form of ceramic decoration with fertility implications is found on Anasazi (Pueblo II to Pueblo IV) pottery of northern Arizona. The "babe-in-cradle" pattern describes the small effigies of infants in their cradle boards that were used to decorate the ladle handles. Because specimens have been found in at

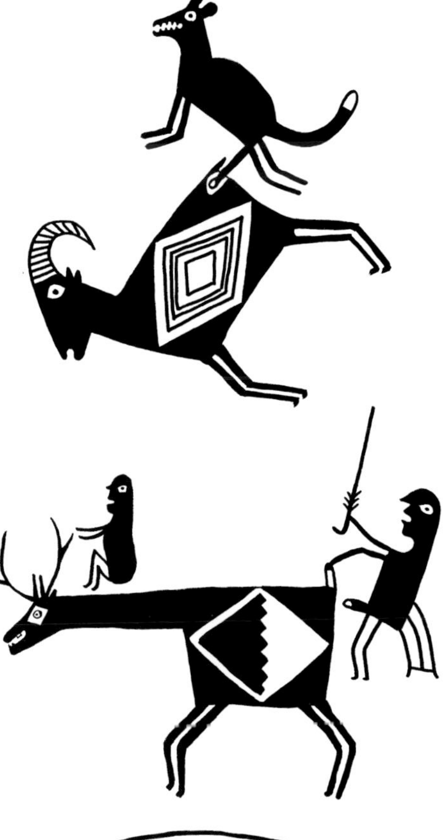

fig. 185. Mimbres bowl painted design of a coyote copulating with a bighorn sheep (after Snodgrass 1977, 281).

fig. 186. Mimbres bowl painted design of an anthropomorph holding a crook-necked staff and copulating with a deer (after Snodgrass 1977, 280).

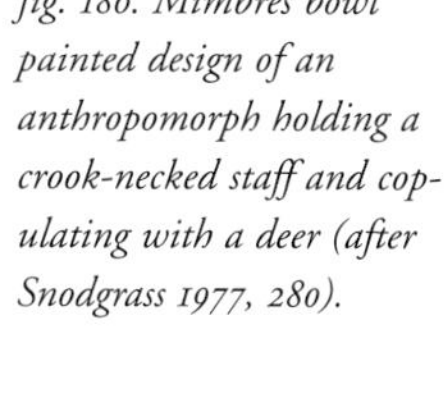

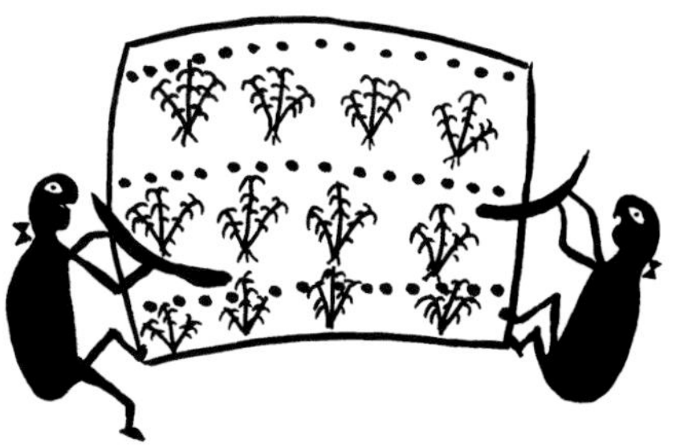

fig. 187. Mimbres bowl painted design of people working in a field or garden (after Campbell 1989, II(3):273).

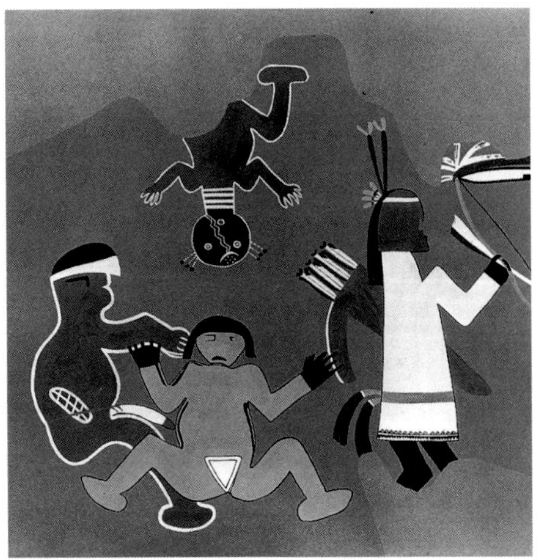

fig. 188. Kiva mural of a fertility rite at Awatovi, Hopi, Arizona (Smith 1952: fig. 53b, neg, no. N20217b. Reprinted courtesy of the Peabody Museum of Archaeology and Ethnology, Harvard University).

least six different sites and spanning three centuries, it has been interpreted as an unusually stable object that undoubtedly relates to an increase cult (Morss 1954, 38–39).

There are nearly as many wall paintings incorporating fertility symbolism as ceramics. Anasazi/Pueblo kiva murals are particularly rich in such symbolic content (Brody 1991; Hibben 1975; Dutton 1963). The following examples illustrate fertility symbolism in this medium.

An elaborate wall painting incorporating fertility themes was found during the excavation of Awatovi, a progressive Hopi village destroyed by neighboring conservative factions during the winter of A.D. 1700 to 1701. On one wall, a humpbacked, phallic figure is depicted in profile, painted blue with a white phallus having a red tip (fig. 188). He has an ear of corn stuck in his narrow red belt, perhaps to offer as a gift to the female, portrayed in frontal view next to him, painted yellow with a white vulva and black hands. The ear of corn may also be symbolic of crop fertility being ritually invoked here. In another kiva mural at Awatovi, a supernatural being or kachina spirit in the receptive female (hocker) position has a spiral on the chest to perhaps represent the life force, and lines extending down from the loins, that may reflect fertility by symbolizing the flow of menstrual blood (fig. 189). Finally, another kiva mural painting from Jemez Pueblo, New Mexico, depicts two figures playing their flutes over baskets of corn sitting on what appear to be cloud terraces with a rainbow arching across the scene—an obvious appeal for fertility in the form of rain for corn crops (Slifer and Duffield 1994, 118).

The remaining media mentioned here, geoglyphs and yarn paintings, are not as significant as ceramics and wall murals in this discussion of fertility themes, but a few illustrations provide an interesting comparison. Geoglyphs, also known as earth figures and intaglios, are large features created on the ground of arid deserts in the lower Colorado and Gila river valleys of Arizona and California (Johnson 1985, von Werlhof 1987). These sprawling sculptures, often nearly invisible except when viewed from the air, were created as messages to the gods by aligning boulders or scraping away a veneer of black, desert-varnished rocks to expose the lighter-colored soil underneath, in much the same way as petroglyphs are created on solid rock. The resulting designs are usually rather simple and abstract, but some are representational, such as the thirty-five-foot-long anthropomorph with an exag-

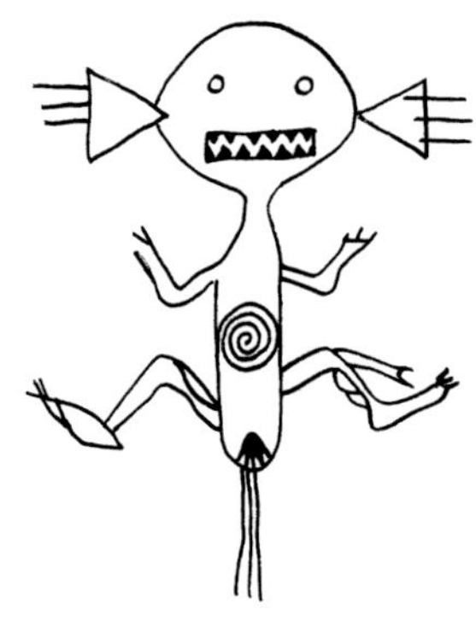

fig. 189. (left) Kiva mural design at Awatovi (Room 529), Hopi, Arizona (after Smith 1952).

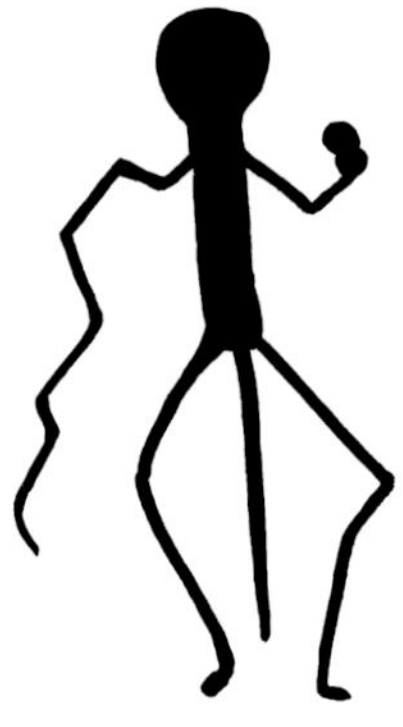

fig. 190. (right) Geoglyph of a phallic anthropomorph (approximately thirty-five feet long), lower Colorado River, California (after Johnson 1985, 108).

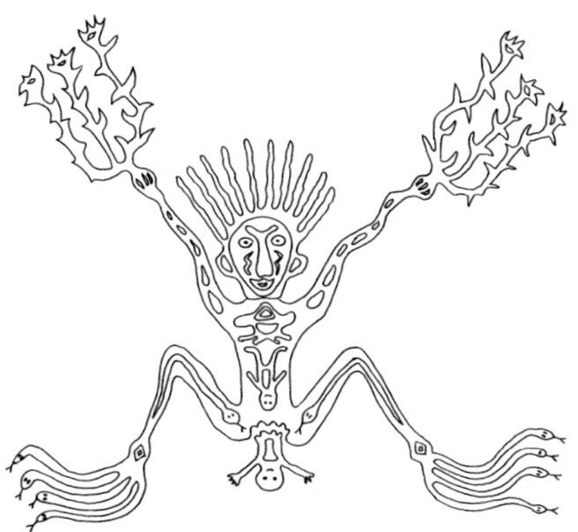

fig. 191. (far left) Huichol Indian yarn painting of Tacutsi, Goddess of Life (after Valadez 1992, 108).

gerated penis (fig. 190). This figure may depict a supernatural or shaman since he holds what may be ritual objects (some spheres and a snake) and expresses potency.

Female power and fertility are emphasized in the spectacular depictions of Tacutsi, Goddess of Life, in Huichol Indian yarn paintings from Mexico (fig. 191 and Plate 16). Tacutsi, also called Our Grandmother by the shamanistic Huichols, is another example of the archetypal Great Mother who gives birth to every living thing. In these renderings she is seen birthing a baby human but is surrounded by a menagerie of creatures as her toes become snakes and her fingers sprout vegetation—all symbolic elements that are also expressed in various ways in rock art images of the Southwest.

Another example of Huichol yarn painting that relates to fertility, described in Chapter 2 (fig. 18), illustrates the tradition of the couvade, where a man ritually shares in his wife's birthing pains. Huichol shamans tend to pregnant and birthing women with rituals that invoke the help of childbirth deities:

> The gods and goddesses bring forth the soul of the infant and determine its sex, based on what the shaman and parents ask for. Throughout the pregnancy, many votive objects are made by the shaman and the parents-to-be, who are constantly in touch with the magical plants and animals that pertain to childbearing (Valadez 1992, 79).

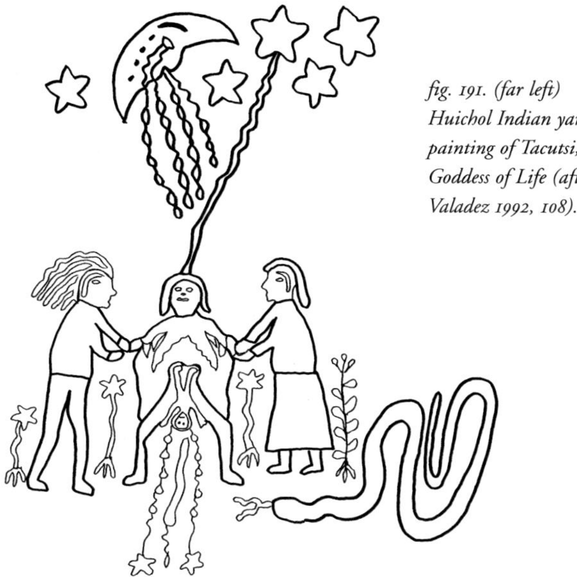

fig. 192. (above) Huichol Indian yarn painting of a birthing scene (after Valadez 1992, 108).

Such assistance by shamans and protection by deities is illustrated in fig. 192, a drawing based on a Huichol yarn painting. The woman giving birth seems to be receiving power from the moon and stars, as well as from magical plants and that omnipresent fertility symbol the serpent.

SEXUAL THEMES IN HISTORIC ROCK ART

Just as it is instructive to consider fertility themes in other media, it is also interesting to compare this theme in historic rock art to that of prehistoric rock art. Although there is much less rock art of historic vintage, it also contains fertility and sexuality themes. Among these depictions, the theme of sexuality occurs more frequently than the theme of fertility, as the images seem to be more about human desire than about the more spiritual concerns with fertility that characterize prehistoric images. Of historic rock art images, not all of which are by Indians, the majority are depictions of nude women and scenes of sexual intercourse, presumably the product of lonely males in remote settings. This is typified by an interesting series of well-executed charcoal sketches on the wall of Cowboy Cave in southeastern Utah. Evidently drawn by

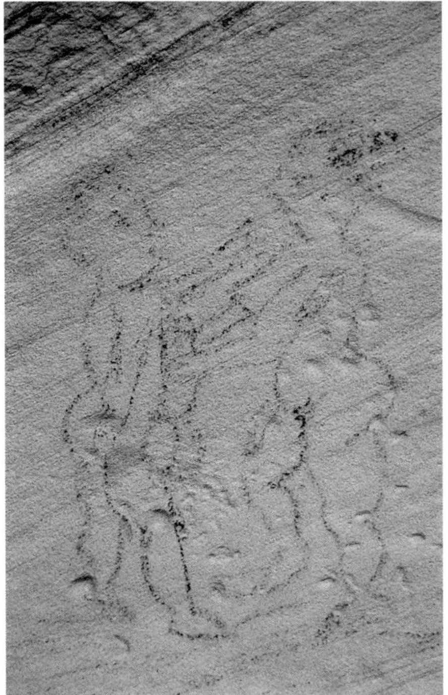

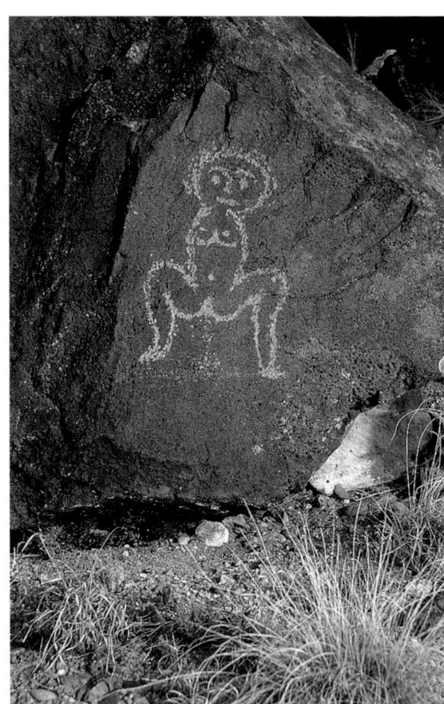

fig. 193. (left) Historic charcoal sketch of a nude couple on the wall of Cowboy Cave, Comb Ridge, Utah.

fig. 194. (right) Historic petroglyph depicting a squatting woman relieving herself, upper Rio Grande near Rinconada, New Mexico.

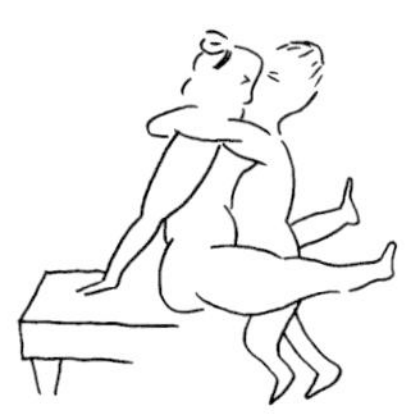

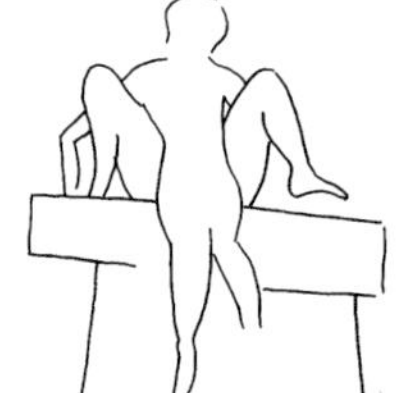

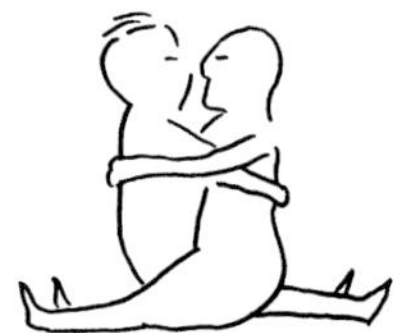

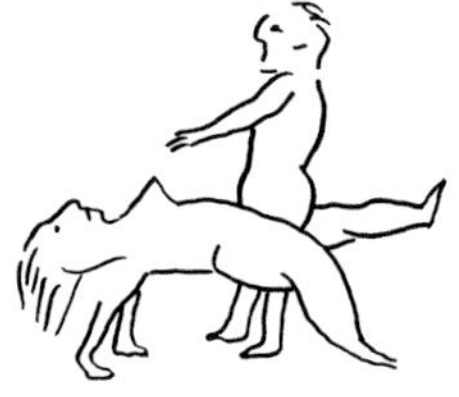

fig. 195. Depictions of sexual intercourse sketched in charcoal on the wall of Cowboy Cave, Comb Ridge, Utah.

the same artist, this collection of vignettes rendered in a quaint, nineteenth-century style portrays the sexual fantasies, or perhaps real adventures, of a bored cowboy or sheepherder who camped here (fig. 193). In addition to scenes of intercourse (fig. 195), there are also images of other activities that are absent from prehistoric rock art, such as oral sex, masturbation, and excretory/toilet functions. Inscribed on the wall of the cave is the crude message in period vernacular: "Heap Fuckem All E Time" —which seems to distinguish the tone of this rock art from the mysterious, awe-inspired visions of prehistoric rock art. From this vulgar sentiment, it is not much of a leap to contemporary pornography and crude tattoos.

The petroglyphs in fig. 200 are somewhat more symbolic in their meaning, although the combination of a church/ecclesiastical design, horse, and erect penis is strange. Perhaps this artist was merely making a statement about the things most important in his (or her) life. Nearby at the same site is the curious image in fig. 198 of an old-time U.S. postman delivering a letter, surrounded by a small herd of cattle—two of which are mating. Invoking fertility for livestock is an understandable theme, but the postman's role in this scene is less obvious—unless he somehow represents abundance in a similar manner as the cargo cults of some other native peoples.

The petroglyphs in fig. 199 from the upper Rio Grande in New Mexico, probably historic based on style and degree of repatination, also express sexual themes. Sexual intercourse is represented by the male and female symbols, and the two adjacent figures appear to be females wearing skirts. At another site nearby, a petroglyph depicts a squatting female apparently relieving herself (fig. 194). Feminine beauty is explicit in the talented

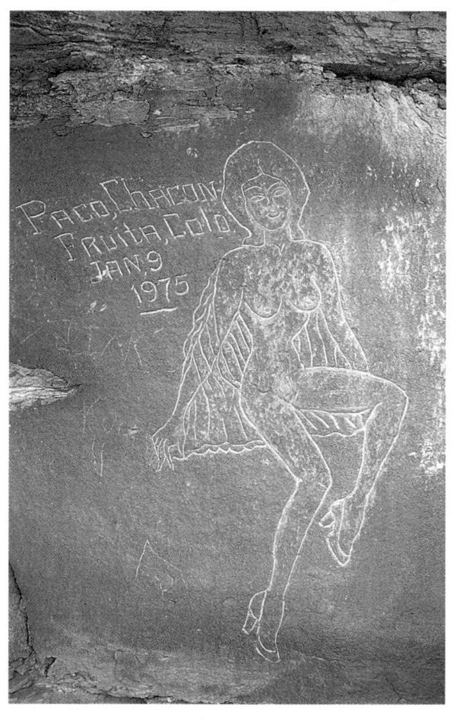

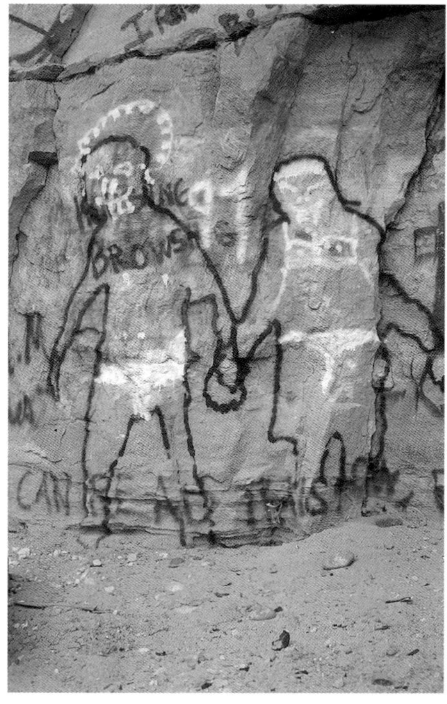

fig. 196. (left) Historic petroglyph depicting a nude woman, signed and dated 1975, Rangely, Colorado.

fig. 197. (right) Graffiti "rock painting" of a man and woman in their underwear, San Juan River near Bluff, Utah.

carving of a nude in fig. 196, which is signed and dated by the artist. A final example of fertility themes in historic rock art is the spray-painted graffiti in fig. 197; this composition of a hand-holding couple in their underwear adorning a cliff face gallery of more inane graffiti that overlies prehistoric Anasazi petroglyphs along the San Juan River near Bluff, Utah, is probably the product of Navajo teens who live nearby.

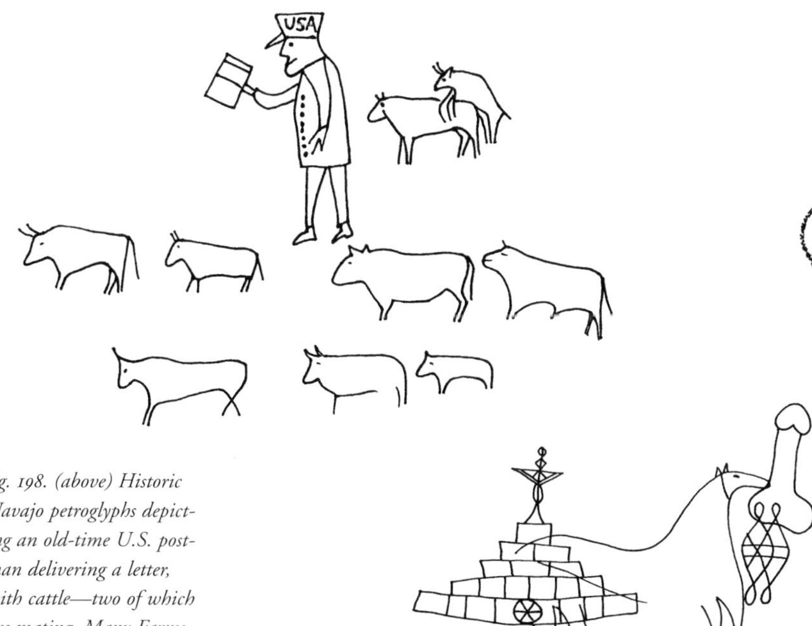

fig. 198. (above) Historic Navajo petroglyphs depicting an old-time U.S. postman delivering a letter, with cattle—two of which are mating, Many Farms, Arizona.

fig. 199. (above) Historic petroglyphs depicting a penis and vulva next to two figures wearing skirts, Velarde, New Mexico.

fig. 200. (left) Historic Navajo petroglyphs depicting a penis, horse, and church symbol, Many Farms, Arizona.

That our mother
May wear a fourfold green robe,
Full of moss,
Full of flowers,
Full of pollen.[41]
—Zuni prayer for summer

At the south
Where the white shell ridges of the earth lie,
Where all kinds of fruit are ripe
We two shall meet.[42]
—Apache Deer Song

It increases and spreads
In the middle of the wide field
The white corn, it increases and spreads
Good and everlasting one, it increases
and spreads.[43]
—Navajo Growth Song

Seeds sprout in the darkness of the ground before they know the summer and the day.
In the night of the womb the spirit quickens into flesh.[44]
—Black Elk, Oglala Sioux

She is the mother of all living things, i.e., of all human kind, all animals,
and all vegetation; plants suck from her breast a nourishing liquid,
it passes up from their roots to their flowers and fruit, and animals
and man eat of this vegetation, hence Tuwa'pontum'si is mother of all life.[45]
— Alexander M. Stephen
"Hopi Journal"

CHAPTER 4

FECUNDITY OF THE EARTH, ANIMALS, AND PLANTS

Fecundity is defined as fruitful in offspring or vegetation—being prolific. Although the term is generally interchangeable with fertility, it is used in this chapter to illustrate those concepts which apply to the natural world beyond human societies. This is, of course, an artificial distinction because indigenous peoples' concerns with fertility are inextricably linked with the fecundity of the earth, plants, and animals. However, while Chapter 3 focused on these topics mainly in connection with human societies, the role of fecundity in the natural world and its expression in rock art are explored here.

Humans have always perceived their own nature and activities reflected in the forces of nature. In early religions, natural phenomena are often seen as behaving in a recognizably human manner. Thus, the fecundity of the earth came to be linked with the fertility and sexual customs of humans. Many cultures perceived a connection between human sexuality and plant and animal fertility and, through sympathetic magic and rituals related to sex, invoked supernatural power in guaranteeing the fruitfulness of the earth. Ideas and beliefs about fecundity of the world, and the images that stem from them, can be considered on two basic levels that correspond to developmental stages of human societies—that of hunter-gatherers and that of agriculturalists. In his *Historical Atlas of World Mythology*, Joseph Campbell called these divisions "The Way of the Animal Powers" and "The Way of the Seeded Earth" (Campbell 1988, 1989).

Beginning with rupestrian art in the Paleolithic painted caves in Europe, abundance of animals has been associated with human sexuality by hunting cultures around the world. Such cultures are very aware that their survival depends on the flesh of other living beings and that the life they take becomes their own. In their myths, humanity often is descended from animals, who are also the source of power and knowledge needed by humans to survive. These gifts from the animal ancestors were frequently granted by sexual means—giving the hunt a connotation of sexual or mystical union. Hunters among some Athabaskan groups claim their knowledge of the animals' ways is because long ago men married them and acquired this knowledge from their animal wives (Bishop 1996, 12). Some Plains tribes believed humanity resulted from a sexual transfer of power between a woman and a buffalo. The Mandans' Buffalo Dance ritualized this ancient event to ensure abundant herds of the animal; during it a woman would have intercourse with a man of great power who represented the buffalo, and would extract the power from the medicine bundle he carried

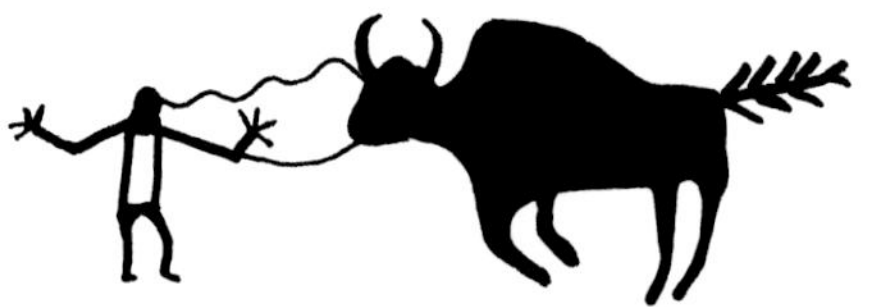

fig. 201. Pictograph representing an exchange of power between a human and a buffalo, Churchill River, Saskatchewan, Canada (after Grant 1967, 147).

(Bishop 1996, 13). An exchange of power between a human and a buffalo is depicted in a rock painting in fig. 201.

Most ancient hunting cultures were shamanic, and their beliefs and rituals concerning fecundity of animals were directed by their shamans. He was responsible for regulating the flow of life force between his people and the animals they depended upon. Sometimes this responsibility involved visiting a supernatural spirit in charge of the animals and negotiating for a sufficient number of animal souls that could be hunted:

> The underlying mythic theme—which occasionally becomes explicit—is of a covenant between the animal and human villages whereby in recognition of the necessities of the way of the will in nature, the animals are given as individuals willingly to the nourishment of the human tribes, with an understanding that through appropriate rites recognition will be rendered in a sacred way . . . and the given lives thus returned in spirit to their living ground (Campbell 1988, II:1:10)

Sometimes ritual prescribed a period of sexual abstinence before a hunt as a means of propitiating animal spirits and producing more power for successful hunting. Among the Desana people of the Amazon, the verb for "to hunt" translates as "to make love to the animals" (Reichel-Dolmatoff 1971). Similar concepts are responsible worldwide for piercing by spear or arrow as a metaphor for sexual penetration. Sometimes hunters would have erotic dreams of animals who presented themselves to be fertilized in order to multiply. Sexually explicit dances were performed to renew life, and shamans in Siberia imitated the rut of elk and reindeer to represent intercourse with the daughter of the Master of Animals. Images depicting these concepts occur in prehistoric art around the world, including the Southwest. Older rock art attributable to the Desert Archaic Period in the Southwest is most likely to have been influenced by shamanism and to exhibit such fecundity themes related to hunting and animals, but even in more recent rock art of agricultural peoples there are vestiges of ancient shamanic hunting rituals along with themes pertaining to plants, rain, and fertility of the soil.

The fertility rituals of agricultural cultures, though sometimes possessing elements from the hunting-gathering past, often center on concerns about rain and seasonal cycles. With the shift from hunting to planting and harvesting, humans focused on the mysteries of the plant world where metamorphosis prevails, and on the celestial elements of sun and rain upon which a fruitful harvest depends. Beliefs about the sky fertilizing the earth with rain and sunlight are nearly universal in the Southwest and elsewhere around the world. In parts of Africa and Australia, women who wish to conceive may go out and lie in a rainstorm. The significance of rain in the myths and rites of southwestern peoples is discussed in Chapter 3, along with rock art images related to moisture, such as cloud terraces (fig. 143), snakes, and dragonflies.

Among both hunting and planting cultures, the rite of Sacred Marriage—where a couple ritually enacts the sexual congress of god and goddess to guarantee the fecundity of the earth—was a widespread ancient practice and is illustrated in prehistoric art from many places throughout the world; southwestern examples are given in Chapter 3, in the section "Fertility Shrines and Rites." Widely know by its Greek name of *hieros gamos*, the first written record of the Sacred Marriage Ceremony is an ancient Sumerian hymn from the third millennium B.C., recorded on clay tablets (Eisler 1995, 66–71). In the "Hymn of Innana," poetic and erotic passages deal with the Sacred Marriage of Innana—Goddess of Love and Procreation. In annual New Year celebrations, Innana's Sacred Marriage to the reigning king of Sumer was enacted by a high priestess representing the Goddess. Key elements of these traditions go back to at least the Neolithic Period. In anticipation of her marriage to the pastoral king/god Dumuzi, Innana is filled with sexual desire and likens her vulva to the horn-shaped crescent moon and a fallow plot of land. She proclaims:

"My vulva, the horn, the Boat of Heaven, is full of eagerness like the young moon. . . . Who will plow my vulva? Who will plow my high field? Who will plow my wet ground?" She is answered by her lover, "Great Lady, the king will plow your vulva. I Dumuzi the King, will plow your vulva." When Innana accepts him, the hymn relates: "At the king's lap stood the rising cedar. Plants grew high by their side. Grains grew high by their side. Gardens flourished luxuriantly" (Eisler 1995, 69).

The hymn continues with language that combines sexuality with the earth's fecundity:

> My caresser of the soft thighs, He is the one my womb loves best, He is lettuce planted by the water.
>
> Oh Lady, your breast is your field.
> Innana, your breast is your field.
> Your broad field pours out plants.
> Your broad field pours out grain.
> Water flows from on high for your servant (Eisler 1995, 69).

This ancient Mesopotamian narrative, as well as numerous images from the Neolithic Period, show that people have long invoked the fecundity of the earth by linking it to sexuality. The sacred sexual union between divine male and female partners helped drive the larger cosmic cycles that energized and fertilized the natural world.

Focusing on fecundity in southwestern rock art, we find that these themes reflect the same ideas as discussed above—concerns with animals and hunting, rain, and the germination and growth of plants. Scenes with animals in implied hunting magic contexts occur in rock art that dates from archaic hunter-gatherers to historic agriculturalists, because even though some southwestern peoples adopted agriculture and herding, they have always been hunters, too. Hunting scenes are, in fact, one of the more common themes in southwestern rock art. The link between hunting and fecundity/sex is sometimes expressed by the presence of hunters with erect phalli (fig. 202), including hunting scenes with phallic, humpbacked flute players (fig 203). However, hunting scenes are not always what they appear to be. In the Great Basin, for example, the frequently repeated scenes depicting the killing of bighorn sheep actually represent a metaphor for the Numic rain shaman falling into a trance. But this is still related to fecundity, because the bighorn sheep was associated with rain, and the shaman's trance was part of a ritual invoking supernatural power in bringing rain and well-being for all things. There are records that shamans traveled from as far as Utah to tap the rainmaking power of the Coso

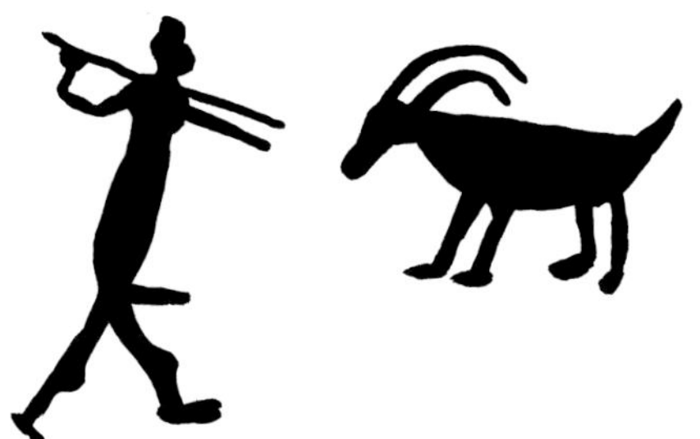

fig. 202. Petroglyphs depicting a phallic hunter hurling a spear at a bighorn sheep, Rochester Creek, Utah.

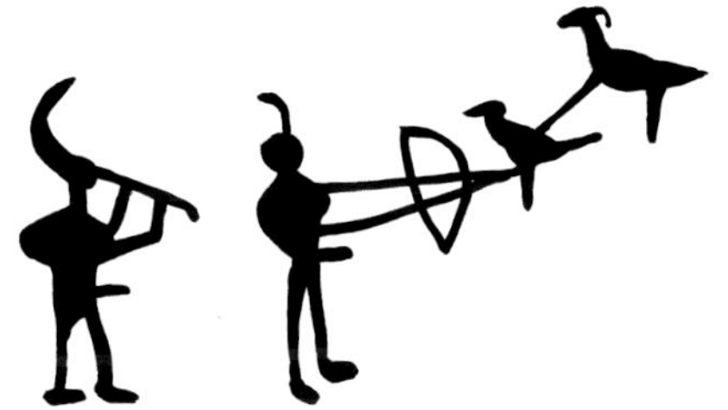

fig. 203. Pueblo petroglyphs depicting a humpbacked, phallic hunter with bow, shooting at a bird and an animal, along with a flute player, La Cienega, New Mexico.

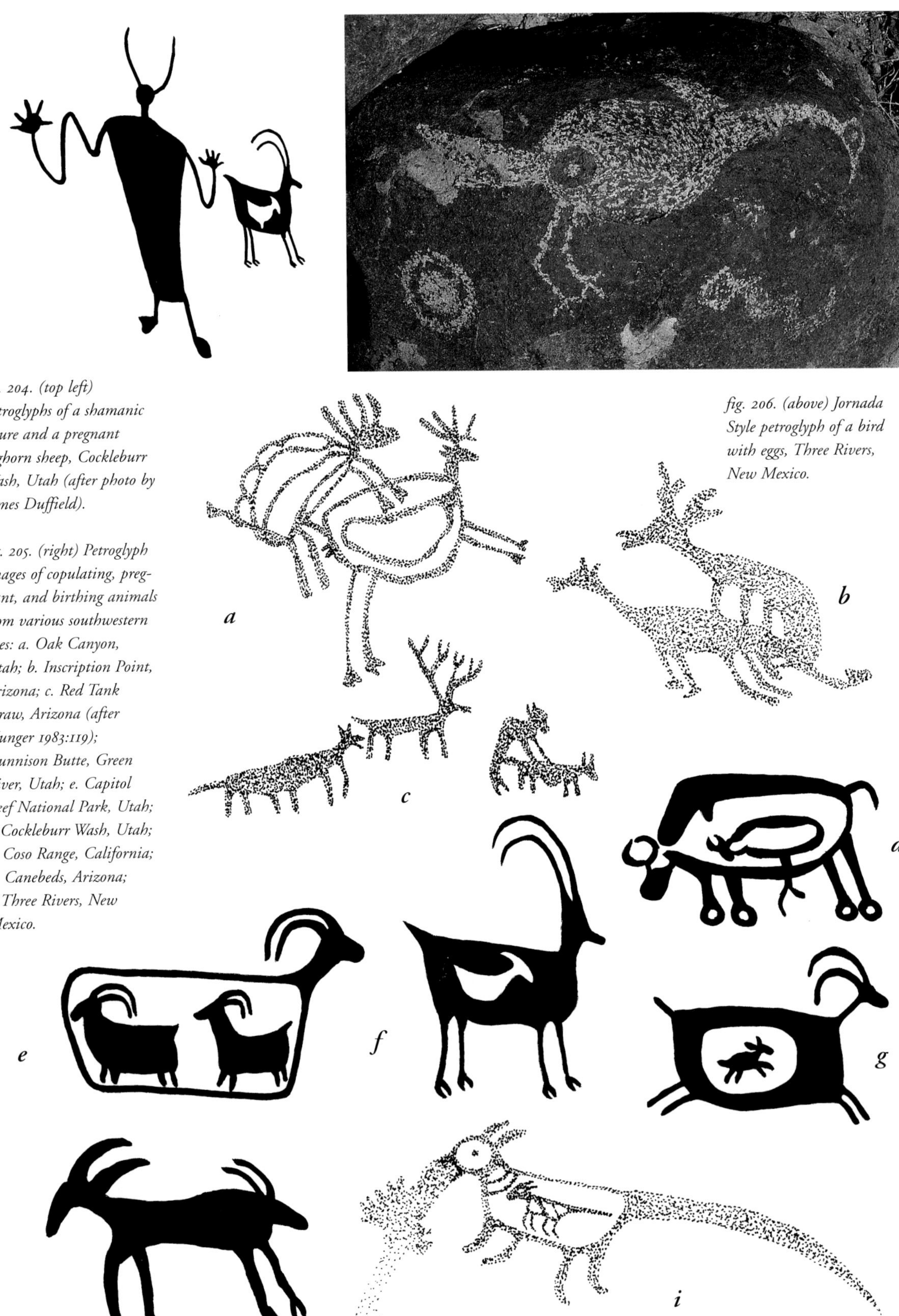

fig. 204. (top left) Petroglyphs of a shamanic figure and a pregnant bighorn sheep, Cockleburr Wash, Utah (after photo by James Duffield).

fig. 205. (right) Petroglyph images of copulating, pregnant, and birthing animals from various southwestern sites: a. Oak Canyon, Utah; b. Inscription Point, Arizona; c. Red Tank Draw, Arizona (after Hunger 1983:119); Gunnison Butte, Green River, Utah; e. Capitol Reef National Park, Utah; f. Cockleburr Wash, Utah; g. Coso Range, California; h. Canebeds, Arizona; i. Three Rivers, New Mexico.

fig. 206. (above) Jornada Style petroglyph of a bird with eggs, Three Rivers, New Mexico.

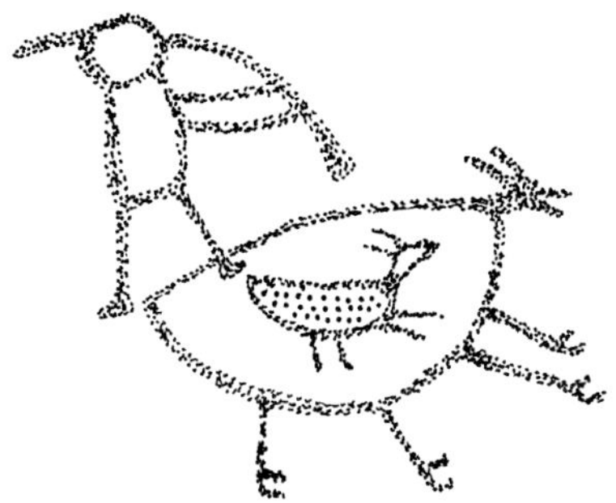

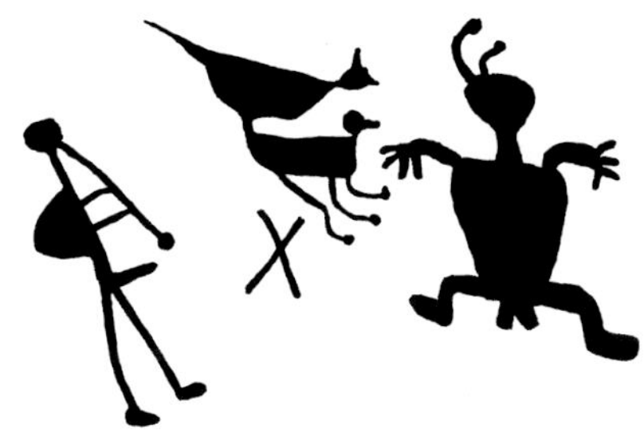

fig. 207. (left) Petroglyphs of a flute player and a pregnant deer, Holiday Mesa, Jemez Mountains, New Mexico.

fig. 208. (right) Petroglyphs of a hump-backed, phallic flutplayer with a female and copulating animals, Santa Fe River, New Mexico.

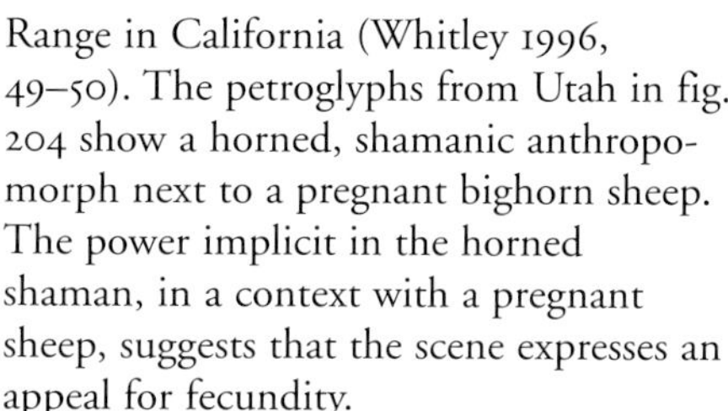

Range in California (Whitley 1996, 49–50). The petroglyphs from Utah in fig. 204 show a horned, shamanic anthropomorph next to a pregnant bighorn sheep. The power implicit in the horned shaman, in a context with a pregnant sheep, suggests that the scene expresses an appeal for fecundity.

Prayers for abundant game are reflected in numerous rock art depictions of pregnant animals and animals giving birth (fig. 205). Moreover, concern with fecundity is especially evident in the scene showing a pregnant deer with spotted fawn inside her next to a flute player (fig. 207) and in the depiction of mating animals near a phallic flute player and a receptive female (fig. 208). A pregnant bison is depicted in the well-crafted petroglyph from Nine Mile Canyon, Utah (fig. 209), and a bighorn sheep gives birth in a petroglyph from the Escalante River, Utah (fig. 210).

A petroglyph panel in Largo Canyon, New Mexico, also illustrates the link between hunting and fecundity of animals (fig. 211). It includes several hunters with bows and a dead deer, in the same scene with two depictions of antlered stags mating with female deer. A prayer for abundant game is also expressed in the long line of animals approaching a lone hunter with bow from Tapia Canyon, New Mexico. Further, abundant game is represented by depictions of enclosures or corral-like traps that were used in communal game drives (fig. 212). Animals such as deer, pronghorn antelope, and rabbits were sometimes herded by long lines of people into brush fences, stockades, or occasionally woven fiber nets, where waiting hunters would dispatch the animals.

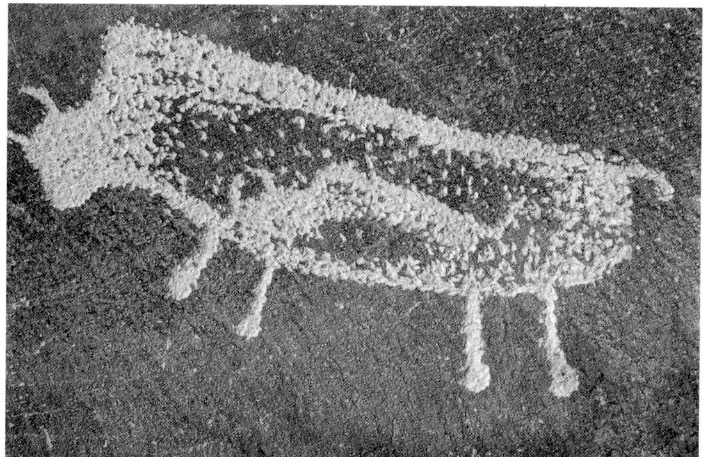

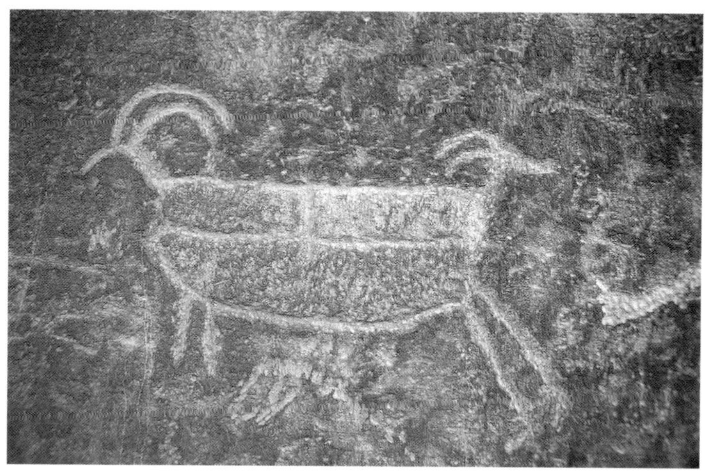

fig. 209. (upper) Petroglyph of a pregnant bison, Nine Mile Canyon, Utah; photo by James Duffield.

fig. 210. (lower) Petroglyph of a bighorn sheep giving birth, Baker Bench, Escalante River, Utah.

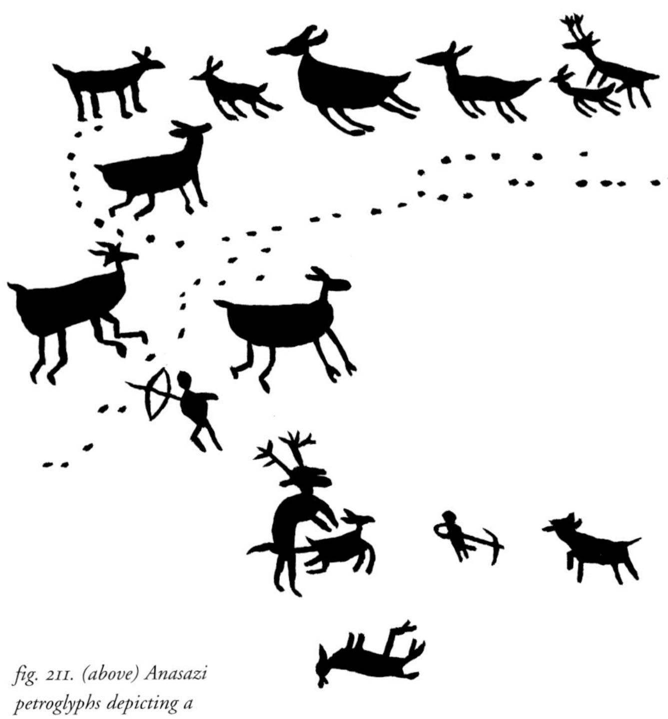

fig. 211. (above) Anasazi petroglyphs depicting a hunting scene with copulating animals, Largo Canyon, New Mexico.

Such U-shaped enclosures are not uncommon in southwestern rock art and sometimes appear as isolated symbols or are depicted with only the hoofprints of the hunted animals. The resemblance of this U-shaped motif to some vulva symbols further emphasizes the fecundity theme.

A ceremony that seems to involve the fertility of humans and pronghorns appears in the petroglyph panel in fig. 213. The pronghorn looks like a pregnant female and is attended by various anthropomorphs, including a pregnant woman holding a staff, a humpbacked figure, and a hunter with his bow. This and other rock art scenes suggest that animals were being portrayed on a supernatural level—perhaps to venerate their powers, ask for their increase, and call upon them for cooperation in the hunt. In Chapter 3 the importance of the increase of animals and the right to kill them is discussed in connection with the Pueblo goddess known as the Mother of Game or Mother of Animals, who gives birth to all the animals and permits hunters to kill them if they have followed prescribed rituals (fig. 98).

A petroglyph in Baja California has been interpreted as a Mother Sea Goddess—perhaps a marine equivalent to the Mother of Animals (fig. 214). This five-foot-tall anthropomorph with a heavily pecked vulva is located near the sea

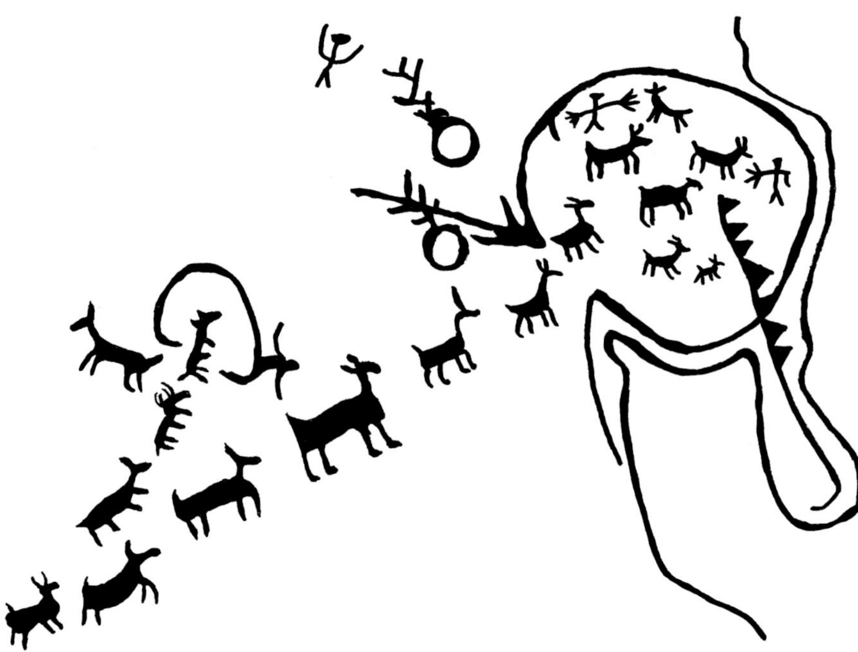

fig. 212. (right) Petroglyph of a game drive into an enclosure, Little Colorado River, Arizona (after McCreery and Malotki 1994, 83).

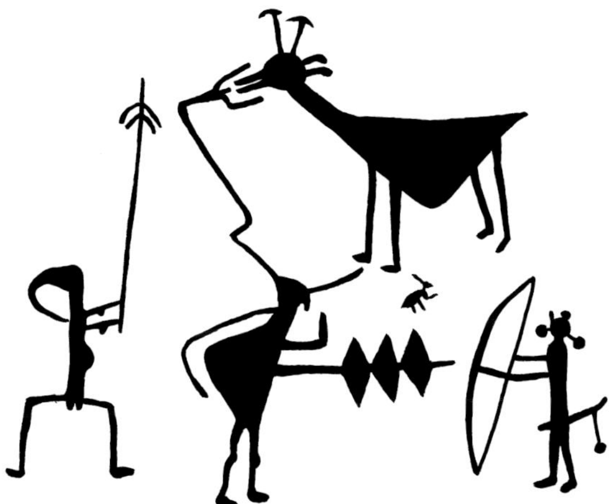

fig. 213. (left) Petroglyphs representing possible ritual activity concerning fertility and pregnancy of humans and antelope, Leroux Wash, Winslow, Arizona.

and is surrounded by a host of marine symbols: "Climbing around the Sea Goddess and her consort gives one the feeling of being inside . . . the sea itself. Perhaps this was the effect that the ancients were trying to create. Such things as sharks, rays, barracuda, dolphin, whales, assorted fish, frogs, turtles, crabs, and other marine organisms are identifiable" (Hampton 1994, 4). It has been documented that vulva symbols are one of the most common elements found in rock art sites in the area of Baja California surrounding this site—supporting the interpretation of this image as concerned with fecundity. Moreover, the prehistoric hunter-gatherers in this area foraged extensively from the sea, as evidenced by the many large shell middens remaining. Sea life would have been an important inspiration for the beliefs and rituals of these people.

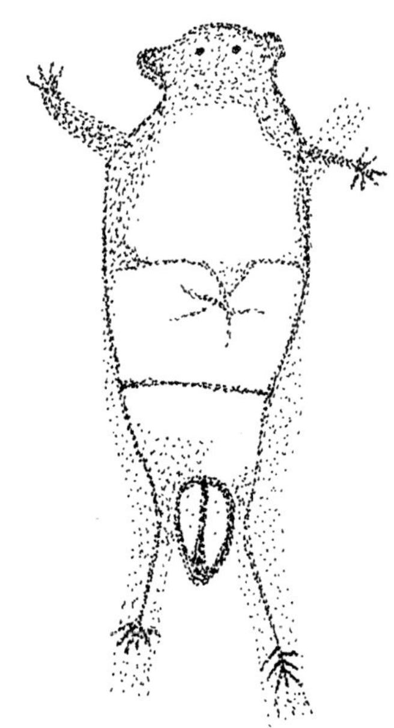

fig. 214. Petroglyph of a female fertility deity with prominent vulva, Sierra de Guadalupe, Baja California (after Crosby 1980, 702).

As a means of invoking fecundity, ritualized or enacted intercourse between animals and shamans or hunters has been documented throughout the ancient world.[46] Several examples among southwestern rock art appear to represent ritual coitus with animals. For instance, Basketmaker petroglyphs from the Little Colorado River in Arizona depict a quadruped being sexually penetrated by an anthropomorph in the presence of a shamanic figure (fig. 215). The petroglyphs in fig. 216 also depict apparent coitus between an animal and a humpbacked figure; a second phallic humpback seems to hold onto the animal, and the presence of the bow and arrow in the scene indicates this image is depicting some sort of

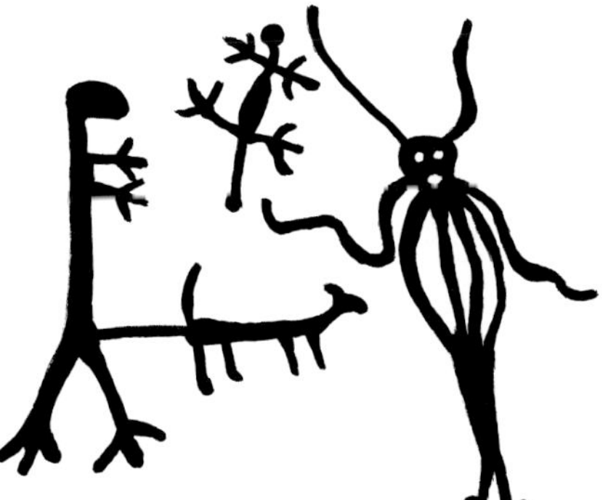

fig. 215. Petroglyphs depicting shamanic figures and copulation with a quadruped, Five Mile Draw, Little Colorado River, Arizona.

hunting/fecundity ritual. Such images may not be portraying actual bestiality, but rather ceremonial or ritualized intercourse between spirits or between humans in animal costumes. This may be the case in the petroglyph from Chaco Canyon, New Mexico, which at first glance seems to express only human intercourse (fig. 217). However, close inspection shows the male partner is wearing horns or antlers and may therefore be acting as an animal representative in an invocation of fecundity. This copulation scene is surrounded by a number of quadrupeds, including a large, antlered animal and bighorn sheep, reinforcing the notion that this petroglyph does not portray an ordinary sex act between people but relates to more supernatural activities concerning the world of animals. This petroglyph may have recorded a public performance between a woman and a man masked as an animal to symbolize ritual coitus with an animal or its spirit. A similar activity may be the intent of a petroglyph from northern Arizona (fig. 218), which portrays a sexual act between two anthropomorphs, one of which has feline-like ears and may represent a person in costume or an animal spirit. Related examples of depictions of apparent copulation between humans and animals in rock art of other regions are shown in Chapter 5 and on the Mimbres bowl in figure 186.

fig. 216. (below) Pueblo petroglyphs showing humpbacked figures ritually copulating with an animal; the bow and arrow link hunting and fecundity with this scene, La Cieneguilla, New Mexico.

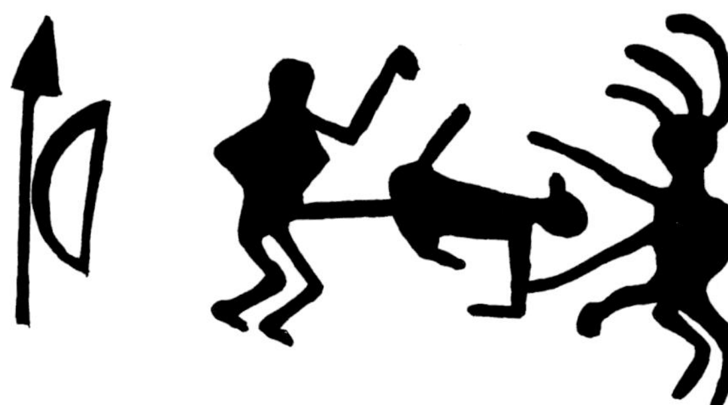

fig. 217. (right) Anasazi petroglyphs of a copulation scene, Chaco Canyon, New Mexico.

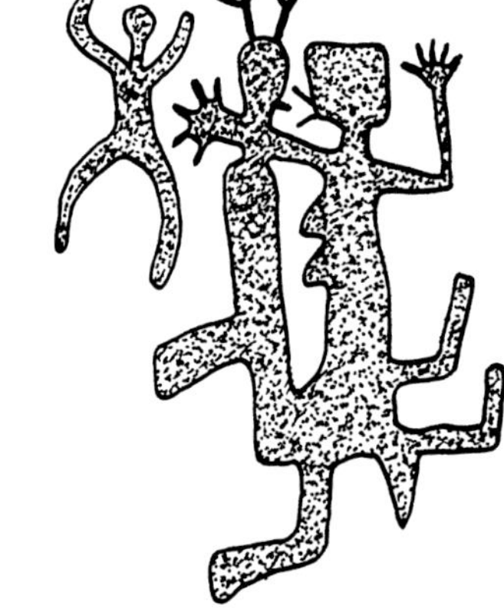

fig. 218. (right) Pictographs of a copulation scene between a man and a partner with feline ears, Coconino National Forest, Arizona.

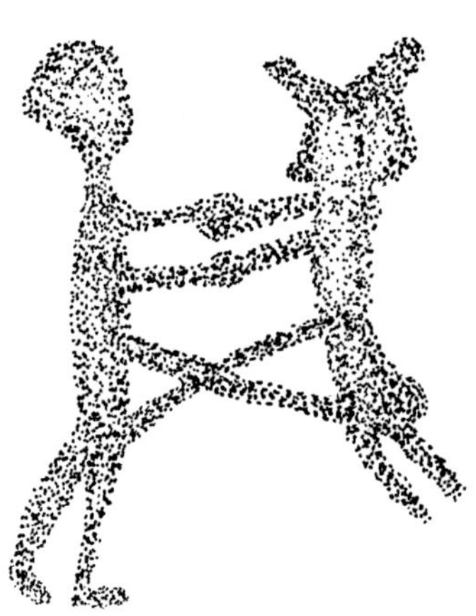

In the transition from hunter-gatherers to agriculturalists, southwestern peoples continued to depict animals and hunting scenes in their rock art, but also incorporated ideas about plants and rain in their expressions of fecundity. The symbolic, fertilizing power of rain is particularly important to the Pueblos and, along with images of seeds, germination, and plant growth, is a dominant theme in ritual and art (fig. 143). Winter ceremonies focus on the return of the sun and its life-affirming warmth, as well as germination and sprouting of seeds. In some pueblos, beans are ritually sprouted inside subterranean, womb-like kivas to prepare for the coming growing season, as described by the following: "During winter solstice we bring in all our seeds and pray that those seeds will be reborn. It teaches you about growth—the seed that you are, the seed that you are becoming" (Trimble 1993, 47). Sprouting seeds are sometimes depicted in Pueblo rock art (fig. 219). For example, in fig. 220 a sprouting seed is shown next to a female who may be giving birth, and others occur in a blanket-like pattern associated with a row of flute players (fig. 221). Flute music was believed to aid germination and promote growth, a

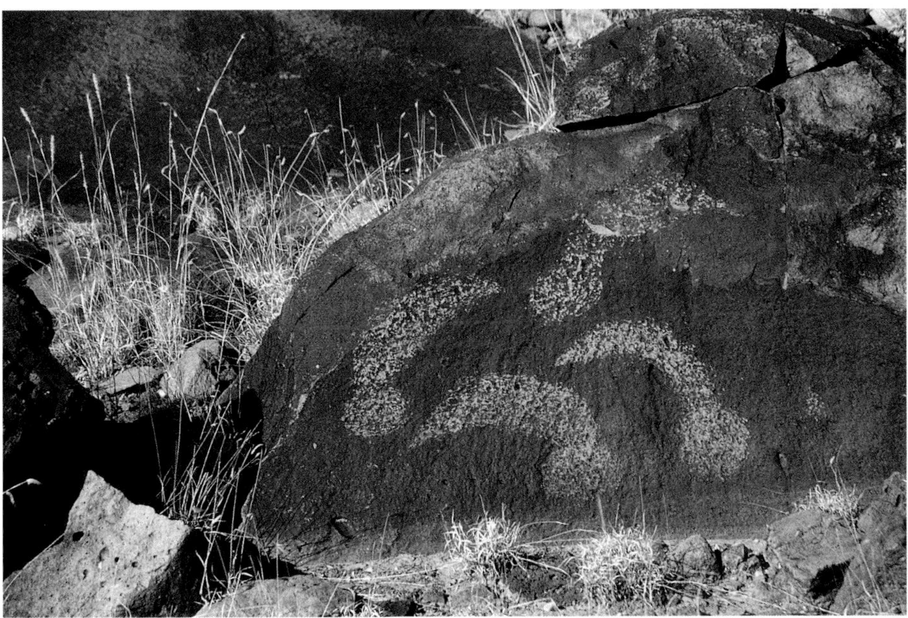

fig. 219. Petroglyphs resembling sprouting seeds, White Rock Canyon, New Mexico.

notion expressed in a petroglyph panel from Canyon de Chelly, Arizona, in which flute players are playing to some sprouting seeds and a snake, while another figure holds a sprouting seed in each hand (fig. 222).

Summer ceremonies celebrate the fecundity of the earth, often focusing on corn—the dietary staple and a profound symbol of fruitfulness. Corn is central to Pueblo religious beliefs, myths, and art. Since growing corn in the desert requires considerable specialized knowledge and adaptation to localized conditions, many types of corn have been developed, including colored strands that have ceremonial significance and in myths are identified with directions and the Corn Maidens. Pueblo ceremonies are based on knowledge of the seasons, especially sun and moon cycles, and this knowledge makes it possible to cultivate corn in a harsh, arid land with risky growing seasons.

Mythic and religious concepts such as the Corn Mother and Corn Maidens (discussed in Chapter 3) typify Pueblo interests in agricultural fecundity. The Christian Virgin Mary was originally presented to native peoples as a type of metamorphosed grain goddess, but in the Southwest by the eighteenth century the

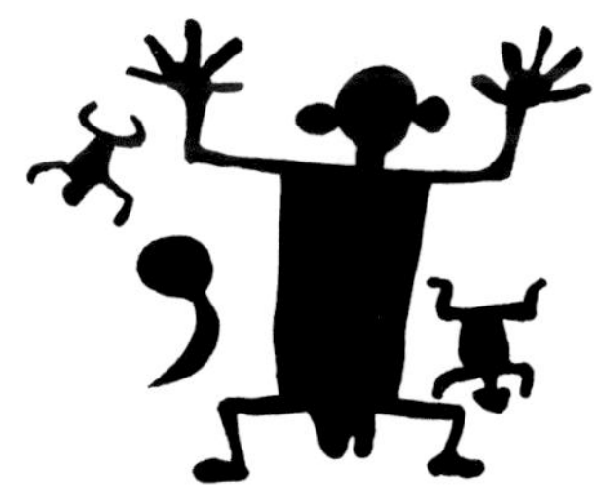

fig. 220. Petroglyphs of a female with babies and a sprouting seed, Velarde, New Mexico.

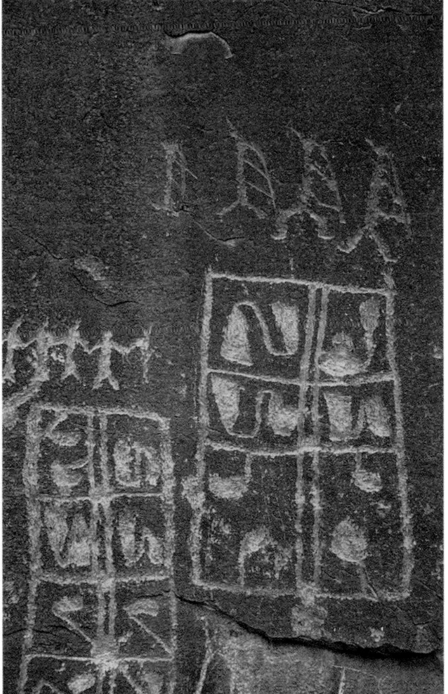

fig. 221. Petroglyphs of flute players with a blanket-like design incorporating possible sprouting seed motifs, Waterflow, New Mexico.

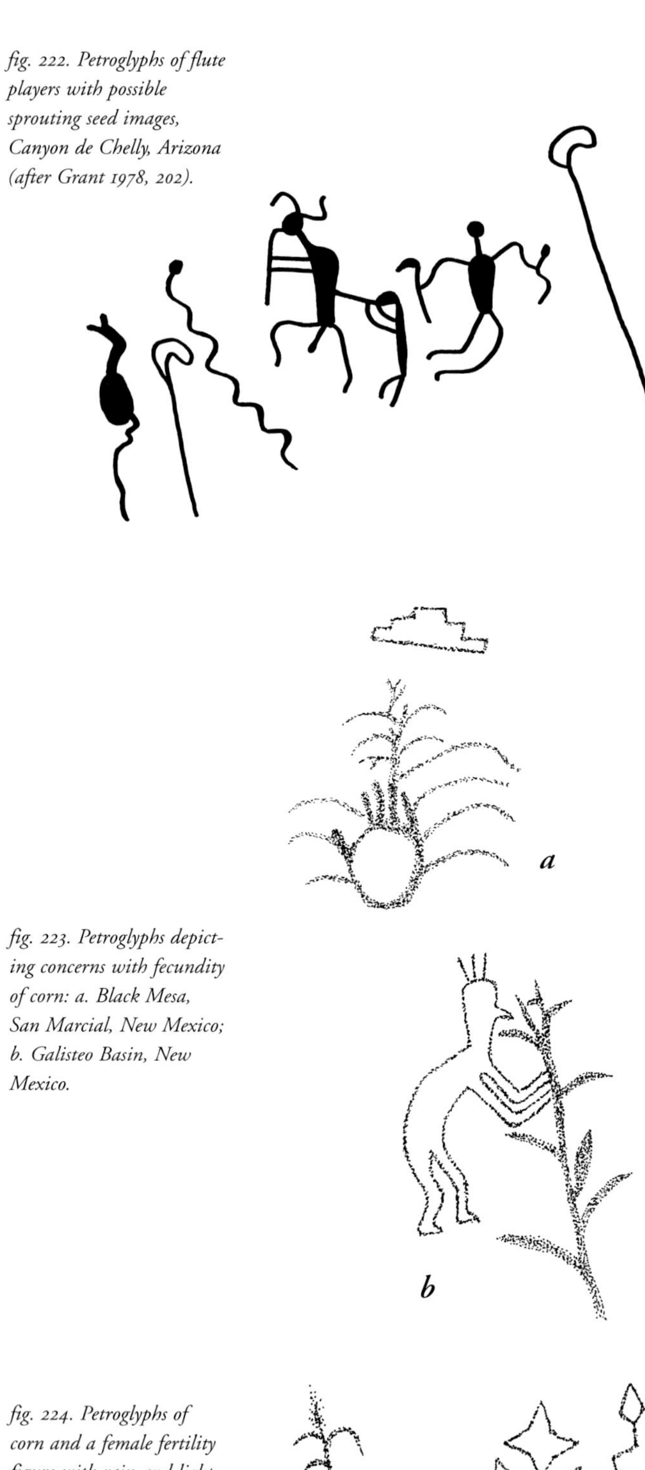

fig. 222. Petroglyphs of flute players with possible sprouting seed images, Canyon de Chelly, Arizona (after Grant 1978, 202).

fig. 223. Petroglyphs depicting concerns with fecundity of corn: a. Black Mesa, San Marcial, New Mexico; b. Galisteo Basin, New Mexico.

fig. 224. Petroglyphs of corn and a female fertility figure with rain and lightning symbolism, First Mesa, Hopi, Arizona (after Schaafsma 1980, 290).

Virgin Mary and the Corn Mothers had merged—the Virgin Mary now appearing in garb with corn ears and surrounded by other Indian symbols of fertility such as butterflies and flowers (Gutierrez 1991, 90–91). Today, Pueblo people still venerate corn as if it were their children, as expressed by a Hopi man: "When a person planted corn, they would be raising these corn plants up as their children. We were taught to sing to our corn, sing to our children, talk to our children, to love our children, to care for them. Corn provides us with food. It is the center of life and the essence of life. Our ceremonies are prayers for rain in order that our corn will grow" (Trimble 1993, 47).

Corn plants are abundantly represented in Anasazi/Pueblo and Navajo rock art, often in ritualized depictions intended to promote fecundity. For example, the petroglyphs in fig. 223 show corn plants being attended to or blessed by an anthropomorph and a human hand. A cloud terrace above the latter symbolizes rain and hence growth and fertility for the corn. Further, a very realistic corn plant is depicted in fig. 224, complete with roots, ears, and tassels, next to a female deity holding rain clouds and lightning symbols. At a Pueblo ruin in the Galisteo Basin in New Mexico, a petroglyph of a corn plant adorns the rock surface above a natural basin that collects water and which probably functioned as a shrine to promote the fecundity of corn (fig. 225); nearby, a flute player and a corn plant adorn the cliff face. Navajo rock art has some of the boldest depictions of corn and associated elements of fecundity. The corn plant in fig. 226 has greatly exaggerated ears and is accompanied by two *Ye'is* (supernaturals) who nurture its growth. The corn in fig. 227 grows from a cloud terrace (symbol for rain) and is flanked by wavy lines suggestive of flowing water along with a humpbacked *Ye'i* known as Ghanaskidi—a fertility symbol whose hump contains mist and seeds of all the plants.

The growth of plants other than corn is also celebrated in southwestern rock art. In Basketmaker Anasazi images, flowering wild plants that were important food and

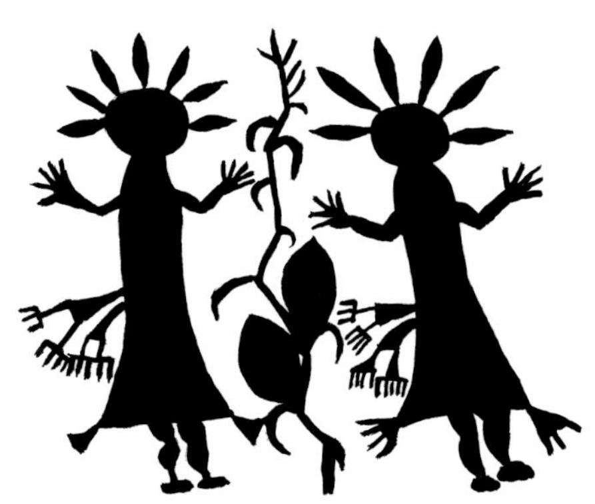

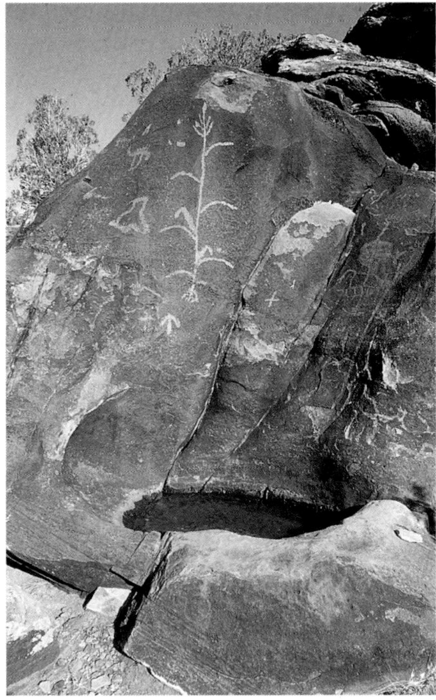

fig. 226. (far left) Navajo petroglyphs of corn and two Ye'i figures, Largo Canyon, New Mexico.

fig. 225. (left) Pueblo petroglyph of a corn plant above a natural rock basin that catches rainwater and probably served as a shrine for moisture and fecundity, San Cristobal, Galisteo Basin, New Mexico.

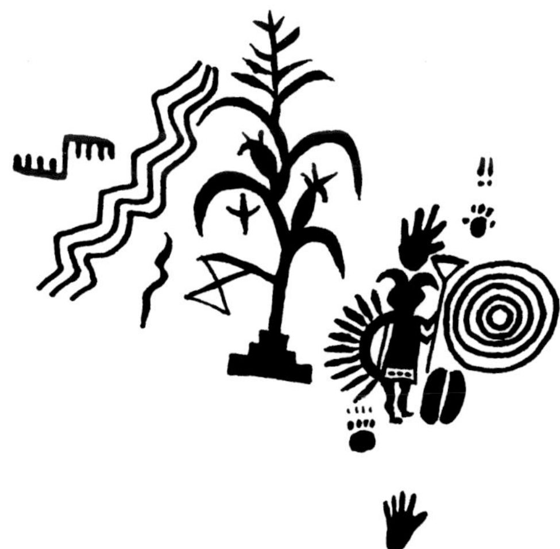

fig. 227. (left) Navajo petroglyphs of corn and a Ye'i figure, Largo Canyon, New Mexico.

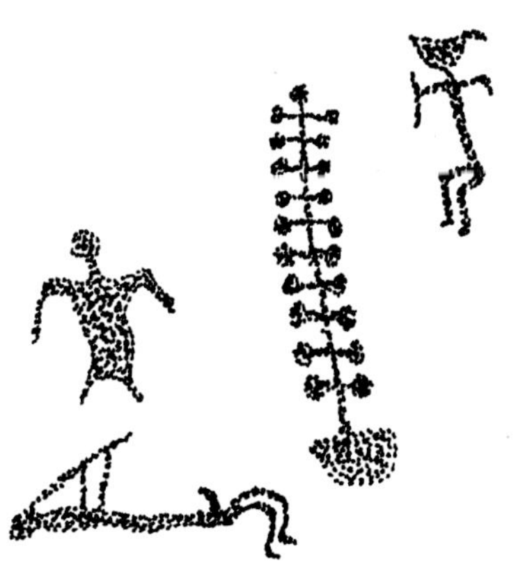

fig. 228. (left) Basketmaker Anasazi petroglyphs celebrating fertility and the fruitfulness of plants, Comb Ridge, Utah.

fiber sources are portrayed in the context of fecundity—such as the flowering yucca-like plant in fig. 228 next to a phallic flute player and bird-headed shaman. Another Basketmaker petroglyph panel depicts a flowering yucca plant near a copulating couple (fig. 86). In even older, Archaic period rock art that predates agriculture, such as the Barrier Canyon Style images from the Harvest Scene in Utah (fig. 165), the bounty and harvest of wild plant foods (Indian rice grass) is symbolized. At another Barrier Canyon Style site in Utah, increase of bighorn sheep seems to be the theme since lines of miniature sheep flow forth from the outstretched arms of a shamanic figure (fig. 229). Further, abundance of both plants and animals is invoked by the Pueblo petroglyphs in fig. 230, where plants have numerous birds perched in them, while nearby a humpbacked flute player copulates with a female to promote growth and fecundity. The relationship between sexuality and the fecundity of plants is beautifully expressed in the Pueblo petroglyph in fig. 231 that depicts a female in the birthing posture with a prominent vulva, over which has been superimposed

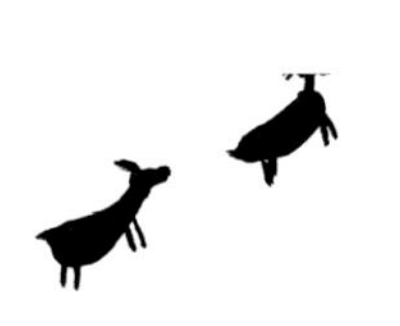

fig. 229. Barrier Canyon Style pictographs of a shaman with spirit helpers and long lines of bighorn sheep, Emery County, Utah.

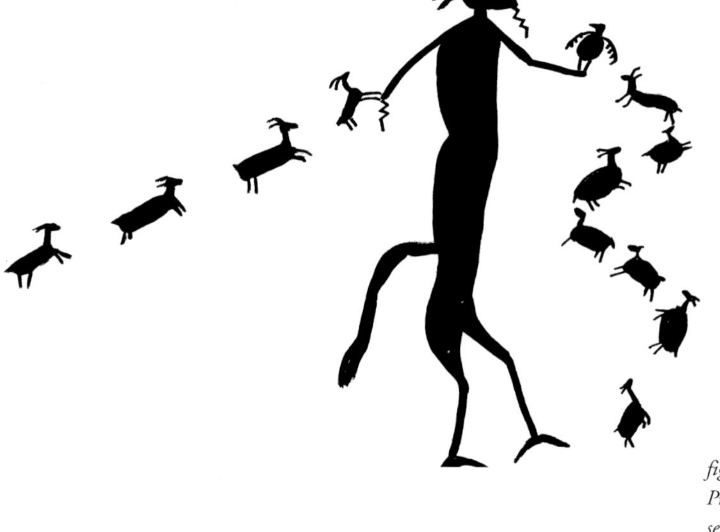

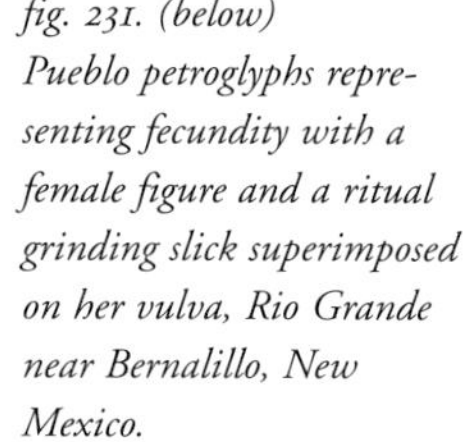

fig. 231. (below) Pueblo petroglyphs representing fecundity with a female figure and a ritual grinding slick superimposed on her vulva, Rio Grande near Bernalillo, New Mexico.

fig. 230.(right) Pueblo petroglyphs representing fecundity with a copulating flute player and numerous birds perched in vegetation, La Cieneguilla, New Mexico.

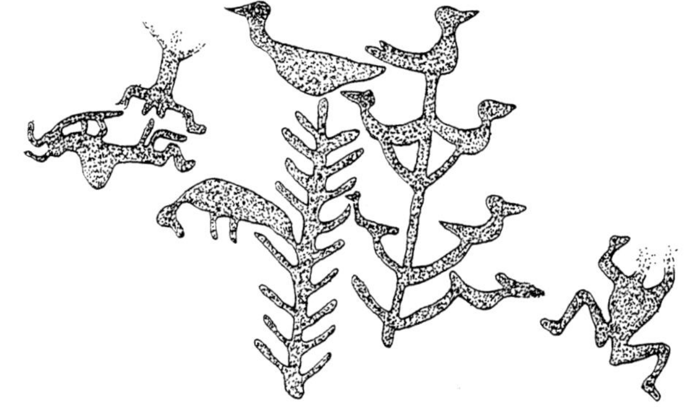

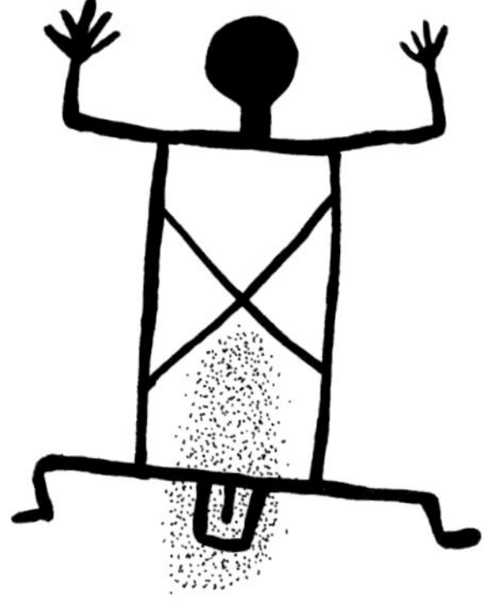

a grinding slick, or bedrock metate, resulting from the milling of grains and seeds. This image seems to express the generative power of the female or Earth Mother to bring forth all the plants needed to sustain the people. In California's Anza-Borrego Desert, similar bedrock slicks occur just below the huge vulva symbols known locally as yoni formations. Native Americans used these slicks to grind and prepare food or drinks, which were sometimes administered to women to assure fertility and pregnancy (Knaak 1988, 58). A juxtaposition of a petroglyph image on a bedrock slick occurs in a cave in southeastern Utah, where a deer and hunter have been carved into the surface of the grinding slick, symbolically linking plants and animals as important elements of fecundity in the survival of the people (fig. 232). Moreover, in the same area of Utah are other rock art sites near ancient fields and granaries, along with deep bedrock grooves used to sharpen stone hoes and which functioned as part of crop fertility rituals (see fig. 125 and the discussion in Chapter 3).

Finally, a compelling Basketmaker petroglyph panel from southeastern Utah (fig. 233) is concerned with the abundance of both plants and animals (in this case, bighorn sheep). A phallic flute player pro-

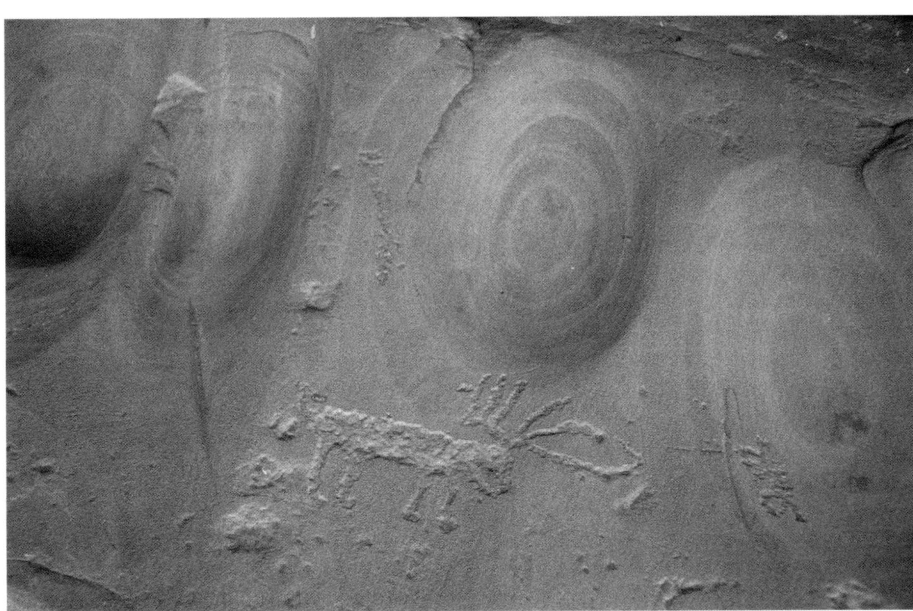

fig. 232. Grinding slick (metate) with superimposed petroglyphs depicting a hunting scene, Cold Spring Cave, Comb Ridge, Utah.

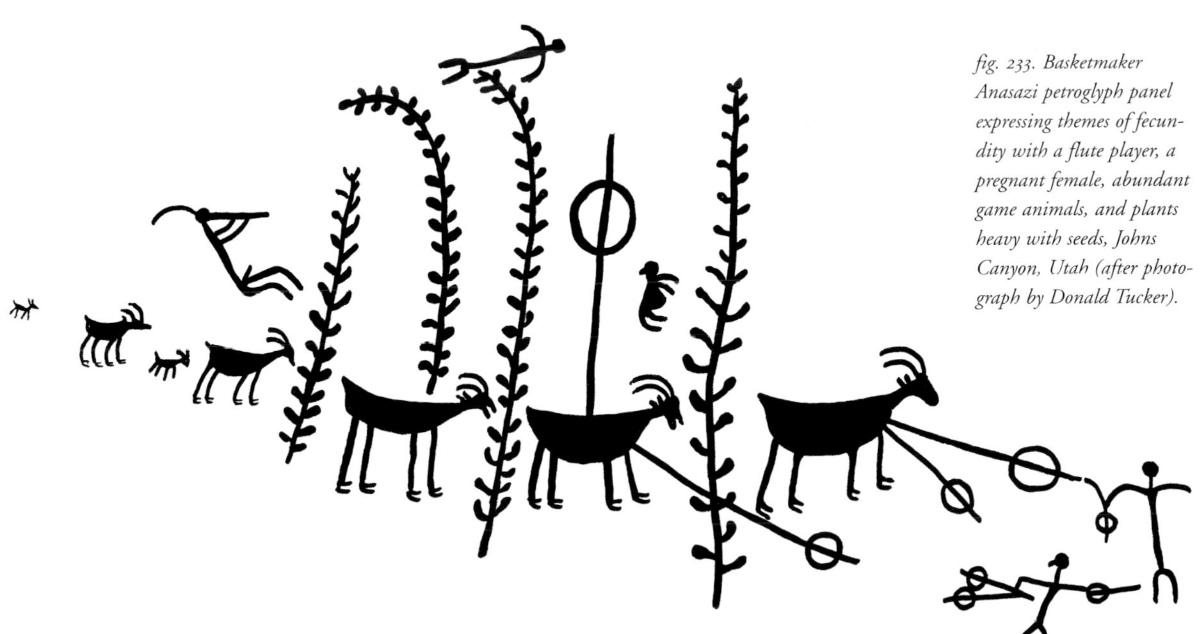

fig. 233. Basketmaker Anasazi petroglyph panel expressing themes of fecundity with a flute player, a pregnant female, abundant game animals, and plants heavy with seeds, Johns Canyon, Utah (after photograph by Donald Tucker).

vides fertility magic as hunters throw atlatl darts into the sheep. In the center of the composition is a small, pregnant figure. Some of the plants bend over as if heavy with seeds or fruit. The line of sheep, graded from large to small, suggests a continuation of generations, while over the plants a horizontal figure hovers—perhaps representing a shaman in spiritual flight as part of his ritual to ensure fecundity and abundance.

Fertility symbols viewed on a worldwide basis show amazing similarities in spite of great geographical distances and vast age differences. The symbols represent a psychic unity of mankind from Neanderthal Man to contemporary primitive cultures. . . . The yoni, the painted abstract fertility signs, the phallic symbol, and the cupules, all were understood by primitive man to be symbols of reproductive powers and were believed responsible for his survival.[47]

—Manfred Knaak
The Forgotten Artist

Sexual morality has undergone many changes, and the strict banishment of all that is overtly erotic from social ceremony is only a development of the past two thousand years or less. Veneration of sexuality and the glorification of reproduction were once the common property and nature of all peoples.[48]

—Burchard Brentjes
African Rock Art

Out of life comes death,
and out of death, life,
Out of the young, the old,
and out of the old, the young,
Out of waking, sleep,
and out of sleep, waking,
The stream of creation and dissolution
never stops.[49]

—Heraclitus

CHAPTER 5

FERTILITY THEMES IN ROCK ART OF OTHER REGIONS

Although this book focuses on rock art of the American Southwest, because themes of fertility and sexuality are so prominent in rock art of indigenous peoples worldwide, a brief overview of these topics is provided to emphasize the archetypal nature of such images. It shows that many of the symbols for fertility and sexuality are similar among diverse cultures separated in time and space. Images such as vulvas, phalli, snakes, mating and birthing, flowering and fruiting plants, the fertilizing powers of rain and sun, the rite of Sacred Marriage, the sexuality of shamans and the hunt, and the Earth Mother are recurring motifs in rock art around the world. The relevance of taking a global view in the study of rock art is being recognized by scholars as described by the following:

> Tribal societies around the world have the common characteristic of producing art, especially rock art. Their visual output is recorded in millions of figures, in thousands of zones distributed in 120 countries on all inhabited continents. Over 70 percent of all known rock art was produced by hunting and gathering societies while less than 30 percent is the work of pastoralists and agriculturalists. The growing interest in this art is caused by the light it projects on the collective memory and on universal conceptual processes.
>
> Through these ancient expressions of the human mind a wide range of submerged memories come back to consciousness, reviving stored chapters of our intellectual heritage. But as important is rock art's historical relevance. Rock art is a sort of pictographic writing which constitutes humanity's largest and most significant archive of its history for 40,000 years until the advent of conventional modern ideographic and then alphabetic writing (Anati 1994b, XII:32).

DIVERSITY AND THE UNIVERSAL

Africa

The African continent, especially southern Africa, may have the greatest concentration of rock art in the world. The oldest African art so far known is from Namibia, where animals painted on stone slabs in a cave date to approximately 25,000 B.P., but there is evidence that suggests such activity goes back to at least 38,000 years

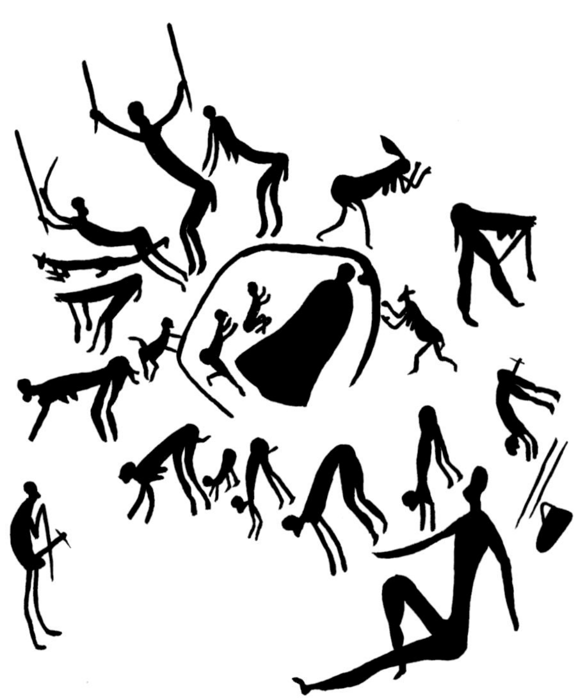

fig. 234. (above) Pictographs of women's Eland Dance for a girl's first menstruation, Fullerton's Rock, Drakensburg, South Africa (after Campbell 1988 I(1):100).

B.P. (Anati 1994b, XII:24). It is appropriate to expect that the continent on which mankind evolved would have the longest occupation by hunter-gatherers, and therefore contain an enormous amount of rock art. Much of our current understanding of shamanic trance imagery in rock art stems from studies of the sophisticated rock paintings and ethnography of the San Bushmen in South Africa.

A story from Africa in the introduction to this book illustrates the universal presence and significance of the vulva symbol for female fertility, and a cave with such a symbol was described by a Zulu spirit-diviner as a "garden of babies," where many women had given birth. The same Zulu man was later taken to another rock painting site, which he described as follows:

> Oh yes, I know it well. This is *Rra-bophelo*, father of life. . . . The spirits have graced this impala with that which all womenfolk are forever seeking, the gift of life. Within her is the seed. And that is why we see *Rra-bophelo* talking through her nostrils, blowing *moya*, the breath of the spirit, into her belly. Do you see the eyes of new awareness shining there, staring out from the womb? The father of life is wearing his usual mask and tail, both of which symbolize fertility. . . .
>
> Moving on to a second impala shown upside down with what looked like blood pouring from her mouth, he said, "When the time came, the mother impala gave birth to her young. It was delivered into this world, but she herself died. . . . The young that have no parents must look after themselves. That is the meaning of this painting. It is the story of life and death. It is what we call *Noka ya bophelo*, the river of life, of continuity. It shows how life is given and life is taken, but Life goes on! (Watson 1982, 106-7).

A South African rock painting that celebrates human fertility and sexuality depicts the women's Eland Dance in honor of a girl's first menstruation (fig. 234). The girl's Rite of the First Menstruation, her passage to maturity, has been described as follows:

> The girl is thought to be charged with a force that must be defended both from the sun's rays and from contact with the earth. Head covered with a kaross, she is carried on a kinswoman's back to a shelter apart, where the women, removing their own karosses, perform the Eland Dance to an eland song that is among the most ancient of Kung musical expressions. At the end, the girl is washed, anointed with eland fat, and painted on her forehead and cheeks with designs the meaning of which has been lost (Campbell 1988, I(1):100).

In the rock painting, women dance around the central figure of the girl in her cloak, while a man with erect penis watches from outside the circle. As in much African rock art, the human figures appear to be mostly naked, but in this image many of the women wear aprons over their buttocks. This is an accurate reflection of San Bushman perception that the buttocks are the most erotic part of the body and must therefore be covered (Garlake 1995, 61).

Other African images seem to portray aspects of courtship, betrothal, and perhaps even abduction. The rock painting from Libya in fig. 235 has been interpreted as a possible depiction of betrothal or bridal customs, as described below:

> A man is leading a woman away by the wrist. . . . The betrothal takes place before migrating to the *pontok* or hut of the husband, and is reckoned as consummated when the man seizes the girl's wrist. But "betrothal" and "marriage" are separated only by the time it takes to walk to the "house," so that the seizing of the forearm can be regarded as the operative part of the marriage, and is fairly violent, the bride allowing herself to be pulled towards the marital home (V. Lebzelter, quoted in Brentjes 1965, 80).

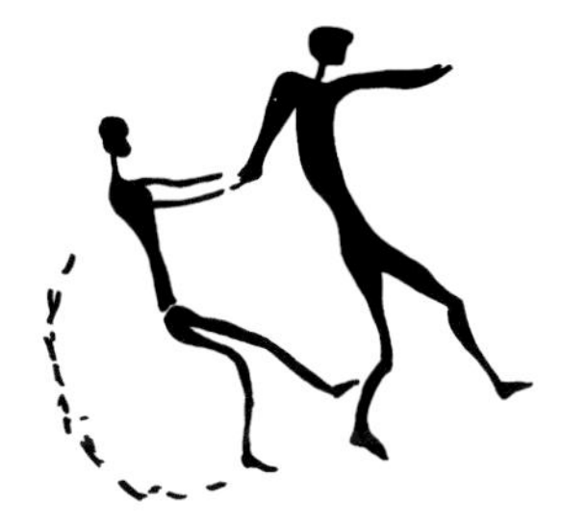

fig. 235. Pictograph representing a betrothal custom, Libya (after Brentjes 1965, 80).

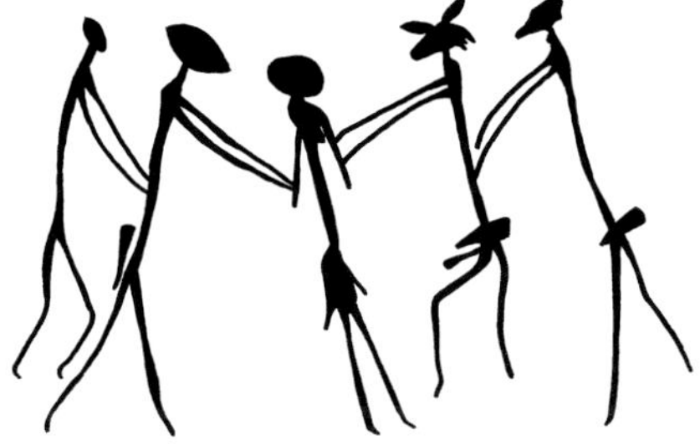

fig. 236. Pictographs representing a possible betrothal custom or an abduction, Kelo, Tanzania (after Leakey 1983, 54).

A similar scene from Tanzania, with four males tugging at the arms of a female, may represent an equivalent bridal custom or a dispute over a woman or even her abduction (fig. 236).

Apparently there are African equivalents in rock art of the ritualized sex known as Sacred Marriage, or *hieros gamos*, discussed in Chapter 4. The copulation scene in fig. 237 is from a shrine as described in the following:

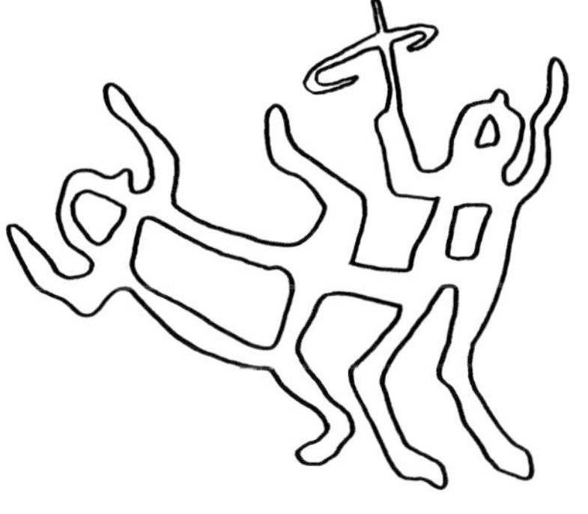

fig. 237. Petroglyph of sexual intercourse that may represent the Sacred Marriage rite, Tell Issaghen, Libya (after Brentjes 1965, 78).

> It is surrounded by groups of copulating lovers. Not far from it are rock faces inscribed with pictures of sheep, cattle, rhinoceroses, and elephants. Masked men and hunters, varans and giraffes cover the cliffs. . . . To this class of cult picture the age-old idea of the *hieros gamos*—sacred wedding—also belongs. We see it as far away as Sweden on rock carvings of the Bronze Age. . . . In Babylon it took the form of the ritual bedding of the king and the High Priestess (the "bride of the god" mating with the king who personated the god). And such "sacred weddings" have been a widespread form of New Year celebration all over Asia and Africa in modern times, intended to promote natural fertility by the stimulation of human sensuality and sexuality. Such scenes are also depicted on the African rocks (Brentjes 1965, 78, 29).

Other scenes of sexual activity occur in rock art from South Africa (fig. 238) and Zimbabwe (fig. 239). A petroglyph from Namibia depicts a woman with an isolated, gigantic penis between her legs (fig. 240). Two scenes of women having intercourse with males who resemble animals occur in Libya (fig. 241). These are probably symbolic expressions of fecundity to invoke an abundance of animals or to pla-

fig. 238. Petroglyphs of sexual intercourse, Townsland, Schweizer Reneke District, Transvaal, South Africa (after Slack 1962, 65).

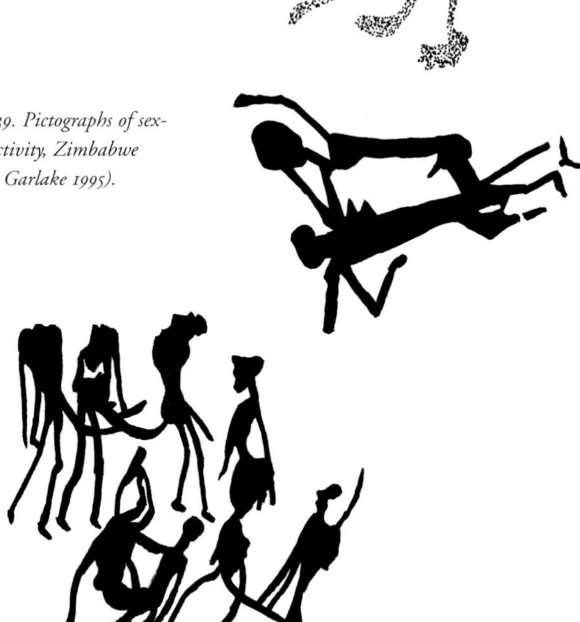

fig. 239. Pictographs of sexual activity, Zimbabwe (after Garlake 1995).

fig. 240. Petroglyphs of a female straddling a giant penis, Gobalis, Namibia (after Anati 1994, 12:95).

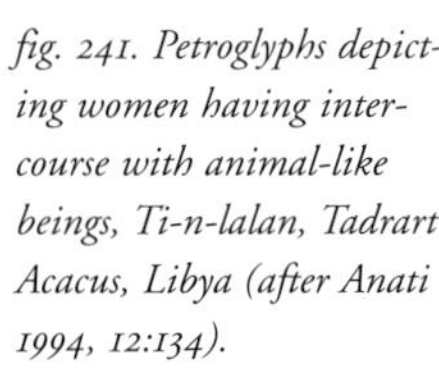

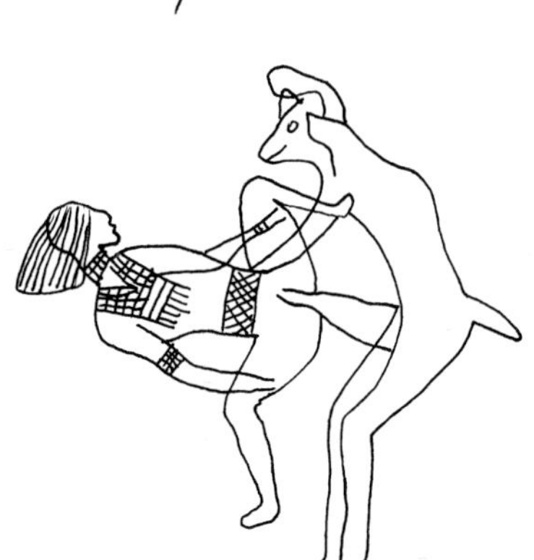

fig. 241. Petroglyphs depicting women having intercourse with animal-like beings, Ti-n-lalan, Tadrart Acacus, Libya (after Anati 1994, 12:134).

cate animal spirits. The male figures may be men wearing masks, or they may represent shamans who have assumed their animal helper's shape during a trance. Such scenes may also portray mythic encounters between animals and humans. These images probably stem from the same concepts as those expressed in some southwestern rock art, such as the copulation scene in Chaco Canyon, New Mexico, discussed earlier (fig. 217). Ritual coitus with an animal may also be depicted in the petroglyph from Nubia in fig. 243.

Another example of a rock art image connecting sex with animals, hunting, and fecundity is a petroglyph panel from Algeria (fig. 242). Here an ostrich hunter with a bow is connected by a long, penile line to the vulva of a figure standing behind him, who may represent not just a woman but a supernatural figure similar to the southwestern Mother of Animals or Mother of Game. By having intercourse with this being, the hunter is probably assuring the fecundity of the animal population. Similar scenes from the same site in Algeria depict sexual connection between couples, one of which involves another bow hunter (fig. 245).

Further, themes of human sexuality and procreation are explicit in pictographs from Tassili (fig. 244); a male with an enormous penis is ejaculating, and around him are women with swollen abdomens and several infants—presumably a testament to the man's potency and fertility. A scene from Zimbabwe shows a mother nursing her child (fig. 246), and in another depiction from Tassili, a couple seems to play with their children (fig. 247).

Other African rock art images depict the shamanic trance and supernatural power experienced in trance, some of which appear to be related to fertility and sex. An example is the long, meandering

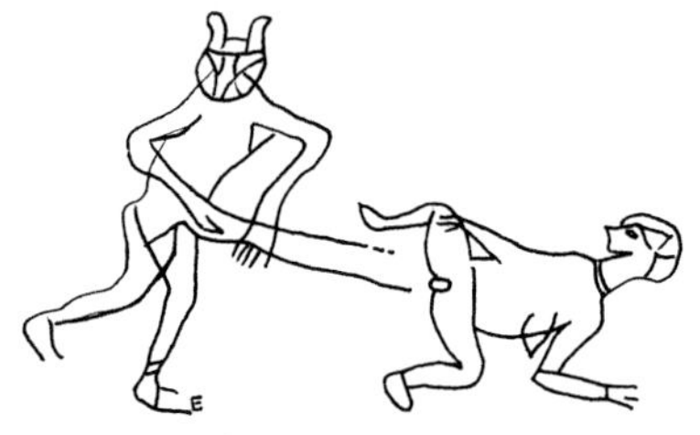

fig. 242. (below) Petroglyphs linking hunting and fertility, Tiout, Atlas Range, Sahara, Algeria (after Frobenius and Obermaier 1925, 79).

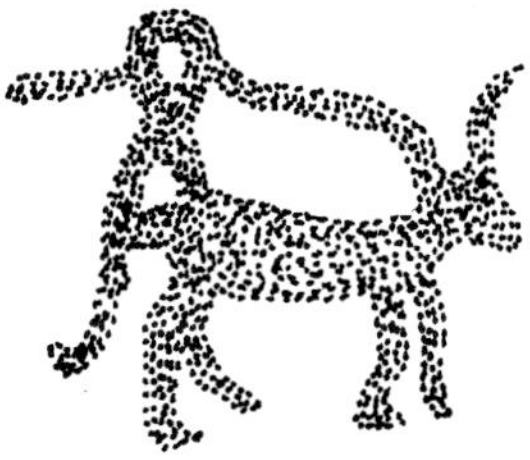

fig. 243. (left) Petroglyph of possible copulation between a man and an animal, Nubia (after Hunger 1983, 123).

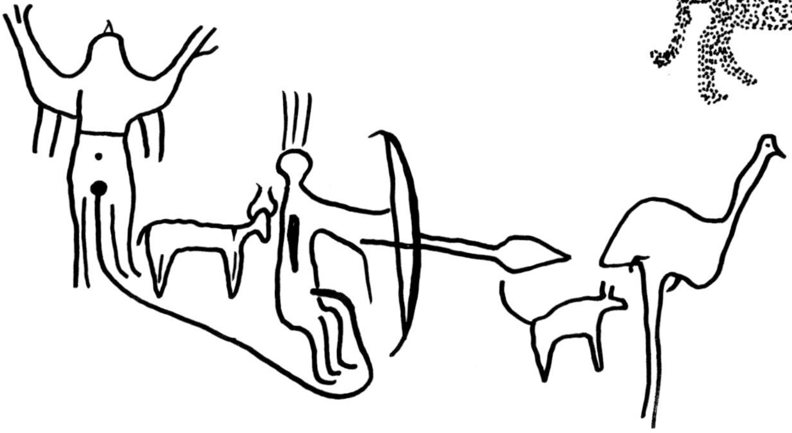

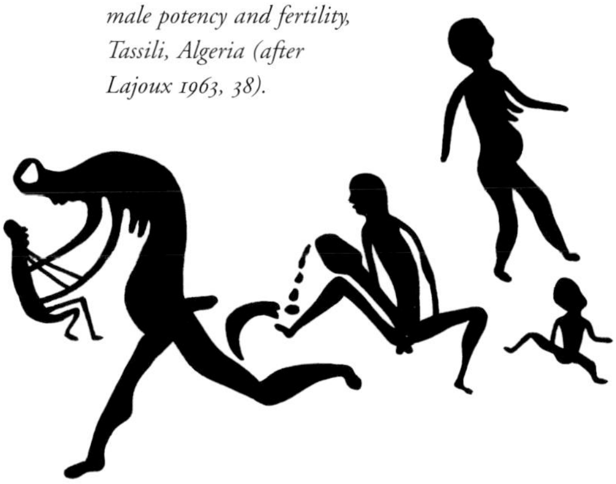

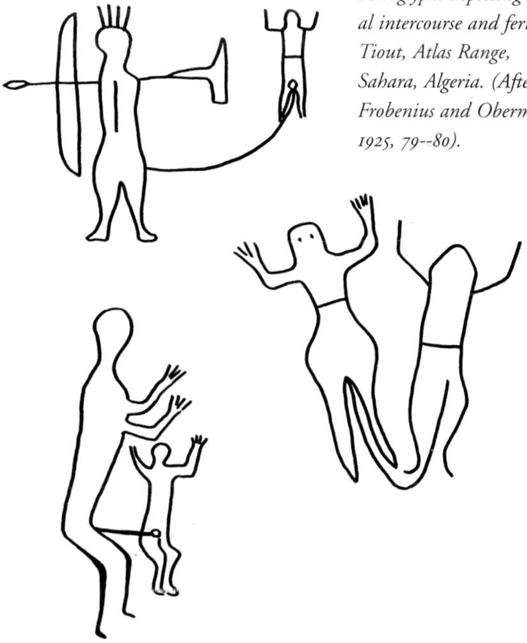

fig. 245. (left) Petroglyphs depicting sexual intercourse and fertility, Tiout, Atlas Range, Sahara, Algeria. (After Frobenius and Obermaier 1925, 79--80).

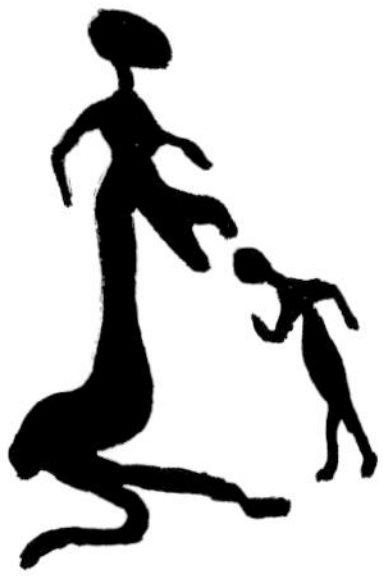

fig. 244. (below) Pictographs representing male potency and fertility, Tassili, Algeria (after Lajoux 1963, 38).

fig. 246. Pictographs of a mother nursing her child, Mazowe, Zimbabwe (after Garlake 1995, 59).

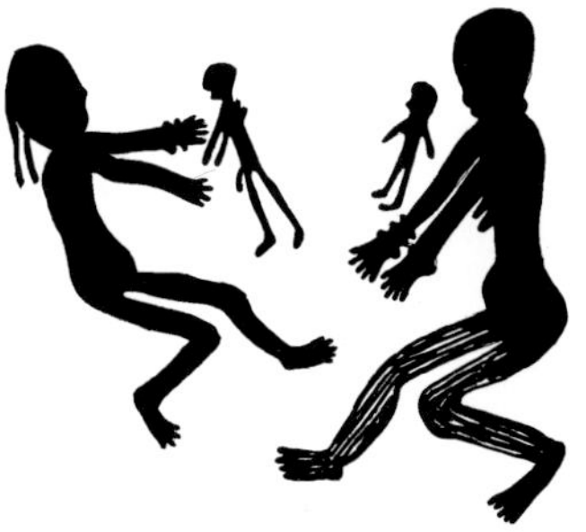

fig. 247. Pictographs of parents with children, Sefar, Tassili, Algeria (after Lajoux 1963, 53).

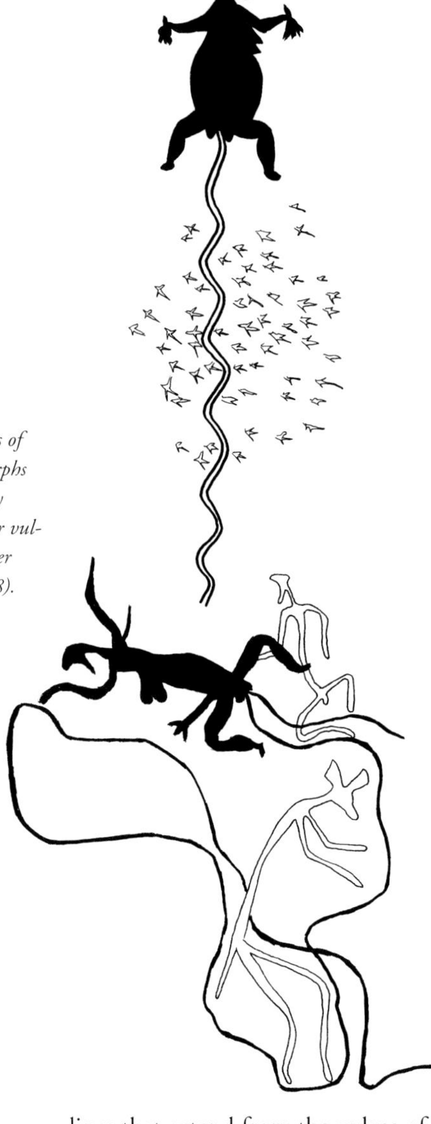

fig. 248. Pictographs of female anthropomorphs with lines of potency extending from their vulvas, Zimbabwe (after Garlake 1995, 89,108).

lines that extend from the vulvas of females in rock paintings from Zimbabwe (figs. 248). The distended abdomens of some of these figures have been interpreted as pregnancy and these figures as symbols of Earth Mothers, but more likely their abdomens are swollen with "boiling" potency (personal spiritual energy) and represent the part of the body the Kung call the *gebesi* (Garlake 1995, 85-89). The fact that potency flows from their genitals is a statement about the power of sex in influencing the fertility of the world. One such rock painting from Zimbabwe shows the meandering lines of potency flowing out from a figure's genitals, but with dozens of small creatures attached to the lines (Garlake 1995, 87)—reminiscent of the long lines of miniature bighorn sheep flowing from the shaman's body in a Utah pictograph (fig. 229).

In many of these African images, males have short lines across their penis or tendril-like lines attached to the penis ending in small tufted shapes. These are probably not adornment or mutilation but rather a means of representing some metaphysical quality inherent in men's bodies that was related to their potency or spiritual energy (Garlake 1995, 136–37).

The power to influence the fertility and natural forces of the world by sexually related ritual is manifest in the pictograph from Rhodesia in fig. 249. This scene has been interpreted as a mythic event involving sacrifice of a young female virgin to bring rain (Brentjes 1965, 26–27). Moreover, the rock art of Mashonaland and Matabeleland is said to illustrate religious concepts of a cult where young girls were sacrificed to obtain water for their people in times of drought as described below:

> The girl was brought through a gap in the wall, which was closed up with stones after her. The priests of sacrifice kept watch that no man should draw near. The girl grew up at the place of sacrifice, for two years, until her breasts began to swell. During those two years no rain fell. All the cattle died, and so did many people. The rivers dried up, and the corn did not sprout. Until one day the maiden came of age. . . . The Wanganga [soothsayers] called on the Mizimu (spirits of the dead) and they strangled the maiden. All the people danced around the place of sacrifice. The Wanganga buried the sacrifice between the roots of the great tree in the termite heap. . . . When the maiden was buried between the roots, the tree began to grow. It grew and grew, all through the night, and for the next three days. And on the last morning the crown of the tree reached the sky. . . . A

> great wind blew up and the leaves of the tree turned into clouds. It began to rain, and it rained for thirty days. Since that time the Wazezuru have always sacrificed a maiden after prolonged drought (L. Frobenius, quoted in Brentjes 1965, 27).

Although such stories may seem heartless, they illustrate the powerful association between puberty/sex and fertility/rain for many tribal peoples, especially those living in arid places. Sacrifice as an element of ritual related to fertility has only been briefly touched upon in this book, yet it occurred widely in the ancient world—a good example being the Aztecs' human sacrifices to the sun and other deities. In the American Southwest, there are stories about sacrifice to huge sacred snakes that were kept in pueblos, including sacrifice of a child to the Horned Water Serpent to bring rain or curtail floods. The practice of scalping in the Southwest was also related to fertility since scalps were used as potent rain fetishes. In the African story above, only a virgin can become the giver of rain, and her death saves the people. This also seems to have a resemblance to certain aspects of the kachina cult in the Southwest—only good, virtuous people can become kachinas (spirits of ancestors who bring rain); in the African story, the spirits of the dead are called upon at the time of sacrifice to help bring rain. In the rock painting that illustrates this story (fig. 249), the sacrificed girl lies below the grave tree. In the upper left, she has become the rain goddess who showers her blessings on the adoring king.

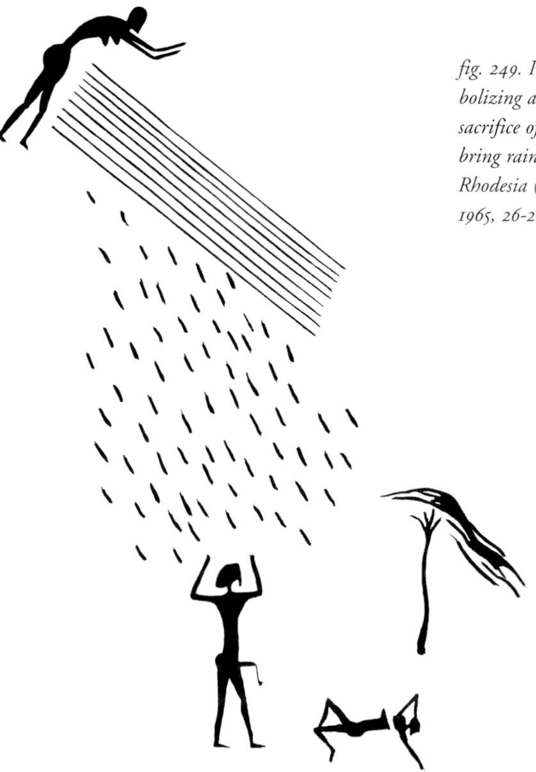

fig. 249. Pictographs symbolizing a myth about the sacrifice of a virgin to bring rain, Rusape, Rhodesia (after Brentjes 1965, 26-28).

Another common symbol of fertility in African rock art, as in the Southwest and elsewhere, is the snake:

> In the beginning, so the story goes, there was the Great Serpent, the first being, whose seven thousand coils set the planet and the stars in motion. This cosmic snake brought life to the earth by gouging out channels for rivers and streams. He can still be seen, moving in the current of a river, or lashing up the waves of the sea. He is the divine python, arching in the form of the rainbow and flashing in the lightning. He lives in a cave deep underground. . . . The symbol of eternity in African lore is a coiled snake with its own tail in its mouth. Snakes are imbued with supernatural powers of wisdom and the secret of eternal youth. They represent the forces of life and regeneration, exercising a profound influence over fertility and good fortune (Watson 1982, 43)

Snake-worshiping cults, which thrived in Africa, focused on resurrection and fecundity. Sacred pythons were kept in villages and venerated as agents of fertility for the earth:

> The snake god *Danh-gbi* . . . was their extreme bliss and general good. . . . Women were very prominent in the cult of *Danh-gbi*. Sometimes the snake appeared to beautiful girls

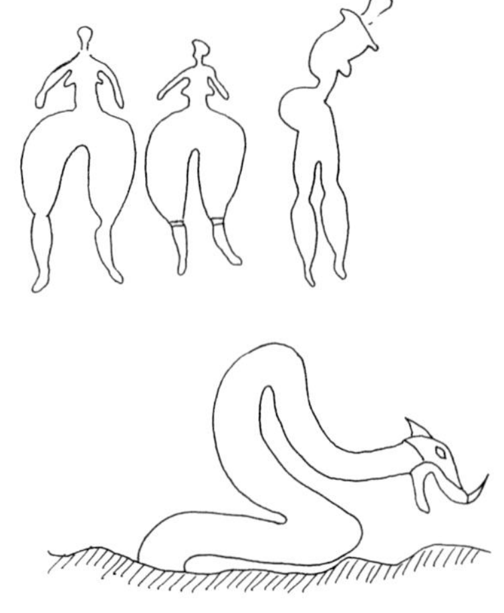

fig. 250. San Bushman rock paintings depicting a giant, Horned Serpent emerging from a crack in the rock, along with women who may represent the snake god's wives, Mahahla's Shelter, East Griqualand, South Africa (after Morris and Morris 1965, 17).

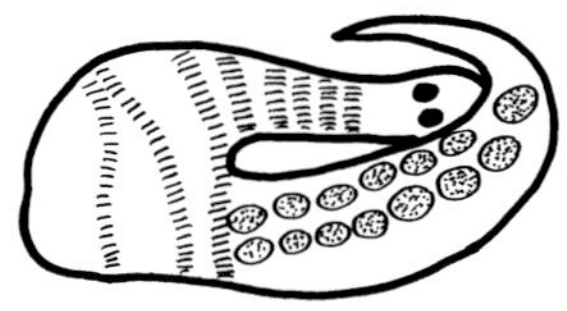

fig. 251. (right) Aboriginal rock painting of a snake with eggs inside its body, Kimberly, Western Australia (after Flood 1997, 297).

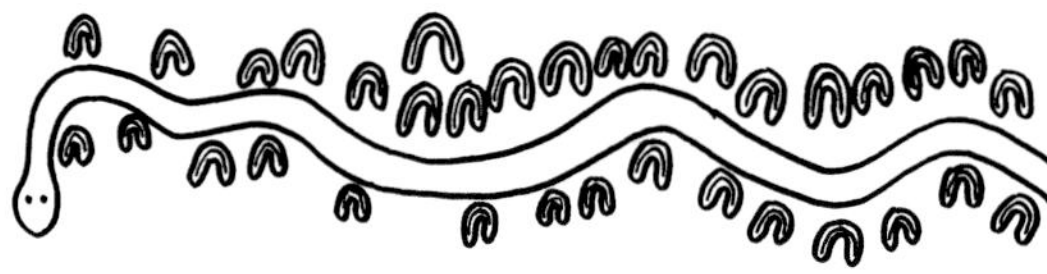

fig. 252. (above) Aboriginal rock painting of a snake with symbols of its unborn spirit children, Ngama Cave, Yuendumu, Australia (after Faulstich 1983, 100).

who became possessed with a kind of madness and entered the service of the snake temple. One of their duties was to dance round with earthen pots on their heads before human sacrifices were made, a ceremony apparently designed to bring rain. Numerous wives were provided for the python. When the millet began to sprout, the old priestesses rushed round the village seizing and carrying off young girls between the age of eight and twelve to be his brides. . . . After due instruction, the snake's wives took part in licentious rites with the priests and eventually became public prostitutes whose services were eagerly sought by the male worshipers when crops were germinating. . . . Since the god directed his wives' activities, no disgrace was attached to their profession (Morris and Morris 1965, 28).

A San Bushman pictograph shows a large horned snake emerging from rocks in the company of women (fig. 250).

Australia and Polynesia

Australian Aboriginal rock art is some of the most beautiful and diverse in the world. More than 100,000 sites are known, including the oldest firmly dated rock art in the world—40,000 years old (Flood 1997, 11–12). Moreover, there is a continuum here with a living tradition, with some Aboriginals still creating and maintaining rock art. Because Australia is an island continent with an ancient human history, the cultural traditions and rock art are unique in some ways, but themes of sexuality and fertility nevertheless resemble those from other regions. For example, snakes figure prominently in Aboriginal religion and rock art. They are very significant in the Dreamtime (the era of creation) and are related to water resources just as in southwestern lore. During the Dreamtime, they formed rivers, springs, and rock cisterns as they traveled across the landscape, before coming to rest in deep pools.

One of the most widespread elements of Aboriginal mythology and rock art is the Rainbow Serpent. This is a great creator spirit who brings the monsoonal rains to end the dry season, at times appearing in the sky as a rainbow. Sometimes the Rainbow Serpent is male, other times female—representing the great fertility mother who gave birth to the First People. Some depictions of the Rainbow Serpent are more than 9,000 years old, suggesting it may represent the world's longest continuous religious tradition. Many spectacular rock paintings of the Rainbow Serpent occur in northern Australia, some more than fifty feet long. These images often have an animal-like head with horns or ears, penis or breasts, and sometimes have eggs inside (fig. 251). There are some parallels between the Aboriginal Rainbow Serpent and the Horned Water Serpent of the southwestern Pueblos—both are intimately related to water, rain, and fertility.

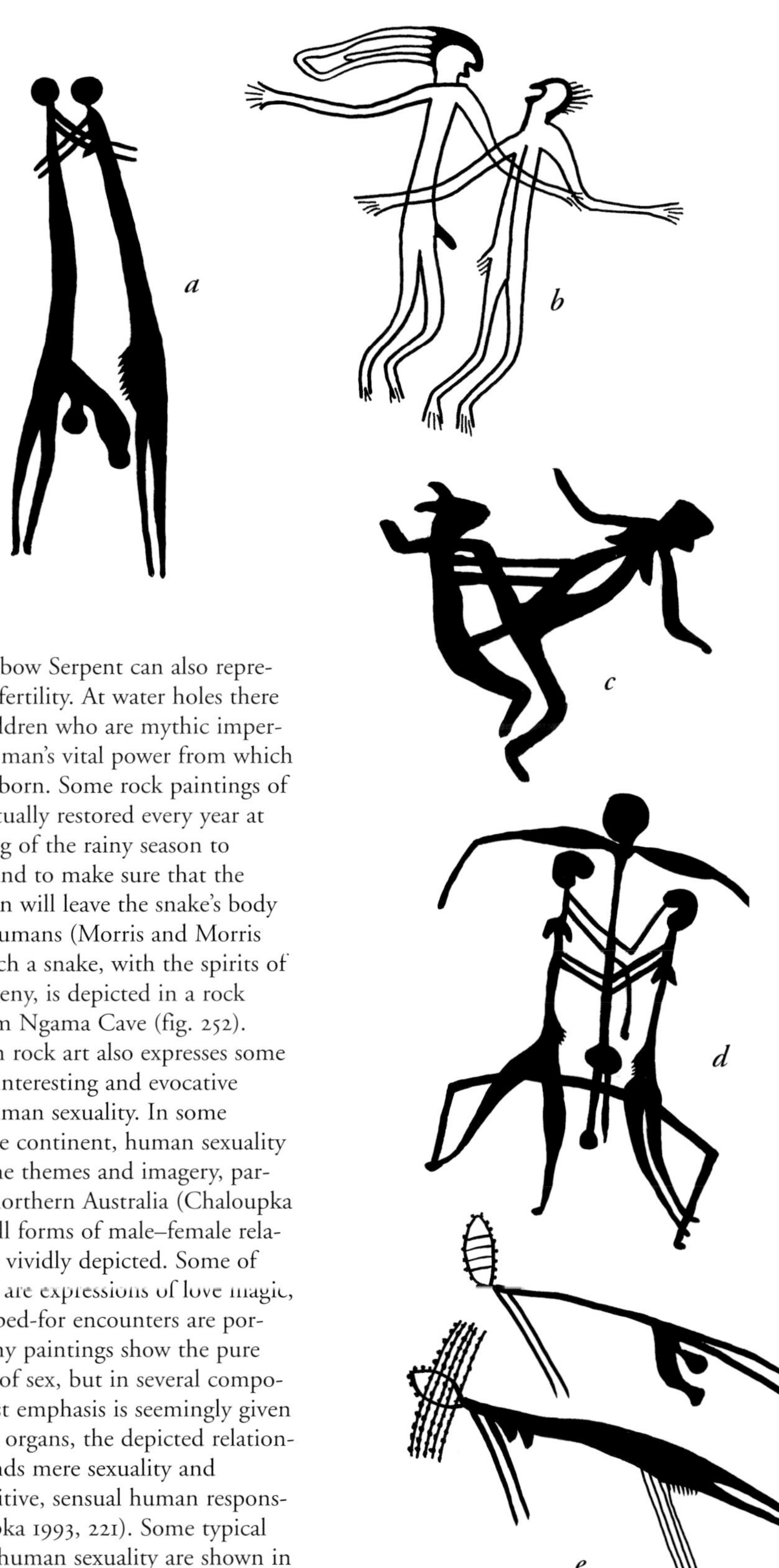

fig. 253. Examples of Aboriginal rock art depicting sexual activity: a. Djuwarr, Arnhem Land (after Chaloupka 1993, 221); b. Kakadu National Park (after Chaloupka 1993, 102); c. Ginga Wardelirrhmeng, Arnhem Land (after Chaloupka 1993, 161); d. Upper East Alligator River (after Brandl 1988, 50); e. Anburdgorrang, Arhem Land (after Chaloupka 1993, 145).

The Rainbow Serpent can also represent human fertility. At water holes there are spirit children who are mythic impersonations of man's vital power from which children are born. Some rock paintings of snakes are ritually restored every year at the beginning of the rainy season to ensure rain and to make sure that the spirit children will leave the snake's body to become humans (Morris and Morris 1965, 21). Such a snake, with the spirits of unborn progeny, is depicted in a rock painting from Ngama Cave (fig. 252).

Australian rock art also expresses some of the most interesting and evocative images of human sexuality. In some regions of the continent, human sexuality dominates the themes and imagery, particularly in northern Australia (Chaloupka 1993, 221). All forms of male–female relationships are vividly depicted. Some of these images are expressions of love magic, in which hoped-for encounters are portrayed: "Many paintings show the pure physicalities of sex, but in several compositions, whilst emphasis is seemingly given to the sexual organs, the depicted relationship transcends mere sexuality and exhibits sensitive, sensual human responses" (Chaloupka 1993, 221). Some typical examples of human sexuality are shown in fig. 253.

Further, at a major pictograph site in Arnhem Land, the artist focused on

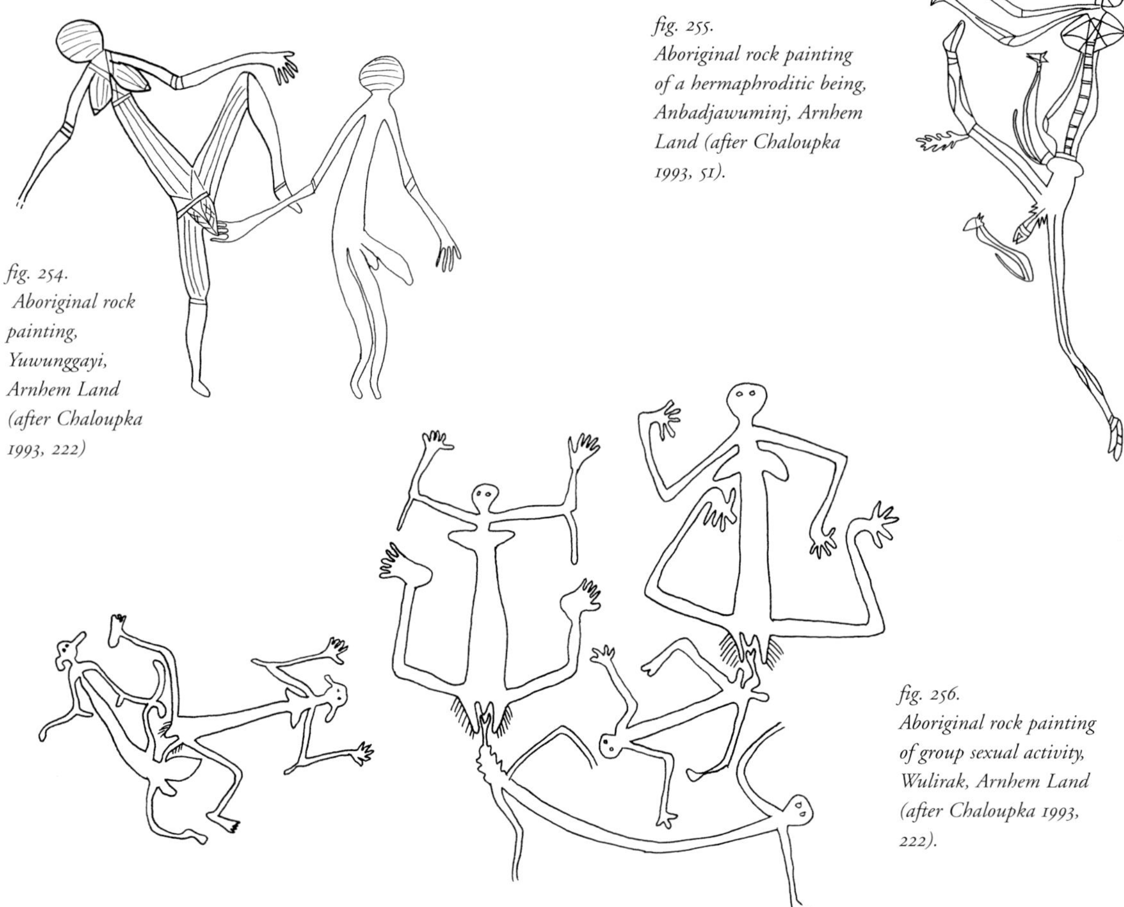

fig. 254. Aboriginal rock painting, Yuwunggayi, Arnhem Land (after Chaloupka 1993, 222)

fig. 255. Aboriginal rock painting of a hermaphroditic being, Anbadjawuminj, Arnhem Land (after Chaloupka 1993, 51).

fig. 256. Aboriginal rock painting of group sexual activity, Wulirak, Arnhem Land (after Chaloupka 1993, 222).

women in a sexual context, depicting them in various stances, including a provocative position with one leg raised to expose the vulva (fig. 254). Triangular vulva symbols are also present and even portrayals of hermaphroditic or bisexual beings with Rainbow Serpents attached (fig. 255). At another rock painting site, three highly stylized couples are shown in sexual union, possibly depicting a ritual act (fig. 256).

An equally interesting scene occurs in a petroglyph panel in western Australia, where two males and three females are sexually connected by lines joining their genitals (fig. 257). The theme of love magic is strongly developed in the rock art of the Wardaman area near Darwin, as explained by an archaeologist who has studied the area:

> Figures associated with love magic were often sexually explicit. Women in the spread-legs position were particularly common, as were copulation scenes. The pronounced sexuality of Wardaman art is causing some embarrassment nowadays, particularly to women, since the development of tourism in the Ingaladdi area in 1989 has brought more strangers into the region. Wardaman women are therefore banning the photographing of sexually explicit female figures, and in some cases visits by men to certain sites.

Murdu-ya (Place of the Dance) in the Ingaladdi area is a large rock shelter associated with women. There are two sections of the shelter—a long area with many stone tools on the floor and paintings and engravings on the back wall, ceiling and boulders with some sexually explicit scenes and female figures in the spread-legged position, and an adjacent sandy area naturally enclosed by rock walls and a few paintings. This place is said to be

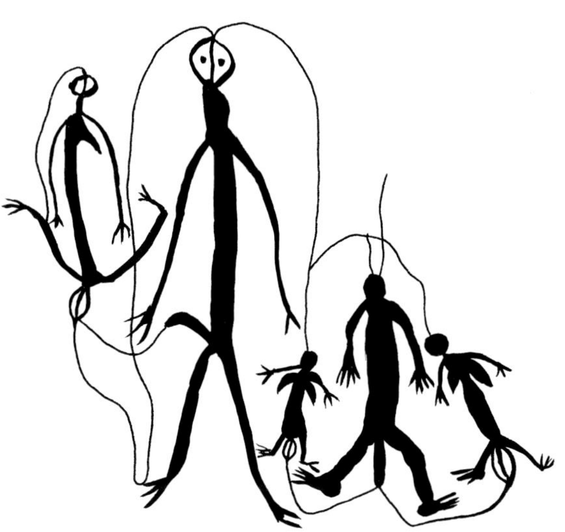

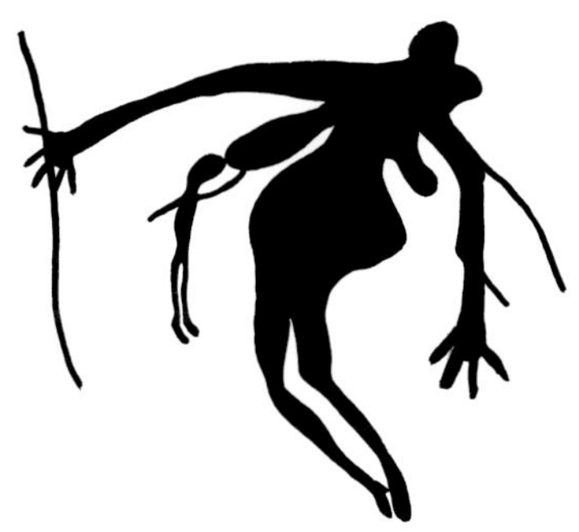

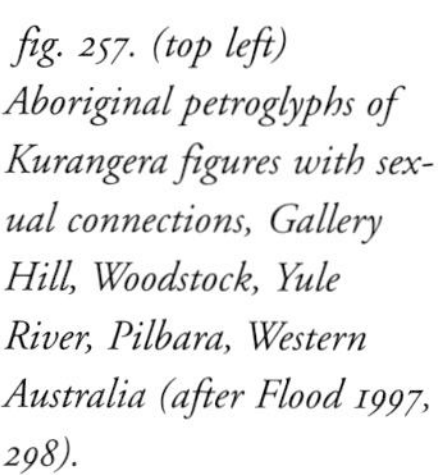

fig. 257. (top left) Aboriginal petroglyphs of Kurangera figures with sexual connections, Gallery Hill, Woodstock, Yule River, Pilbara, Western Australia (after Flood 1997, 298).

fig. 258. (top right) Aboriginal pictograph of mother and nursing child, Anumeri, King Edward River, northwestern Australia (after Brodrick 1948, Plate 55).

> where the women danced, starting at one end and moving in a line down to the other end and back. This dance, *murdu*, is performed with rapid hopping steps, and is used by women in love magic rites in this region. Privacy was desired so the dancing took place in remote parts of the bush or in enclosed places such as this (Flood 1997, 313).

Some Australian rock art contains simple symbolic motifs that depict aspects of fertility and sex, such as circles that represent breasts of young girls and barred double circles that represent the pendant breasts of old women, as explained in the following:

> Circles have more often been thought to symbolize the female genitals than breasts, but lactation is, of course, all-important in traditional hunter-gatherer life, where a baby will die if a mother's milk does not flow. Because most early anthropologists and ethnographers were male, little has ever been recorded about female ceremonies and rites of passage, but there is evidence that rituals were performed by girls to promote lactation. For example, in the Western Desert Pitjandjatjara women had a ceremonial stone against which young girls press themselves to cause their breasts to grow and their milk to flow (Flood 1997, 160).

In a representational depiction, a nursing mother with large, lactating breasts suckles her child in a pictograph in northwestern Australia (fig. 258). A maternal theme is also expressed in the petroglyph portraying a running, pregnant woman in western Australia (fig. 259).

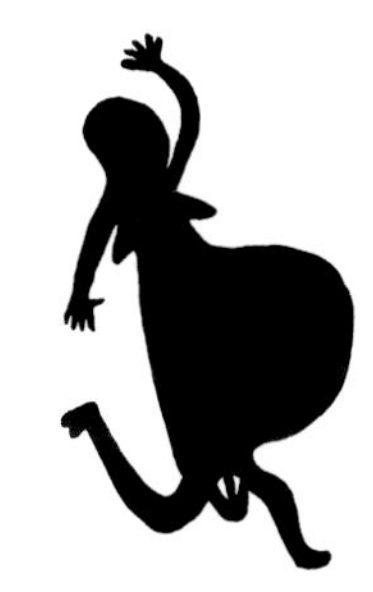

fig. 259. Aboriginal petroglyph of pregnant woman, Maynard Hill, Western Australia (after Flood 1990, 65).

In addition to depicting the themes of love magic and motherhood, some Australian rock art displays malevolent elements of sorcery by portraying images of intended victims, who have grotesque, deformed bodies, sometimes pierced with barbs, being eaten by creatures, or having grossly distorted sexual organs (Chaloupka 1993, 208). For example, shown in fig. 260 is a sorcery painting of a copulating couple described by the following:

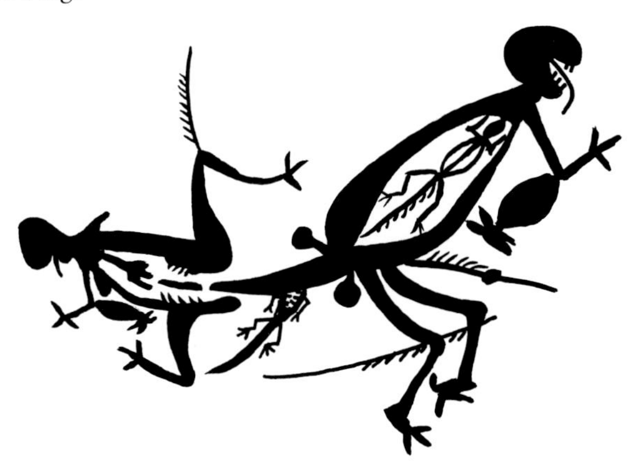

fig. 260. (below) Aboriginal pictograph of a copulating couple with sorcery elements, Yuwunggaya, Arnhem Land (after Chaloupka 1993, 208).

> Each of the victims is depicted with a flying fox hanging from one arm and with a spear through one knee. An additional spear is piercing the male's pubic region, and a freshwater crocodile is biting his penis, while another crocodile, seen within his body cavity, devours his organs. Both figure are shown with painful grimaces and protruding tongues (Chaloupka 1993, 208).

A particular form of Aboriginal sorcery is a lethal phallic rite of magic known as the "pointing bone," which has been characterized by anthropologists in the following manner:

> Black or hostile magic is predominantly phallic in Australia. . . . If a man has been "boned," his dream will show it. First he sees a crack, an opening in the ground, and then two or three men walking toward him within the opening. When they are near they draw a bone out of their own body. It comes from the flesh between the scrotum and the rectum. The sorcerer, before he actually "bones" his victim, makes him fall asleep by strewing in the air some semen or excrement which he has taken from his own penis or rectum. The man who uses the bone holds it under his penis, as if a second penis were protruding from him. . . . The victim is asleep and the bone goes straight into his scrotum (Campbell 1988, I (1):66).x

The subject of sexual taboos is also expressed in Australian rock art. Probably used as a means of instructing each generation about such prohibition, the Moon Dreaming site in the Wardaman region graphically depicts the tribal law against a man having intercourse with his mother-in-law:

> Here, the moon, Gandawag, whilst his wives were out foraging, had sex with his mother-in-law, and she kept his large penis in her dilly bag. Moon was severely punished, and Moon Dreaming was one of the very few rock art sites in Wardaman country which was considered a "dangerous place," in that disturbance of it is believed to bring unpleasant results. We were told not to look too long at the paintings, lest something bad should happen to us, such as becoming sick. A deposit of iridescent pinkish-red ochre, liwin, lies in the creek bed not far from the site, and is believed to be blood from Moon's sub-incised penis. One Wardaman woman collected some of this, and thereupon became deaf for several days (Flood 1997, 311).

A final example of Australian rock art illustrates how an image might be wrongly interpreted in the absence of ethnographic or cultural background. fig. 261 shows two stick-figure anthropomorphs running, one of which has a swollen abdomen containing smaller figures. At first glance, this seems to depict a pregnant female full of

fig. 261. (bottom left) Aboriginal pictographs representing the people-eating spirit Adungun being pursued, Australia (after Mountford 1964, Plate 13).

fig. 262. (bottom right) Petroglyphs of birthing scenes, Hawaii (after Cox and Stasack 1970, 46).

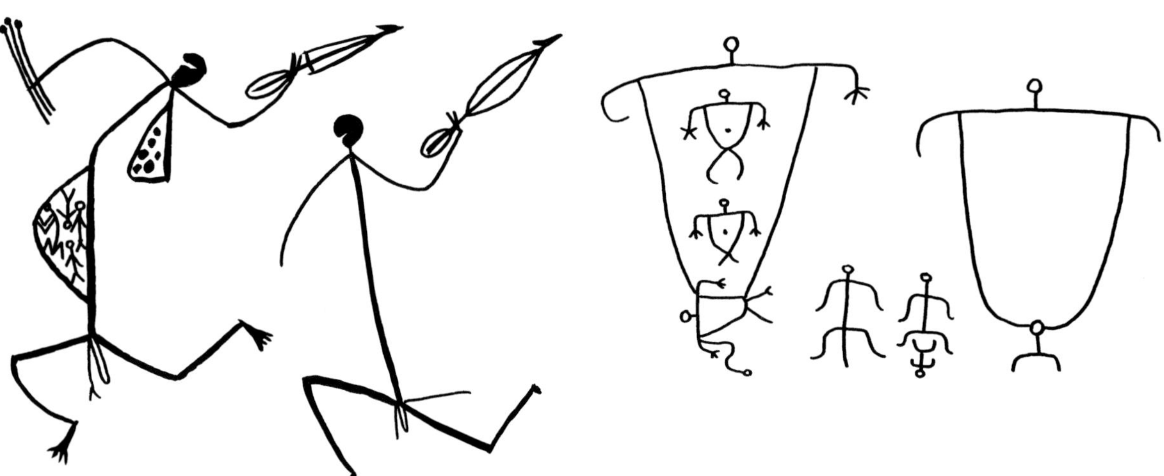

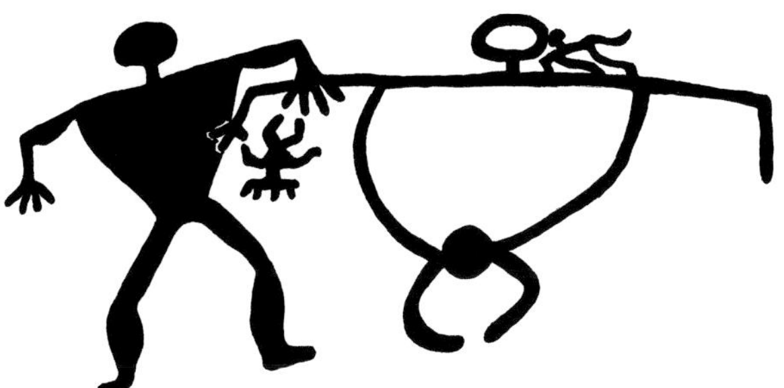

fig. 263. (left) Petroglyphs of a family scene, Hawaii (after Cox and Stasack 1970, 47).

babies, but in fact it is a portrayal of Adungun—a dangerous monster who wanders around the country eating people and whose belly is full of the dead (Mountford 1964, 13).

Australia is part of a large region of the Pacific Ocean known as Oceania that includes New Zealand, New Guinea, and many smaller island countries in Polynesia. Because of their extreme isolation, these places have very diverse cultures and rock art. The island complex of Polynesia, including the Hawaiian islands, contains rock art in nearly every area where suitable surfaces occur, but nowhere else in the Pacific are there such dense concentrations as in Hawaii (Cox and Stasack 1970, 2). Some of this rock art depicts family scenes, pregnancy, and birth (fig. 262). The man and woman in fig. 263 show that the sexes were portrayed differently—men with solidly pecked, muscular, triangular bodies, and women outlined. The vulva on this female is a large circular cavity that is much deeper than any surrounding marks—suggesting repeated use of this petroglyph for fertility rites. In Hawaii, Papa, the Earth Mother, is also patron of childbirth and agriculture. At one time Hawaiians venerated rock formations resembling paired male and female genitals, and the complementary nature of the genders is central to traditional Hawaiian religious beliefs.

Moreover, the vulva symbol is a common motif throughout Polynesia, where rock surfaces and pebbles are covered with it:

> On Easter Island, for example, two-lobed vulva forms with abstractly rendered clitorises are engraved on a rock at the site of Orongo. The engraved stone was used in the girl's clitoris-stretching ceremony; during the *te manu mo ta poki* or "bird child" ceremony (still part of living memory in 1919), girls stood on a rock where their enlarged clitorises were examined by five priests, who then carved the images on the rocks (Taylor 1996, 126).

Asia

Major concentrations of rock art exist in Central Asia and the Far East—in China, Afghanistan, Pakistan, Mongolia, Siberia, and India. However, little research has been conducted in these areas compared to other continents, and much remains to be learned about the rock art of this region. For example, in China, although major sites have been discovered in recent decades, it is estimated that perhaps 90 percent of Inner Mongolia's petroglyphs remain to be discovered (Bahn 1993, 2). Nevertheless, according to current knowledge it is clear that themes of sexuality and fertility can be found here also. At a Chinese petroglyph site in Hutubi is an interesting sexual scene involving a central female surrounded by at least four phallic males in what is probably a ritual activity (fig. 264). Further, some Mongolian sites (fig. 265) depict images of "ancestral mothers" (an equivalent of the Earth Mother) often showing successive births (Martynov 1991, 272). Other images from this region include a fertility goddess with snakes in her hands. Among many northern Asian peoples there was a close relationship between the ideas of fertility, the

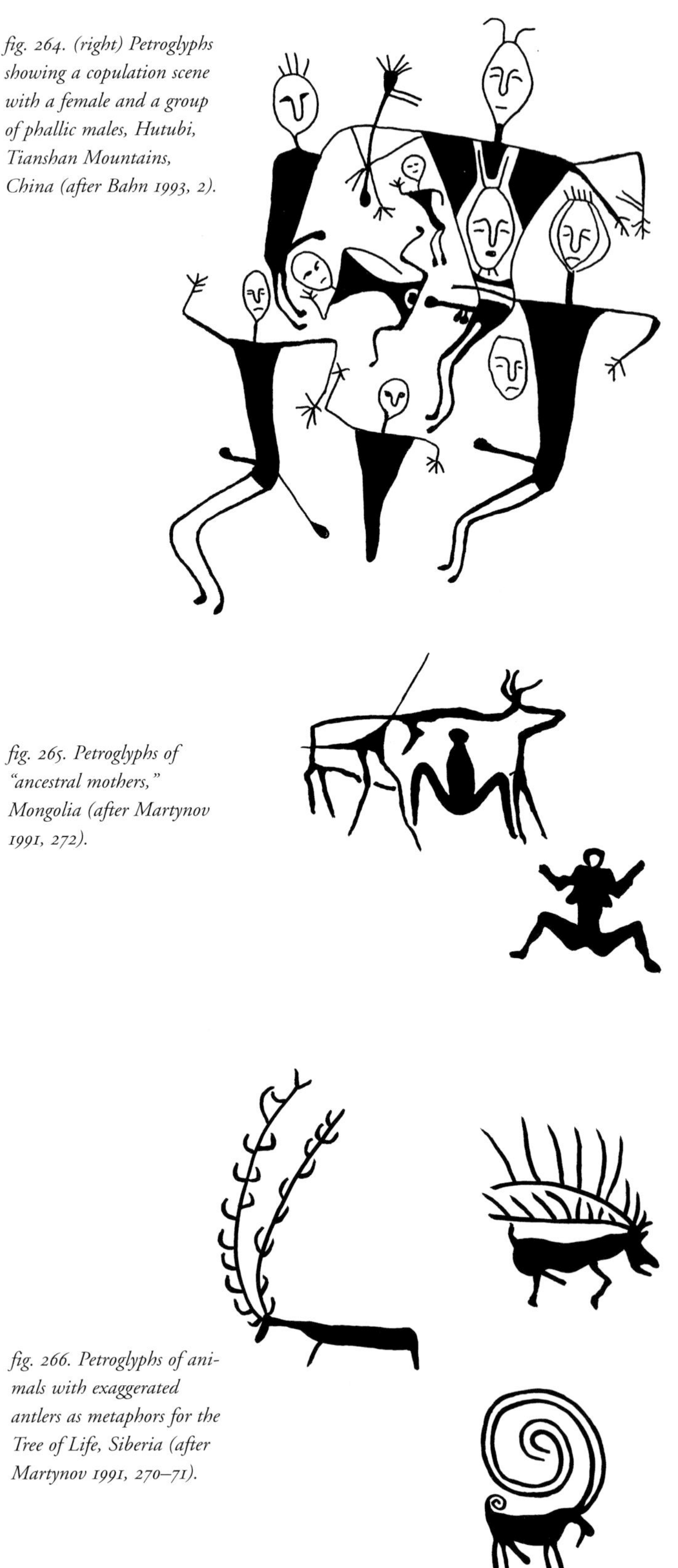

fig. 264. (right) Petroglyphs showing a copulation scene with a female and a group of phallic males, Hutubi, Tianshan Mountains, China (after Bahn 1993, 2).

fig. 265. Petroglyphs of "ancestral mothers," Mongolia (after Martynov 1991, 272).

fig. 266. Petroglyphs of animals with exaggerated antlers as metaphors for the Tree of Life, Siberia (after Martynov 1991, 270–71).

sun, snakes, and vegetative growth. Certain plant cults depicted a goddess of fertility as a face or mask with young sprouts and shoots growing from the head, along with many sun symbols. These sinuous vine-like lines emerging from the head could also represent snakes as well as vegetation since both snake and vegetation cults were common.

A major mythological theme expressed in rock art of northern Asia and the Near East is the Tree of Life—a fertility symbol and cult that represents the dying and resurrecting power of nature. This basic, underlying worldview of the cyclicity of nature is common throughout human prehistory, including Asia:

> In the materials of the art of northern Asia three artistic and semantic images clearly appear as symbols of dying and reawakening nature, its circulation, and the cyclicity and mystery of its life-creating power. One of these we may term the "Tree of Life." That tree with its branches is also a metaphor expressed equally well by branching antlers, hence its manifestation in animals. Finally, a woman giving birth provides still another expression of the Tree of Life. . . . These different embodiments are not accidental, for they embrace three basic spheres of life, vegetative, animal, and human, in a religious and mythological understanding of life. Sometimes we do not perceive in north Asiatic art a clear separation of these images but, on the contrary, their union (Martynov 1991, 101).

Variations of the Tree of Life fertility cult transposed concepts of vegetative fecundity to animals and their reproduction. The animal manifestation had the same meaning—at its core is the cyclic nature of all life, whether it be mating, birthing, dying, or seasonal vegetative renewal. In Asia the substitution of deities was expressed in cultures more dependent on hunting and animal husbandry than on agriculture. The fecund power of growth in the branches of the Tree of Life was reanimated as great branching or curving antlers and horns (fig. 266). Because antlers can be shed and regrown, they also convey the idea of renewal of life. Petroglyph depictions of this theme are numerous in some parts of northern Asia (Martynov, 1991, 107). Such hypertrophied horns sometimes give the impression they are tree symbols connected to an animal:

> In these images all is unreal, unlifelike. All attention is focused on the enormous antler-trees, each represented in the form of two many-branched trunks. Thus the hunters and herdsmen of northern Asia widely employed a formulation of the Tree of Life as horns or antlers distinctive in artistry and meaning (Martynov 1991, 107).

Images of animals with unnaturally large antlers also occur in Southwest U.S. rock art; they convey an impression of power and fecundity, but it is unknown if they relate to vegetative cults like the Tree of Life concepts.

In rock art of southern Siberia, there are depictions of women giving birth and of eroticized women who are always shown with animals as described in the following (fig. 265):

> Moreover, these women are often shown with protruding or pendant abdomens, i.e., pregnant or soon after giving birth. Women's images in definitely erotic postures are repeatedly found in south Siberian petroglyphs. Such a representation is calculated. Women are shown with parted legs bent at the knees and with arms bent and raised overhead, together with drawings of bulls or fantastic beasts. The repetitiveness of these images shows that they were executed as a defined compositional unit—woman and animal—according to defined stylistic traditions (Martynov 1991, 107).

The ancient Indo-European mythic basis for the association of an erotic female image and a bull is expressed in the *Rig Veda*, where the creation of the world is explained:

> In this myth, Heaven is a male principle personified as a bull, while Earth is a woman giving life. "They are spouses: Father Heaven and Mother Earth. The rain let down from Heaven to Earth is seed from which is born all that is living" (Martynov 1991, 108).

Conversely, symbolic inversion may be responsible for images of men fertilizing animals, as depicted in a Siberian petroglyph (fig. 268). Fecundity and abundance of animals, in this case moose, are implied in such images, as they are in scenes like the moose giving birth to a calf, from the same site (fig. 269). A Siberian Mother of Fertility Goddess, Ayisyt, also bestowed fertility on women; three days after a child was born, ceremonies for Ayisyt employed images of moose, reindeer, and horses carved on birchbark (Martynov 1991, 109).

Images of fertility and sexuality in rock art also occur in India, including snake and vulva symbols and depictions of pregnancy and birth, among humans and animals (fig. 270). The symbolic connection between hunting and fecundity of animals is also present, as illustrated in fig. 271. Finally, human sexuality and procreation are well represented by the graceful, pregnant woman depicted in an Indian pictograph in fig. 267.

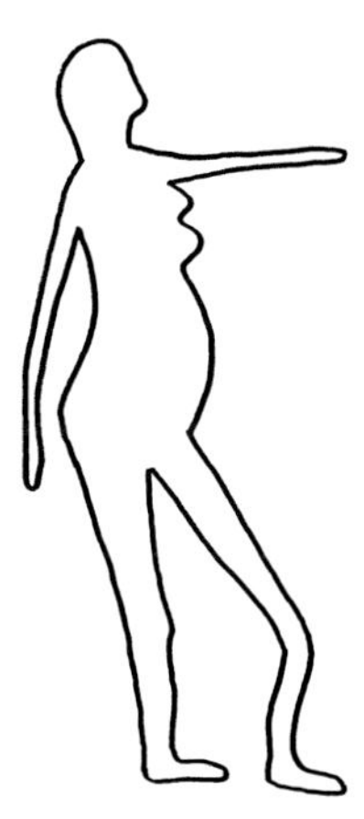

fig. 267. (above) Pictograph of a pregnant woman, Bhimbetka, India (after Brooks and Wakankar 1976, 55).

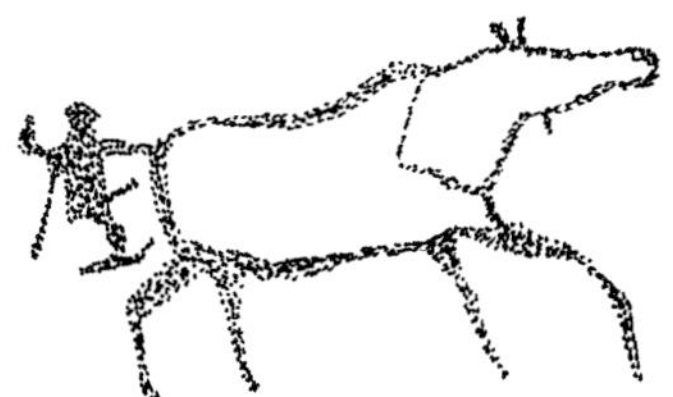

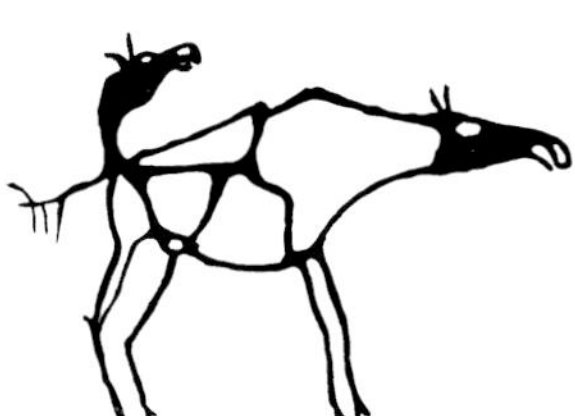

fig. 268. (far left) Petroglyphs of a moose and a man on skis apparently attempting intercourse, Tom River, Siberia (after Martynov 1991, 153).

fig. 269. (left) Petroglyph depicting a moose giving birth, Tom River, Siberia (after Martynov 1991, 156).

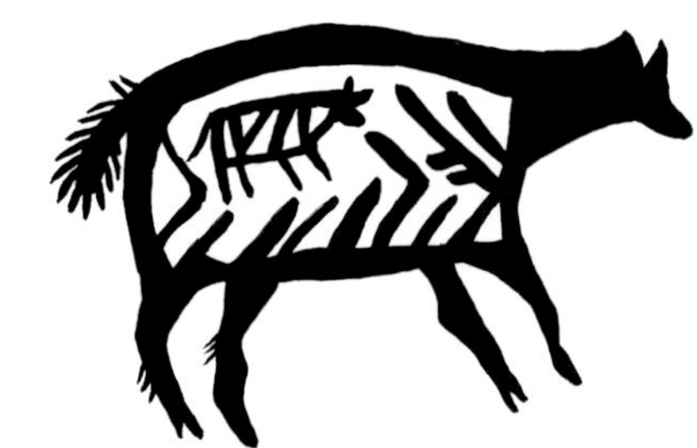

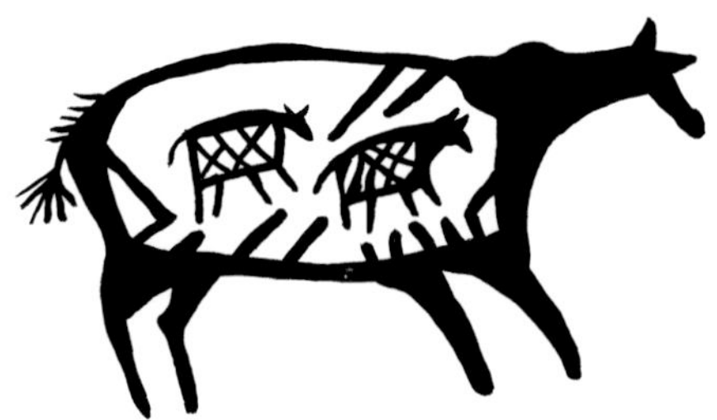

fig. 270. Pictographs of pregnant animals, Hathi Tol Shelter, Raisen, India (after Brooks and Wakankar 1976, 84).

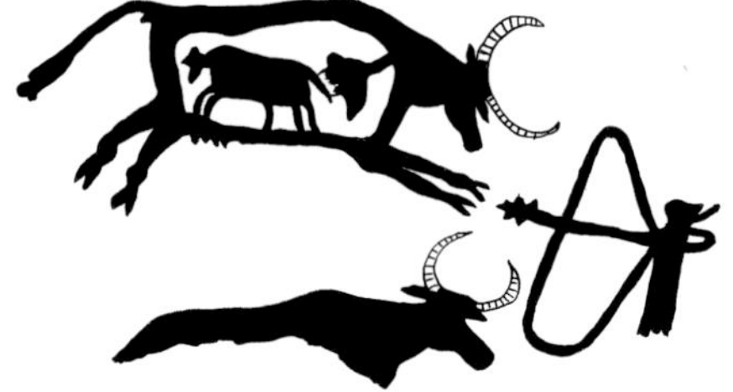

fig. 271. Pictographs of hunter and a pregnant buffalo, Chibbadnala, upper Chambal Valley, India (from Rock Art Research, 1993, 10:2).

Europe and the Middle East

European rock art was some of the first to be studied seriously following the discovery in the late 1800s of the Paleolithic painted caves, the oldest of which are now dated at 32,000 years B.P. (Chauvet, Deschamps, and Hillaire 1996, 131). This ancient art from the Ice Age has inspired many people with its aesthetic sophistication. The caves are regarded as religious sanctuaries for rites of initiation and shamanic activities. Scholars have long discussed their apparent fertility themes, which seem to focus on seasonal renewal of life, fecundity and abundance of Pleistocene animals, shamanic trance imagery, and the caves as symbolic of the womb of the earth, the source of all life.

The cave art consists mostly of animals, but there are enough images of women emphasizing their procreative power that fertility themes seem implicit (figs. 1, 2, 4, 5). Approximately a thousand images of the female form, including sculptures, reliefs, and engravings, are known from the Paleolithic era, spanning the major part of Europe (Husain 1997, 12). The fertility symbolism of the many carved female figurines from Ice Age sites throughout Europe are discussed in the introduction to this book. In the Pleistocene cave art of Europe, actual copulation scenes are rare (fig. 273), and vulva and phallic images occur sparingly (figs. 7 and 272), suggesting that early sexual interpretations may have been overemphasized (Bahn and Vertut 1988, 159–76). Nonetheless, a general concern with

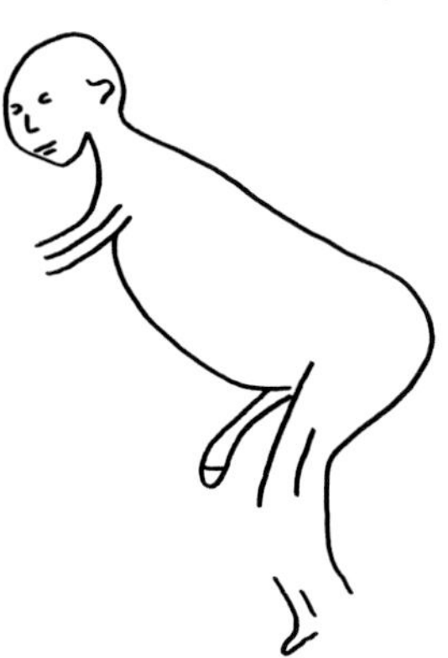

fig. 272. (below) Rock carving in an Ice Age cave, Saint Cirq, France (after photograph by Burt Alpert).

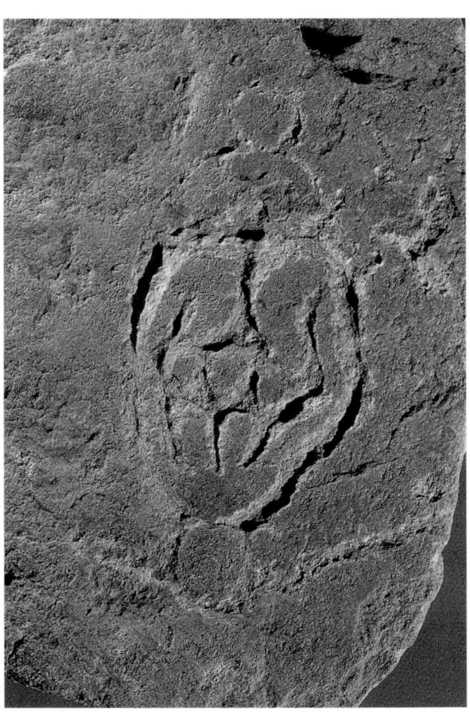

fig. 273. (right) Although copulation scenes in European Paleolithic art are rare, this carving from a rock shelter at Laussel, France, may be such a depiction. The French have dubbed it "la carte à jouer" (the playing card) because, like a playing card, it looks the same either way up (courtesy of the Musee d' Aquitaine Bordeaux; photo by Jean-Michel Arnaud).

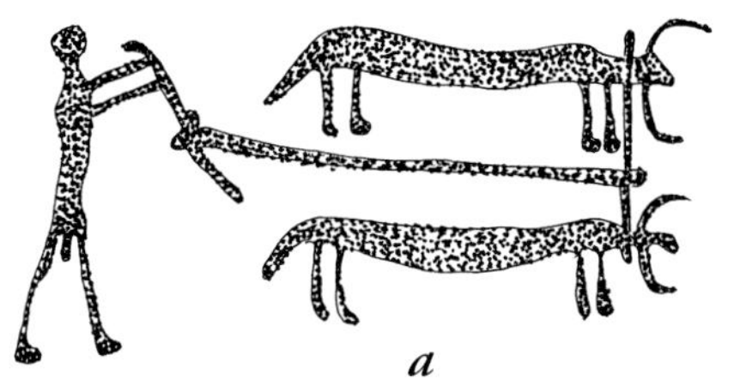

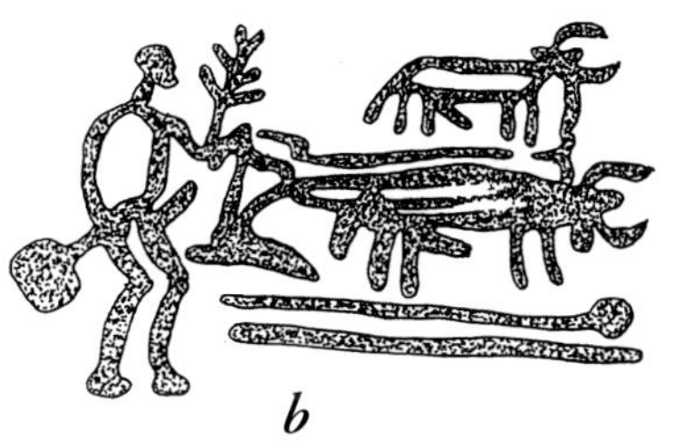

fig. 274. Petroglyphs of phallic men plowing the soil: a. Val Camonica, Italy (after Anati 1994, 124); b. Littlesby, England (after Burl 1979, 224).

fecundity was undoubtedly a motivating factor in creating these images.

From the painted caves and figurines of ancient Europe, as well as rock art of the adjacent areas such as the Mediterranean and the Middle East, the classical concepts of the cult of the Great Goddess, or Earth Mother, arose. These images have been perhaps the most persistent feature in the archaeological record of this part of the ancient world—the Great Goddess prevailed throughout the Paleolithic and Neolithic in Europe and the Bronze Age in the Mediterranean region (Gimbutas 1989, 321). The Earth Goddess cult, which focused on the unity and celebration of life, is the dominant motif in art and ideology of ancient Europe:

> The Goddess in all her manifestations was a symbol of the unity of all life in nature. Her power was in water and in stone, in tomb and cave, in animals and birds, snakes and fish, hills and flowers. Hence the holistic and mytho-poeic perception of the sacredness and mystery of all there is on Earth. . . . The question of mortality was of profound concern but the deep perception of the periodicity of nature based on the cycles of the moon and the female body led to the creation of a strong belief in the immediate regeneration of life at the crisis of death. There was no simple death, only death *and* regeneration. And this was the key to the hymn of life reflected in this art (Gimbutas 1989, 321).

Rock art with elements of the Great Goddess cult, mostly petroglyphs, stretches from the British Isles, Scandinavia, and the Alps into Siberia and beyond—suggesting a continuous tradition by early herders and farmers from the Neolithic into historic times.

Moreover, aspects of the Earth Mother, or divine feminine principle, have survived to the present day. With the development of agriculture, ritual and art show a mystical connection between the fertility of the soil and human sexuality, especially the creative energy of females. The symbol of the fruitful earth womb of the Ice Age hunters evolved into various earth fertility and grain goddesses. Related to this transition, petroglyphs from England and Italy depict phallic men plowing the soil, thereby associating the fertility of the soil (Earth Mother) with human fertility and sexuality (fig. 274). The sexual metaphors about "plowing my vulva" in the ancient Sumerian "Hymn of Innana" discussed in Chapter 4 further express the symbolism of phallic plow and feminine earth. Further, the petroglyph from Litsleby, England, depicts a phallic man and ox team:

> It is obvious that he is engaged in the first ploughing of the year to awaken the earth's fruitfulness after the sleep of winter with the phallus of the plow, the ploughshare. . . . The man's enormous phallus and the highly exaggerated reproductive organs of the oxen speak for themselves. The branch in his hand is a "may tree," a feature of the spring fertility cult (Burl 1979, 223).

Other petroglyphs from Bronze Age Europe depict sexual rites of fecundity between men and animals (fig. 275), as well as images of a man and a woman

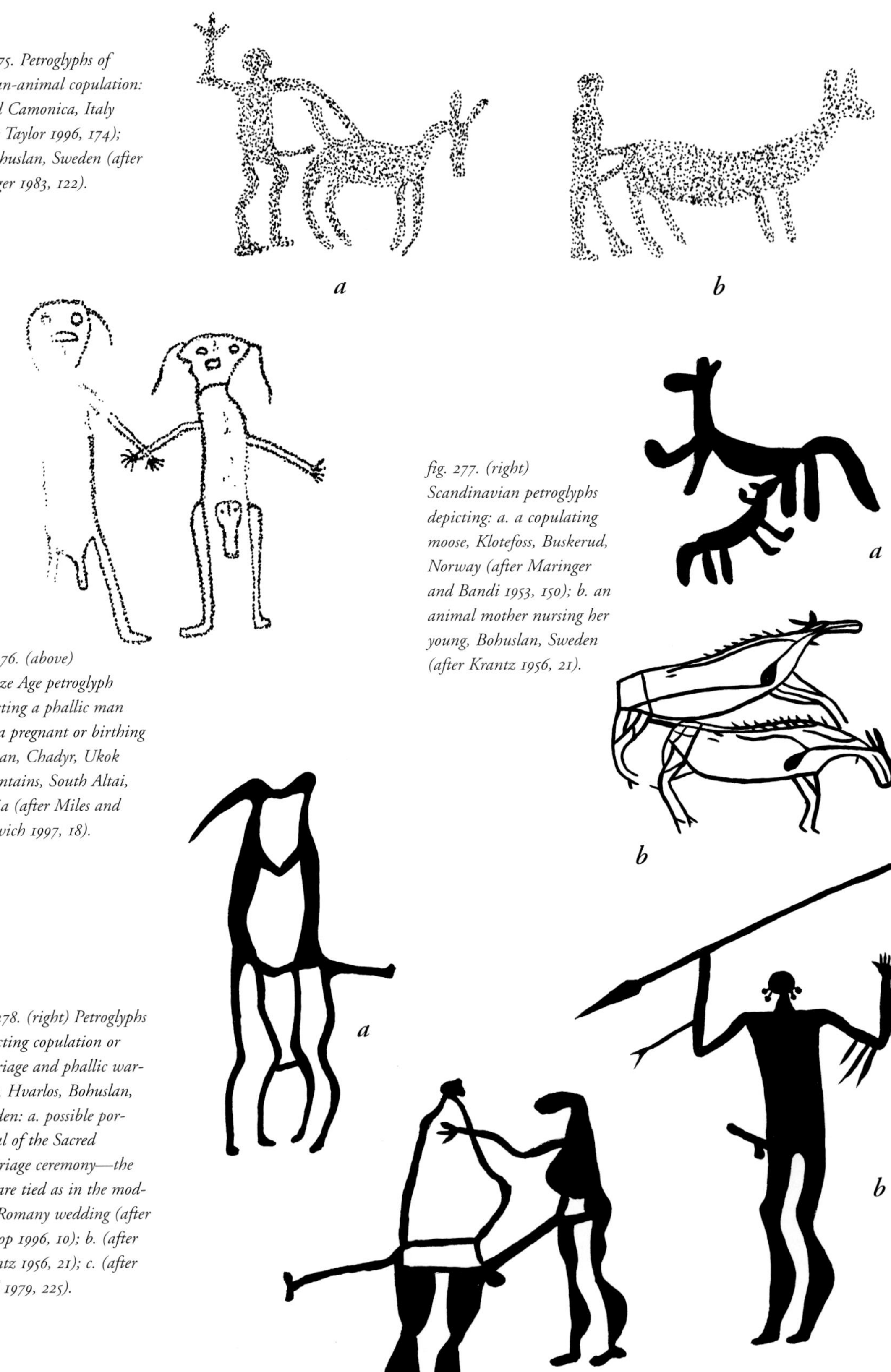

fig. 275. Petroglyphs of human-animal copulation: a. Val Camonica, Italy (after Taylor 1996, 174); b. Bohuslan, Sweden (after Hunger 1983, 122).

fig. 276. (above) Bronze Age petroglyph depicting a phallic man and a pregnant or birthing woman, Chadyr, Ukok Mountains, South Altai, Russia (after Miles and Norwich 1997, 18).

fig. 277. (right) Scandinavian petroglyphs depicting: a. a copulating moose, Klotefoss, Buskerud, Norway (after Maringer and Bandi 1953, 150); b. an animal mother nursing her young, Bohuslan, Sweden (after Krantz 1956, 21).

fig. 278. (right) Petroglyphs depicting copulation or marriage and phallic warriors, Hvarlos, Bohuslan, Sweden: a. possible portrayal of the Sacred Marriage ceremony—the legs are tied as in the modern Romany wedding (after Bishop 1996, 10); b. (after Krantz 1956, 21); c. (after Burl 1979, 225).

who seems to be pregnant or giving birth (fig. 276). A petroglyph near Hoghem, England, portrays a "spring wedding" between a man and a woman and a man mating with a cow (Burl 1979, 223). Such imitative magic to enhance the fertility of the earth and its animals is also pictured in rock art of other continents, including the American Southwest (see Chapter 4).

In addition, petroglyphs of animals mating and nursing their young (fig. 277) can be found in Norway and Sweden. Further, the Swedish site at Bohuslan depicts very phallic men with spears and axes and copulating couples, some of whom may be ritual participants in a Sacred Marriage ceremony (fig. 278).

Concerns with fertility in ancient Europe led to development of phallic cults in numerous cultures (Scott 1966). In many Neolithic and Bronze Age images, the penis is emphasized to the point of hyperbole (fig. 279). The obvious nature of this symbolism was described obliquely by an eighteenth-century scholar: "The great characteristic attribute was represented by the organ of generation in that state of tension and rigidity which is necessary to the due performance of its functions" (Richard Payne Knight, 1786, in Knight and Wright 1957). The fertilizing power of the penis would have been paramount to herders as well as hunters, since managing animals involves controlling their mating patterns. Phallicism led to the erection of many stone monoliths throughout the landscape of northern Europe, where they were reported to have the power to make sterile women fruitful. Veneration of phallic power is also behind the awesome geoglyph known as the Cerne Abbas Giant on a hillside near Dorset, England (fig. 280). This 150-foot-long figure of a phallic man wielding a club is carved into chalk bedrock and has long served as an ancient fertility locale for a related folk ritual:

> The great prehistoric chalk-hill figure of Cerne Abbas, who once stood guard on the outer slope of a hill fort, wielding a club, his penis erect in a show of virility . . . played host to a midsummer's-eve orgy of village lads and lasses. Young women who were having difficulty getting pregnant would walk up the hill to spend the night sleeping on the giant's penis (Taylor 1996, 223).

Likewise, the many ancient stone circles in the British Isles were probably sites where themes of fertility, death, and resurrection were ritually enacted. Further, passage graves were built as large earthen mounds with vulvar-like entrances that symbolized both womb and tomb for sacred burials, some functioning as solstice markers that allowed the sun's rays to penetrate into the earth womb in symbolic fertilization on winter solstice as described below:

> The idea conveyed by the whole is of the sun as a male fertilizing power, whose shafts of light have analogies with the fertilizing penises of men and stud animals, as well as connections with the earth-penetrating power of the plow and the fork (*Fork* is an Indo-European word that was originally at one with *fuck*). The idea of the female sex as a field into which grain is sown is common among farming cultures and can be found in Talmudic, Egyptian, and Vedic writings. . . . The resurrection of the bodies of the dead is symbolically connected to the resurrection of the year itself—the point of exact midwinter, after which the sun must begin to come back or there will be no spring (Taylor 1996, 187).

Phallic veneration can also incorporate homosexual elements, as documented throughout the world. Although examples are rare in rock art, in Mongolia there are reportedly depictions of figures with touching penises, as well as a sex scene with a woman fellating one man while having intercourse with another (Taylor 1996, 173). The fertilizing power of the penis has since been celebrated widely throughout the continent, leading to worship of various deities such as Priapus, Dionysius, Pan, and Bacchus.

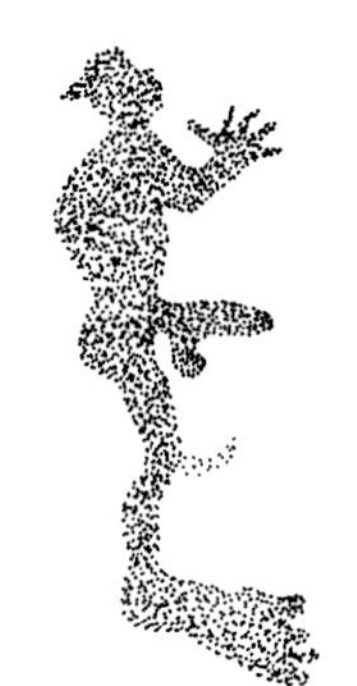

fig. 279. Petroglyph of a phallic male, northern Russia (after Vastokas and Vastokas 1973, 87).

fig. 280. The Cerne Abbas Giant, a geoglyph carved in chalk on a hillside in Dorset, England (after Taylor 1996, 223).

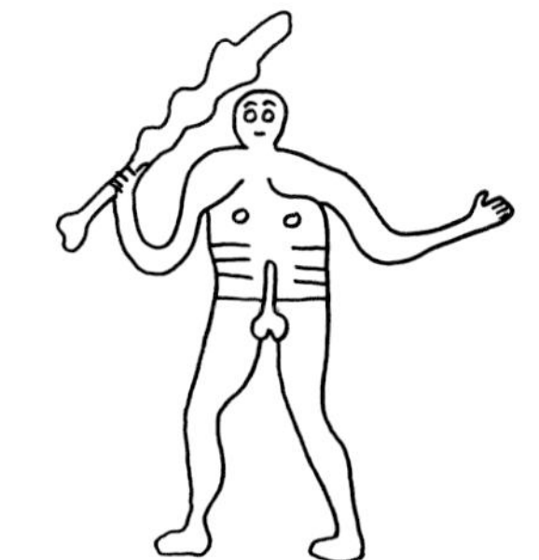

In medieval Europe, there were harvest festivals celebrated with festive processions where large phallic statues were drawn through villages on carts, on which women placed garlands. The May Day celebration of spring is based on ancient fertility rites where the maypole is a phallic symbol. Until at least the sixteenth century in rural Europe, as part of the traditional May Day, young women and men partook in orgiastic sexual rites and a specially chosen virgin (the May Queen) coupled with a man dressed in green, representing vegetative fecundity and the greater fertility of the world. About these various forms of sexual rites, it has been said: "It would be unjust to treat these orgies as a mere outburst of unbridled passion; no doubt they are deliberately and solemnly organized as essential to the fertility of the earth and the welfare of man" (Sir James Frazer, quoted in Burl 1979, 221).

An intriguing symbol of the ancient merging of fertility cults and sexual activity is found engraved on the sandstone lid of a Bronze Age cremation urn from Maltegard, Denmark (fig. 281):

> Engraved on it the matchstick figure of a man, his extended penis touching the edge of the hole, holds out his hands to a woman on the other side of the perforation. Behind her is a May Tree, the forerunner of the Maypole, that symbol of fecundity described by Philip Stubbes, the puritan, as a "stinking idol" because of the depravity he knew its raising in the villages of Elizabethan England, when "all the young men and maides, old men and wives, run gadding overnight to the woods, groves, hills and mountains, where they spend the night in plesant [sic] past-times."... the whole scene from Maltegard, sometimes called the Sacred Wedding, is encircled by what may be a wreath of spring flowers. If the central hole represented the underground presence of the rich Earth for whom such mating was essential, the holed Ring Stone could have stood for the same principle of ritual mating at the time of sowing. The Maltegard lid demonstrated that death in the form of the cremated bones, life and generation were not separate concepts in the prehistoric mind (Burl 1979, 223).

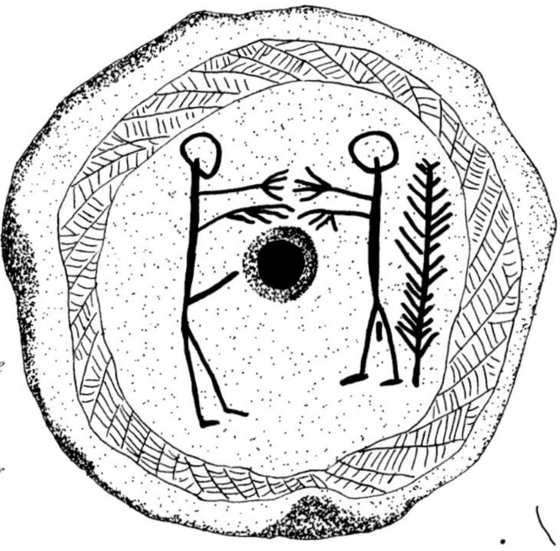

fig. 281. Engraved depiction of the Sacred Marriage ceremony on the stone lid of a cremation urn, Maltegard, Denmark (after Burl 1979, 222).

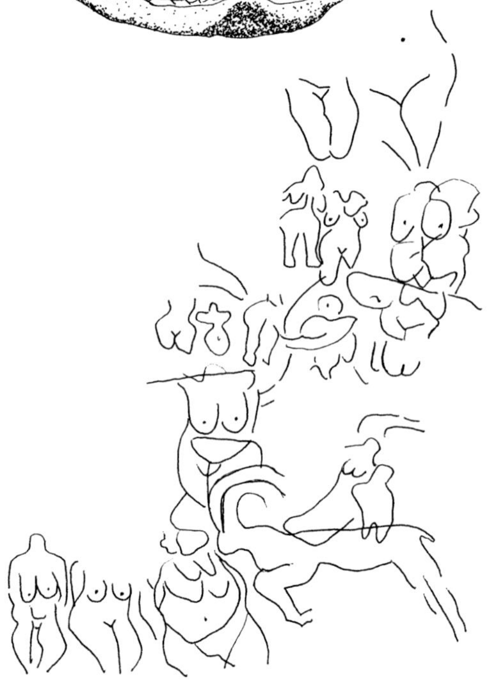

fig. 282. (left) Petroglyphs of nude women, Alam, Saudi Arabia (after Anati 1994, 12:94).

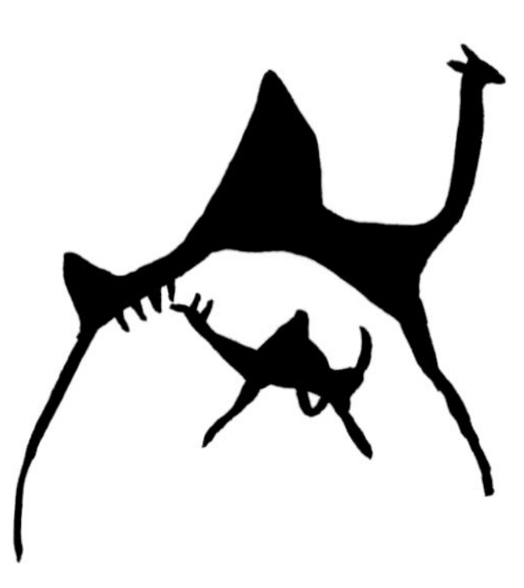

fig. 283. (right) Petroglyph of a nursing camel, Nahal Odem, Southern Negev, Israel (after Anati 1994, 12:135).

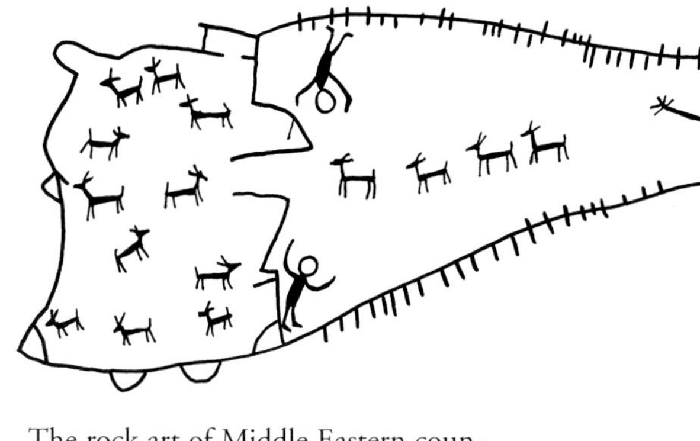

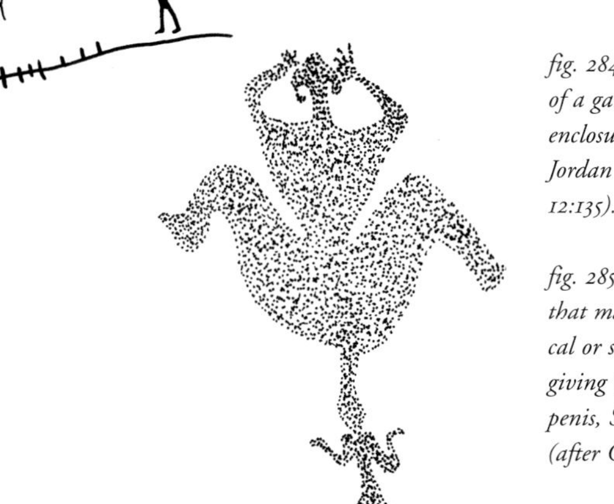

fig. 284. (left) Petroglyphs of a game drive into an enclosure, Rujum Hani, Jordan (after Anati 1994, 12:135).

fig. 285. (right) Petroglyph that may portray a mythical or supernatural male giving birth through his penis, Sabaean, Yemen (after Getty 1990, 43).

The rock art of Middle Eastern countries, although less thoroughly researched, nevertheless contains images of fertility and sexuality. Petroglyphs from Saudi Arabia depict a group of nude women in fig. 282. Animal fertility and abundance are represented in the Israeli petroglyph of a camel nursing her young (fig. 283), and a petroglyph from Jordan shows a game drive or herders corralling animals into an enclosure (fig. 284).

In some early cultures—India, Egypt, and the ancient Middle East—male gods usurped the feminine power of giving birth and claimed their supremacy by giving birth and bringing forth creation in unusual ways, such as from their heads, thighs, mouths, or penes. Moreover, according to ancient Sanskrit scripture, a god named Sukra (Seed) was born from Shiva's penis after living in his belly for a hundred years (Walker 1983, 106). In other cultures, male deities gave birth to primal couples from their penis by masturbating. As strange as these concepts appear, the fact that ancient patriarchal societies attempted to cloak their authority in symbols of motherhood is well documented. The petroglyph from Yemen in fig. 285 may represent such concepts. The large anthropomorph appears to be phallic, and the small size of the lower figure suggests this is a birthing scene (from the penis) rather than a depiction of intercourse.

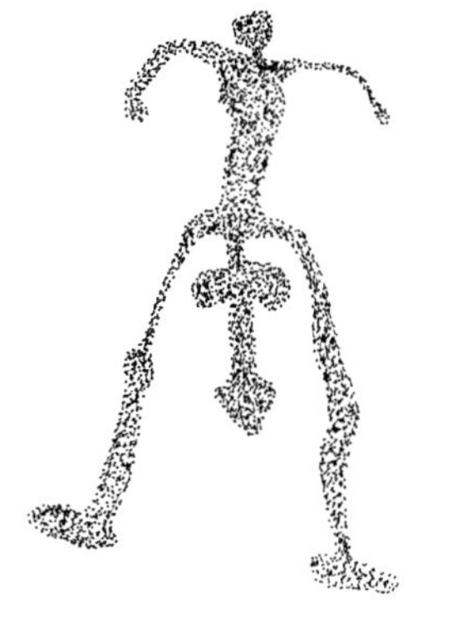

fig. 286. (left) Petroglyph of a male with exaggerated phallic attributes, Peterborough, Ontario, Canada (after Vastokas 1973).

North America

Although the American Southwest has the greatest concentration of rock art on the continent, there are other notable areas of rock art in North America, including the Canadian Shield, Columbia River Basin, the Northwest Coast and the High Plains of the United States and Canada, and Mexico. A site that is particularly significant for its images of fertility and sexuality is the Peterborough, Ontario, petroglyphs (Vastokas 1973). On a massive outcrop of white, crystalline limestone, ancestors of the Algonkian peoples pecked more than nine hundred petroglyph images. A major site for recording ritual, visionary, and shamanic art, it is characterized by an unusual abundance of fertility symbolism. There are numerous female figures, phallic males (fig. 286), vulva symbols, scenes of symbolic copulation (fig. 287), snakes, turtles (fig. 288), and other symbols of fertility and sexuality. The artists may have been drawn to the site by the appearance of the rock, which is weathered into many holes and crevices that seem to penetrate to the underworld, and by the muffled sounds of underground waters that can be heard flowing within the crevices of the rock. Seen as an

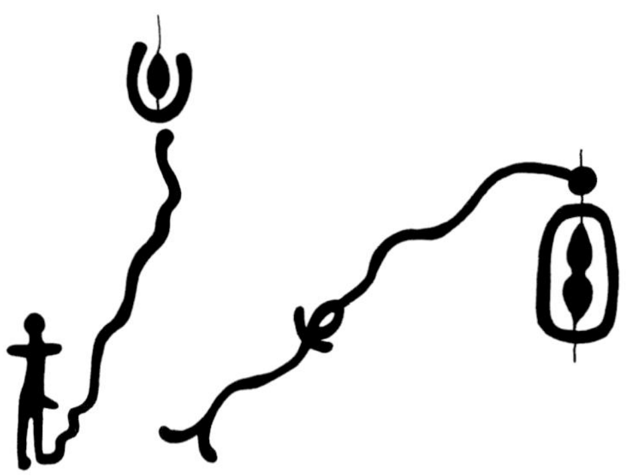

fig. 287. (above) Petroglyphs of symbolic copulation, Peterborough, Ontario, Canada (after Vastokas 1973).

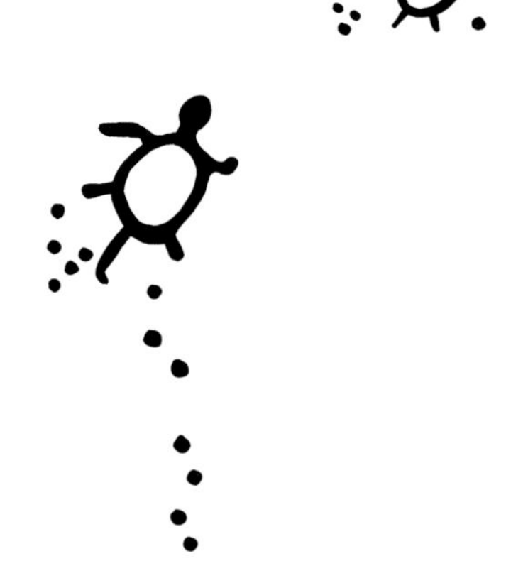

fig. 288. (right) Petroglyphs of turtles and eggs, Peterborough, Ontario, Canada (after Vastokas 1973, 106).

obvious source of supernatural power, this landscape feature was probably selected as a place for images that venerate spirits residing there.

Perhaps the most striking image at the Peterborough site is a five-foot-long, full-figured female who straddles a natural seam in the rock and whose vulva is an enlarged hole in the crevice (fig. 68). The symbolic significance of this image and its placement on the rock have been described by several scholars as follows:

> Her main axis coincides with a natural fissure in the rock . . . .The woman's genital region is represented by a fusiform enlargement of this rock fissure. The suspicion that the ancient artist deliberately modeled his figure around this "natural vagina" is strengthened by the presence of iron oxide compounds along the edges of the fissure. The resulting reddish-brown discoloration of the rock is particularly striking in the genital region (Wellman 1974b, 9).
>
> The rendering of this image was no doubt directly inspired by the crevice and the red seam and, perhaps, the female itself was seen as pre-existent at the site (Vastokas 1973, 80).

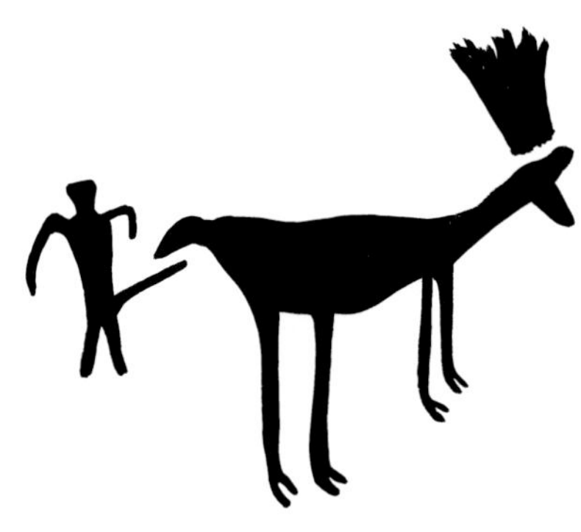

fig. 289. (left) Pictographs of an anthropomorph apparently copulating with a large animal, Tramping Lake, Grass River, Manitoba (after Steinbring 1998, 63 and 149).

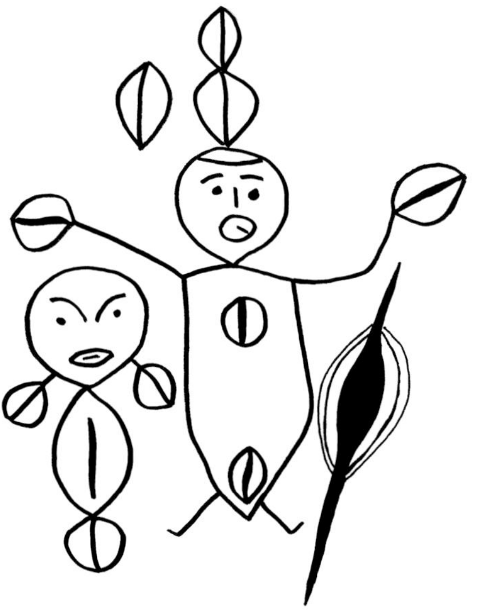

fig. 290. (right) Petroglyphs of two anthropomorphs and twelve vulva symbols, one of which incorporates a natural crevice in the rock, Cape Alava, Washington (after Hill and Hill 1974, 67).

Two other female figures and six vulva symbols are also carved around natural fissures at the site. It is likely that the ancient Algonkian shamans believed such fissures, some red and thus symbolic of menstrual blood, represented the womb of the Earth Mother and led to power deep inside the rock—to the uterus where the gestation of fauna takes place. The female figures at this site are probably best interpreted as manifestations of earth spirits or a conceptual equivalent of the Earth Mother, whereas the phallic male images probably represent shamans. The Wabeno shamans of the Algonkians were particularly concerned with fertility and sexual practices, enacting spring rites with erotic songs and imagery. It is in this light that the site has been explained:

> The Algonkian shaman is capable of penetrating other worlds, of entering and making communion with the spiritual world in order to foster the fertility and well-being of animals and men. Once again it is within the context of shamanism that the most plausible interpretation for the iconography of the Peterborough petroglyphs lies. The site itself, a pierced and perforated rock, may be read as an ideal feminine symbol; it is a symbolic uterus and a means of access for the shaman to the hidden power or sexual energy of nature upon which he can draw for the benefit of mankind (Vastokas 1973, 89).

Further west in the Canadian province of Manitoba are found many pictographs along the Grass River. One of these seems to depict a human copulating with a large, cloven-hoofed quadruped (fig. 289) (Steinbring 1998, 63).

Among the petroglyphs of the Pacific Northwest coastal area of Puget Sound in Washington and British Columbia, there are depictions of stylized anthropomorphs in contexts of fertility and sexuality. In the area of the Salish/Nootkan cultures particularly, there is an emphasis on sexual symbolism, with both phallic representations and female figures showing breasts and vulvas (Hill 1974, 280–81).

Moreover, at the Cape Alava site in Washington, vulva symbols are conspicuous elements. Here two anthropomorphs are portrayed with at least twelve vulva symbols, one of which incorporates a natural opening in the rock (fig. 290). At the Clo-oose site on the west side of Vancouver Island, there is a depiction of copulation and a female figure whose vulva is a deep natural fissure in the rock and whose breasts are elongated depressions (fig. 291). Isolated vulvas also occur at Pachena Point. A composite of various images with sexual symbolism from these sites is shown in fig. 292. In addition to the rock art, the sexual symbolism of these sites themselves has been noted:

> The Clo-oose petroglyph site is on the coast, on sandstone with holes and fissures, above an oval beach enclosed by two rock points which almost meet, so that the rising tide pours in through a narrow gap, filling and emptying the basin with every change of tide. Pachena Point is a cave. The Cape Alava site is a rocky point dominated by a sheer pinnacle rising several hundred feet above the petroglyph site. Thus the site itself can be viewed as having sexual connotations (Hill and Hill 1974, 281).

In the same general region, Eskimo art also contains scenes of sexual activity and

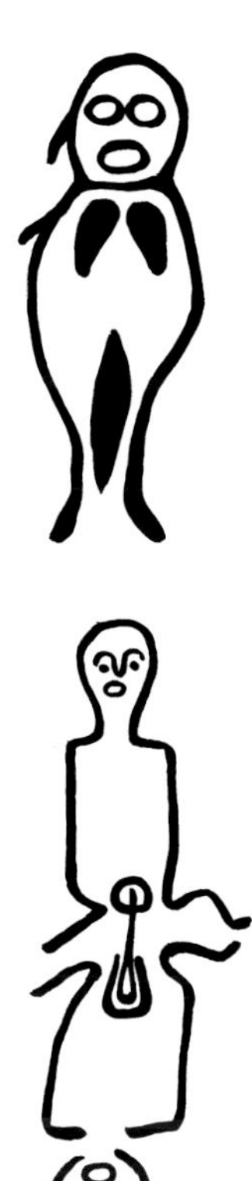

fig. 291.(above) Petroglyphs of two anthropomorphs copulating and a female figure incorporating a natural crevice in the rock, Clo-oose, Vancouver Island, British Columbia, Canada (after Hill 1974, 74,79).

fig. 292. (below) Petroglyphs depicting females, vulva symbols, and copulation from the Puget Sound area of Washington and British Columbia, Canada (after Hill 1974).

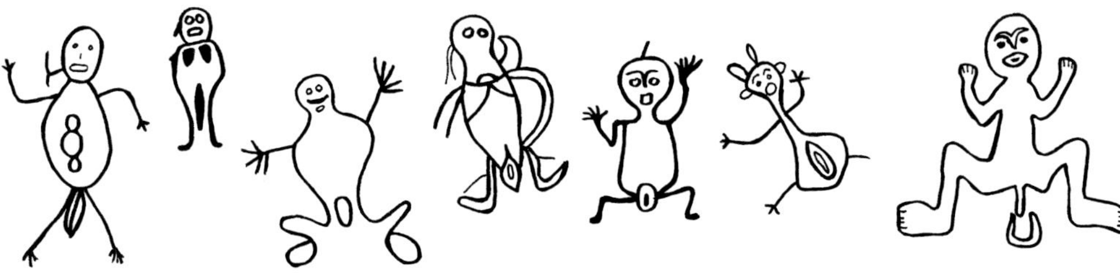

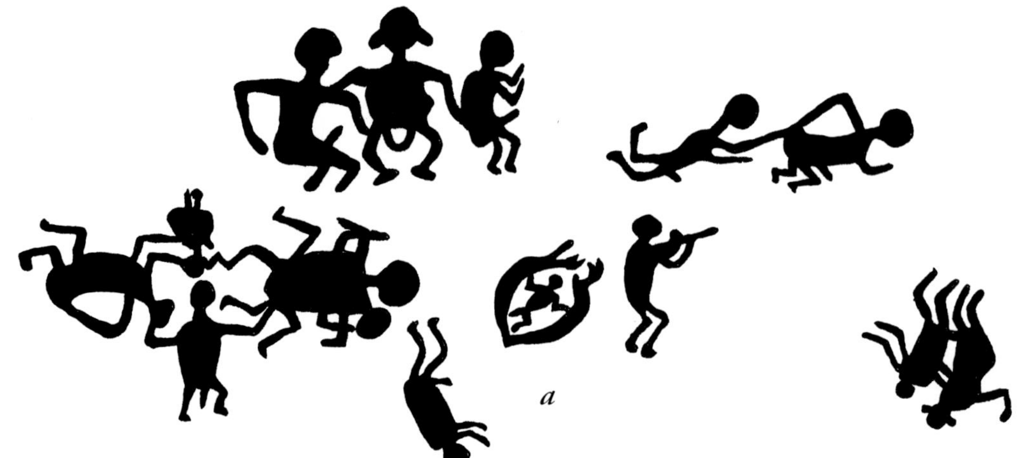

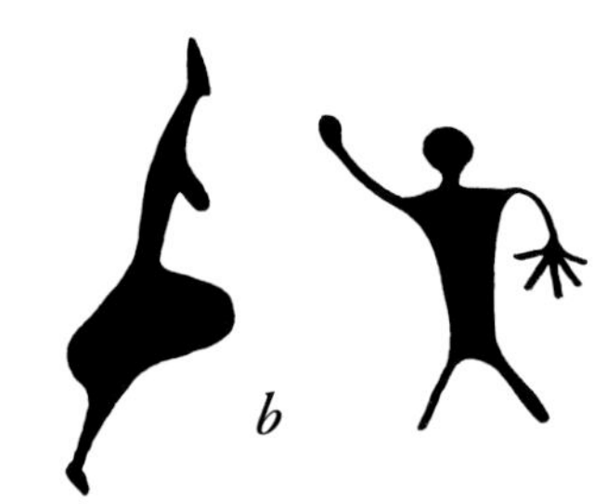

fig. 293. (above & right) Eskimo pictographs with fertility themes: a. a scene of copulation and other sexual activity, southwestern Alaska (after Dening 1996, 35); b. pregnant female, Cook Inlet, Alaska (after Grant 1967, 8).

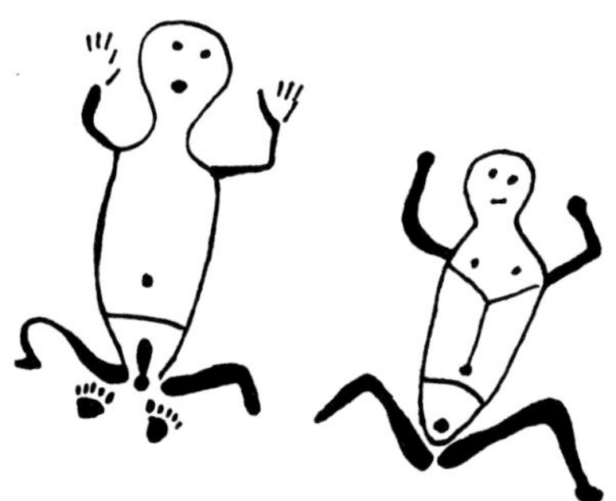

fig. 294. (right) Petroglyphs of two females in the spread-legged posture, Feather Rock, Preston County, West Virginia (after Fowler 1977).

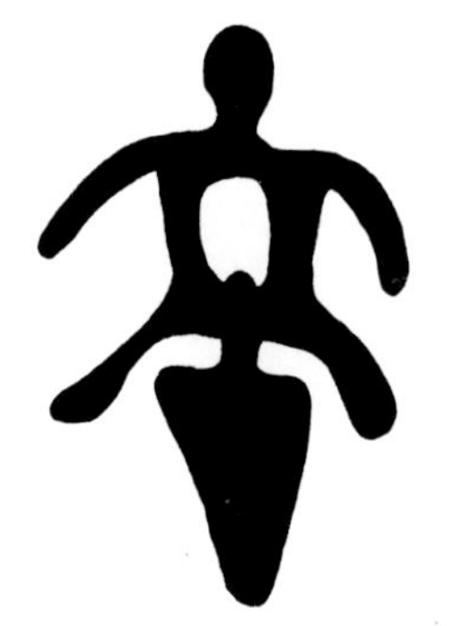

fig. 295.(right) Petroglyph depicting birthing, Washington State Park, Missouri (after Wellman 1979).

depictions of pregnancy (fig. 293).

Curiously similar in style to the Northwest coast figures are two female figures at a petroglyph site in West Virginia (fig. 294). Glyphs made in soft clay deep inside Crumps Cave in Kentucky depict a Horned Serpent and two anthropomorphs with nipples that are thought to represent pregnant females and which have been dated to 30 B.C. (Faulkner 1997, 151). From midcontinent, a Missouri petroglyph seems to depict a birthing scene (fig. 295), and other sites in this area contain pecked vulva symbols.

Rock art of Plains Indians contains some interesting scenes of fertility and sexuality as well. A petroglyph at Spriggs Rocks, Kansas, has a highly stylized phallic figure in symbolic intercourse with a bifurcated, box-like vulva symbol (fig. 296). A Black Hills petroglyph depicts a female in a spread-legged position above an isolated penis (fig. 297); a woman in a similar position, wearing a skirt and leggings, squats over a phallic male lying on his back in a petroglyph from Joliet, Montana (fig. 298). Further, the Castle Gardens petroglyph site in Wyoming contains a number of figures with vulvas and phallus, both human and animal (fig. 299), as well as depictions of intercourse and pregnancy (fig. 300). Several more coital scenes from this site are relatively unique for the long, U-shaped phallus by which the artists depicted the sex act (fig. 42). Finally Plains-style rock art sites in southeastern Colorado also contain scenes of sexual activity (fig. 301).

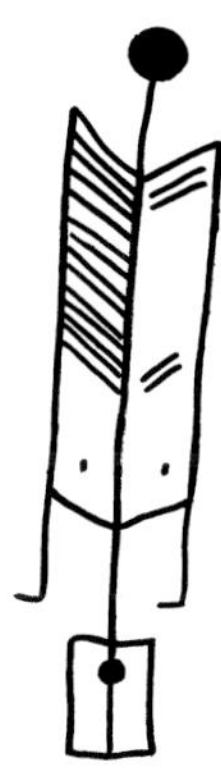

fig. 296. (above) Petroglyph of a stylized male figure copulating with a box-like vulva symbol, Spriggs Rocks, near Little River, Kansas (after Wellman 1979, 649).

fig. 297. (below) Plains Style petroglyph of a stylized female figure and an isolated phallic symbol, Black Hills, South Dakota (after Sunstrom 1982, 195).

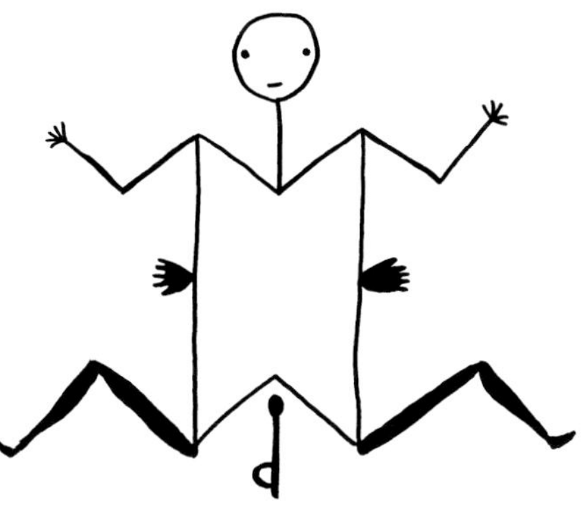

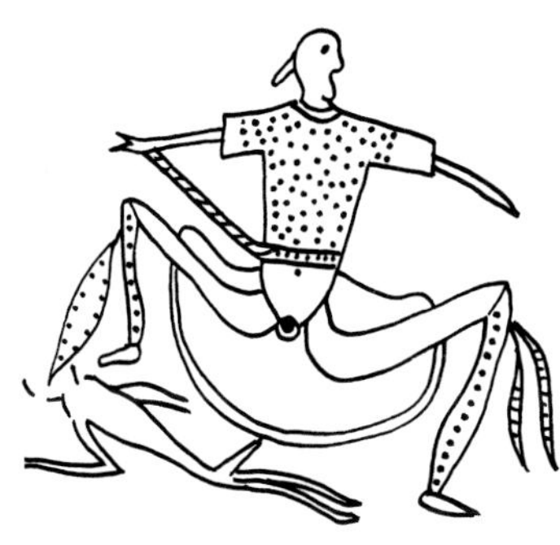

fig. 298.(above) Plains Style petroglyph of a female wearing a skirt and leggings, having sex with a phallic male lying beneath her, Joliet, Montana (after Wellman 1974, 8).

fig. 299. (below) Plains Style petroglyphs depicting male and female figures, a deer, and several prominent vulva symbols, Castle Gardens, Wyoming (after Wellman 1979, 648).

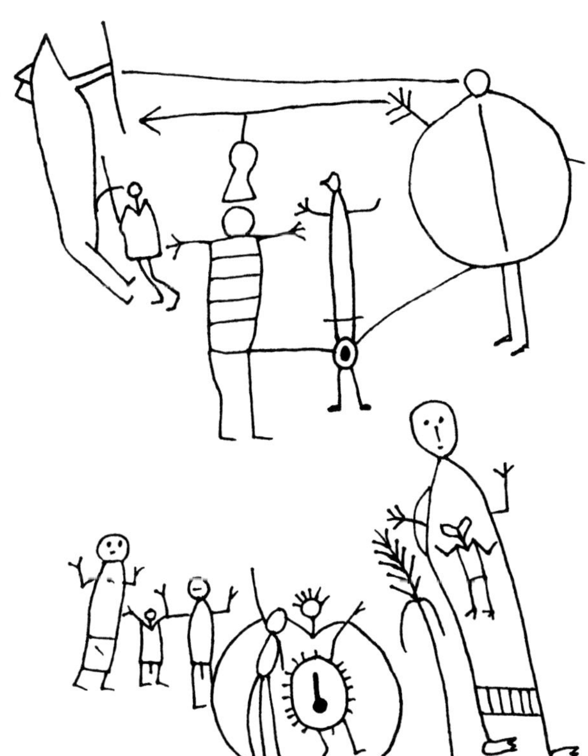

fig. 300. (above) Plains Style petroglyphs depicting male and female figures, sexual intercourse, pregnancy, and several prominent vulva symbols, Castle Gardens, Wyoming (after Renaud 1936, 14-15).

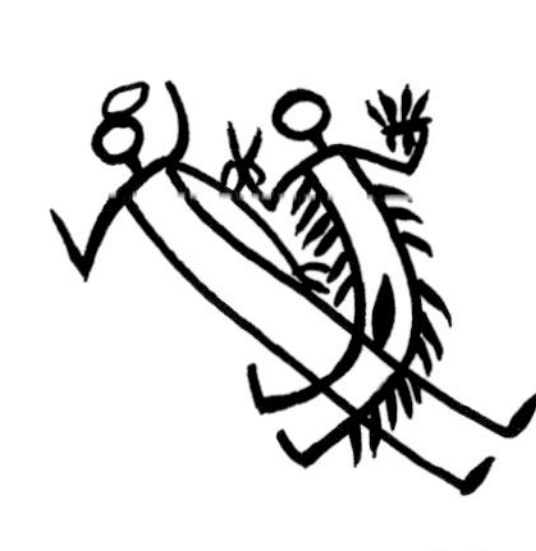

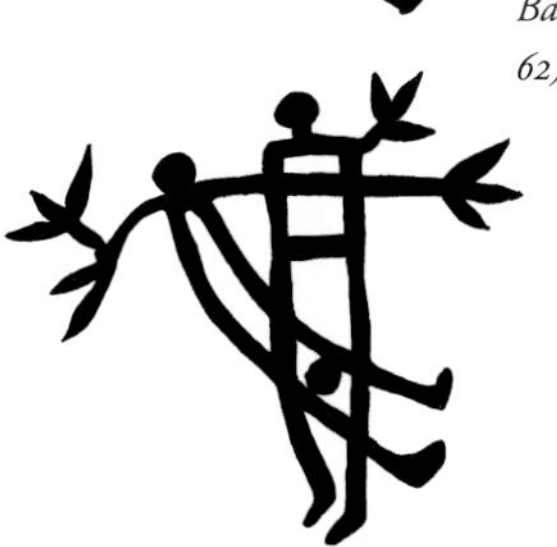

fig. 301. (left) Incised petroglyphs in the Plains Biographic Style depicting sexual intercourse, southeastern Colorado (after McGlone, Barker, and Leonard 1994, 62).

South and Central America

Major rock art sites are known to occur in the South American and Central American countries of Argentina, Bolivia, Brazil, Chile, Colombia, Ecuador, Guatemala, Peru, and Venezuela. In the Americas, apparently the oldest rock art dated so far comes from sites in Brazil and Argentina, where radiocarbon dating has produced a range of 10,000 to 15,000 years B.C. (Anati 1994, vol. 12, 25). Although recording and analysis of South American and Central American rock art iconography is still in an early stage, the archetypal themes of fertility and sexuality will undoubtedly be well represented there, too. A cursory view of some of the continent's ethnography demonstrates that these themes were prominent in many native cultures.

An example of sexual ritual used as imitative magic to promote fecundity of plant growth is illustrated by the following:

> For four days before they committed the seed to the earth the Pipiles of Central America kept apart from their wives in order that on the night before planting they might indulge their passion to the fullest extent; certain persons are even said to have been appointed to perform the sexual act at the very moment when the first seeds were deposited in the ground (Sir James Frazer 1922, quoted in Burl 1979, 221).

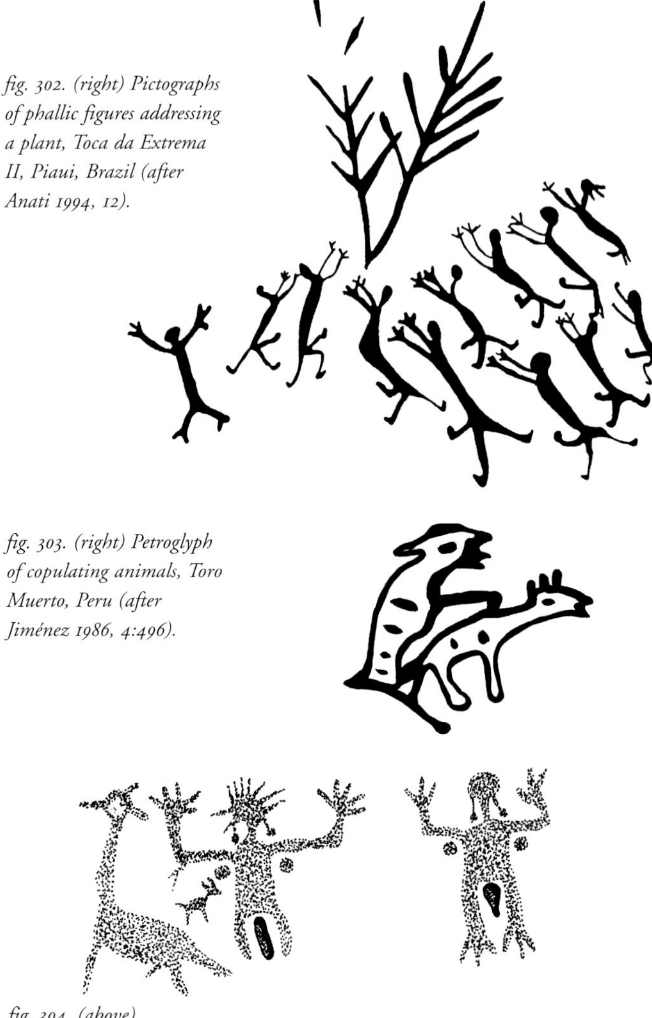

fig. 302. (right) Pictographs of phallic figures addressing a plant, Toca da Extrema II, Piaui, Brazil (after Anati 1994, 12).

fig. 303. (right) Petroglyph of copulating animals, Toro Muerto, Peru (after Jiménez 1986, 4:496).

fig. 304. (above) Petroglyphs of animals and two anthropomorphs incorporating natural holes in the rock. The upraised arms, twin disks under the arms, and associated animals are elements also found in depictions of the Mother of Animals deity in southwestern Anasazi rock art. Toro Muerto, Peru (after Jiménez 1986, 4:413).

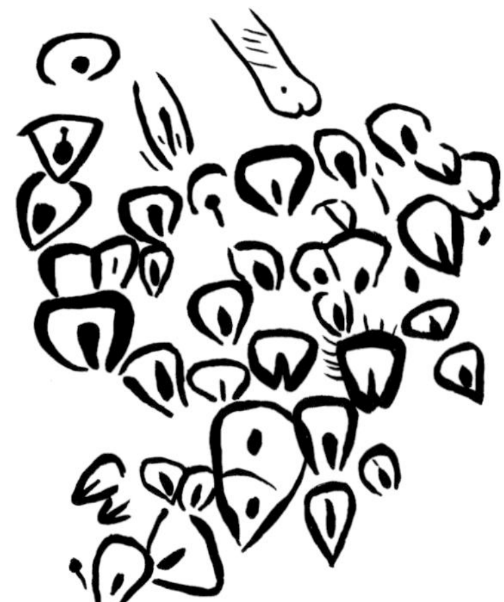

fig. 305. (right) Cluster of vulva symbols and a sole phallic symbol, Pachene, Chimanes, Bolivia (after Anati 1994, 12:74).

In a related image, the connection between human sexuality and plant fecundity is expressed in a pictograph from Brazil that shows a group of phallic men with arms outstretched in apparent supplication toward a large, branching plant (fig. 302).

Animal fertility is expressed in the Peruvian petroglyph of copulating animals in figure 303.

In a petroglyph panel from Bolivia, a single penis at the top seems to watch over a thick cluster of vulva symbols (fig. 305). In Venezuela, both petroglyphs and pictographs contain depictions of phallic males and stylized females showing vulvas and pregnancy (fig. 306). Elsewhere, elaborate carvings focus on themes of fertility and genitals among the enigmatic Los Danzantes figures of Monte Alban in Mexico (fig. 307):

> In one *danzante* a curved line representing liquid comes from the head of a god drawn on a man's chest. It joins another stream which flows from his sex organs. The streams flow outward together to create what looks like the forked tongue of a serpent. It is as if god and man have merged to create a symbol of the life force. The concept of the stream of life is illustrated in dancer after dancer. From the genitals come flowers, symbols of wind and water, and intricate scrolls of unknown meaning (Smith 1968, 42).

The diverse and spirited sexuality of many Indian cultures in Latin America has been recorded in early Spanish records from the time of conquest. Particularly in Peru and Mexico, where there was a rich artistic tradition of erotic art, sexual customs were depicted in detail, including homosexual behavior (Williams 1992, 134–37). The Spanish found that same-sex acts were common, and because this was an inflammatory subject given their strict religious views, it became a major justification for conquest and subjugation of the Indians. Thus much pre-Columbian

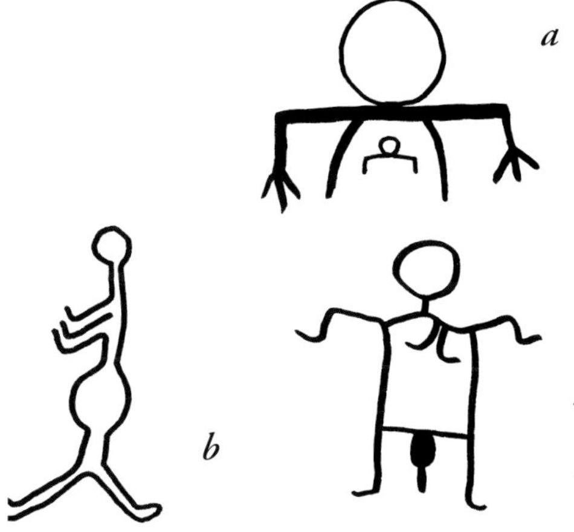

fig. 306. (left & above) Pictographs of male and pregnant female figures, southwestern Venezuela: a. (after Greer and Greer 1998, 85-88); b. Cueva Iglesias, (after Greer 1994, 53).

art that expressed these themes was systematically destroyed, but some pieces survived. In his exploration of the Yucatán in 1517, Bernal Díaz observed many clay idols which depicted sodomy. The king's chronicler, Fernandez de Oviedo, saw such examples in intricate gold artwork:

> In some part of these Indies, they carry as a jewel a man mounted upon another in that diabolic and nefarious act of Sodom, made in gold relief. I saw one of these jewels of the devil in twenty pesos gold in weight. . . . I broke it down with a hammer and smashed it under my own hand (Guerra 1971, 56, quoted in Williams 1992, 136).

In opposition to the Spanish contempt, we get an indication of not only native acceptance but spirituality related to sexuality in some of the Spanish observations:

> The Spanish were also amazed that homosexuality was often associated with cross-dressing, and that the practice had religious connotations. Cieza de Leon reported in 1553 that he punished the Indians of Puerto Viejo in Peru because of temple prostitution. He wrote in disgust: "The devil held such sway in this land that, not satisfied with making them fall into so great sin, he made them believe that this vice was a kind of holiness and religion" (Williams 1992, 136).

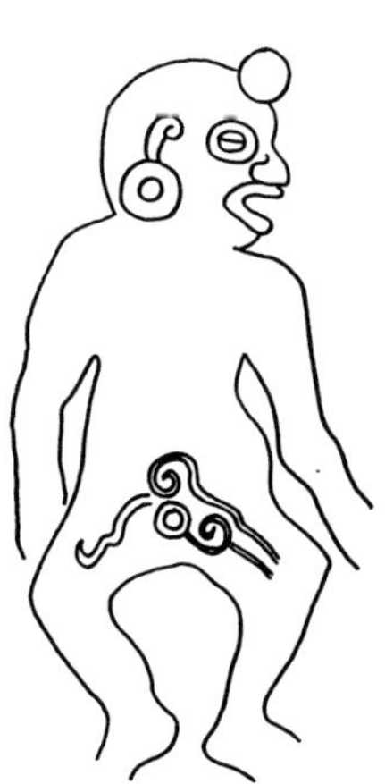

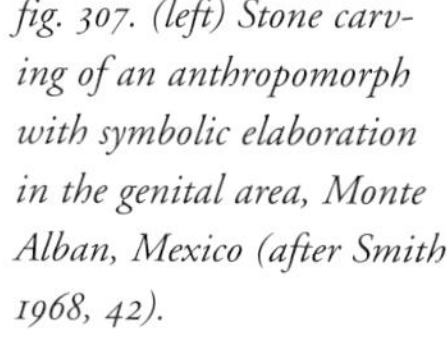

fig. 307. (left) Stone carving of an anthropomorph with symbolic elaboration in the genital area, Monte Alban, Mexico (after Smith 1968, 42).

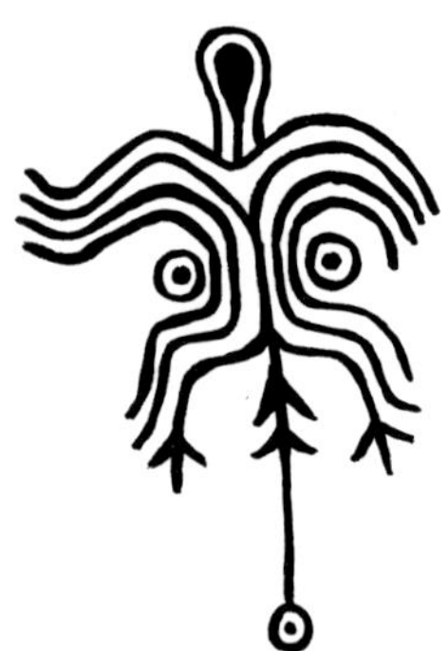

fig. 308. Desana petroglyph perhaps representing the Master of Animals, Amazon, South America (after Campbell 1989, II(3):341).

Perhaps the most important ethnographic record of native concepts concerning fertility and sexuality from South America is a brilliant study of the Amazonian Desana (Tukano) Indians on the border of Colombia and Brazil (Reichel-Dolmatoff 1971). The worldview of the Desana is replete with sexual symbolism, and nature is endowed with vaginal and phallic imagery. One of their origin myths, for example, tells of a River of Milk down which the first men were brought in a Maternal Snake Canoe named Fermentation Placenta, with spiritual guides named Fermentation Man and Flowing Forth (Ejaculating) Man. This origin myth has been explained as follows:

> All human beings are connected in their lives by an invisible umbilical cord that runs back through the rivers to the cosmic womb in the River of Milk, and the Snake Canoe that traced the journey is the sign of that connection (Campbell 1989, II(3):340).

A further Desana origin myth relating to incest taboo was presented in the section on "The Flute Player" in Chapter 3. The Desana people also believe the moon descends at night in the form of a man, as a celestial incubus to have intercourse with women in their sleep and incite their sexuality. Dew is called by them *dihsiko*, the "saliva of the moon," and is thought to be a seminal liquid that fertilizes nature, not only promoting plant growth but aiding the gestation of pregnant women, who sit outside at night to receive the moon's fecund power (Reichel-Dolmatoff 1971, 72).

Many Desana dances represent the fertility of game animals, and the sexual symbolism of their rock art is a graphic expression of this same concern. Animals and female figures are frequently depicted in an obvious state of pregnancy, and males are represented with erect phallus (Reichel-Dolmatoff 1967, 108). An example is the bold petroglyph image pecked on a large boulder near where the Pirapirana River crosses the equator, which is said to represent an episode in Desana mythology (fig. 308). This image may be male or female, but the spread-legged posture and the two disks beneath the arms bear an uncanny resemblance to the Mother of Animals deity from the Pueblo area of the Southwest (see fig. 98). Desana mythologies are composites, mixing elements of hunting and fishing with horticulture: "Although the Old Stone Age mythic figure of the Animal Master looms large in their rites and thinking, the structuring energies of their universe are mixed of female and male aspects . . . ." (Campbell 1989, II(3):340). The being depicted in fig. 308 may therefore represent an equivalent to the Mother of Game, or a bisexual composite, but is most likely the phallic Master of Animals, who is in charge of the fertility of game animals.

The shaman who acquires attributes of this being is phallic in essence. He carries a phallic, ritualistic quartz crystal that symbolizes semen and fertilization. In fact, the Desana term for shaman is from words meaning "to cohabit" and "penis," attesting to the universal belief that shamans influence the process of fertility (just as the Southern Paiute had a term for their shamans that translates as "having semen," mentioned in Chapter 3). The principal task of the Desana shaman is to visit in his trance the abode of the Animal Master (Vai-mahse) to negotiate an exchange of game animals for human souls, who are then reincarnated as more animals. The Animal Master is described as a mercurial dwarf with a red-painted body, but he can also appear as a lizard who likes to bite menstruating or pregnant women. He is especially interested in girls who have not yet reached puberty, for whom he lies in wait. After biting these women, they fall asleep and he has intercourse with them. After a short time they die, and the place where the act occurred later teems with animals or fish. Vai-mahse, as a sort of insatiable satyr, is jealous of human sexuality. Easily excited, he watches the sexual life of society by spying through cracks in walls. Hunters distract his attention in the forest by carving sexual symbols on trees to excite him.

Some Desana rock art sites are thus sacred places where the Master of Animals lives in the rock and controls the supply of animal life. These rock formations, known as "houses of the hills," are imagined as large uterine storehouses where animals are conceived, fertilized, and born through the shaman's supplications:

> The large rocky hills that rise in lonely places in the jungle are the uteri where the animals of the forest live; and the deep pools at the foot of the rapids are the subaquatic uteri where the fish live. . . . The cracks, caverns, and tunnels are the entrances to the interior of the hills, to the great malocas of the animals. There, within their dark interior, the gigantic prototypes of each species exist, and thousands of animals are kept—deer, tapirs, peccaries, monkeys, rodents, and many more, in a great community similar to that of human beings (Reichel-Dolmatoff 1971, 63, 81).

Sometimes the shamans go to these sites, not in their trances but in reality, to affirm their requests for fertility:

> On many of the hills today the rock walls are covered with pictographs representing various animals and fertility symbols, where generations of payes [shamans] have drawn, in red, yellow, or black, the forms of game animals. The drawings show deer, tapirs, monkeys, rodents, turtles, and birds, together with phallic and uterine symbols. . . . Sometimes these rock walls are true palimpsests with a superposition of drawings . . . (Reichel-Dolmatoff 1971, 83).

> Next to the figures, or within their bodies, they paint the signs which . . . symbolize fertility: rows of dots that signify drops of semen, lines in zigzag which signify the succession of generations, or lines which fill up the body of the animal and signify its fecundity (Reichel-Dolmatoff 1967, 111).

The religion of the Desana and other hunting tribes in the Amazon is based on the belief that the world of living things consists of a limited potential of vital energy of fertility and fecundity, and that all creatures, including humans, participate in a kind of great energy circuit. Hunters, in killing animals, diminish this potential and must balance it by restraining their own energy with fasts, vigils, and sexual abstinence. This concern for maintaining a biotic equilibrium in the circuit between man and animal is therefore expressed in terms of procreation, fertility, and multiplication of the species (Reichel-Dolmatoff 1967, 109).

This native worldview that creatures of the forest and rivers are in a relationship of fertilization between the hunter and his prey, and by extension all of society, is yet another aspect of the universally conceived flow of life force among indigenous peoples. The nature of the life force as observed by these Amazonian peoples applies to all peoples—to their myths, religion, and art: "The larger circuit of fertilization-fecundity, or the attraction of two fundamental complementary elements, embraces all the biosphere, all the Cosmos, in a grand synthesis of the structure of the Universe" (Reichel-Dolmatoff 1971, 55). In contemplating the sacred, earth-uterine places of incubation for the Amazonian animals, one cannot help but be amazed at the symbolic similarity with the Ice Age painted caves of Europe—separated by as much as 30,000 years and 10,000 miles but united by the timeless, universal nature of the life force embodied in the human soul and mind.

AFTERWORD: PROTECTING ROCK ART

It is assumed that readers of a book such as this would not condone intentional damage to fragile, irreplaceable cultural resources such as rock art. Senseless desecration, including target shooting at images, stealing and damaging panels, painting and carving graffiti, digging in archaeological areas, and littering, is hopefully on the decline due to increasing public awareness and more aggressive law enforcement. But even if we have good intentions we need to be aware of the potential harm to archaeological sites from the cumulative impact of increasing numbers of people visiting rock art sites. Today, at some of the more popular sites the number of monthly visitors probably exceeds the total Indian population of the area in prehistoric times. As rock art becomes more popular, we risk loving these sites to death. Thus, unintentional damage caused by visitors is also a serious preservation challenge.

We are the guardians of the rich heritage of rock art, and as such we must make every effort to preserve this legacy from destruction. Although deterioration from natural causes is inevitable, unfortunately much rock art has been damaged or destroyed by human activity. Rock art is a fragile treasure—once destroyed it cannot be replaced. It is important, therefore, to instill a code of ethics in visitors to these sites through education about low-impact behavior. Absolute basics of site visitation are: stay on the trail (if there is one) and never touch the rock art. Rock art should never be touched, since salt, moisture, and oils from skin will hasten deterioration of both petroglyphs and pictographs. Moreover, chalk or other mate rial should not be used to highlight rock art for photography, as such materials may alter the natural patination process of the rock, and their application confuses the dating of overlapping images. Further, a person applying chalk may incorrectly interpret dim or faded portions of a design, thereby giving erroneous impressions to subsequent viewers. Likewise, making rubbings of petroglyphs is damaging because the rock is unnaturally eroded, and patination, lichen growth, and other natural processes are disrupted by repetitive stress and placement of adhesive tapes.

Unfortunately, bullet holes and graffiti are fairly common conditions encountered at rock art sites today. Furthermore, we see evidence of stolen rock art where fresh scars from chisels or saws and broken slabs of rock mark the previous locations of petroglyphs. Ironically, such shameful and criminal activities often result in destruction of the sought-after treasure since the rock usually fractures into small pieces. In the West, much rock art is on public land and is, therefore, protected by federal and state antiquity laws.

In addition to bullet holes and other physical damage, photographers and other individuals have negatively impacted rock art by building bonfires in front of panels to obtain dramatic lighting effects. This harms the rock art through smoke damage or thermally induced exfoliation of the rock surface. Similarly, the burning of votive candles and incense can damage sensitive sites, especially those in caves. Moreover, soil erosion due to foot traffic around heavily visited sites can alter original conditions and damage archaeologically significant features.

Studies of visitor behavior at rock art sites have concluded that children pose the greatest risk to these sites. If children are not responsibly controlled, they are more likely to touch and rub against the rock art, climb on the rocks and other areas that should not be tread upon, and pick up artifacts. Children also often make inappropriate noise, which tends to spoil other visitors' appreciation of a site. Therefore, adults need to use good judgment in taking children to rock art sites, always keeping the safety of the rock art in mind. If you visit a rock art site, do so with the utmost care and respect. Tread lightly and do not touch the rock art—ever. The conservation adage "take nothing but pictures, leave nothing but footprints" is especially true for visiting rock art sites. Many of these sites are sacred to Native Americans. Behave as you would in other sacred places.

All groups and individuals who go to rock art sites need to realize that any visit may endanger the rock art. A rock art site is not just images on rocks but includes surrounding rocks, cliffs, or ruins. For researchers and individuals to appreciate a site, the images and their environment should be kept as closely as possible to their state when the panel was created. To visit a site responsibly, adhere to the following guidelines:

1. Minimize the number of vehicles going to the site. Stay on existing roads. Do not "pioneer" vehicle trails or parking areas. Leave all gates as you found them (open or closed).

2. Do not camp or build fires within .25 mile of rock art.

3. Do not disturb rock arrangements, artifacts, and other site features.

4. Stay on trails where they exist. Do not disturb rocks, vegetation, or microbiotic soil crusts.

5. Do not climb rocks or cliffs at rock art sites.

6. Do not touch the rock art.

7. Do not attempt to remove graffiti, chalking, lichens, or bird droppings from rock art.

8. Do not apply any substance, including liquid, powder, plastic, cloth, or paper, to rock art.

9. Do not allow children or careless associates to behave improperly around rock art.

10. Use binoculars and a telephoto lens to study or record high panels instead of attempting to climb steep slopes or ledges.

11. Be constantly aware of the effects of your actions and the actions of others at rock art sites. Make your behavior a model. Speak out when necessary to prevent others from damaging rock art.

ROCK ART PRESERVATION LAWS

Preservation laws protect historic and prehistoric archaeological resources. The remains of structures (even the most obscure rock piles), artifacts of all kinds, fire hearths and kilns, trash deposits and middens, and trail markers, as well as petroglyphs and pictographs, are important protected resources. Laws stipulate that only those with permits may dig in archaeological sites. Federal felony, misdemeanor, and civil convictions can result in fines, vehicle confiscation, and imprisonment. Most states also have preservation laws that provide penalties for appropriating, excavating, removing, or destroying archaeological materials on state lands. Moreover, many states and some municipalities enforce burial laws to protect human remains and associated materials found on private property.

There are several federal and state laws that deal with archaeological resources on federal and Native American lands. The following acts protect our national heritage from the behavior of both serious looters and casual visitors who slip potsherds or arrowheads into their pockets as souvenirs. Please become familiar with these acts, respect them, and report any violation to appropriate authorities:

- **1906, Antiquities Act:** This act protects all historic and prehistoric sites on federal lands and prohibits excavation or destruction of such antiquities unless a permit (Antiquities Permit) is obtained from the secretary of the department that has jurisdiction over those lands. It also authorizes the president to declare areas of public lands as national monuments and to reserve or accept private lands for that purpose.

- **1966, National Historic Preservation Act:** This act supplements the provisions of the Antiquities Act of 1906. The law makes it illegal to destroy, excavate, or remove cultural resources from federal or Indian lands and to remove any archaeological resources without a permit from the land manager. Permits may be issued only to educational or scientific institutions and only if the resulting activities will increase knowledge about archaeological resources.

- **1979, Archaeological Resources Protection Act:** This act requires federal agencies to provide notice to the Secretary of the Interior of any dam constructions and, if archaeological resources are found, for recovery or salvage of them. The law applies to any agency whenever it receives information that a direct or federally assisted activity could cause irreparable harm to prehistoric, historic, or archaeologic data. Further, it increases the penalty for stealing or vandalizing to $500,000 and up to five years in prison.

- **1990, Native American Graves Protection and Repatriation Act (NAGPRA)**: This act assigns ownership and control of Native American cultural items, human remains, and associated funerary objects to Native Americans. It also establishes requirements for the treatment of Native American human remains and sacred or cultural objects found on federal land. In addition, it provides for the protection, inventory, and repatriation of Native American cultural items, human remains, and associated funerary objects.

To report illegal activities involving cultural resources, contact the National Park Service's toll-free, twenty-four-hour hotline at 1-800-227-7286 or the U.S. Bureau of Land Management's law enforcement hotline at 1-800-722-3998.

NOTES

1. Marija Gimbutas, *The Language of the Goddess*, 139.

2. Jay von Werlhof, *Spirits of the Earth*, 7.

3. Edgar L. Hewitt, *Pajarito Plateau*, 1.

4. Quoted in Lyall Watson, *The Lightning Bird*, 169.

5. At the extensive petroglyph site at Inscription Point, near Wupatki National Monument in Arizona, numerous depictions of copulating people and animals indicate this was once a major fertility shrine. Sometime after 1983 an unknown person rubbed out most of the sex scenes. Rumor has it that a fundamentalist preacher was responsible, ostensibly to avoid exposing members of his church group to the "obscene" material on a field trip to the site. Fortunately, images at the site were documented before this happened. Before-and-after illustrations from this site are given in Figures 8 and 9. It is ironic that the blatantly obvious sexual and fertility aspects of this site were apparently overlooked by two authors of a report on *Petroglyphs of Wupatki* (Davin and Dolphin 1973, 1 and 5), who wrote that "A mystery surrounding Inscription Point, and indeed all prehistoric petroglyph sites, is the conspicuous absence of any petroglyphs representing women, women's occupation, human reproduction, or human fertility in general."

6. Edward Abbey, *The Serpents of Paradise*, 310.

7. Porter, quoted in Kay Sutherland, "Spirits from the South," ii.

8. Some notable exceptions are the Archaic pictograph styles of the Pecos River in Texas and Barrier Canyon in Utah, which are dated as old as 4,000 years. Certain pictographs in Australia are believed to be up to 20,000 years old, and some of the Paleolithic cave paintings in Europe are dated at 35,000 years.

9. From Mesoamerica trade items included macaws, seashells, and copper bells; from the Plains Indians, buffalo hides and other items; from the Salinas Pueblo area east of the Manzano Mountains, salt was a commodity.

10. Scalps and whole-head scalps have been unearthed from Fremont sites, the shape and decorations of which resemble certain objects being held by Fremont Style anthropomorphs.

11. Campbell Grant, *Rock Art of the American Indian*, is a good general introduction to the rock art of California. For more up-to-date and detailed information about rock art in southern California, see David S. Whitley, *A Guide to Rock Art Sites: Southern California and Southern Nevada*.

12. Quoted in Martin B. Duberman, "Documents in Hopi Indian Sexuality: Imperialism, Culture and Resistance," 110.

13. This quotation is from an English subtitle to words spoken by the actor Jean-Paul Belmondo in Jean-Luc Godard's film *Pierrot-Le-Fou*, released in 1965. Cited in Timothy Taylor, *The Prehistory of Sex: Four Million Years of Human Sexual Culture*, 1.

14. Havelock Ellis, *The New Spirit*, quoted in *Bartlett's Familiar Quotations*, 119.

15. See Mircea Eliade, *Patterns in Comparative Religion*, for some of the scholarly and original work on this topic. Sir James Frazer's *The Golden Bough* is also a classic work containing a wealth of information about fertility rites and the anthropological evolution of religion. More recent and general discussions can be found in Clifford Bishop, *Sex and Spirit*, and Riane Eisler,

Sacred Pleasure: Sex, Myth, and the Politics of the Body.

16. A recent and excellent work on this subject is *The Prehistory of Sex*, by archaeologist Timothy Taylor. Much of the summary material that follows in the text is synthesized from this source.

17. Also, for examples of repressive, antisexual attitudes in the Southwest, see Martin B. Duberman, "Documents in Hopi Indian Sexuality." This collection of letters and depositions was collected from U.S. government sources and informants in the early 1900s in an effort to repress the expression of sexuality in ceremonial contexts. The comments by prudish, narrow-minded white observers include such phrases as "quite impossible to describe the dance in polite language"; "a carnival of promiscuous carnal indulgence"; "these dances are too loathsome and repugnant for me to describe"; and "pornographic in the extreme."

18. Ekkehart Malotki, personal communication, April 30, 1999.

19. In this autobiographical account of a Hopi Indian, there are dozens of descriptions of various rituals and ceremonies for which the men prepared themselves in part by abstaining from sexual relations with women for a period of days. See also Carolyn Niethammer, *Daughters of the Earth: The Lives and Legends of American Indian Women*, 208-212, and Hamilton A.Tyler, *Pueblo Gods and Myths*, 197.

20. There are numerous firsthand accounts of such affairs in Don C. Talayesva, *Sun Chief.* See also Martin B. Duberman, "Documents in Hopi Indian Sexuality," 111, 115, 119.

21. See also Henry Hay, "The Hammond Report," 19. The Hammond report was written in 1887 by William Hammond, a surgeon general of the U.S. Army. While Hammond's observation of Pueblo Indians in New Mexico between 1850 and 1852 is not the work of a trained anthropologist, the report contains several salient points concerning secret ceremonies involving berdaches and their role in spring fertility rituals. Hay's summary includes an equitational ritual following a secret pederastic ceremony with a "bull-virgin" (essentially a still-virile berdache in training), in which "the practice upon him of excessive masturbation transforms him into a phallic spigot, sowing in wide broadcast the previously deposited seeds of the Pueblo's fertility to fecundate both the flora and fauna of the sacred mesa being traversed."

22. Bronislaw Malinowski, *The Sexual Life of Savages in North-Western Melanesia.*

23. Siegfried Giedion, *Eternal Present: The Beginnings of Art*, quoted in J. Halley Cox and Edward Stasack, *Hawaiian Petroglyphs*, 2.

24. An additional anecdote is told of a government nurse undressing a female baby during a healthy baby contest on the reservation. The hall quickly emptied because of the perceived danger to the audience from an exposed vulva.

25. An interesting example of Native American views about the special power of menstrual blood was illustrated in a December 1999 news story in New Mexico. A painting made with a female artist's menstrual blood was displayed in a public setting, but was quickly removed from the show following strong objections from the Native American community.

26. Mircea Eliade, *Patterns in Comparative Religion*, 368-369.

27. Joseph Campbell, *Historical Atlas of World Mythology*, vol. 2, *The Way of the Seeded Earth*, Part 3, 292. This excerpt is taken from Campbell's description of the Hopi Lakon ceremony.

28. "We arrived at the shrine where Hopi salt gatherers carve their clan emblems on the rocks. Our ancestors had gathered salt for many generations, and there were hundreds of clan emblems cut into the rocky base of the shrine. Every traveler, on each successive trip, had carved another symbol to the left of his original one."

29. Sites mentioned by Krupp (1983) include Window Rock on Vandenburg Air Force Base, a birth tunnel and pictograph site in Joshua Tree National Monument, the Chumash House of the Sun pictograph cave on Sierra Madre Ridge in the Los Padres National Forest, and a Yokuts painted shelter in Round Valley, California.

30. About the mating ceremonies at the fertility shrine on Lake Peak, Hewett goes on to say, "There has been some hazy knowledge of this, which should remain hazy, among the white people. It has been the source of much unjust though well meant, criticism."

31. Far western groups in southern California and Nevada believed the supernatural was distinct from mythic time-space, and accordingly their rock art does not depict mythic themes. The exception to this is the Colorado River groups (Yuman speakers), who did equate the supernatural with mythic time-space, so their rock art depicts this theme. Rock art of the lower Colorado River is likely to represent a shaman's connection to certain mythic beings or events and not an entire tale.

32. Although numerous primary sources are cited throughout this discussion of the flute player figure, the most comprehensive synthesis of this information is found in Dennis Slifer and James Duffield, *Kokopelli: Flute Player in Rock Art*, from which portions of this section are adapted.

33. "Several of the old men were said to have this power. One of them shook all the time and had to move from place to place because the power was so strong in him."

34. Juzhong Zhang, Changsui Wang, and Zhaochen Kong, "Oldest Playable Musical Instruments," 366–68.

35. Some of the more comprehensive and interesting descriptions of the origins and importance of snakes and snake symbolism include: Ramona and Desmond Morris, *Men and Snakes*; Marija Gimbutas, *The Language of the Goddess*, 121-137; Barbara G. Walker, *The Woman's Encyclopedia of Myths and Secrets*, 903–09; and Joseph Campbell, *The Mythic Image*, 281–301.

36. Crook-necked staffs and wooden sticks with curved handles have fertility associations based on archaeological and historical ceremonial evidence. More than three hundred were removed from a room containing a high-status burial excavated at Pueblo Bonito in Chaco Canyon, New Mexico.

37. J. Walter Fewkes also suggests that the crooked stick's symbolism of an ancient weapon may represent an implement akin to a throwing stick, by which he probably is referring to the atlatl.

38. John Neihardt, *Black Elk Speaks*, as quoted in Salvatore Mancini, *On the Edge of Magic*, 13.

39. This publication is an anthology of articles by David S. Whitley, Polly Schaafsma, Solveig A.. Turpin, Ken Hedges, and Lawrence Loendorf. I have borrowed mainly from the articles by Whitley and Schaafsma for the present discussion. They in turn acknowledge the seminal work on shamanism by Mircea Eliade and on shamanism themes in San Bushman rock art by David Lewis-Williams and Thomas Dowson.

40. Within the greater Southwest, rock art with shamanic implications is found in three principal regions: southern California and the Great Basin, the Colorado Plateau, and the lower Pecos River in Texas. These are addressed by articles from Solveig A. Turpin, *Shamanism and Rock Art in North America*. The first region is discussed by David S. Whitley, "Shamanism, Natural Modeling and the Rock Art of Far Western North American Hunter-Gatherers." Several Colorado Plateau rock art styles are discussed by Polly Schaafsma, "Trance and Transformation in the Canyons: Shamanism and Early Rock Art on the Colorado Plateau." The Pecos River shamanic rock art is discussed by Solveig Turpin, "On a Wing and a Prayer: Flight Metaphors in Pecos River Art."

41. Quoted in Ruth L. Bunzel, "Introduction to Zuni Ceremonialism," 483f.

42. Apache Deer Song excerpt from Salvatore Mancini, *On the Edge of Magic*, 41.

43. Navajo Growth Song excerpt from Salvatore Mancini, *On the Edge of Magic*, 44.

44. Excerpt from John Neihardt, *Black Elk Speaks*, as quoted in Salvatore Mancini, *On the Edge of Magic*, 17.

45. Alexander M. Stephen, "Hopi Journal," 1313: quoted in Hamilton Tyler, *Pueblo Gods and Myths*, 133.

46. In interpreting several European rock art depictions of men copulating with animals, Heinz Hunger provides this description by a twelfth-century visitor to Ireland: "One of the northern Irish tribes used to inaugurate their chief or king by having him enact or simulate sexual intercourse with a white mare. Once this was done, the beast was immediately slain and ritually eaten by all the liege men of the new feudal lord of that province." Heinz Hunger, "Ritual Coition with and among Animals," 122.

47. Manfred Knaak, *The Forgotten Artist: Indians of Anza-Borrego and Their Rock Art*, 61.

48. Burchard Brentjes, *African Rock Art*, 27.

49. Quoted in David Cohen, *The Circle of Life: Rituals from the Human Family Album*, 4.

BIBLIOGRAPHY

Abbey, Edward. 1990. *Desert Solitaire: A Season in the Wilderness.* New York: Simon and Schuster.

_______. 1995. *The Serpents of Paradise.* New York: Henry Holt and Company.

Anati, Emmanuel. 1994a. Valcamonica Rock Art: A New History for Europe. *Studi Camuni* 13. Valcamonica, Italy: Edizioni del Centro.

_______. 1994b. World Rock Art: The Primordial Language. *Studi Camuni* 12. Valcamonica, Italy: Edizioni del Centro.

Bahn, Paul G. 1993. The Rock Art of China: The Longest Known and Least Known. *American Indian Rock Art* 19:1–8. American Rock Art Research Association.

Bahn, Paul G., and Jean Vertut. 1988. *Images of the Ice Age.* Leicester, England: Windward.

Bandelier, Adolph F. 1890. Final Report of Investigations among the Indians of the Southwestern United States, Part I. *Papers of the Archaeological Institute of America,* American Series, No. 3.

Bartlett, John. 1953. *The Shorter Bartlett's Familiar Quotations*, ed. Christopher Morley. New York: Pocket Books, Inc.

Beaglehole, Ernest and Pearl. 1976. Hopi of the Second Mesa. *Memoirs of the American Anthropological Association* 44. Millwood, N.Y.: Krauss Reprint Company.

Begole, Robert S. 1984. Fertility Symbols in the Anza-Borrego Desert. *Pacific Coast Archaeological Society Quarterly* 20, no. 4: 13–28.

Benedict, Ruth. 1953. *Patterns of Culture.* New York: Mentor Books.

_______. 1969. Zuni Mythology. *Columbia University Contributions to Anthropology* 21, no. 2. New York: AMS Press.

Berrin, Kathleen, ed. 1978. *Art of the Huichol Indians.* New York: Harry N. Abrams and Fine Arts Museums of San Francisco.

Bierhorst, John. 1979. *A Cry from the Earth: Music of the North American Indian.* Santa Fe, N.M.: Ancient City Press.

Bishop, Clifford. 1996. *Sex and Spirit.* Boston: Little, Brown and Company.

Boyd, Douglas K., and Bobbie Ferguson. 1988. *Tewa Rock Art in the Black Mesa Region.* Amarillo, Tex.: U.S. Department of the Interior, Bureau of Reclamation, Southwest Region.

Brandl, E. J. 1988. *Australian Aboriginal Paintings in Western and Central Arnhem Land.* Canberra, Australia: Aboriginal Studies Press.

Brentjes, Burchard. 1965. *African Rock Art.* New York: Clarkson N. Potter, Inc.

Broderick, Alan Houghton. 1948. *Prehistoric Painting.* London: Avalon Press Ltd.

Brody, J. J. 1977. *Mimbres Painted Pottery.* Santa Fe and Albuquerque: School of American Research and University of New Mexico Press.

_______. 1990. *The Anasazi.* New York: Rizzoli.

_______. 1991. *Anasazi and Pueblo Painting.* Albuquerque and Santa Fe: University of

New Mexico Press and School of American Research.

Brody, J. J., and Rina Swentzell. 1996. *To Touch the Past: The Painted Pottery of the Mimbres People*. New York: Hudson Hills Press.

Brooks, Robert R. R. and Vishnu S. Wakankar. 1976. *Stone Age Painting in India*. New Haven: Yale University Press.

Bunzel, Ruth L. 1932. Introduction to Zuni Ceremonialism. *Forty-Seventh Annual Report of the American Bureau of Ethnology*. Washington, D.C.: Government Printing Office.

Burkholder, Grace. 1992. An Introduction to Mount Schrader, Nye County, Nevada. In *Rock Art Papers* 9:67–71. San Diego Museum Papers No. 28.

Burl, Aubrey. 1979. *Prehistoric Avebury*. New Haven, Conn.: Yale University Press.

Campbell, Joseph. 1974. *The Mythic Image*. Princeton, N.J.: Princeton University Press.

_______. 1988. *Historical Atlas of World Mythology*, vol. 1, parts 1 and 2: *The Way of the Animal Powers*. New York: Harper and Row.

_______. 1989. *Historical Atlas of World Mythology*, vol. 2, parts 1, 2, and 3: *The Way of the Seeded Earth*. New York: Harper and Row.

Castleton, Kenneth B. 1978. *Petroglyphs and Pictographs of Utah, Volume 1, The East and Northeast*. Salt Lake City: Utah Museum of Natural History.

_______. 1979. *Petroglyphs and Pictographs of Utah, Volume 2, The South, Central, West, and Northwest*. Salt Lake City: Utah Museum of Natural History.

Chaloupka, George. 1993. *Journey in Time: The World's Longest Continuing Art Tradition*. Chatswood, Australia: Reed.

Chauvet, Jean-Marie, Eliette Brunel Deschamps, and Christian Hillaire. 1996. *Dawn of Art: The Chauvet Cave: The Oldest Known Paintings in the World*. New York: Harry N. Abrams.

Cohen, David, ed. 1991. *The Circle of Life: Rituals from the Human Family Album*. San Francisco: HarperCollins Publishers.

Cole, Sally J. 1989. Iconography and Symbolism in Basketmaker Rock Art. In *Rock Art of the Western Canyons*, eds. Jane S. Day, Paul D. Friedman, and Marcia J. Tate. *Colorado Archaeological Society Memoir* 3:59–85. Denver, Col.: Denver Museum of Natural History.

_______. 1990. *Legacy on Stone: Rock Art of the Colorado Plateau and Four Corners Region*. Boulder, Colo.: Johnson Books.

Collier, Jane F. 1988. *Marriage and Inequality in Classless Societies*. Stanford: Stanford University Press.

Cordell, Linda S. 1984. *Prehistory of the Southwest*. New York: Academic Press.

Cordell, Linda S., and George J. Gumerman, eds. 1989. *Dynamics of Southwest Prehistory*. Washington, D.C.: Smithsonian Institution Press.

Cox, J. Halley, and Edward Stasack. 1970. *Hawaiian Petroglyphs*. Honolulu: Bishop Museum Press.

Crawford, O. G. S. 1991. *The Eye Goddess*. Oak Park, Ill.: Delphi Press.

Crosby, Harry. 1980. Baja's Murals of Mystery. *National Geographic* 158, no. 5.

_______. 1984. *The Cave Paintings of Baja California*. La Jolla, Calif.: Copley Books.

Cundle, James R., and Markus A. Jacquemain. 1995. *Stone Magic of the Ancients: Petroglyphs, Shamanic Shrine Sites, Ancient Rituals*. Phoenix, Ariz.: Golden West Publishers.

Curtis, Edward S. 1926. *The North American Indian*, vol. 17. Norwood: The Plimpton Press.

Cushing, Frank Hamilton. 1896. Outlines of Zuni Creation Myths. *Bureau of American Ethnography Thirteenth Annual Report, 1891–92*. Washington, D.C.: Government Printing Office.

_______. 1979. *Zuni*. Lincoln: University of Nebraska Press.

Davin, Eric, and Gabrielle Dolphin. 1973. *Petroglyphs of Wupatki. Southwestern Lore*, vol. 39, no. 1: 1–8. Colorado Archaeological Society.

Davis, John. 1978. *Prehistoric Art of Cave Valley*. Transactions of the 13th Regional Archaeological Symposium for Southeastern New Mexico and Western Texas, 39–59.

Dedrick, Philip. 1958. *An Analysis of the Human Figure Motif on North American Prehistoric Painted Pottery*. Master's thesis, University of New Mexico.

Dening, Sarah. 1996. *The Mythology of Sex*. New York: Macmillan.

Dorsey, George A. 1902. *The Arapaho Sun Dance: The Ceremony of the Offerings-Lodge*. Field Columbian Museum, Anthropology Series 4.

Duberman, Martin B., ed. 1979. Documents in Hopi Indian Sexuality: Imperialism, Culture and Resistance. *Radical History Review* 20:99–130.

Durham, Dorothy. 1955. Petroglyphs at Mesa de los Padillas. *El Palacio* 62, no. 1:3–17.

Dutton, Bertha P. 1963. *Sun Father's Way: The Kiva Murals of Kuaua*. Albuquerque: University of New Mexico Press.

Eisler, Riane. 1995. *Sacred Pleasure: Sex, Myth, and the Politics of the Body*. San Francisco: HarperCollins.

Eliade, Mircea. 1958. *Patterns in Comparative Religion*. New York: World Publishing Company.

———. 1964. *Shamanism: Archaic Techniques of Ecstasy.* Princeton, N.J.: Princeton University Press.

Ellis, Havelock. 1969. *The New Spirit.* Millwood, N.Y.: Krauss Reprint.

Englehardt, Zephyrin. 1921. San Luis Rey Mission. In *The Missions and Missionaries of California, New Series Local History*. San Francisco: James H. Barry Company.

Erdoes, Richard, and Alfonso Ortiz. 1984. *American Indian Myths and Legends*. New York: Pantheon Books.

Ewing, Eve. 1986. Pintadita: A Newly Discovered Painting Complex in the Sierra de San Francisco, Baja, California. *Rock Art Papers* 3:52–74. San Diego Museum Papers No. 21.

_______. 1989. Serpiente: New Discoveries. *Rock Art Papers* 6:49–72. San Diego Museum Papers No. 24.

Ewing, Eve, and Marc Robin. 1987. Sunlight and Shadow. *Rock Art Papers* 5:110–25. San Diego Museum Papers No. 23.

Faris, Peter K. 1986. A Fertility Ceremony Illustrated in the Cave of Life, Petrified Forest National Park, Arizona. *Southwestern Lore* 52, no. 1:4–6.

Faulkner, Charles. 1997. Four Thousand Years of Native American Cave Art. *Journal of Cave and Karst Studies.* Vol. 59, no. 3. National Speleological Society.

Faulstich, Paul E. 1983. Australian Aboriginal Rock Art and the Sense of Place. *American Indian Rock Art* 9:96–113. American Rock Art Research Association.

Fewkes, J. Walter. 1914. Archeology of the Lower Mimbres Valley, New Mexico. *Smithsonian Miscellaneous Collections* 63, no. 10. Washington, D.C.: Smithsonian Institution. In J. Walter Fewkes, 1989. *The Mimbres: Art and Archaeology*. Albuquerque, N.M.: Avanyu Publishing.

_______. 1919. Designs on Prehistoric Hopi Pottery. *Thirty-Third Annual Report of the Bureau of American Ethnography to the Secretary of the Smithsonian Institution 1911–12*. Washington, D.C.: Government Printing Office.

Fire, John, and Richard Erdoes. 1972. *Lame Deer, Seeker of Visions*. New York: Simon and Schuster.

Flandrin, Jean-Louis. 1975. Contraception, Marriage, and Sexual Relations in the Christian West. In *Biology of Man in History,* eds. Robert Forster and Orest A. Ranum. Baltimore, Md.: Johns Hopkins University Press.

Flood, Josephine. 1990. *The Riches of Ancient Australia*. Queensland: University of Queensland Press.

_______. 1997. *Rock Art of the Dreamtime.* Sydney, Australia: HarperCollins Publishers.

Foucault, Michael. 1990. *The History of Sexuality: An Introduction*. Harmondsworth, Great Britain: Penguin.

Fowler, Daniel B. 1977. Indian Petroglyphs Recently Discovered in West Virginia. *American Indian Rock Art* 3:38–46. American Rock Art Research Association.

Frazer, Sir James. 1993. *The Golden Bough*. Hertfordshire, UK: Wordsworth Editions.

Frobenius, Leo, and Hugo Obermaier. 1925. *Hadschra Maktuba*. Munich: Kurt Wolff Verlag.

Furst, Peter T. 1974. Ethnographic Analogy in the Interpretation of West Mexican Art. In *The Archaeology of West Mexico*, ed. Betty Bell. Ajijic, Jalisco, Mexico: West Mexican Society for Advanced Study.

Garlake, Peter. 1995. *The Hunter's Vision: The Prehistoric Art of Zimbabwe*. Seattle: University of Washington Press.

Geertz, A. W., and M. Lomatuway'ma. 1987. *Children of Cottonwood: Piety and Ceremonialism in Hopi Indian Puppetry*. Lincoln: University of Nebraska Press.

Getty, Adele. 1990. *Goddess: Mother of Living Nature*. London: Thames and Hudson.

Giedion, Siegfried. 1962. *Eternal Present: The Beginnings of Art*. New York: Pantheon Books.

Gimbutas, Marija. 1989. *The Language of the Goddess*. San Francisco: Harper and Row.

Gough, Galal R. 1996. *The Shaman's Poro (Sacred Crook) in Native American Rock Art.* Presented at the Utah Rock Art Research Association Symposium on August 31, 1996, Green River, Utah.

_______. 1998. Native American Encircled and Enclosed Crosses Having Prehistoric Puberty/Fertility Symbolism. *Rock Art Papers* 13:45–51. San Diego Museum Papers No. 35.

Grant, Campbell. 1967. *Rock Art of the American Indian.* Dillon, Colo.: Vistabooks.

_______. 1978. *Canyon de Chelly: Its People and Rock Art.* Tucson: University of Arizona Press.

Grant, Campbell, James W. Baird, and J. Kenneth Pringle. 1968. *Rock Drawings of the Coso Range.* Ridgecrest, Calif.: Maturango Press.

Greer, John. 1994. The Painted Rock Art of Southwestern Venezuela: Context and Chronology. *American Indian Rock Art* 20:45–58. American Rock Art Research Association.

Greer, John, and Mavis. 1998. 1995 Rock Art Fieldwork in Southwestern Venezuela. *American Indian Rock Art* 22:79–94. American Rock Art Research Association.

Gregg, Josiah. 1845. *Commerce of the Prairies.* New York: J. and Henry G. Langley.

Guerra, Francisco. 1971. *The Pre-Columbian Mind.* London: Seminar Press.

Gutierrez, Ramon A. 1991. *When Jesus Came, The Corn Mothers Went Away: Marriage, Sexuality, and Power in New Mexico, 1500–1846.* Stanford, Calif.: Stanford University Press.

Hadlock, Harry L. 1980. Ganaskidi: The Navajo Humpback Deity of the Largo. *Papers of the Archaeological Society of New Mexico* 5:179–210.

Hamilton, Tyler. 1964. *Pueblo Gods and Myths.* Norman: University of Oklahoma Press.

Hampton, O. Winston. 1994. Piedras Pintas: A Trinary Petroglyph Site of Major Importance, Baja California Sur, Mexico. *Rock Art Papers* 11. San Diego Museum Papers No. 31.

Harris, James. 1982. The War Twin Petroglyph and a Tentative Interpretation. *American Indian Rock Art* 7 and 8:165–76. American Rock Art Research Association.

_______. 1983. Zion Park Petroglyph Canyon Panel. *American Indian Rock Art* 10:40–47. American Rock Art Research Association.

_______. 1993. Corn Maidens in Anasazi Rock Art. *American Indian Rock Art* 12:123–32. American Rock Art Research Association.

Haury, Emil W. 1976. *The Hohoka: Desert Farmers and Craftsmen.* Tucson: University of Arizona Press.

Hawley, Florence. 1937. Kokopelli of the Prehistoric Southwestern Pueblo Pantheon. *American Anthropologist* 39:644–46.

Hay, Henry. 1963. The Hammond Report: A Deposition with Subsequent Commentary on the Conspiracy of Silence anent Social Homophilia. *One Institute Quarterly* 6:6–21.

Hays, Kelley Ann. 1994. Kachina Depictions on Prehistoric Pueblo Pottery. In *Kachinas in the Pueblo World*, ed. Polly Schaafsma. Albuquerque: University of New Mexico Press.

Hedges, Ken. 1983. A Re-examination of Pomo Baby Rocks. American Indian Rock Art 9. American Rock Art Research Association.

_______. 1986. The Sunwatcher of La Rumarosa. *Rock Art Papers* 4:17–32. San Diego Museum Papers No. 21.

Heizer, R. F., and M. A. Baumhoff. 1962. *Prehistoric Rock Art of Nevada and Eastern California.* Berkeley: University of California Press.

Hewett, Edgar L. 1953. *Pajarito Plateau and Its Ancient People.* Albuquerque and Santa Fe: University of New Mexico Press and School of American Research.

Hibben, Frank C. 1975. *Kiva Art of the Anasazi at Pottery Mound.* Las Vegas, Nev.: KC Publications.

Highwater, Jamake. 1990. *Myth and Sexuality.* New York: Penguin.

Hill, Beth, and Ray Hill. 1974. *Indian Petroglyphs of the Pacific Northwest.* Seattle: University of Washington Press.

Hultkrantz, Ake. 1987. *Native Religions of North America: The Power of Visions and Fertility.* San Francisco: Harper and Row.

Hunger, Heinz. 1982. Ritual Coition as Sacred Marriage in the Rock Art of North America. *American Indian Rock Art* 9:1–9. American Rock Art Research Association.

_______. 1983. Ritual Coition with and among Animals. *American Indian Rock Art* 10:116–24. American Rock Art Research Association.

________. 1993. Ritual Coition with Inanimate Objects. *American Indian Rock Art* 12:75–80. American Rock Art Research Association.

Husain, Shahrukh. 1997. *The Goddess.* New York: Little, Brown and Company.

Jimenez, Antonio Nunez. 1986. *Petroglifos del Peru: Panorama Mundial del Arte Rupestre.* Havana, Cuba: Ministerio de Cultura.

Johnson, Boma. 1985. Earth Figures of the Lower Colorado and Gila River Deserts: A Functional Analysis. *The Arizona Archaeologist.* Arizona Archaeological Society, No. 20.

Keyser, James D. 1992. *Indian Rock Art of the Columbia Plateau.* Seattle: University of Washington Press.

Kidder, Alfred V. 1932. The Artifacts of Pecos. In *Papers of the Southwestern Expedition 6.* New Haven: Published for Phillips Academy by Yale University Press.

Kidder, Alfred Vincent, and Samuel J. Guernsey. 1919. Archaeological Explorations in Northeastern Arizona. *Bureau of American Ethnology Bulletin 65.* Washington, D.C.: Government Printing Office.

Kirkland, Forrest, and W. W. Newcomb. 1967. *Rock Art of Texas Indians.* Austin: University of Texas Press.

Knaak, Manfred. 1988. *The Forgotten Artist: Indians of Anza-Borrego and Their Rock Art.* Borrego Springs, Calif.: Anza-Borrego Desert Natural History Association.

Knight, Richard Payne, and Thomas Wright. 1957. *Sexual Symbolism: A History of Phallic Worship.* New York: Bell Publishing Company.

Krantz, Lars. 1956. *Bronze Age Pictures: Photographs from the Rock Carvings in Bohuslan, Sweden.* Gothenburg, Sweden: The Gothenburg Art Gallery.

Krupp, E. C. 1983. Emblems of the Sky. In *Ancient Images on Stone*, ed. JoAnne Van Tilburg. 38–45. Los Angeles: The Institute of Archeology.

________. 1997. *Skywatchers, Shamans and Kings: Astronomy and the Archaeology of Power.* New York: John Wiley and Sons.

Laeberlin, H. K. 1916. The Idea of Fertilization in the Culture of the Pueblo Indians. *The American Anthropological Association, Memoir 3.*

Laird, Carobeth. 1976. *The Chemehuevis.* Banning, Calif.: Malki Museum Press.

________. 1984. *Mirror and Pattern: George Laird's World of Chemehuevi Mythology.* Banning, Calif.: Malki Museum Press.

Lajoux, Jean-Dominique. 1963. *The Rock Paintings of Tassili.* New York: World Publishing Co.

Leakey, Mary. 1983. *Africa's Vanishing Art: The Rock Paintings of Tanzania.* Garden City, N.Y.: Doubleday and Company.

Lewis-Williams, David, and Thomas Dowson. 1989. *Images of Power: Understanding Bushman Rock Art.* Cape Town, South Africa: National Book Printers.

Linne, S. 1943. Humpbacks in Ancient America. *Ethnos* 8:161–86.

Loeb, Edwin M. 1924. Pomo Folkways. *University of California Publications in American Archaeology and Ethnology* 1:147–409.

McCreery, Pat and E. Malotki. 1994. *Tapamveni, the Rock Art Galleries of Petrified Forest and Beyond.* Petrified Forest, Ariz.: Petrified Forest Museum Association.

McGlone, Bill, Ted Barker, and Phil Leonard. 1994. *Petroglyphs of Southeastern Colorado and the Oklahoma Panhandle.* Kamas, Utah: Mithras, Inc.

McGlone, William R., Phillip M. Leonard, James L. Guthrie, Rollin W. Gillespie, and James P. Whittall, Jr. 1993. *Ancient American Inscriptions: Plow Marks or History?* Sutton, Mass.: Early Sites Research Society.

McGowan, Charlotte. 1978. Female Fertility and Rock Art. *American Indian Rock Art* 4:26–40. American Rock Art Research Association.

________. 1982. *Ceremonial Fertility Sites in Southern California.* San Diego Museum Papers No. 14. San Diego, Calif.: Museum of Man.

Malinowski, Bronislaw. 1929. *The Sexual Life of Savages in North-Western Melanesia.* New York: Harcourt, Brace, and World.

Mallery, Garrick. 1893. Picture Writing of the American Indians. *Bureau of American Ethnology, Tenth Annual Report, 1888–89.* Washington, D.C.: Government Printing Office.

Malotki, Ekkehart. 1983. The Story of the "Tsimonmamant" or Jimson Weed Girls: A Hopi Narrative Featuring the Motif of the Vagina Dentata. In *Smoothing the Ground: Essays on Native American Literature*, ed. Brian Swann. Berkeley: University of California Press.

_______. 1997. The Dragonfly: A Shamanistic Motif in the Archaic Rock Art of the Palavayu Region in Northeastern Arizona. *American Indian Rock Art* 23:57–72. American Rock Art Research Association.

Mancini, Salvatore. 1996. *On the Edge of Magic: Petroglyphs and Rock Paintings of the Ancient Southwest.* San Francisco: Chronicle Books.

Manning, Steven J. 1992. The Lobed-Circle Image in the Basketmaker Petroglyphs of Southeastern Utah. *Utah Rock Art* 10:149–208. Utah Rock Art Research Association.

Maringer, Johannes, and Hans-Georg Bandi. 1953. *Art in the Ice Age.* New York: Frederick A. Praeger.

Marshack, Alexander. 1972. *The Roots of Civilization: The Cognitive Beginnings of Man's First Art, Symbol and Notation.* New York: McGraw Hill Book Co.

Martynov, Anatoly I. 1991. *The Ancient Art of Northern Asia.* Chicago: University of Illinois Press.

Miles, Christopher, and John Julius Norwich. 1997. *Love in the Ancient World.* New York: St. Martin's Press.

Miller, Jay. 1975. Kokopelli. In *Collected Papers in Honor of Florence Hawley Ellis*, ed. T. R. Frisbie. Archaeological Society of New Mexico Papers 2:371–80.

Mixco, Mauricio. 1984. *Paipai Literature. Spirit Mountain.* Tucson: Sun Tracks and University of Arizona Press.

Morss, Noel. 1954. Clay Figurines of the American Southwest. *Papers of the Peabody Museum of American Archaeology and Ethnology*, 40, no. 1. Cambridge, Mass.: Harvard University.

Morris, Earl H. 1925. Exploring the Canyon of Death. *National Geographic* 48, no. 3: 263–300.

_______. 1951. Basketmaker III Human Effigies from Northeast Arizona. *American Antiquity* 17:33–40.

Morris, Elizabeth Ann. 1980. Basketmaker Caves in the Prayer Rock District, Northeastern Arizona. *Anthropological Papers of the University of Arizona No.35.*

Morris, Ramona and Desmond. 1965. *Men and Snakes.* New York: McGraw Hill Book Company.

Moulard, Barbara L. 1984. *Within the Underworld Sky: Mimbres Art in Context.* Pasadena, Calif.: Twelvetrees Press.

Mountford, Charles P. 1964. *Aboriginal Paintings from Australia.* New York: New American Library of World Literature, Inc.

Neihardt, John. 1961. *Black Elk Speaks: Being the Life History of a Holy Man of the Oglala Sioux.* Lincoln: University of Nebraska Press.

Neuman, Erich. 1955. *The Great Mother:. An Analysis of the Archetype.* Princeton, N.J.: Princeton University Press.

Niethammer, Carolyn. 1977. *Daughters of the Earth: The Lives and Legends of American Indian Women.* New York: Touchstone Books.

Noxon, John S., and Deborah A. Marcus. 1985. *Significant Rock Art Sites in the Needles District of Canyonlands National Park, Southeastern Utah.* A report submitted to the National Park Service, Moab, Utah.

Packard, Gar and Maggy. 1974. *Suns and Serpents: The Symbolism of Indian Rock Art.* Santa Fe, N.M.: Packard Publications.

Parkman, E. Breck. 1996. Pomo Concepts of Power, Spirit, and Place. In *Rock Art as Visual Ecology*, ed. Paul Faulstich. Tucson, Ariz.: American Rock Art Research Association.

Parrinder, G. 1980. *Sex in the World's Religions.* London: Sheldon Press.

Parsons, Elsie Clews. 1919. Mothers and Children at Zuni. *Man* 19:168–82.

_______. 1938. The Humpbacked Flute Player of the Southwest. *American Anthropologist* 40, no. 2: 337–38.

_______. 1939. *Pueblo Indian Religion.* Chicago: University of Chicago Press.

_______. 1974. *The Pueblo of Isleta.* Albuquerque, N.M.: University of Albuquerque, Calvin Horn Publishers.

Patterson, Alex. 1992. *A Field Guide to Rock Art Symbols of the Greater Southwest.* Boulder, Colo.: Johnson Books.

_______. 1994. *Hopi Pottery Symbols.* Boulder, Colo.: Johnson Books.

Patterson-Rudolph, Carol. 1990. *Petroglyphs and Pueblo Myths of the Rio Grande.* Albuquerque, N.M.: Avanyu Publishing Inc.

Rafter, John. 1982. Shelter Rock of the Providence Mountains. *Rock Art Papers* 5:25–31. San Diego Museum Papers No. 23.

_______. 1990. The Bernasconi Hills Discovery. *Rock Art Papers* 7:33–40. San Diego Museum Papers No. 26.

_______. 1995. Sun and the Lone Woman of the Cave. *Rock Art Papers* 12: 31–37. San Diego Museum Papers No. 33.

Reichard, Gladys A. 1950. *Navajo Religion: A Study of Symbolism.* Vols. 1 and 2. New York: Stratford Press.

Reichel-Dolmatoff, Gerardo. 1967. Rock Paintings of the Vaupes: An Essay of Interpretation. Folklore Americas 27, no. 2: 107–13.

_______. 1971. *Amazonian Cosmos: The Sexual and Religious Symbolism of the Tukano Indians.* Chicago: University of Chicago Press.

Renaud Etienne B.. 1936. Pictographs and Petroglyphs of the High Western Plains. *8'th Report - Archaeological Survey Series.* Denver, Colo.: University of Denver.

Schaafsma, Polly. 1963. Rock Art in the Navajo Reservoir District. *Museum of New Mexico Papers in Anthropology* 7. Santa Fe, N.M.: Museum of New Mexico Press.

_______. 1971. The Rock Art of Utah. *Papers of the Peabody Museum of American Archaeology and Ethnology* 65. Cambridge, Mass.: Harvard University Press.

_______. 1975. Rock Art in the Cochiti Reservoir District. *Museum of New Mexico Papers in Anthropology* 16. Santa Fe, N.M.: Museum of New Mexico Press.

_______. 1980. *Indian Rock Art of the Southwest.* Santa Fe and Albuquerque: School of American Research and University of New Mexico Press.

_______. 1994. Trance and Transformation in the Canyons: Shamanism and Early Rock Art on the Colorado Plateau. In *Shamanism and Rock Art in North America*, ed. Solveig Turpin. San Antonio, Tex.: Rock Art Foundation.

_______. 1999. Tlalocs, Kachinas, Sacred Bundles, and Related Symbolism in the Southwest and Mesoamerica. In *The Casas Grandes World*, eds. Curtis F. Schaafsma and Carroll L. Riley. Salt Lake City: University of Utah Press.

Schaafsma, Polly and Curtis F.. 1974. Origins of the Pueblo Katchina Cult. *American Antiquity* 39, no. 4:535–45.

Scott, George Ryley. 1966. *Phallic Worship: A History of Sex and Sexual Rites.* London: Random House UK, Ltd.

Slack, Lina N. 1962. Rock Engravings from Driekops Eiland and Other Sites Southwest of Johannesburg. London: Centaur Press Ltd.

Slifer, Dennis and James Duffield. 1994. *Kokopelli: Flute Player Images in Rock Art.* Santa Fe, N.M.: Ancient City Press.

Slifer, Dennis. 1998. *Signs of Life: Rock Art of the Upper Rio Grande.* Santa Fe, N.M.: Ancient City Press.

Smith, Bradley. 1968. *Mexico: A History in Art.* Garden City, N.Y.: Doubleday and Company, Inc.

Smith, Gerald A., and Steven M. Freers. 1994. *Fading Images: Indian Pictographs of Western Riverside County.* Riverside, Calif.: Riverside Museum Press.

Smith, Ron. 1986a. Male and Female Symbolism in the Great Mural Paintings of the Sierra de San Francisco, Baja, California. *Rock Art Papers* 4:107–20. San Diego Museum Papers No. 22.

_______. 1986b. Serpent Cave. *Rock Art Papers* 3:27–50. San Diego Museum Papers No. 20.

_______. 1987. Rock Feature Incorporation. *Rock Art Papers* 5: 127–39. San Diego Museum Papers No. 23.

Smith, Watson. 1952. Kiva Mural Decorations at Awatovi and Kawaika-a. *Papers of the Peabody Museum of Archaeology and Ethnology* 37. Cambridge, Mass.: Harvard University Press.

Snodgrass, O. T. 1975 and 1977. *Realistic Art and Times of the Mimbres Indians.* El Paso, Tex.: O. T. Snodgrass.

Staniford, Phillip S. 1977. Inside Out: Anthropological Communication of Alternate Realities. *New Directions in the Study of Man* 1, no. 1:36–46. Phoenix, Ariz.

Steinbring, Jack. 1998. Aboriginal Rock Painting Sites in Manitoba. *Manitoba Archaeological Society* 8, nos. 1 and 2.

Stephen, A. M. 1939. Hopi Indians of Arizona. *The Masterkey* 8, no. 6. Los Angeles: Southwest Museum.

Stephen, Alexander M. 1936. Hopi Journal, ed. E. C. Parsons. *Columbia University Contributions to Anthropology* 23, parts 1 and 2. New York: Columbia University Press.

Stevenson, Matilda Coxe. 1904. The Zuni Indians: Their Mythology, Esoteric Fraternities and Ceremonies. *Twenty-Third Annual Report of the Bureau of American Ethnology for the Years 1901–1902.* Washington, D.C.: Government Printing Office, 1915.

Sundstrom, Linea. 1982. A Rock Art Chronology for the Black Hills. *American Indian Rock Art* 7 and 8: 177–204. American Rock Art Research Association.

Sutherland, Kay. 1975. A Classification and Preliminary Analysis of Pictographs at Hueco Tanks State Park, Texas. *American Indian Rock Art—Papers Presented at the 1974 Symposium*, ed. Shari T. Grove, 61–80. Farmington, N.M.: San Juan County Museum Association.

_______. 1995. *Rock Paintings at Hueco Tanks State Historical Park*. Austin, Tex.: Texas Parks and Wildlife Press.

_______. 1996. Spirits from the South. *The Artifact* 34, nos 1 and 2: 1–101. El Paso Archaeological Society.

Swentzell, Rina. 1993. Mountain Form, Village Form—Unity in the Pueblo World. In *Ancient Land, Ancestral Places: Paul Logsdon in the Pueblo Southwest,* Paul Logsdon. Santa Fe: Museum of New Mexico Press.

Switzer, Ronald R. 1972. *The Origin and Significance of Snake-Lightning Cults in the Pueblo Southwest*. El Paso, Tex.: El Paso Archaeological Society Special Report No. 11.

Talayesva, Don C. 1942. *Sun Chief: The Autobiography of a Hopi Indian*. New Haven, Conn.: Yale University Press.

Tannahill, Reay. 1980. *Sex and History*. New York: Stein and Day.

Taylor, Timothy. 1996. *The Prehistory of Sex: Four Million Years of Human Sexual Culture*. New York: Bantam Books.

Tedlock, Dennis. 1972. *Finding the Center: Narrative Poetry of the Zuni Indians*. Lincoln: University of Nebraska Press.

Thomas, J. J. 1982. Rock Art and the Religion of Sky. *American Indian Rock Art* 7 and 8:33–37. American Rock Art Research Association.

Titiev, Mischa. 1939. The Story of Kokopele. *American Anthropologist* 41, no.1:91–98.

_______. 1972. *The Hopi Indians of Old Oraibi: Change and Continuity*. Ann Arbor: University of Michigan Press.

Trimble, Stephen. 1993. *The People: Indians of the American Southwest*. Santa Fe, N.M.: School of American Research.

True, D. L., C. W. Meighan, and Harvey Crew. 1974. Archaeological Investigations at Molpa, San Diego County, California. *University of California Publications in Anthropology* 11.

Turner, Christy G. II. 1963. *Petrographs of the Glen Canyon Region*. Flagstaff: Museum of Northern Arizona Bulletin 38, Glen Canyon Series 4.

_______. 1971. Revised Dating for Early Rock Art of the Glen Canyon Region. *American Antiquity* 36:469–71.

Turpin, Solveig A. 1990. Speculations on the Age and Origin of the Pecos River Style, Southwestern Texas. *American Indian Rock Art* 16:99–122. American Rock Art Research Association.

_______, ed. 1994. *Shamanism and Rock Art in North America*. San Antonio, Tex.: Rock Art Foundation, Inc.

_______. 1994. On a Wing and a Prayer: Flight Metaphors in Pecos River Art. In *Shamanism and Rock Art in North America*, ed. Solveig A. Turpin. San Antonio, Tex.: Rock Art Foundation.

Tyler, Hamilton A. 1964. *Pueblo Gods and Myths*. Norman: University of Oklahoma Press.

_______. 1979. *Pueblo Birds and Myths*. Norman: University of Oklahoma Press.

Valadez, Susana. 1992. *Huichol Indian Sacred Rituals*. San Francisco: Amber Lotus.

Van Tilburg, Jo Anne, ed. 1983. *Ancient Images on Stone*. Los Angeles: The Institute of Archaeology.

Vastokas, Joan and Romas. 1973. *Sacred Art of the Algonkians: A Study of the Peterborough Petroglyphs*. Peterborough, Ontario: Mannard Press.

von Werlhof, Jay. 1987. *Spirits of the Earth: A Study of Earthen Art in the North American Deserts*. El Centro, Calif.: Bernard Mannis, Inc.

Vuncannon, Delcie H. 1985. Fertility Symbols at the Chalfont Site, California. *Rock Art Papers* 2:119–26. San Diego Museum Papers No. 20.

Wade, Edwin L., and Lea S. McChesney. 1980. *America's Great Lost Expedition: The Thomas Keam Collection of Hopi Pottery from the Second Hemenway Expedition, 1890–1894*. Phoenix, Ariz.: The Heard Museum.

Walker, Barbara G. 1983. *The Woman's Encyclopedia of Myths and Secrets*. San Francisco: Harper and Row.

Wallace, Henry D. 1991. Pictures in the Desert: Hohokam Rock Art. In *The Hohokam: Ancient People of the Desert*, ed. David Grant Noble. Santa Fe, N.M.: School of American Research Press.

Warner, Jesse E. 1982. The "Enclosure Petroglyph" Motif: One Possible Interpretation. *American Indian Rock Art* 7 and 8. American Rock Art Research Association.

Warner, Judith. 1983. An Intuitive View of Waterflow, New Mexico. *American Indian Rock Art* 10:29–39.

———. 1991. Female Sexual Identification in Rock Art: A Problem of Gender and Values. *Utah Rock Art* 8:1–27. Utah Rock Art Research Association.

Watson, Lyall. 1982. *The Lightning Bird.* New York: Simon and Schuster.

Wellman, Klaus. 1970. Kokopelli of Indian Paleology: Hunchbacked Rain Priest, Hunting Magician, and Don Juan of the Old Southwest. *Journal of the American Medical Association* 212:1678–82.

———. 1974a. The Indomitable Hump-back Returns. *La Pintura* 1:2–4. American Rock Art Research Association.

———. 1974b. Some Observations on Human Sexuality in American Indian Rock Art. *Southwestern Lore* 40, no.1:1–12.

———. 1979. *A Survey of North American Indian Rock Art.* Graz, Austria: Akademische Druck-u, Verlagsanstalt.

———. 1981. Shades of Dr. Jekyll and Mr. Hyde: Conceptual Dichotomy as Expressed in North American Indian Rock Drawings. *American Indian Rock Art* 6:1–10.

Whitley, David S. 1994. Shamanism, Natural Modeling and the Rock Art of Far Western North American Hunter-Gatherers. *Shamanism and Rock Art in North America*, Special Publication No. 1., ed. Solveig Turpin. San Antonio, Tex.: Rock Art Foundation.

———. 1996. *A Guide to Rock Art Sites: Southern California and Southern Nevada.* Missoula, Mont.: Mountain Press.

Williams, Walter. 1992. *The Spirit and the Flesh: Sexual Diversity in American Indian Culture.* Boston: Beacon Press.

Young, M. Jane. 1988. *Signs from the Ancestors.* Albuquerque: University of New Mexico Press.

———. 1994. The Interconnection Between Western Puebloan and MesoAmerican Ideology/Cosmology. *Kachinas in the Pueblo World*, ed. Polly Schaafsma. Albuquerque: University of New Mexico Press.

Zhang, Juzhong, Changsui Wang, and Zhaochen Kong. 1999. Oldest Playable Musical Instruments Found at Jiahu Early Neolithic Site in China. *Nature* 401:366–68.

Zimmerman, Larry J. 1996. *Native North America.* Boston: Little, Brown and Company.

INDEX

Note: Pages with illustrations are noted **in bold**.